STUDIES IN EARLY MODERN CULTURAL,
POLITICAL AND SOCIAL HISTORY

Volume 52

THE UNIVERSITIES OF SCOTLAND,
IRELAND, AND NEW ENGLAND DURING
THE BRITISH CIVIL WARS

Studies in Early Modern Cultural, Political and Social History

ISSN: 1476-9107

Series editors
Tim Harris – Brown University
Stephen Taylor – Durham University
Andy Wood – Durham University

Previously published titles in the series
are listed at the back of this volume

THE UNIVERSITIES OF SCOTLAND, IRELAND, AND NEW ENGLAND DURING THE BRITISH CIVIL WARS

CONTESTED SEMINARIES

Salvatore Cipriano

THE BOYDELL PRESS

© Salvatore Cipriano 2024

All Rights Reserved. Except as permitted under current legislation no part of this work may be photocopied, stored in a retrieval system, published, performed in public, adapted, broadcast, transmitted, recorded or reproduced in any form or by any means, without the prior permission of the copyright owner

The right of Salvatore Cipriano to be identified as the author of this work has been asserted in accordance with sections 77 and 78 of the Copyright, Designs and Patents Act 1988

First published 2024
The Boydell Press, Woodbridge

ISBN 978-1-78327-786-5

The Boydell Press is an imprint of Boydell & Brewer Ltd
PO Box 9, Woodbridge, Suffolk IP12 3DF, UK
and of Boydell & Brewer Inc.
668 Mt Hope Avenue, Rochester, NY 14620-2731, USA
website: www.boydellandbrewer.com

A catalogue record for this book is available
from the British Library

The publisher has no responsibility for the continued existence or accuracy of URLs for external or third-party internet websites referred to in this book, and does not guarantee that any content on such websites is, or will remain, accurate or appropriate

For Kerrie

Contents

List of Illustrations   viii
Acknowledgements   ix
Conventions   xi
List of Abbreviations   xii

Introduction   1
1   Charles I, William Laud, and the Universities, c. 1625–37   22
2   The Scottish Universities, c. 1638–50   59
3   Ireland and New England, c. 1637–50   97
4   The Cromwellian Conquest and the Universities   133
5   The Scottish Universities, c. 1652–60   166
6.   Ireland, New England, and New College Projects, c. 1655–60   199
Conclusion   234

Bibliography   241
Index   281

Illustrations

Figure

5.1	Excerpt from the Dictates of Thomas Craufurd, March 1653	170

Tables

1.1	Trinity College, Dublin Staff during Laud's Chancellorship	36–7
2.1	The Scottish Professoriate on the Eve of the Covenanting Revolution, c. 1638	62–3
2.2	The Scottish Professoriate under the Covenanters, c. 1642–7	85–6
2.3	University Staff Removals under the Covenanters, c. 1638–47	91
3.1	Trinity College, Dublin Staff in the 1640s	115–16
3.2	Harvard College Staff, c. 1636–50	125–6
4.1	Harvard College Staff, c. 1650–4	140
4.2	Trinity College, Dublin Staff, c. 1651–5	148
4.3	Anti-Engager Purges at the Scottish Universities, c. 1647–51	151–2
5.1	The Scottish Professoriate, c. 1652–60	186–7
6.1	Trinity College, Dublin Staff, c. 1655–60	210
6.2	Harvard College Staff, c. 1654–60	225

Acknowledgements

My parents had always emphasised to my siblings and me the importance of going to 'college', something they never had the opportunity to do themselves. I did not know much about college, but I knew it was important, for some reason. But why was it important? Who was it for? What was its purpose? These questions have driven my curiosity in higher education for a long time. The university is a thousand years old, but for me, it was something else – it was new, extraordinarily so. This juxtaposition fascinated me, and it has oriented my intellectual and professional journey, with this book being one of the ways in which I have continued to engage with these questions. I am therefore very thankful to my parents for sparking my lasting curiosity in universities and, most importantly, providing their children with the opportunity to go to college.

More immediately, this book has benefited enormously from the expertise and insight of many great historians. Christopher Maginn was instrumental to the project's earliest stages. Susan Wabuda, David Myers, Brendan Kane, Christopher Rose, Jonathan Woods, and Karie Schultz provided invaluable insight on chapters and drafts over the years. Steven Reid and Chris R. Langley read, and re-read, various drafts and provided much-needed guidance in the manuscript's final stages. Robert Landrum, Steve Murdoch, Jamie Reid-Baxter, Alan Ford, and Coleman Dennehy shared their expertise on different topics and provided access to and insight on primary sources that enhanced the scope of the study. I am also incredibly grateful to Michael Middeke and the editorial team at Boydell for thoughtfully and amiably shepherding this project along. I have thus benefited from the knowledge and guidance of a gracious community of scholars. It goes without saying that any errors and omissions in this work are entirely my own.

I am thankful to have received funding from Fordham University and the Huntington Library that facilitated research at a number of archives and libraries across Scotland, England, Ireland, and the United States. I am grateful to the staffs at the university libraries of Aberdeen, Edinburgh, Glasgow, St Andrews, and Trinity College, Dublin; the National Library of Scotland; the National Records of Scotland; the New College Library, Edinburgh; the British Library; the Huntington Library; the Harvard University Archives; and the Massachusetts Historical Society. I am especially grateful for the librarians at Fordham University's Walsh Library, Boston College's O'Neill Library, and Harvard University's Widener Library for their ability to secure resources.

I owe a heavy debt of gratitude to family and friends. My parents and siblings seemed to have always known when, and when not, to ask about the book's progress, and I am appreciative of their love and support for all my personal and professional endeavours. My friends – from Long Island to New York City, Boston, California, and beyond – have been a constant source of encouragement, and escape, during the long process of research and writing. I am also thankful for my colleagues at the Boston College Career Center and Stanford Career Education who provided support, and an extra dose of inspiration, as I pursued a scholarly project alongside our work with students.

Finally, my deepest appreciation and affection are reserved for my wife, Kerrie. She was there from day one. She was ever supportive of a project that necessitated prolonged periods apart, whether that meant travelling to other countries for months at a time or holing up to write on most nights and weekends. And, on more than a few occasions, she listened with understanding as I vented about research and writing. Ultimately, then, this book is for Kerrie, my partner in PhD.

Conventions

All quotations maintain original spelling and syntax. Abbreviations and superscripts have been expanded silently. All translations are my own unless noted otherwise. The New Year is taken to begin on 1 January.

Abbreviations

Acts and Ordinances	C.H. Firth and R.S. Rait (eds), *Acts and Ordinances of the Interregnum* (3 vols, London, 1911)
Alumni Dublinenses	George D. Burtchaell and Thomas U. Sadleir (eds), *Alumni Dublinenses: A Register of the Students, Graduates, Professors and Provosts of Trinity College in the University of Dublin (1593–1860)* (Dublin, 1935)
Anderson, *Officers and Graduates*	P.J. Anderson (ed.), *Officers and Graduates of University and King's College Aberdeen, MVD–MDCCCLX* (Aberdeen, 1893)
AUL	Aberdeen University Library
Baillie, *L&J*	David Laing (ed.), *The Letters and Journals of Robert Baillie* (3 vols, Edinburgh, 1841)
BL	The British Library, London
CJ	*The Journals of the House of Commons, 1547–1660* (7 vols, London, 1802)
CJI	*The Journals of the House of Commons of the Kingdom of Ireland, Vol. I, 1613–1666* (Dublin, 1796)
Cotton, *Fasti*	Henry Cotton, *Fasti Ecclesiæ Hibernicæ: The Succession of the Prelates and Members of the Cathedral Bodies of Ireland* (6 vols, Dublin, 1851–78)
Cromwellian Union	C.S. Terry (ed.), *The Cromwellian Union: Papers Relating to the Negotiations for an Incorporating Union between England and Scotland 1651–1652* (Edinburgh, 1902)
Cromwell Writings	W.C. Abbott (ed.), *The Writings and Speeches of Oliver Cromwell* (4 vols, Cambridge, MA, 1937–47)
CSPC	Noel Sainsbury, ed., *Calendar of State Papers, Colonial Series Volume 1: 1574–1660* (London, 1860)
CSPD	*Calendar of State Papers, Domestic Series, of the Reign of Charles I and the Interregnum* (36 vols, London, 1858–97)

ABBREVIATIONS

CSPI	Robert Pentland Mahaffy (ed.), *Calendar of State Papers Relating to Ireland, 1625–1660* (3 vols, London, 1900–08)
DIB	*Dictionary of Irish Biography* (Cambridge, 2009) [http://dib.cambridge.org/]
Evidence	*Evidence, Oral and Documentary, Taken and Received by the Commissioners Appointed by His Majesty George IV., July 23d 1826; and Re-Appointed by His Majesty William IV., October 12th, 1830; for Visiting the Universities of Scotland* (4 vols, London, 1837)
EUA	Edinburgh University Archives
EUL	Edinburgh University Library
Fasti Aberdonenses	Cosmo Innes (ed.), *Fasti Aberdonenses: Selections from the Records of the University and King's College of Aberdeen* (Aberdeen, 1854)
FAM	P.J. Anderson and J.F.K. Johnstone (eds), *Fasti Academiae Mariscallanae Aberdonensis: Selections from the Records of Marischal College and University, MDXCIII–MDCCCLX* (3 vols, Aberdeen, 1889)
GUA	Glasgow University Archives
GUL	Glasgow University Library
HCR	*Harvard College Records*, Publications of the Colonial Society of Massachusetts (4 vols, Boston, MA, 1925–75)
HL	Henry E. Huntington Library, San Marino, CA
HP	Mark Greengrass, et al. (eds), *The Hartlib Papers* (Sheffield, 2013) [https://hrionline.ac.uk/hartlib/]
HUA	Harvard University Archives
HUE	Hilde de Ridder-Symoens (ed.), *A History of the University in Europe, Volume II: Universities in Early Modern Europe (1500–1800)* (Cambridge, 1996)
Ireland under the Commonwealth	Robert Dunlop (ed.), *Ireland under the Commonwealth: Being a Selection of Documents Relating to the Government of Ireland from 1651 to 1659* (2 vols, Manchester, 1913)
Laing, *Catalogue*	David Laing (ed.), *A Catalogue of the Graduates of the Faculties of Arts, Divinity, and Law of the University of Edinburgh, Since Its Foundation* (Edinburgh, 1858)

ABBREVIATIONS

Laud Works	W. Scot and J. Bliss (eds), *The Works of the Most Reverend Father in God, William Laud* (7 vols, Oxford, 1847–60)
MA	Massachusetts Archives
Massachusetts Records	Nathaniel B. Shurtleff (ed.), *Records of the Governor and Company of the Massachusetts Bay in New England* (5 vols, Boston, MA, 1853–4)
MAUG	Cosmo Innes (ed.), *Munimenta Alme Universitatis Glasguensis: Records of the University of Glasgow, from Its Foundation till 1727* (4 vols, Glasgow, 1854)
MHS	Massachusetts Historical Society, Boston, MA
Morison, *Founding*	Samuel Eliot Morison, *The Founding of Harvard College* (Cambridge, MA, 1935)
Morison, *HCSC*	Samuel Eliot Morison, *Harvard College in the Seventeenth Century* (2 vols, Cambridge, MA, 1936)
NCL	New College Library, Edinburgh University
NLS	National Library of Scotland, Edinburgh
NRS	National Records of Scotland, Edinburgh
ODNB	*Oxford Dictionary of National Biography* (Oxford, 2004) [www.oxforddnb.com/]
PCSM	*Publications of the Colonial Society of Massachusetts*
Plymouth Records	Nathaniel B. Shurtleff and David B. Pulsifer (eds), *Records of the Colony of New Plymouth in New England* (12 vols, Boston, MA, 1855–61)
Records of the Kirk	Alexander Peterkin (ed.), *Records of the Kirk of Scotland, Containing the Acts and Proceedings of the General Assemblies from the Year 1638 Downwards* (Edinburgh, 1843)
RCGA	Alexander F. Mitchell and James Christie (eds), *The Records of the Commissions of the General Assemblies of the Church of Scotland* (3 vols, Edinburgh, 1892–1909)
RPS	Keith M. Brown, *et al.* (eds), The Records of the Parliaments of Scotland to 1707 (St Andrews, 2007–17) [www.rps.ac.uk/].

ABBREVIATIONS

Scotland and the Commonwealth	C.H. Firth (ed.), *Scotland and the Commonwealth: Letters and Papers Relating to the Military Government of Scotland, from August 1651 to December 1653* (Edinburgh, 1895)
Scotland and the Protectorate	C.H. Firth (ed.), *Scotland and the Protectorate: Letters and Papers Relating to the Military Government of Scotland from January 1654 to June 1659* (Edinburgh, 1899)
Scott, *Fasti*	Hew Scott, *Fasti Ecclesiæ Scoticanæ: The Succession of Ministers in the Church of Scotland from the Reformation* (7 vols, Edinburgh, 1915–28)
StAUL	St Andrews University Library
Strafford Letters	William Knowler (ed.), *The Earl of Strafforde's Letters and Despatches* (2 vols, London, 1739)
TCD	Trinity College, Dublin Library
Thurloe State Papers	Thomas Birch (ed.), *A Collection of the State Papers of John Thurloe* (7 vols, London, 1742)
TNA	The National Archives, Kew, London
Ussher Correspondence	Elizabethanne Boran (ed.), *The Correspondence of James Ussher, 1600–1656* (3 vols, Dublin, 2015)
Ussher Works	Charles R. Elrington (ed.), *The Whole Works of the Most Rev. James Ussher, D.D.* (17 vols, Dublin, 1847–64)
VCA	Virginia Company Archives [http://virginiacompanyarchives.amdigital.co.uk/]
Winthrop Journal	Richard S. Dunn, James Savage, and Laetitia Yeandle (eds), *The Journal of John Winthrop, 1630–1649* (Cambridge, MA, 1996)
Winthrop Papers	Stewart Mitchell, Allyn B. Forbes, and Malcolm Freiberg (eds), *The Winthrop Papers* (6 vols, Boston, MA, 1929–92)
YUL	Yale University Library

Introduction

> The very truth is, that all wise princes respect the welfare of their estates, and consider that schools and universities are (as in the body) the noble and vital parts, which being vigorous and sound, send good blood and active spirits into the veins and arteries, which cause health and strength: or if feeble or ill affected, corrupt all the vital powers; whereupon grow diseases, and in the end death itself.[1]

Writing in his history of Oxford University under his chancellorship, William Laud, archbishop of Canterbury, underlined the crucial function of the university in society. For Laud, the university was a vital organ – the heart – that, when functioning properly, circulated ministers and magistrates into the structures of state power – the veins and arteries – which they administered in orderly, and obedient, fashion. But, when infected – be it from disobedience, laxity, or nonconformity – the university's intramural corruption could metastasise, spreading through extramural society and generating instability. Charles I likewise noted in a 1628 missive to the earl of Pembroke, Laud's predecessor as Oxford's chancellor, that 'The examples which spread from such places are able to infect a whole State.'[2] For Charles and Laud, the universities were central to maintaining intellectual, religious, and political conformity across secular and religious governing structures and society at large. Kevin Sharpe wrote that Laud's Oxford was for Charles 'a utopia of order and sobriety, the promise of a perfect commonweal in the future'.[3] The university was a model for discipline and virtue, but, importantly, it was also an instrument to impose obedience and conformity.[4] At the heart of a healthy society was the university, which trained governing elites, thereby ensuring the long-term stability of the realm.

The same was true for the universities in the realms that the early Stuart composite monarchy ruled from afar, and which also drew the monarchy's intrusive energies. This book examines the universities of Scotland,

---

[1] *Laud Works*, V, p. 130.
[2] Anthony à Wood, *The History and Antiquities of the University of Oxford* (2 vols, Oxford, 1796), II, p. 362.
[3] Kevin Sharpe, 'Archbishop Laud and the University of Oxford', in Hugh Lloyd-Jones, Valerie Pearl, and Blair Worden (eds), *History and Imagination: Essays in Honour of H.R. Trevor-Roper* (London, 1981), pp. 146–64, at 150.
[4] Kenneth Fincham, 'Oxford and the Early Stuart Polity', in Nicholas Tyacke (ed.), *The History of the University of Oxford, Vol. IV Seventeenth-Century Oxford* (Oxford, 1997), pp. 179–210, at 198–9.

Ireland, and New England during the mid-seventeenth century, when, amid pronounced upheaval, fluid structures of secular and religious power contested for control of these institutions. These disputes highlighted the university's essential role in promoting social order, specifically as it was defined by rival authorities. Laud's preoccupation with perpetuating an ordered society influenced his conception of the university, and both his Oxford chancellorship and his planned reforms for Cambridge University attest to his conviction that England's universities were to be models of order in the service of the state.[5] His vision also underscored the role higher education played in creating and maintaining social order in early modern Europe. In Britain, Ireland, and New England between 1625 and 1660, the universities were regularly exploited to meet the needs of shifting centres of power; their strategic significance during the turmoil of the Civil Wars bore out Laud's aphorism that the universities were the 'noble and vital parts' of a society, as they emerged as contested political and religious spaces in the struggle between the monarchy and its opponents. Caroline and Cromwellian interventions in the universities were key parts of wider programs of state building, which themselves stimulated responses from opponents in Scotland, Ireland, and New England, who viewed their universities as bulwarks against such intrusions. This book examines how the universities were employed to realise competing conceptions of ordered, godly commonwealths.

* * *

Scholars have long highlighted the importance of educational institutions to the development of states and the construction of social order in pre-modern societies. Talcott Parsons viewed schools as microcosms of wider society, underlining their utility as purveyors of different brands of social order.[6] As Émile Durkheim and later Eric Carlton argued, schools and universities had to exemplify and inculcate what governing authorities defined as the normative customs and values of the societies in which they resided.[7] The early modern university's utility was rooted in creating and preserving a type of societal homogeneity that conformed to authorised norms; it socialised students into the values of a particular culture via the inculcation of normative political and religious orthodoxies and authorised knowledge, thus preserving the wider social order.[8]

---

[5] Fincham, 'Oxford and the Early Stuart Polity', pp. 199–209; John Twigg, *The University of Cambridge and the English Revolution, 1625–1688* (Woodbridge, 1990), pp. 30–41.
[6] Talcott Parsons, 'The School Class as a Social System: Some of Its Functions in American Society', in A.H. Halsey, Jean Floud, and C. Arnold Anderson (eds), *Education, Economy, and Society: A Reader in the Sociology of Education* (New York, 1961), pp. 434–55.
[7] Émile Durkheim, *Education and Sociology*, trans. Sherwood D. Fox (New York, 1956), pp. 56–62; Eric Carlton, *Ideology and Social Order* (London, 1977), pp. 77–9.
[8] Michel Foucault, *Discipline and Punish: The Birth of the Prison*, trans. Alan Sheridan, 2nd edn (New York, 1995), pp. 170–7; Jonathan Davis, 'The Ideal Student: Manuals of Student

INTRODUCTION

In early modern Europe and its overseas colonies, higher education perpetuated normative orthodoxies via the distillation of known bodies of inherited, Christian knowledge and Scholastic philosophy, which were understood to have provided the bedrock of ordered societies for centuries.[9] The medieval and early modern university – indeed, the university as it existed largely prior to the nineteenth century and the emergence of the research university – was not a space of knowledge creation, but rather an institution that taught 'old and established principles which were beyond the reach of argument' in order to instil morality and virtue.[10] Even as Christendom fractured in the wake of the Reformation, university curricula remained largely rooted in its foundational, medieval antecedents: instruction, in Latin, of the 'higher' faculties of canon and civil law, theology, and medicine, in addition to Scholastic commentaries on the Greek texts of Aristotle.[11] In Protestant universities – including those of Scotland, Ireland, and New England – this curriculum was crucial both to instil doctrine and train able ministers, elders, and schoolmasters.[12] This training was essential to what Durkheim contended was the 'methodical socialisation' of younger generations according to the needs of individual societies. University students were socialised into the norms defined by ruling authorities, which fashioned conformity and obedience via higher education.[13]

Behaviours in Early Modern Italy', in Richard Kirwan (ed.), *Scholarly Self-Fashioning and Community in the Early Modern University* (Burlington, VT, 2013), pp. 21–37; Richard Kirwan, 'Scholarly Careers and the Confessional University in Early Modern Germany', in Arthur der Weduwen and Malcolm Walsby (eds), *Reformation, Religious Culture and Print in Early Modern Europe: Essays in Honour of Andrew Pettegree, Volume 1* (Leiden, 2022), pp. 101–15, at 101–2.

[9] Helga Robinson-Hammerstein, 'Royal Policy and Civic Pride: Founding a University in Dublin', in David Scott (ed.), *Treasures of the Mind: Trinity College, Dublin Quatercentenary Exhibition Catalogue* (London, 1992), pp. 1–16, at 2–3.

[10] Lawrence Stone, 'Social Control and Intellectual Excellence: Oxbridge and Edinburgh, 1560–1983', in Nicholas Phillipson (ed.), *Universities, Society and the Future* (Edinburgh, 1983), pp. 3–30, at 3–5. On the evolution and emergence of the research university in the nineteenth century, see Chad Wellmon, *Organizing Enlightenment: Information Overload and the Invention of the Modern Research University* (Baltimore, MD, 2015).

[11] Hastings Rashdall, *The Universities of Europe in the Middle Ages* (2 vols, Oxford, 1895), I, pp. 4–5; A.B. Cobban, *The Medieval Universities: Their Development and Organization* (London, 1975), pp. 23–5; Olaf Pedersen, *The First Universities: Studium Generale and the Origins of University Education in Europe*, trans. Richard North (Cambridge, 1997), pp. 122–54; James Axtell, *Wisdom's Workshop: The Rise of the Modern University* (Princeton, NJ, 2016), chap. 1.

[12] See e.g., Gerald Strauss, *Luther's House of Learning: Indoctrination of the Young in the German Reformation* (Baltimore, MD, 1978); John Morgan, *Godly Learning: Puritan Attitudes towards Reason, Learning and Education, 1560–1640* (Cambridge, 1986); Olaf Pedersen, 'Tradition and Innovation', *HUE*, pp. 452–88; Paul Grendler, 'The Universities of the Renaissance and Reformation', *Renaissance Quarterly*, 57:1 (2004), 1–42.

[13] Durkheim, *Education and Sociology*, pp. 62–3.

The early modern university itself was a space reserved primarily for elite identity formation. It was an idealised microcosm of, and model for, society at large. It was also the machinery that supplied society with ruling elites to govern the social order that ensured the endurance of a healthy commonwealth. As Carlton emphasises, the transmission of knowledge and principles – that is, a particular way of life – in the university was reserved for the sons of governing elites, which perpetuated the cycle of elite formation and preserved the social hierarchy and wider social order through careers as ministers, statesmen, lawyers, and other officials.[14] As such, the university was wedded closely to early modern governing structures, thus underscoring its essential link to the apparatuses of elite power and state formation.[15] Both the founding and the control of institutions of higher education were vital processes to the formation of states in Europe and the emergence of European settlements in imperial spaces. By viewing the university as both an instrument of socialisation and a venue of elite formation, this book necessarily explores the application of higher education in the service of emerging states and settler communities in early modern Scotland, Ireland, and New England.

In an early modern Europe divided increasingly by confessions, scholars – especially those who have examined education and state formation in central Europe – have identified how schools and universities became vital machinery of the state, for controlling education was central to inculcating 'true' religion and learning.[16] In examining seventeenth-century Scotland, Ireland, and New England, this book understands the university as one of the many institutions that constituted a wider system of governance that exercised political, religious, and social power; but, crucially, it was also the institution that provided essential personnel who constituted and controlled these sources of power.[17] Michael Braddick's analysis of political power in its confessional

---

[14] Carlton, *Ideology and Social Order*, p. 90. See also Willem Frijhoff, 'Graduation and Careers', *HUE*, pp. 355–415.

[15] Notker Hammerstein, 'Relations with Authority', *HUE*, pp. 114–53, at 116–18; Maria Rosa di Simone, 'Admission', *HUE*, pp. 285–325; R.A. Houston, *Literacy in Early Modern Europe: Culture and Education 1500–1800* (London, 2002), pp. 90–9; Richard Kirwan, 'Introduction: Scholarly Self-Fashioning and the Cultural History of Universities', *Scholarly Self-Fashioning*, pp. 1–20, at 2–3.

[16] See e.g., Notker Hammerstein, 'Universitäten - Territorialstaaten - Gelehrte Rätem', in Roman Schnur (ed.), *Die Rolle Der Juristen Bei Der Entstehung de Mondernen Staates* (Berlin, 1986), pp. 687–737; Anton Schindling, 'Schulen Und Universitäten Um 16. Und 17. Jahrhundert. Zehn Thesen Zu Bildungsexpansion, Laienbildung Und Konfessionalisierung Nach Reformation', in Walter Brandmüller, Herbert Immenkötter, and Erwin Iserloh (eds), *Ecclesia Militans: Studia Zur Konzilien Und Refomartionsgeschichte Remigius Bäumer Zum 70. Geburtstag Gewidmet* (Paderborn, 1988), pp. 561–70; Brad S. Gregory, *The Unintended Reformation: How a Religious Revolution Secularized Society* (Cambridge, MA, 2012), pp. 327–49.

[17] Foucault, *Discipline and Punish*, pp. 176–7; Steve Hindle, *The State and Social Change*

'crystallisation' has especial resonance for conceptualising the vital role universities played. Early modern political legitimacy was rooted, in part, in the 'defence' of true religion that ruling authorities – monarchs, prelates, nobles, statesmen, church synods, and, as will also be highlighted in this study, powerful clerical factions – defined and enforced.[18] Indeed, as Howard Hotson shows, in the era of confessional rivalry following the Reformation, student demand was met by the growth of confessionalised academic institutions to meet the needs of established and emerging states.[19] The overarching ecclesiastical apparatus that served as the governing structure of religious power – itself a type of ideological power – could take the form of an established church, as was the case in England, Scotland, and Ireland, or through the highly structured congregational communities that defined early New England.[20] In areas where Reformed Protestantism was ascendant, the university was connected closely to this structure of ideological power. It emerged as both a purveyor of 'true' religion – through perpetuating forms of knowledge thought to promote order and discipline – and a tool of political power.[21]

In his analysis of Calvinism and state formation, Philip Gorski argued that a state's strength was determined by two core infrastructural elements: its ideological infrastructure, in which ruling authorities harnessed the loyalties of administrators and subjects to distil collective identities; and its administrative infrastructure, through which authorities regulated individual conduct.[22] This book contends that universities in seventeenth-century Scotland, Ireland, and New England developed as vital infrastructures of power – sites of political, theological, and administrative control – in which both of these processes played out.[23] What this study also seeks to emphasise was that this was often a chaotic, contingent process. As Charles Tilly has highlighted, European state formation was characterised by pronounced conflict and resistance. Ruling authorities often encountered

---

in *Early Modern England, 1550–1640* (Basingstoke, 2000), pp. 18–19; Michael Mann, *The Sources of Social Power, Volume I: A History of Power from the Beginning to A.D. 1760* (Cambridge, 1986), pp. 9–10.

[18] Michael J. Braddick, *State Formation in Early Modern England, c. 1550–1700* (Cambridge, 2000), pp. 287–90.

[19] Howard Hotson, *The Reformation of Common Learning: Post-Ramist Method and the Reception of the New Philosophy, 1618–1670* (Oxford, 2020), p. 4.

[20] Mann, *Sources of Social Power*, pp. 22, 27.

[21] Philip S. Gorski, 'Calvinism and State-Formation in Early Modern Europe', in George Steinmetz (ed.), *State/Culture: State-Formation after the Cultural Turn* (Ithaca, NY, 1999), pp. 147–81, at 148–50. See also Walter Rüegg, 'Themes', *HUE*, pp. 3–42, at 24; Willem Frijhoff, 'Patterns', *HUE*, pp. 43–110, at 53–4, 64–5; Helga Robinson-Hammerstein, 'The "Common Good" and the University in the Age of Confessional Conflict', in Ciaran Brady and Jane H. Ohlmeyer (eds), *British Interventions in Early Modern Ireland* (Cambridge, 2005), pp. 73–96.

[22] Gorski, 'Calvinism and State-Formation', pp. 156–7.

[23] Mann, *Sources of Social Power*, pp. 9, 27–8.

severe opposition to their interventionist policies as they sought to marshal and create institutions to be effective instruments of policy, cultivate social order, and engineer homogeneity to norms – like state religions – in order to solidify political power and, crucially, survive for future generations.[24] This study endeavours to demonstrate that within both metropolitan and colonial spaces during an era of civil war, universities were key venues where this conflict and resistance took place.

In examining this phenomenon as it played out in universities on either side of the Atlantic, this study conceives of early modern universities as contested spaces – sites, imbued with meaning, where rival exertions of power projected their authority and became entangled with one another.[25] Kirsteen MacKenzie applies this concept to the analysis of the burgh of Glasgow during the Cromwellian conquest and occupation, in which she demonstrates how a 'force from the outside challenges the long established authority in a given area to displace or manipulate existing representations of authority to its own advantage'. MacKenzie elucidates the processes by which an occupying power controlled social and political structures and how this authority was resisted by groups and individuals loyal to the old order.[26] This idea is especially instructive for an examination of the universities. But this book also seeks to take this idea of a contested space further. The university was not only a space where power was projected, it was also a space where power was refined through the training of future governing elites – or so it was assumed. With the concept of contested spaces in mind, the university also emerges as a place of resistance to the forces of domination. The agency of the men who staffed the universities – their backgrounds and education, their idiosyncrasies, and their actions – is thus of vital importance. Universities were not passive institutions that acquiesced repeatedly to the whims of territorial rulers; rather, they were dynamic, highly politicised arenas, where the decisions, expertise, foibles, and biases of individuals mattered.[27] While dominating forces often won the day, the universities of Scotland, Ireland, and New England were

---

[24] Charles Tilly, 'Reflections on the History of European State-Making', in Charles Tilly (ed.), *The Formation of National States in Western Europe* (Princeton, NJ, 1975), pp. 3–83, at 17–19, 23–5, 28, 40–4.

[25] See e.g., Joanne P. Sharp *et al.*, 'Entanglements of Power: Geographies of Domination/Resistance', in Joanne P. Sharp *et al.* (eds), *Entanglements of Power: Geographies of Domination/Resistance* (New York, 2000), pp. 1–42, at 1, 20–4; David Storey, *Territories: The Claiming of Space*, 2nd edn (London, 2012), chap. 1; Martin Jones *et al.*, *An Introduction to Political Geography: Space, Place and Politics* (London, 2015), pp. 97–8.

[26] Kirsteen M. MacKenzie, 'A Contested Space: Demonstrative Action and the Politics of Transitional Authority in Glasgow 1650–1653', in Kate Buchanan, Lucinda H.S. Dean, and Michael Penman (eds), *Medieval and Early Modern Representations of Authority in Scotland and the British Isles* (New York, 2016), pp. 68–82.

[27] Braddick, *State Formation*, p. 1; Mann, *Sources of Social Power*, p. 37. On the utility of expertise in early modern state-building, see Eric H. Ash, 'Introduction: Expertise and the Early Modern State', *Osiris*, 25:1 (2010), 1–24.

nevertheless spaces where competing conceptions of true religion, sober learning, and political conformity were debated, contested, and coerced. As such, they were spaces where the conflicts and struggles endemic to European state formation manifested often.

The nature of the early modern British composite monarchy and its overseas empire meant that, particularly during the Civil Wars, there were overlapping and rival foci of authority that competed for control of higher education to realise their competing conceptions of the wider social order. The early Stuart monarchy, the Cromwellian regime, the independent kingdom of Scots, and New English settlers in Ireland all vied for control of institutions of higher learning. But resisting the encroachments of a centralising monarchy also saw the founding of new institutions to support communities whose relationship with royal power was being redefined. Indeed, in an era of confessional and political rivalry, competing authorities set doctrinal and institutional boundaries to define communities, with the universities mobilised to endorse divergent political and religious agendas.[28] This book therefore underlines the crucial role universities played in their specific, seventeenth-century settings. It investigates how rival groups and individuals vied for control of higher education to highlight how the universities of Scotland, Ireland, and New England were fundamental to the construction of states, the extension of governing authority, and the resistance to intrusions.

* * *

In 1975, the historian of universities Charles Schmitt noted that, 'we are sorely in need of synthetic and comparative studies relating several universities to one another'.[29] This book seeks to provide one such comparative analysis by focusing specifically on the smaller, Reformed institutions of higher learning of the British Atlantic world. Alison Games argues that the Atlantic framework is concerned not only with 'literal points of contact' and empire building, but also with exploring 'transformations, experiences, and events' in various locales in the Atlantic basin.[30] This work thus examines the shared, and at times interconnected processes that marked early modern higher education on either side of the Atlantic by highlighting its relationship to the formation of states and communities in three locales. In doing so, it employs a type of 'trans-Atlantic' framework to make comparisons between the higher educational experiences in these spaces in the mid-seventeenth century.[31] J.G.A. Pocock's formative articulation of a 'new British history', which argued

---

[28] Gorski, 'Calvinism and State-Formation', p. 173.
[29] Quoted in Walter Rüegg, 'Foreword', *HUE*, pp. xix–xxiii, at xxii.
[30] Alison Games, 'Atlantic History: Definitions, Challenges, and Opportunities', *American Historical Review*, 111:3 (2006), 741–57, at 747.
[31] David Armitage, 'Three Concepts of Atlantic History', in David Armitage and Michael J. Braddick (eds), *The British Atlantic World, 1500–1800*, 1st edn (New York, 2002), pp. 11–27, at 19–21.

for a holistic approach to the study of Britain, Ireland, and the empire, has spawned a prodigious amount of scholarship that has investigated, among other subjects, Britain's composite monarchy, state formation, and religion in their archipelagic and Atlantic contexts.[32] Historians have especially come to appreciate the 'British' dimension of the seventeenth-century Civil Wars: their causes, nature, and conclusion must be understood in their wider archipelagic settings.[33] But, as Pocock also recognised, as the British empire expanded in the seventeenth century, so too should our interpretive framework.[34]

Carla Pestana's scholarship, which provides a crucial historiographic basis for many elements of this study, highlighted how the British Isles' religious tensions migrated throughout the Atlantic, thus reframing our understanding of the conflict's impact.[35] This book contends that such a wider perspective will also help to shape our understanding of the universities that dotted the peripheries of the British Atlantic by viewing these institutions as contested spaces where early modern conceptions of power and identity were negotiated. It seeks to illuminate how the universities figured into attempts to solve the problem of multiple monarchy; highlight the nature of conflict and resistance in the universities; and elucidate the connectedness and mobility of ideas concerning higher learning and social order as they migrated throughout Britain, Europe, and America. In doing so, this study highlights the development and application of common, 'British' ideas about the universities, and higher learning in general, in vastly different contexts.[36]

---

[32] J.G.A. Pocock, 'British History: A Plea for a New Subject', *Journal of Modern History*, 47:4 (1975), 601–21; idem, 'The Limits and Divisions of British History', *American Historical Review*, 87:2 (1982), 311–36. The 1990s witnessed the publication a number of important edited volumes on British history, including Steven G. Ellis and Sarah Barber (eds), *Conquest and Union: Fashioning a British State, 1485–1725* (London, 1995); Alexander Grant and Keith J. Stringer (eds), *Uniting the Kingdom? The Making of British History* (New York, 1995); Brendan Bradshaw and John Morrill (eds), *The British Problem, c. 1534–1707: State Formation in the Atlantic Archipelago* (New York, 1996); Brendan Bradshaw and Peter Roberts (eds), *British Consciousness and Identity: The Making of Britain, 1533–1707* (Cambridge, 1998); Glenn Burgess (ed.), *The New British History: Founding a Modern State 1603–1715* (London, 1999); Allan I. Macinnes and Jane H. Ohlmeyer (eds), *The Stuart Kingdoms in the Seventeenth Century: Awkward Neighbours* (Dublin, 2002).

[33] See e.g., Conrad Russell, *The Fall of the British Monarchies, 1637–1642* (Oxford, 1991); J.G.A. Pocock, 'The Atlantic Archipelago and the War of the Three Kingdoms', *British Problem*, pp. 172–91; Austin Woolrych, *Britain in Revolution 1625–1660* (Oxford, 2002); Allan I. Macinnes, *The British Revolution, 1629–1660* (Basingstoke, 2005); Tim Harris, *Rebellion: Britain's First Stuart Kings, 1567–1642* (Oxford, 2014).

[34] Pocock, 'Limits and Divisions', pp. 318–19, 323.

[35] See especially Carla Gardina Pestana, *The English Atlantic in the Age of Revolution, 1640–1661* (Cambridge, MA, 2004). See also eadem, *Protestant Empire: Religion and the Making of the British Atlantic World* (Philadelphia, PA, 2009), chap. 3.

[36] Alison Games, 'Beyond the Atlantic: English Globetrotters and Transoceanic Connections', *William and Mary Quarterly*, 63:4 (2006), 675–92, at 687; John Roberts, Águeda M. Rodríguez Cruz, and Jurgen Herbst, 'Exporting Models', *HUE*, pp. 256–82.

INTRODUCTION

Oxford and Cambridge's centrality to the religious and political policies of the British monarchy and their relationships to shifting centres of power during the Civil Wars has been well studied in existing historiography.[37] This literature provides an important comparative element for examining the universities in this study. As this book's main units of analysis, Scotland's five university centres and the universities of Ireland and New England – Trinity College, Dublin and Harvard College – all, crucially, bore the marks of a particular type of institution of higher learning that began appearing throughout Europe during the Reformation, which ultimately set them apart from their English counterparts. Rooting this study in European trends also provides a richer perspective through which to investigate these British and Atlantic institutions. Beginning in the mid-sixteenth century, Europe saw a proliferation of institutions of higher learning, especially in the Reformed world, with the growth of smaller colleges and 'academies' that were better able to respond to the needs of small, religiously homogenised communities.[38] Karin Maag's analysis of academies in Switzerland, France, and the Holy Roman Empire emphasises that these institutions were highly versatile and combined pre-university education for youths, Latin instruction in the arts, and university-level training in higher faculties to educate clerics and civil servants in an era of pronounced confessional conflict.[39]

These institutions were not altogether new, but rather hybrids that blended elements of the archetypal university with novel organisational structures and instruction.[40] The nature of university learning in the medieval territorial universities – like Oxford and Cambridge – remained rooted in rote instruction of the Aristotelian *Organon*, which was, as Hotson notes, better suited for producing ecclesiastics and scholars of larger, territorial churches

---

[37] See e.g., Nicholas Tyacke (ed.), *The History of the University of Oxford, Vol. IV Seventeenth-Century Oxford* (Oxford, 1997); Christopher Brooke and Victor Morgan, *A History of the University of Cambridge, Vol. II 1546–1750* (Cambridge, 2004); Twigg, *Cambridge and the English Revolution*. See also Victor Morgan, 'Approaches to the History of the English Universities in the Sixteenth and Seventeenth Centuries', in Grete Klingenstein, Heinrich Lutz, and Gerard Stourzh (eds), *Bildung, Politik Und Gesellschaft* (Vienna, 1978), pp. 138–64; Mark H. Curtis, *Oxford and Cambridge in Transition, 1558–1642: An Essay on Changing Relations between the English Universities and English Society* (Oxford, 1959).

[38] Frijhoff, 'Patterns', pp. 70–3.

[39] Karin Maag, 'The Reformation and Higher Education', in Thomas A. Howard and Mark A. Noll (eds), *Protestantism after 500 Years* (Oxford, 2016), pp. 121–37. See also *eadem, Seminary or University? The Genevan Academy and Reformed Higher Education, 1560–1620* (Aldershot, 1995), pp. 1–3; *eadem*, 'The Huguenot Academies: Preparing for an Uncertain Future', in Raymond A. Mentzer and Andrew Spicer (eds), *Society and Culture in the Huguenot World 1559–1685* (Cambridge, 2002), pp. 139–56.

[40] John F. Padgett and Walter W. Powell, 'The Problem of Emergence', in John F. Padgett and Walter W. Powell (eds), *The Emergence of Organizations and Markets* (Princeton, NJ, 2012), pp. 1–29, at 2.

than it was for effectively training ministers and magistrates.[41] What was required was a streamlined pedagogical approach that offered practical training for authorities to meet the needs of societies in contested confessional spaces, such as the fragmented Holy Roman Empire. There, the Augsburg principle of *cuius regio, eius religio* played out in an academic context as rulers founded, or re-founded, Lutheran, Reformed, and Catholic universities to consolidate state control.[42] Within this central European crucible, innovative pedagogies flourished. Many of these ideas were rooted in the methods of the French Reformed humanist Petrus Ramus (1515–72), who sought to standardise the Aristotelian corpus in pursuit of a streamlined arts course that instilled in students practical tuition in logic and rhetoric.[43] In Reformed institutions, pure Ramist pedagogy was largely repudiated by the early seventeenth century. Yet the Heidelberg philosopher Bartholomäus Keckermann (1572–1609) refined the Ramist method and developed a new system of philosophical instruction that was distilled via scholarly and refugee networks to universities throughout the Reformed world.[44] The pedagogy was especially useful for institutions, like the Scottish universities, Trinity, and Harvard, on confessional and cultural borders that sought practical training for clerics and civil servants to support smaller, self-fashioned godly communities.[45] It was a pragmatic training that supported education in smaller states and settler communities within and beyond Europe that consolidated along confessional lines. In many ways, these institutions exemplified Steve Hindle's assertion that certain societal apparatuses acted as tools of state formation – such as the university – that shifted and responded as societal needs evolved.[46]

Like Protestant academies on the continent, the universities of Scotland, Ireland, and New England were small, centralised 'college-universities'.

---

[41] Hotson, *Reformation of Common Learning*, p. 8. See also Laurence Brockliss, 'Curricula', HUE, pp. 565–620, at 565–9; Hugh Kearney, *Scholars and Gentlemen: Universities in Pre-Industrial Britain, 1500–1700* (Ithaca, NY, 1970), chap. 3.

[42] See e.g., Hammerstein, 'Universitäten'; Ian Hunter, *The Secularisation of the Confessional State: The Political Thought of Christian Thomasius* (Cambridge, 2007), pp. 2–3, 34–45.

[43] Howard Hotson, *Commonplace Learning: Ramism and Its German Ramifications, 1543–1630* (Oxford, 2007), pp. 43–51.

[44] Hotson, *Reformation of Common Learning*, chap. 1; idem, 'The Ramist Roots of Comenian Pansophia', in Steven J. Reid and Emma Annette Wilson (eds), *Ramus, Pedagogy and the Liberal Arts: Ramism in Britain and the Wider World* (Aldershot, 2011), pp. 227–52, at 228–31; Steven J. Reid, 'Reformed Scholasticism, Proto-Empiricism and the Intellectual "Long Reformation" in Scotland: The Philosophy of the "Aberdeen Doctors", c. 1619–c. 1641', in John McCallum (ed.), *Scotland's Long Reformation: New Perspectives on Scottish Religion, c. 1500–c. 1660* (Leiden, 2016), pp. 149–78; Emma Annette Wilson, 'The International Nature of Britannic Ramism', in Sarah Knight and Emma Annette Wilson (eds), *The European Contexts of Ramism* (Turnhout, 2019), pp. 109–31.

[45] Howard Hotson, '"A Generall Reformation of Common Learning" and Its Reception in the English-Speaking World, 1560–1642', in Polly Ha and Patrick Collinson (eds), *The Reception of Continental Reformation in Britain* (Oxford, 2010), pp. 193–228.

[46] Hindle, *State and Social Change*, p. 16.

They were all degree-granting institutions of higher learning that brought students through an arts course and offered varied training in higher faculties, especially divinity.[47] But they also possessed key differences that marked each institutions' early history. Only St Andrews University (founded 1410/13) had more than one constituent college; it comprised St Salvator's (f. 1450), St Leonard's (f. 1512), and St Mary's (f. 1538). Trinity College, Dublin (f. 1592) was the 'mother' of a university, the founding and still the only college of the University of Dublin.[48] Though modelled on the Cambridge colleges, Trinity possessed a marked degree of autonomy in the early seventeenth century that was derived from its Elizabethan charter, which authorised provosts to make their own statutes and fellows to elect their own provost. The provost was the college head and shared teaching and governing duties with up to sixteen fellows. Trinity's chancellorship, traditionally occupied by a high-ranking political figure in England, was prior to the 1630s mostly a ceremonial position, with successive chancellors intervening in the college only superficially prior to Laud's tenure.[49] Meanwhile, each of Scotland's 'medieval' universities – St Andrews, Glasgow University (f. 1451), and King's College, Aberdeen (f. 1495) – were founded via papal bull and had university structures in which the local bishop served as chancellor. Edinburgh University (f. 1583) and Marischal College, Aberdeen (f. 1593), meanwhile, owed their existence, rights, and privileges to the patronage of the local nobility and town councils.[50] Despite the differences in these foundations, each Scottish university had a principal (called provost at St Salvator's) who helmed each institution and often served as a divinity professor. Each had four teaching regents, normally made up of more capable recent graduates, who guided students through the arts course, in addition to specialised professors.[51] Finally, Harvard College (f. 1636) owed its foundation to the General Court of Massachusetts, and in its infancy the college possessed a master and tutor who shared teaching and disciplinary responsibilities, though this arrangement was scrapped by 1640, when the Court established the office of the president. Throughout the 1640s, the president shared responsibilities with an advisory committee of ministers and magistrates, the Board of Overseers, and teaching responsibilities with

---

[47] Morison, *HCSC*, I, pp. 70–3.
[48] John Pentland Mahaffy, *An Epoch in Irish History: Trinity College, Dublin, Its Foundation and Early Fortunes, 1591–1660* (London, 1903), p. 63.
[49] For Trinity's founding charter, see Hercules H.G. MacDonnell (ed.), *Chartæ et Statuta Collegii Sacrosanctæ et Individuæ Trinitatis Reginæ Elizabethæ, Juxta Dublin* (Dublin, 1844), pp. 1–9.
[50] Michael Lynch, 'The Origins of Edinburgh's "Toun College": A Revision Article', *Innes Review*, 33 (1982), 3–14; Steven J. Reid, 'Aberdeen's "Toun College": Marischal College, 1593–1623', *Innes Review*, 58:2 (2007), 173–95; Miles Kerr-Peterson, *A Protestant Lord in James VI's Scotland: George Keith, Firth Early Marischal (1554–1623)* (Woodbridge, 2019), chap. 8.
[51] Alasdair Raffe, 'Academic Specialisation in the Early Modern Scottish Universities', in Bo Lindberg (ed.), *Early Modern Academic Culture* (Stockholm, 2019), pp. 177–88.

tutors consisting of recent graduates. It was not until the charter of 1650, which established a formal corporation, that fellows became part of the college dynamic.

Within an Atlantic context, we are thus presented with a group of small, malleable, college-universities, which were easily controllable and made to adapt to the needs of their respective societies.[52] External control by governing authorities was a key feature of Reformed institutions of higher learning.[53] But as a machinery of state formation and contested spaces, the intentions, actions, and impacts of the groups and individuals who vied for control of these universities was just as important as the institutions themselves. Thus a further comparative element crucial to the examination of the universities of Scotland, Ireland, and New England was that each of the communities that the universities served was, to varying degrees, 'puritan'. Puritanism refers to the particularly intense form of Reformed Protestantism that germinated in late sixteenth-century England and Scotland, whose proponents opposed the overly sacramental, hierarchical, and 'popish' elements that remained in the established churches. Puritans, broadly speaking, favoured plain and unadorned forms of worship and total adherence to the Bible, stressed unconditional election, promoted strict sabbatarianism, discipline, and personal devotion, and harboured a virulent anti-Catholicism.[54] This brief definition speaks to the general beliefs held by puritans that spanned England, Ireland, and Scotland, expatriates in Europe, and settlers in New England, all of which differed in terms of government, church membership, and baptism.[55]

Grounding this study in a shared – though highly diversified – trans-Atlantic puritanism allows for an examination into the types of confessionalised

---

[52] Frijhoff, 'Patterns', p. 65.
[53] Maag, 'Reformation and Higher Education', p. 136; Anja-Silvia Goeing, 'Sixteenth Century Higher Education in Zurich and Its Ties to the City-State Government', in Anja-Silvia Goeing, Glyn Parry, and Mordechai Feingold (eds), *Early Modern Universities: Networks of Higher Learning* (Leiden, 2021), pp. 63–82.
[54] See e.g., Patrick Collinson, *The Elizabethan Puritan Movement* (Oxford, 1967); idem, 'Sects and the Evolution of Puritanism', in Francis J. Bremer (ed.), *Puritanism: Transatlantic Perspectives on a Seventeenth-Century Anglo-American Faith* (Boston, MA, 1993), pp. 147–66; Stephen Foster, *The Long Argument: English Puritanism and the Shaping of New England Culture, 1570–1700* (Chapel Hill, NC, 1991), pp. 5–25; John Coffey and Paul C.H. Lim, 'Introduction', in John Coffey and Paul C.H. Lim (eds), *The Cambridge Companion to Puritanism* (Cambridge, 2008), pp. 1–15. See also Evan Haefeli, *Accidental Pluralism: America and the Religious Politics of English Expansion, 1497–1662* (Chicago, IL, 2021), chap. 4.
[55] David D. Hall, *The Puritans: A Transatlantic History* (Princeton, NJ, 2019). See also Pestana, *Protestant Empire*, p. 45; Margo Todd, 'The Problem of Scotland's Puritans', *Cambridge Companion to Puritanism.*, pp. 174–88; David G. Mullan, *Scottish Puritanism 1590–1638* (Oxford, 2000); Alan Ford, 'The Church of Ireland, 1558–1634: A Puritan Church?', in Alan Ford, James McGuire, and Kenneth Milne (eds), *As By Law Established: The Church of Ireland Since the Reformation* (Dublin, 1995), pp. 52–68.

societies that these groups, and their opponents, wished to build in these spaces, and how they employed the universities to ensure they would endure for successive generations through the socialisation of future governing elites.[56] The religious tensions endemic to Charles I's reign were exported to New England, as English 'Separatist' communities sought to escape the Laudian Church of England and established godly communities of the elect.[57] In New England, membership within a polity rooted in congregational church communities was, initially, strictly limited, with full membership based on evidence of authentic conversion. In Massachusetts, secular and religious authorities worked in tandem to maintain the Bible commonwealth, enacting legal codes rooted in Scripture and supporting churches in each of the towns within the colony.[58] This was the society that Harvard was founded to sustain. In Scotland, conceptions of an autonomous, anti-episcopal Kirk were based on an imaginary Dalriadic heritage.[59] Though its polity oscillated between episcopacy and Presbyterianism, the Kirk possessed a Reformed confession and comprised a system of courts, from the local kirk session to the national General Assembly, which regulated discipline and fostered an identity as a covenanted nation undergirded by a national church.[60] As will be examined in this study, Charles I's reforms of the Kirk and the Scottish universities prompted leading Scottish divines, operating under the revolutionary aegis of the 1638 National Covenant, to retake control of the universities in order to support a reinvigorated, Presbyterian Church of Scotland.

In Ireland, three main religious and ethnic groups, in addition to Scottish settlers in Ulster, constituted the kingdom's population: the native Irish, broadly of Catholic religion and Gaelic culture, and the overwhelming majority of Ireland's population; the Old English, the descendants of the twelfth-century Norman conquerors who intermixed with the native Irish and remained largely Catholic following the Reformation; and the New English, the Protestant English settlers and their descendants who planted

---

[56] Tilly, 'Reflections', p. 40; Braddick, *State Formation*, p. 287.
[57] Pestana, *Protestant Empire*, chap. 3.
[58] Francis J. Bremer, *The Puritan Experiment: New England Society from Bradford to Edwards*, rev. edn (Hanover, NH, 1995), pp. 56–62; Virginia DeJohn Anderson, 'New England in the Seventeenth Century', in Nicholas Canny (ed.), *The Oxford History of the British Empire, Vol. I: The Origins of Empire* (Oxford, 1998), pp. 193–217, at 204–7; Francis J. Bremer, 'The New England Way Reconsidered: An Exploration of Church Polity and the Governance of the Region's Churches', in Elliot Vernon and Hunter Powell (eds), *Church Polity and Politics in the British Atlantic World, c. 1635–66* (Manchester, 2020), pp. 155–73.
[59] Colin Kidd, *British Identities before Nationalism: Ethnicity and Nationhood in the Atlantic World, 1600–1800* (Cambridge, 1999), pp. 128–31.
[60] R. Scott Spurlock, 'Polity, Discipline and Theology: The Importance of the Covenant in Scottish Presbyterianism, 1560–c. 1700', *Church Polity and Politics in the British Atlantic World*, pp. 80–103; Margo Todd, *The Culture of Protestantism in Early Modern Scotland* (New Haven, 2002), pp. 402–12.

Ireland in the sixteenth and early seventeenth centuries.[61] With its particular attention to Trinity College, Dublin, this study focuses on the New English, who also exercised authority in the Irish government. In a quasi-colonial setting, the New English were animated by the idea that they were a distinct people, superior to both the native Irish and Old English.[62] The religious element reinforced this distinctiveness. With the failure of the Reformation, the Church of Ireland developed as an institution staffed initially by English puritans.[63] It also possessed a distinct Reformed doctrine formalised in the Irish Articles of 1615, and its theology set out an apocalyptic vision that dissociated its adherents from Catholics, thus underpinning a distinct identity as a godly community amongst the damned.[64] Similar to the Kirk's imagined past, James Ussher, archbishop of Armagh, crafted an identity for the Irish church, basing its independence from the Church of England on the imaginary heritage of an autonomous Celtic church.[65] Trinity served this confessional milieu. It was a Reformed seminary whose New English students were educated via a Ramist method and were armed with anti-Catholic polemic to fight the Anti-Christ.[66] Like New England, in Ireland, the local university reinforced an insular settler population's communal identity.

By viewing the mid-seventeenth century universities as contested instruments of socialisation, we see them not as intellectual backwaters, divorced

---

[61] See e.g., Kidd, *British Identities*, pp. 146–77; Aidan Clarke, 'Colonial Identity in Early Seventeenth-Century Ireland', in T.W. Moody (ed.), *Nationality and the Pursuit of National Independence*, Historical Studies XI (Belfast, 1978), pp. 57–71; Pádraig Lenihan, *Consolidating Conquest: Ireland 1603–1727* (London, 2008), pp. 68–70.

[62] Nicholas Canny, 'Identity Formation in Ireland: The Emergence of the Anglo-Irish', in Nicholas Canny and Anthony Pagden (eds), *Colonial Identity in the Atlantic World, 1500–1800* (Princeton, NJ, 1987), pp. 159–212; idem, *Making Ireland British, 1580–1650* (Oxford, 2001), pp. 42–58.

[63] Ford, 'Church of Ireland', pp. 53–4. See also idem, *James Ussher: Theology, History, and Politics in Early-Modern Ireland and England* (Oxford, 2007), pp. 23–5; Ute Lotz-Heumann, 'Confessionalisation in Ireland: Periodisation and Character, 1534–1649', in Alan Ford and John McCafferty (eds), *The Origins of Sectarianism in Early Modern Ireland* (Cambridge, 2005), pp. 24–53.

[64] Alan Ford, 'Apocalyptic Ireland: 1580–1641', *Irish Theological Quarterly*, 78:2 (2013), 123–48.

[65] Kidd, *British Identities*, pp. 162–77; Alan Ford, 'Dependent or Independent? The Church of Ireland and Its Colonial Context, 1536–1649', *The Seventeenth Century*, 10 (1995), 163–87; idem, 'James Ussher and the Creation of an Irish Protestant Identity', *British Consciousness and Identity*, pp. 185–212; idem, 'Shaping History: James Ussher and the Church of Ireland', in Mark Empey, Alan Ford, and Miriam Moffitt (eds), *The Church of Ireland and Its Past: History, Interpretation and Identit* (Dublin, 2017), pp. 19–35.

[66] Alan Ford, 'Who Went to Trinity? The Early Students of Dublin University', *European Universities in the Age of Reformation and Counter Reformation*, pp. 53–74, at 73–4; Elizabethanne Boran, 'Ramism in Trinity College, Dublin, in the Early Seventeenth Century', in Mordechai Feingold, Joseph S. Freedman, and Wolfgang Rother (eds), *The Influence of Petrus Ramus* (Basel, 2001), pp. 177–99.

from the realities of the day, but rather as contemporaries saw them: as strategic institutions upon which the endurance of competing visions of social order rested. This book thus also seeks to contribute to scholarship that has aimed to examine early modern universities beyond their purely institutional contexts. Indeed, the Scottish universities, Trinity, and Harvard do not lack for narrative histories. St Andrews and its colleges, Glasgow, King's, Edinburgh, and Marischal, boast a litany of histories,[67] while Trinity has been served by several institutional histories.[68] Harvard also possesses a strong historiographical tradition, especially through Samuel Eliot Morison's tercentenary histories.[69] Beyond these institutional studies, the nature of the historiography that has defined the universities is highly varied.

Trinity, specifically, has been served well by studies that situate its founding and early function in the seventeenth-century constitutional and confessional contexts. This is tied to interest in the failure of the Reformation in Ireland, in which schooling played a key role.[70] Much of Helga Robinson-Hammerstein's important work on Trinity has proceeded from the fact that it was an English institution meant to consolidate control of Ireland. It was founded in 1592 to train a Protestant ministry, civilise the native Irish, and

---

[67] On St Andrews, see Ronald G. Cant, *The University of St Andrews: A Short History*, 2nd edn (Edinburgh, 1970); idem, *The College of St Salvator: Its Foundation and Development Including a Selection of Documents* (Edinburgh, 1950). On Glasgow, see James Coutts, *A History of the University of Glasgow From Its Foundation in 1451 to 1908* (Glasgow, 1909); J.D. Mackie, *The University of Glasgow 1541–1951: A Short History* (Glasgow, 1954). On both colleges of Aberdeen, see Robert S. Rait, *The Universities of Aberdeen: A History* (Aberdeen, 1895); John M. Bulloch, *A History of the University of Aberdeen 1495–1895* (London, 1895). There are many histories of Edinburgh, beginning with Thomas Craufurd, *History of the University of Edinburgh, from 1580 to 1646* (Edinburgh, 1808); Alexander Bower, *The History of the University of Edinburgh; Chiefly Compiled from Original Papers and Records, Never before Published* (2 vols, Edinburgh, 1817); Andrew Dalzel, *History of the University of Edinburgh from Its Foundation* (2 vols, Edinburgh, 1862); Alexander Grant, *The Story of the University of Edinburgh during Its First Three Hundred Years* (2 vols, London, 1884); D.B. Horn, *A Short History of the University of Edinburgh 1556–1889* (Edinburgh, 1967); Gordon Donaldson (ed.), *Four Centuries Edinburgh University Life: 1583–1983* (Edinburgh, 1983).

[68] Mahaffy, *Epoch in Irish History*; John William Stubbs, *The History of the University of Dublin, from Its Foundation to the End of the Eighteenth Century* (Dublin, 1889); William Urwick, *The Early History of Trinity College Dublin 1591–1660, As Told in Contemporary Records on Occasion of Its Tercentenary* (Dublin, 1892); Harold L. Murphy, *A History of Trinity College Dublin from Its Foundation to 1702* (Dublin, 1951); R.B. McDowell and D.A. Webb, *Trinity College Dublin 1592–1952: An Academic History* (Dublin, 2004).

[69] Morison, *Founding*; idem, *HCSC*; idem, *Three Centuries of Harvard, 1636–1936* (Cambridge, MA, 1936). See also Josiah Quincy, *The History of Harvard University* (Cambridge, MA, 1840) and more recently, George H. Williams, *First Light: The Formation of Harvard College in 1636 and Evolution of a Republic of Letters in Cambridge* (Göttingen, 2014).

[70] Colm Lennon, 'Education and Religious Identity in Early Modern Ireland', *Paedagogica Historica*, 35, supplement (1999), 57–75.

stem the flow of Irish boys to Catholic universities on the continent. But Trinity's founding was too little too late, and the college failed to produce a Protestant clergy and extirpate popery.[71] Trinity instead became a haven for nonconforming, hard-line Calvinists who desired further religious reform and who had become increasingly unwelcome in England's universities and ministry.[72] Among its founders were graduates of its namesake Trinity College and Emmanuel College, Cambridge. This resulted in the creation of a hotly Protestant seminary increasingly at odds with the English monarchy.[73]

Until recently, studies of the seventeenth-century Scottish universities have been influenced by long-standing scholarly focus on the eighteenth-century Enlightenment.[74] This has led to problematic portrayals of the preceding century.[75] A generation of historians applied this interpretation to the universities.[76] The universities' attachment to Aristotle and the Scots' dogmatism

---

[71] See e.g., Robinson-Hammerstein, 'Royal Policy and Civic Pride'; eadem, 'Trinity College, Dublin, in the Early Seventeenth Century: Institutional Isolation and Foreign Contacts', in John M. Fletcher and Hilde de Ridder-Symoens (eds), *Lines of Contact* (Gent, 1994), pp. 43–56; eadem, 'Archbishop Adam Loftus: The First Provost of Trinity College, Dublin', *European Universities in the Age of Reformation and Counter Reformation*, 34–52; eadem, 'Aspects of the Continental Education of Irish Students in the Reign of Elizabeth I', *Historical Studies*, 8 (1971), 137–54; James Murray, 'St Patrick's Cathedral and the University Question in Ireland c. 1547–1585', *European Universities in the Age of Reformation and Counter Reformation*, pp. 1–33; Thomas O'Connor, 'The Domestic and International Roles of Irish Overseas College, 1590–1800', in Liam Chambers and Thomas O'Connor (eds), *College Communities Abroad: Education, Migration and Catholicism in Early Modern Europe* (Manchester, 2017), pp. 90–114.

[72] Alan Ford, *The Protestant Reformation in Ireland, 1590–1641*, 2nd edn (Dublin, 1997), pp. 155, 161.

[73] Elizabethanne Boran, 'Perceptions of the Role of Trinity College, Dublin, from 1592 to 1641', in Andrea Romano (ed.) *Università in Europa: Le Istituzioni Universitarie Del Medio Evo Ai Nostri Giorni Strutture, Organizzazione, Funzionamento* (Messina, 1995), pp. 257–66.

[74] Richard B. Sher, *Church and University in the Scottish Enlightenment: The Moderate Literati of Edinburgh* (Edinburgh, 1985); Roger L. Emerson, 'Scottish Universities in the Eighteenth Century, 1690–1800', *Studies on Voltaire and the Eighteenth Century*, 167 (1977), 453–74; idem, *Academic Patronage in the Scottish Enlightenment: Glasgow, Edinburgh, and St Andrews Universities* (Edinburgh, 2008); David Allan, 'The Universities and the Scottish Enlightenment', in Robert Anderson, Mark Freeman, and Lindsay Paterson (eds), *The Edinburgh History of Education in Scotland* (Edinburgh, 2015), pp. 97–113; Kelsey Jackson Williams, *The First Scottish Enlightenment: Rebels, Priests, and History* (Oxford, 2020), chap. 2.

[75] For discussions on periodisation and origins, see Williams, *First Scottish Enlightenment*, chap. 1; Paul Wood, 'Defining the Scottish Enlightenment', *Journal of Scottish Philosophy*, 15:3 (2017), 299–311. On portrayals of the seventeenth century, see e.g., Hugh Trevor-Roper, 'Scotland and the Puritan Revolution', in *Religion, the Reformation and Social Change* (London, 1967), 392–444; idem, 'The Scottish Enlightenment', in John Robertson (ed.), *History and the Enlightenment* (New Haven, CT, 2010), pp. 17–33.

[76] See for instance Cant, *St Andrews*, p. 72; idem, 'Origins of the Enlightenment in Scotland: The Universities', in R.H. Campbell and Andrew S. Skinner (eds), *The Origins*

were construed as stunting intellectual growth.[77] Recent scholarship has revised these teleological conclusions, and has shown that Scottish academics and intellectuals were on the vanguard of contemporary philosophical and theological thought, which was reinforced by close intellectual and familial links with continental intellectuals.[78] The universities' use of regenting, in which a single teacher brought a class through the entire four-year arts course, and of the Aristotelian course, despite incorporating post-Ramist method, also found contemporary corollaries and was thus not unique to the Scottish context.[79] Steven Reid has demonstrated that the curriculum of the Covenanters was built on the practical instruction of logic, rhetoric, and divinity to ensure students could apply their skills effectively.[80] This scholarship represents a significant revision to our understanding of early modern Scottish academic life. There has also been important recent work on the educational initiatives of reformer Andrew Melville, who sought to mould the universities into the service of the Presbyterian Kirk by introducing new instruction based on the method of Petrus Ramus, whom Melville studied under at the University of Paris in the 1560s, and new Protestant constitutions in an attempt to rid the universities of their popish elements.[81] While

---

and Nature of the Scottish Enlightenment (Edinburgh, 1982), pp. 42–64; Roger L. Emerson, 'Scottish Cultural Change 1660-1710 and the Union of 1707', in John Robertson (ed.), *A Union for Empire: Political Thought and the British Union of 1707* (Cambridge, 1995), pp. 121–44; Keith M. Brown, 'Scottish Identity in the Seventeenth Century', *British Consciousness and Identity*, pp. 236–58, at 252–3.

[77] Ronald G. Cant, 'The Scottish Universities in the Seventeenth Century', *Aberdeen University Review*, 43:143 (1970), 223–33; Christine M. Shepherd, 'Newtonianism in Scottish Universities in the Seventeenth Century', *Origins and Nature of the Scottish Enlightenment*, pp. 65–85. For Shepherd's important study of learning in the seventeenth-century Scottish universities, see *eadem*, 'Philosophy and Science in the Arts Curriculum of the Scottish Universities in the 17th Century' (PhD thesis, University of Edinburgh, 1974).

[78] See e.g., Alasdair Raffe, 'Intellectual Change before the Enlightenment: Scotland, the Netherlands and the Reception of Cartesian Thought, 1650–1700', *Scottish Historical Review*, 94:238 (2015), 24–47; Giovanni Gellera, 'The Reception of Descartes in the Seventeenth-Century Scottish Universities: Metaphysics and Natural Philosophy (1650–1680)', *Journal of Scottish Philosophy*, 13:3 (2015), 179–201; Esther Mijers, '"Addicted to Puritanism": Philosophical and Theological Relations between Scotland and the United Provinces in the First Half of the Seventeenth Century', *History of Universities*, 29:2 (2016), 69–95; Karie Schultz, 'Protestant Intellectual Culture and Political Ideas in the Scottish Universities, ca. 1600–50', *Journal of the History of Ideas*, 83:1 (2022), 41–62.

[79] Steven J. Reid, 'On the Edge of Reason: The Scottish University between Reformation and Enlightenment, 1560–1660', in Alexander Broadie (ed.), *Scottish Philosophy in the Seventeenth Century* (Oxford, 2020), pp. 33–49.

[80] Steven J. Reid, '"Ane Uniformitie in Doctrine and Good Order": The Scottish Universities in the Age of the Covenant, 1638-1649', *History of Universities*, 29:2 (2016), 13–41.

[81] See especially Steven J. Reid, *Humanism and Calvinism: Andrew Melville and the Universities of Scotland, 1560–1625* (Aldershot, 2011). See also James Kirk, '"Melvillian"

this book examines developments in learning, it mainly focuses on the universities' political and religious utility to competing centres of power, and thus aims to complement recent historiography that has reassessed Scottish intellectual life in the universities. Indeed, save for scholarship on the universities during the Reformation, there has been much less focus on the study of the Scottish universities beyond the classroom, especially after 1625.[82]

Like the Scottish universities, Harvard's history has been mired in a teleology that has viewed the college as part of a wider, uniquely American progression towards a liberal society.[83] Morison's histories of Harvard tower over the field, and they are highly useful to the historian interested in a coherent narrative account of Harvard's early history. He asserted that Harvard was less a religious institution than a forum of secular learning that contributed to the unique 'New England Way'.[84] This conclusion is difficult to reconcile given the highly confessionalised nature of New England society. Perry Miller's study of the New England mind, which viewed Ramism as the bedrock of the entire New England system, also reiterated Morison's claims about Harvard, which fuelled scholarly perceptions of New England's unique *mentalité*.[85] Yet New England was a 'Bible Commonwealth' bent on maintaining orthodoxy and built on a strictly defined sense of church membership of 'visible saints'.[86] Its uniqueness lay not in its status as the progenitor of a liberal, democratic society, but in the closeness with which secular and religious authorities endeavoured to ensure religious orthodoxy.[87] Additionally, analyses of Harvard situate

---

Reform in the Scottish Universities', in Alasdair A. MacDonald, Michael Lynch, and Iain B. Cowan (eds), *The Renaissance in Scotland: Studies in Literature, Religion, History and Culture* (Leiden, 1994), pp. 276–300.

[82] For a recent overview, see David Allan, '"For the Advancement of Religion and Learning": University and Society in Seventeenth-Century Scotland', *Scottish Philosophy in the Seventeenth Century*, pp. 11–32. On the Scottish universities and the Reformation, see Cant, *St Andrews*, pp. 45–51; James K. Cameron, ed., *The First Book of Discipline: With Introduction and Commentary* (Edinburgh, 1972), pp. 58–62, 137–55; Alec Ryrie, *The Origins of the Scottish Reformation* (Manchester, 2006), pp. 29, 97–8; Gordon Donaldson, 'Aberdeen University and the Reformation', *Northern Scotland*, 1:2 (1973), 129–42; David Stevenson, *King's College, Aberdeen, 1560–1641: From Protestant Reformation to Covenanting Revolution* (Aberdeen, 1990), pp. 7–19. The protestantisation of Scotland's universities led to the creation of Scots Catholic colleges abroad. See Tom McInally, *The Sixth Scottish University: The Scots Colleges Abroad: 1575 to 1799* (Leiden, 2012), pp. 6–43.

[83] See especially Michael Sletcher, 'Historians and Anachronisms: Samuel E. Morison and Seventeenth-Century Harvard College', *History of Universities*, 19:2 (2004), 188–220.

[84] Morison, *Founding*, chaps 1–3, 8–10.

[85] Perry Miller, *The New England Mind: The Seventeenth Century* (Boston, MA, 1954), pp. 74–6, chap. 5, pp. 490–1.

[86] Edmund S. Morgan, *Visible Saints: The History of a Puritan Idea* (Ithaca, NY, 1963); David D. Hall, *A Reforming People: Puritanism and the Transformation of Public Life in New England* (Chapel Hill, NC, 2011), pp. 24–38, chap. 3.

[87] Bremer, *Puritan Experiment*, chap. 6; Darren Staloff, *The Making of an American Thinking Class: Intellectuals and Intelligentsia in Puritan Massachusetts* (New York, 1998).

the college's founding and early history within the context of a particularly American educational trajectory as a way to understand America's national development.[88] This ignores the religious and imperial contexts within which Harvard was founded. Harvard's founding and early history resemble closely the experiences of the seventeenth-century Scottish universities and Trinity. In one of the only comparative studies of early Harvard and Trinity, Helga Robinson-Hammerstein and Elizabethanne Boran recognise both institutions' links to supporting puritan settlers in colonial spaces – Catholic Ireland and North America.[89] This book contributes to this comparative thread. Harvard may have been founded in New England, but the idea of a college to sustain godly expatriates was highly mobile: it travelled with communities as they navigated the religious and political tumult of the seventeenth century.

During the mid-seventeenth-century Civil Wars, the universities' contested uses in the construction of emerging states and societies on either side of the Atlantic was amplified. Controlling these institutions meant controlling the lifeblood of the church and state and setting higher learning's confessional character, thereby perpetuating it for future generations. In a time of heightened political, religious, and social upheaval, this study contends that, by investigating the ways in which rival authorities in Britain and Ireland, and in expatriate communities abroad, exerted control over universities, we can gain unique insights into competing conceptions of how these authorities envisioned ordered societies.

* * *

This study is rooted in an examination of each university's substantial corpus of published and archival sources. However, in seeking to understand more clearly the ways in which universities interacted with shifting centres of authority, and how groups and individuals sought to wield the universities to their ends, this study also looks beyond university records to better understand the interaction between the institutions of higher education and the Civil Wars. A range of manuscript letters, visitation records, parliamentary records, local town and church records, and state papers were scrutinised alongside university records to delineate a more complete picture of the universities' utility and their strategic standing as contested spaces. These

---

[88] Starting with Bernard Bailyn, *Education in the Forming of American Society: Needs and Opportunities for Study* (New York, 1960). See also Lawrence A. Cremin, *American Education: The Colonial Experience, 1607–1783* (New York, 1970); James Axtell, *The School Upon a Hill: Education and Society in Colonial New England* (New Haven, CT, 1974); Roger L. Geiger, *The History of American Higher Education: Learning and Culture from the Founding to World War II* (Princeton, NJ, 2014), p. 1.

[89] Elizabethanne Boran and Helga Robinson-Hammerstein, 'The Promotion of "Civility" and the Quest for the Creation of a "City of Peace": The Beginnings of Trinity College, Dublin and of Harvard College, Cambridge, Mass.', *Paedagogica Historica*, 34:2 (1998), 479–505.

primary sources – especially visitation records, which offer rich insight into how political decisions were carried out and received in the universities – offer a unique view of the universities' dynamism during this era of upheaval.

This book opens with an examination of Charles I and Laud's university policies for Scotland, Ireland, and communities abroad. This chapter revisits a core question that has engaged many historians over the past three decades: did Charles, and Laud, seek uniformity, or a lesser form of agreement, between the established churches of the three kingdoms? This chapter considers the monarchy's intended reforms for the universities as an extension of its ecclesiastical policy. It highlights Charles' actions to engender conformity to Laudian norms via the reform of the universities and argues that the long-term goal of this policy was religious uniformity. Understanding that these policies had ramifications beyond the British Isles, this chapter shows that such policies led expatriates to found their own colleges during their migrations in Europe and then ultimately across the Atlantic. Chapter 2 investigates the Scottish response to Charles' policies and provides a systematic overview of the Covenanters' administration of the universities in the 1640s. It examines how the Covenanters sought to break the universities' royalism in order to calibrate them towards a Presbyterian confessional ideal. This is followed by an analysis of the Covenanters' supervision of university affairs, which examines how conformity to the Covenant was refined through visitations, the reform of the professoriate, and the implementation of a unified curriculum. Chapter 3 examines both Trinity and Harvard in the 1640s. For Trinity, the decade was calamitous, while for Harvard, this embryonic period saw the college emerge as a key institution in the formation of a godly society. This chapter first examines the New English response to the Laudian reform of Trinity via the dismantling of Laud's Trinity reforms. The aim was to return Trinity to its function as a seminary that served its small settler population. Similarly, this chapter examines how New England's authorities sought to support their fledgling college and maintain autonomy of colonial governance. This chapter underscores how Harvard and Trinity shared a common purpose, to sustain settlers in colonial spaces in a decade of pronounced turmoil.

Chapter 4 explores how the Cromwellian regime sought to control the universities, viewing the Scottish and Irish universities, in particular, as tools to consolidate conquest in the period 1649–52. But these were policies that were pursued with the wider empire in mind. The chapter explores the Commonwealth's approaches to the universities by examining twin acts for the propagation of the gospel in Ireland and New England, which reveals the regime's varying priorities for each territory. It also examines how the regime planted masters at the universities of Scotland and Ireland in order to coerce allegiance to the regime. Like Chapter 1, this chapter underlines the significance of universities as mechanisms by which English rulers could consolidate power and thus socialise governing elites to their religious and political agendas. Chapter 5 examines how the Scottish universities, though envisioned as spaces to cultivate Cromwellian mores, emerged as spaces of resistance. It also considers the universities' place in the factional rivalry that emerged in the Kirk. At the heart of this division was a struggle over what should constitute the true parameters of the Scottish church and state, and which confessional ideal the universities should serve. Chapter 6 assesses Trinity and Harvard during the 1650s, and analyses how the proliferation of Protestant sects and the growth of heterodox ideas destabilised university operations and impacted Cromwellian policy, especially towards Trinity. This chapter contends that religious controversy in the universities played a key part that sparked a series of schemes to found new colleges in Ireland, New England, and northern England. It also examines the charged political and religious atmosphere of the latter 1650s and the rivalries that emerged, which had lasting ramifications for both Harvard and Trinity.

Far from being cloistered, austere institutions in the pre-Enlightenment era, this book seeks to more fully situate the Scottish universities, Trinity, and Harvard into the narrative of the mid-seventeenth century and illuminate what has been a hitherto unexplored dimension of the Civil War era. In doing so, it underscores the contested nature of universities in this period and their crucial place not only as tools that supported state power, but as refineries that could support, and sustain, distinctive Reformed communities on either side of the Atlantic.

1

Charles I, William Laud, and the Universities, c. 1625–37

William Laud viewed England's universities as the bedrock upon which to realise Charles I's vision of an ordered society that obeyed the doctrine and ceremony of the Church of England. The Laudian vision of the church, and the wider English state, was built upon an arguably Arminian framework that was predicated on mitigating schism, fostering order in all practices, invigorating the ecclesiastical hierarchy, and promoting avant-garde ceremonialism.[1] At Oxford and Cambridge, future governing elites would be socialised into these norms. Laud himself was a prime example of how higher education could condition students' outlooks, as his own religious inclinations were symptomatic of the anti-Calvinist sentiment that pervaded St John's College, Oxford, his *alma mater*.[2] As chancellor of Oxford from 1630, he pursued comprehensive reform of the university, highlighted by the completion of new statutes in 1636, while as metropolitan he intended to visit both Oxford and Cambridge to reform religious practice he found disagreeable.[3]

---

[1] Peter Marshall, *Reformation England 1480–1642*, 2nd edn (New York, 2012), pp. 216–26; Kenneth Fincham, 'Avant-Garde Conformity and the English Church, c. 1590–1625', in Kenneth Fincham and Nicholas Tyacke (eds), *Altars Restored: The Changing Face of English Religious Worship, c. 1547–c.1700* (Oxford, 2007), pp. 74–125; Peter Lake, 'The Laudian Style: Order, Uniformity and the Pursuit of the Beauty of Holiness in the 1630s', in Kenneth Fincham (ed.), *The Early Stuart Church, 1603–1642* (Stanford, CA, 1993), pp. 161–86. Scholars have debated whether these policies were the culmination of an 'Arminian revolution' in the English church or were simply emblematic of conservative religious mores. See Nicholas Tyacke, *Anti-Calvinists: The Rise of English Arminianism, c. 1590–1640* (Oxford, 1987), chap. 8; Kevin Sharpe, *The Personal Rule of Charles I* (New Haven, CT, 1992), pp. 279–80, 327–33; Julian Davies, *The Caroline Captivity of the Church: Charles I and the Remoulding of Anglicanism, 1625–1641* (Oxford, 1992), pp. 16–18, 205–50, 297–305.

[2] Scholars have assigned especial influence to Laud's tutor at St John's College, John Buckeridge. See Charles Carlton, *Archbishop William Laud* (London, 1987), pp. 1–15; Nicholas Tyacke, 'Archbishop Laud', *Early Stuart Church*, pp. 51–70; Anthony Milton, 'Laud, William (1573–1645)', *ODNB*.

[3] On Laud's Oxford reforms and the statutes of 1636, see Sharpe, 'Archbishop Laud and the University of Oxford'; John Griffiths (ed.), *Statutes of the University of Oxford Codified in the Year 1636 Under the Authority of Archbishop Laud* (Oxford, 1888). On Laud

Both the king and archbishop also turned their attention to Scotland, Ireland, and the growing puritan communities on the continent and across the Atlantic. Scholarly focus on Caroline policy in Scotland and Ireland has focused primarily on the extent that the Church of Ireland and the Church of Scotland were reformed in the image of the English church. A key historiographical debate that marked the heyday of 'new British history' focused on the nature and intent of these policies. Did Charles and Laud seek to build uniformity between the established churches or were they intent on achieving a level of agreement in religious matters?[4] John Morrill argued for the latter in an influential essay on 'ecclesiastical imperialism' under the early Stuarts, contending that Charles, and his father James VI/I, sought an acceptable degree of 'congruity' between the churches and not outright uniformity under English hegemony. Policies viewed as offensive to local sensibilities were indicative of Charles' absolutism and ignorance of local customs.[5] Morrill's argument generated important scholarship that has probed much more acutely the nature of these policies in their Scottish and Irish contexts before the outbreak of the Civil Wars.[6] The universities, however, have not been fully integrated into these considerations.[7]

Closer scrutiny of university policies complicates the argument that Charles' monarchy sought congruity. Drawing on the interpretive framework that views the universities as agents of socialisation in the construction of well-ordered realms provides a way to rethink the nature of Caroline religious policy. When examining the universities, we see a policy focused, in the long term, on building a type of homogenised uniformity across the monarchy's realms to an increasingly Laudian English church. When we consider efforts by royal authorities to coerce university reform in Scotland and Ireland and among expatriate communities abroad, the university emerges as both model and machinery: it was the institution that modelled the ideal of an ordered commonwealth for the rest of society and the machinery that authorities

---

and Cambridge, and on the disorders at Cambridge that prompted his review, see Victor Morgan, 'The Electoral Scene and the Court: Royal Mandates 1558–1640', *History of the University of Cambridge*, pp. 388–436; Charles Henry Cooper (ed.), *Annals of Cambridge* (5 vols, Cambridge, 1842–1908), III, pp. 279–83.

[4] Conrad Russell was most vocal in his contention that the English crown sought uniformity. See Russell, *Fall of the British Monarchies*, pp. 109–30; idem, *The Causes of the English Civil War* (Oxford, 1990), pp. 36–49.

[5] John Morrill, 'A British Patriarchy? Ecclesiastical Imperialism Under the Early Stuarts', in Anthony Fletcher and Peter Roberts (eds), *Religion, Culture and Society in Early Modern Britain: Essays in Honour of Patrick Collinson* (Cambridge, 1994), pp. 209–38.

[6] See especially John McCafferty, *The Reconstruction of the Church of Ireland: Bishop Bramhall and the Laudian Reforms* (Cambridge, 2007); Leonie James, *'This Great Firebrand': William Laud and Scotland, 1617–1645* (Woodbridge, 2017).

[7] The notable exception, which provides essential insight for this chapter, is Alan Ford, '"That Bugbear Arminianism": Archbishop Laud and Trinity College, Dublin', *British Interventions in Early Modern Ireland*, pp. 135–60.

sought to control to produce the governing elites who would go on to build order and conformity to their competing visions of a healthy commonwealth.[8] The university's dual function also underlined its reality as a contested space, where royal authorities intent on building uniformity clashed with opponents who upheld competing visions of the church and state.

Lifting the gaze to consider Ireland, Scotland, and English expatriates in continental and Atlantic spaces suggests a coherent place for university reform within the crown's ecclesiastical program, a type of imperial Laudianism that focused on higher education. Crucially, each of the universities in Ireland, Scotland, the Netherlands, and New England resembled the Protestant academies that proliferated in the Reformed international. Within the British Isles this made them prime targets for intervention. By contrast, abroad, these institutions provided key seminaries to support religious groups who were suppressed at home. The first part of this chapter examines Trinity College, Dublin, where Laud was elected chancellor in 1633. It considers how Laud composed new statutes and reformed Ireland's only university as part of a broader push to reform the Church of Ireland. The second part examines the Scottish universities in the 1630s and the ways the monarchy intervened in university affairs. Laud's revision of the Scottish canons, which emphasised well-ordered universities, was central to reform. The third part examines the monarchy's interactions with puritan communities in the Netherlands and New England, setting the founding of Harvard in 1636 within the context of this imperial Laudianism. This chapter's episodic approach is meant to clarify policies as they were pursued in each locale while highlighting the near simultaneous nature of their rollout. This suggests a 'British' policy that laid the groundwork for building uniformity in the three kingdoms while, rather unintentionally, prompting the founding of the precise type of institution that Laud wished to eradicate across the Atlantic.

Trinity College, Dublin

Trinity's utility to constructing a church and state amenable to the English crown predated Laud's intervention. Founded in part to train a native clergy, by the time of Archbishop of Canterbury George Abbott's chancellorship, Trinity had made little progress.[9] During James VI/I's reign, the king, archbishop, and their acolytes in Ireland clashed often with Trinity's provosts and fellows. In 1610 James endowed Trinity with lands in the Ulster plantation in order to provide revenues to cultivate capable ministers to convert the native Irish, but ten years later he reproached Trinity for its failure to do so.[10]

[8] Tilly, 'Reflections', p. 40.
[9] Nicholas Canny, *Making Ireland British, 1580–1650* (Oxford, 2001), p. 362.
[10] The College received 10,000 acres in Ulster: 6,000 in Armagh and 4,000 in Donegal. See HL, EL 7055; TCD, MS 571, fol. 3r; Timothy Corcoran (ed.), *State Policy in Irish*

Combined with this failure was Trinity's intransigence in matters of ceremony. Provost William Temple repeatedly defended Trinity from the 'imputacon of puritanisme', while James and Abbott exhorted the provost and fellows to follow proper decorum so that the seminary 'of obedience' would not devolve into a 'ground plotte of disorder and disobedience'.[11] Provost Temple also defended Trinity from accusations that it was overrun with 'foreigners' to the detriment of 'Natives', and that it was 'of no use & service to the Church'.[12] Temple objected to attracting and admitting the native Irish. He argued instead for admitting the sons of the New English – 'natives' who were born in Ireland – and produced lists of Trinity-educated preachers to highlight its seminary function.[13] But subsequent crown reports, including that of the 1622 commission, underlined Trinity's failure to furnish Protestant ministers and to provide a viable university for natives to attend.[14] Royal authorities, seeking to employ Trinity to consolidate control of Ireland, viewed Trinity's relative autonomy and its Reformed ethos as the causes of disorder and disobedience in the college.

The difficulties that the king and Archbishop Abbott confronted at Trinity foregrounded the tumult that would arrive with Laud's chancellorship. In September 1633, Laud was made Trinity's chancellor, which he thereafter held in tandem with the Oxford chancellorship.[15] Under Laud's regime, Trinity was a contested space, one in which rival forces clashed over the type of institution the college was to be, and ultimately the type of society it was to serve. Though the chancellorship had been largely ceremonial, archbishop of Armagh James Ussher, Trinity's vice chancellor and staunch defender of his *alma mater* and the Irish church, recognised the need to reform Trinity's problematic constitution and remedy internecine problems that plagued college operations. He considered Laud the man to do so.[16] But in Laud, Trinity would acquire no ceremonial figurehead. The new chancellor would be more exacting, and work not only to correct 'disorder', but to undercut Trinity's autonomy and religious identity to remould the institution to serve a new confessional ideal.

Laud's reform of Trinity was part of a concurrent process of Irish ecclesiastical reform in the 1630s, which sought to realign the Church of Ireland with the Church of England. Trinity would have to be reformed to socialise students

---

Education A.D. 1536 to 1816: Exemplified in Documents Collected for Lectures to Postgraduate Classes (Dublin, 1916), pp. 65–6.

[11] TCD, MUN/P/1/69, 70, 72.

[12] TCD, MUN/P/1/129.

[13] TCD, MUN/P/1/126, 127, 128, 130.

[14] Victor Treadwell (ed.), *The Irish Commission of 1622: An Investigation of the Irish Administration, 1615–1622, and Its Consequences, 1623–1624* (Dublin, 2006), pp. 128–30, 169–71, 294; TCD, MS 808, fols 28–40; TNA, SP 63/248, fol. 140r.

[15] TNA, SP 63/254, fol. 270.

[16] *Ussher Works*, XV, pp. 574–5.

into a reconstructed, Laudian-endorsed Church of Ireland. On the ground in Ireland, John Bramhall, bishop of Derry, and lord deputy Thomas Wentworth aimed to conform the Irish church to its English counterpart: in a letter to Laud, Wentworth wrote that, 'reducing of this Kingdom to a conformity in Religion with the Church of England, is no doubt deeply set in his Majesty's pious and prudent Heart'.[17] Regarding the Irish church, Bramhall opined that 'I doubt much whether the clergy be very orthodox, and could wish both the Articles and Canons of the Church of England were establish'd here by Act of Parliament, or State; that as we live all under one king, so we might both in doctrine and discipline observe an uniformity.'[18] Laud agreed, noting that 'I easily beleeve the best of theire Country-men would be glad enough to live under an English bishop.'[19] This was a vision of the Irish church diametrically opposed to an autonomous Church of Ireland.

The Irish Convocation in 1634 portended both the Laudian tenor of Trinity's subsequent reform and the nature of the clashes that would envelope the college. The settlement that Convocation concluded did not impose the jurisdiction of Canterbury over Ireland, nor did it impose the English liturgy on Ireland; rather, as John McCafferty has highlighted, in a conclusion echoing Morrill's thesis, it achieved a level of agreement between the churches.[20] The canons that Convocation produced integrated portions of the 1615 Irish Articles, and the new code nominally preserved the Church of Ireland's independence.[21] Crucially, however, the 1634 code's educational strictures signalled an additional flank on which a longer-term process of reform would be pursued. The canons included educational requirements for ministers and mandated that all expectants be in good standing with a university education.[22] Educational requirements such as these were laden with deeper meaning: ministers not only had to be educated, but they also had to be educated in a correct, authorised manner in order to promote distinctive visions of the church.

The codes regarding education bore the marks of Laudianism, as they were interested in structures of government as much as dress and ceremony. All university members were required to wear 'Gownes with standing Collars, and

---

[17] TCD, MS 1038, fol. 106v; *Strafford Letters*, I, p. 187; Canny, *Making Ireland British*, pp. 276–8; John McCafferty, *The Reconstruction of the Church of Ireland: Bishop Bramhall and the Laudian Reforms* (Cambridge, 2007), pp. 33–9.
[18] A.W. Haddan (ed.), *The Works of the Most Reverend Father in God, John Bramhall, D.D.* (5 vols, Oxford, 1842–5), I, pp. lxxix–lxxxii.
[19] HL, HA 15153.
[20] McCafferty, *Reconstruction*, chap. 3.
[21] Ibid., pp. 112–13.
[22] *Ussher Works*, I, pp. xxxi–l; *Constitutions and Canons Ecclesiasticall, Treated upon by the Archbishops, and Bishops, and the Rest of the Cleargie of Ireland…Anno Dom. 1634* (Dublin, 1635), pp. 44–5.

Sleeves streight at the bands; or wyde sleeves, as is used in the Universities, with Hoods, or Tippets or like or farcenet, and square Caps in places and times convenient'.[23] The canons underlined the Laudian preoccupation with dress and ceremony and foreshadowed Laud's subsequent reforms of academic garb at both Oxford and Trinity. For Laud it was important that students acculturate to proper order at university, for deference to ceremony served as 'the hedge and the fence of those things which are of far greater consequence'.[24] The canons also curtailed Trinity's nonconformist streak.

The 1634 canons prefigured Trinity's Laudian reform, but the college's autonomy had been gradually eroding since the beginning of Charles' reign. As Alan Ford notes, Provost Temple's death in 1627 sparked a succession crisis that had important implications for the college's autonomy.[25] Alongside the provost, Trinity's seven senior fellows were responsible for governing the college, while all sixteen fellows performed a range of duties, which included lecturing on arts and divinity and serving as dean, catechist, librarian, bursar, or auditor. According to Trinity's charter, the fellows were also empowered to select a new provost.[26] Their first choice was Richard Sibbes, the puritan preacher and Cambridge graduate.[27] Though they had sole authority to elect their provost, the fellows sought royal backing because they feared that there were opponents in London 'who wish us no good', who would attempt to plant an 'Arminian' in the provostship. The fellows identified Sibbes as 'conformable to the orders of this church' and fit to train 'a sound ministrie in that poore Countrie free from Popperie & Arminianisme', a telling assertion, for in 1626 this meant that they viewed Sibbes as amenable to the Irish church based on the 1615 code. Archbishop Ussher also petitioned Sibbes on Trinity's behalf.[28] Sibbes, however, declined, prompting a dispute between the fellows.[29] The ambiguity of Trinity's constitution became apparent: the senior fellows maintained that they alone had the right to elect a provost, while the juniors believed it to be the duty of all fellows.[30] The seniors chose Joseph Mede, the puritan biblical scholar and Greek lecturer, though he also declined. The juniors, meanwhile, sought to elect Trinity alumnus Robert

---

[23] *Irish Canons*, pp. 57, 88–9.
[24] Quoted in Fincham, 'Oxford and the Early Stuart Polity', pp. 202–3.
[25] Ford, 'That Bugbear Arminianism', pp. 139–41.
[26] For the fellows' responsibilities, see TCD, MUN/V/5/1, pp. 23, 29, 35, 37, 41, 60; TCD, MUN/V/5/2, pp. 6, 8, 17.
[27] Mark E. Dever, 'Sibbes, Richard (1577?–1635)', *ODNB*.
[28] TNA, SP 63/268, fol. 52r; *Ussher Works*, XV, pp. 361–4.
[29] Mark Empey (ed.), 'The Diary of Sir James Ware, 1623–66', *Analecta Hibernica*, 45 (2014), 53–146, at 71.
[30] Murphy, *History of Trinity College Dublin*, p. 68.

Ussher, the archbishop's nephew.[31] The provostship eventually fell to William Bedell, a graduate of Emmanuel College.[32]

The affair over Temple's successor laid bare both Trinity's Reformed inclinations and the fractious nature of its constitution. Bedell, who was surprised to have been offered the position by a college he knew little about, was agreeable to Trinity's ethos – mostly. He sought to remove distractions from worship and added the study of law and medicine. But he also inaugurated lectures in Irish.[33] This initiative highlighted Bedell's linguistic interests and his concern with improving clerical tuition in Irish; such lectures doubtlessly had a missionary impulse. But despite Trinity's Jacobean pretences to spread Protestantism, Bedell's Irish lectures clashed with the New English community's providential self-definition as an elect amidst the reprobate, largely uninterested in proselytising.[34]

Academic interest in the Irish language notwithstanding, Bedell became Trinity's provost, a move that, as Ford highlights, came at a cost to Trinity's autonomy.[35] Crucially, the fellows had elected Bedell only after Charles assented, which set a precedent for future elections and would only accelerate the college's development into a contested space.[36] Issues inherent in Trinity's constitution also continued under Bedell, especially after he returned to England in September 1627 to collect his family. Bedell's absence meant that his deputy, Vice-Provost John Floyd, a Welshman, deputised for him. With newfound, if temporary, authority, Floyd immediately installed his cousin, William, in a senior fellowship.[37] Ussher argued that the promotion of Floyd's cousin was injurious to Trinity's 'natives', those resident, Irish-born scholars who were eligible for promotion. By contrast, William was a Welshman, a 'stranger' and 'nonresident'. To appear impartial, Ussher urged Floyd to wait for Bedell's return.[38] Ussher's appeal, however, fell on deaf ears. Floyd continued his gambit, but Trinity's fellows denied him, which prompted

---

[31] TCD, MUN/V/5/1, p. 13; TCD, MS 543/2/1; *Ussher Works*, XVI, pp. 455–6.

[32] TCD, MUN/P/1/185; *Ussher Works*, XV, pp. 402–5, XVI, pp. 442–3.

[33] *Ussher Works*, XV, pp. 395–6, XVI, pp. 458–60; E.S. Shuckburgh (ed.), *Two Biographies of William Bedell, Bishop of Kilmore* (Cambridge, 1902), pp. 270–1, 295.

[34] Canny, 'Identity Formation in Ireland', pp. 175–6. On Bedell's initiatives, see Aidan Clarke, 'Bishop William Bedell (1571–1642) and the Irish Reformation', in Ciaran Brady (ed.), *Worsted in the Game: Losers in Irish History* (Dublin, 1989), pp. 61–72.

[35] Ford, 'That Bugbear Arminianism', p. 140.

[36] On the election and Bedell's subsequent translation to Ireland, see John Pentland Mahaffy (ed.), *The Particular Book of Trinity College, Dublin: A Facsimile from the Original* (London, 1904), fols 97r–99v; TNA, SP 63/244, fol. 301; TCD, MUN/P/1/178, 181, 183.

[37] Mahaffy identifies Floyd as Welsh, while entries in the Trinity register refer to William Floyd as the vice provost's 'countryman'. See TCD, MUN/V/5/1, p. 14; Mahaffy, *Epoch in Irish History*, p. 196.

[38] BL, Add MS 4274, fol. 34r. Elizabethanne Boran misidentifies the appeal's recipient as Robert Ussher. John Floyd was elected vice provost in May 1627. See *Ussher Correspondence*, II, pp. 402–3; TCD, MUN/V/5/1, p. 13. See also *Alumni Dublinenses*, p. 294.

Floyd to halt all elections. This provoked several candidates to petition then-lord deputy Henry Cary, viscount Falkland, who circumvented the fellows' authority and issued orders to admit William Floyd and two others to vacancies 'for the good of that Society, which greatly imports the welfare of the whole Realme'.[39] Angered by this interference, the junior fellows called for a visitation and urged Bedell to return.[40] Four junior fellows – William Fitzgerald, David Thomas, Richard Jordan, and Thaddeus Lysaght – argued that Floyd preferred his 'countrmen' over 'natives' and that he 'kept some of the Colledge rents' and discharged them without the bursar's consent.[41] In the end, the visitors, which included Ussher in his role as vice chancellor, deposed Floyd, while Falkland was forced to rescind his orders.[42] This affair highlighted the need for Trinity to have a strong, resident provost who could compose coherent statutes that would guard against constitutional ambiguity that bred disorder. Persistent instability not only kept the fellows from performing their duties, but it also invited external intrusion into Trinity's affairs. This episode also underlined the contested idea of whom Trinity was for. Despite the college's string of English provosts, and the fact that most of its students were New English, English, or Welsh scholars, the promotion of a Welshman was considered detrimental to 'natives' – those born in Ireland, Protestants of the New or Old English communities.[43] These tensions would only increase under Laud's chancellorship.

Bedell's task was to draft new statutes, the provost's prerogative as defined by Trinity's charter.[44] He found Temple's existing statutes 'part latin, part English, and in sheets of Paper some stich'd together, some loose, a heape without order, with long preambles, and sometime unnecessary, and in many thinges defective'.[45] He sought initially to base his new code on Emmanuel's, but in the end he changed little from Temple's statutes.[46] He made no changes to either the order of preferment of fellows or the length of fellowships. Similarly, the provost would continue to share power with the fellows.[47]

---

[39] The others were Thomas Vesey and George Cottingham. See TCD, MUN/P/1/195, 196.
[40] TCD, MUN/V/5/1, p. 14; TCD, MUN/P/1/203, 206, 208. Ussher also requested that Bedell return immediately. TCD, MS 3812.
[41] TCD, MUN/V/5/1, p. 14.
[42] Ibid.; Ussher Works, XV, pp. 391–2, XVI, pp. 468–9; Shuckburgh, Bedell, p. 284.
[43] Ford, 'Who Went to Trinity', pp. 61–7.
[44] TCD, MUN/V/5/1, p. 13; Mahaffy, Particular Book, fol. 98v.
[45] Shuckburgh, Bedell, p. 272.
[46] Ibid., p. 273; Stubbs, History of the University of Dublin, pp. 398–400; Mahaffy, Epoch in Irish History, pp. 327–75.
[47] Mahaffy, Epoch in Irish History, pp. 335–9; Ussher Works, XV, p. 389; Shuckburgh, Bedell, p. 274. For the qualifications of fellows at Emmanuel, see Frank H. Stubbings (ed.), The Statutes of Sir Walter Mildmay for Emmanuel College (Cambridge, 1983), pp. 52–3; Sarah Bendall, Christopher Brooke, and Patrick Collinson, A History of Emmanuel College, Cambridge (Woodbridge, 1999), pp. 23–30.

Bedell's statutes did not rectify Trinity's governing structure or guard against disputes over vacancies.

Bedell's tenure did not last long, and with his translation to the bishopric of Kilmore and Ardagh in spring 1629 came Laud's explicit entry into Trinity's affairs. In April, Ussher received a letter from the Trinity alumnus Archibald Hamilton, the son of the archbishop of Cashel. In the letter, Hamilton warned that it was urgent that the college secure a successor sympathetic to Trinity's Reformed ethos:

> Some fear there is conceived, that one or other hence may put upon the house, who will not, it may be, so truly aim at the religious education of the students; for some are, deeply tainted with the Arminian tenets, putteth in close to be recommended thither by his Majesty, and thinks to prevail by that means. This I thought good to certify, that your grace may give timely warning thereof to the fellows, that they may make a wary and safe election of some sound scholar and orthodox divine.[48]

Hamilton, who as an alumnus was sensitive to Trinity's identity, suggested a familiar name, Joseph Mede.[49] Ussher's contact was clearly suspicious of anti-Calvinist designs on Trinity, noting that it was Laud who had moved to translate Bedell to the bishopric in an attempt to plant an amendable divine in the provostship.[50] Hamilton was likely aware of Laud's distaste for puritanism, and he was witness to mounting religious disaffection in England. A year earlier, the English Commons had accused Laud and Bishop Richard Neile of Durham of Arminianism, only for Charles to forbid all discussion of the doctrine of predestination. And, a month before Hamilton wrote to Ussher, the Commons issued a protest making a 'capital enemy' anyone who sought to introduce 'Popery or Arminianism'.[51] Hamilton viewed Bedell's translation through the lens of the controversies smouldering across the Irish Sea. It was part of a Laudian plot to breathe Arminianism into Trinity.

Because Bedell's 1627 election effectively transferred electoral power to London, Falkland prohibited the fellows from electing a new provost without royal approval.[52] In response, Ussher, Bedell, and the fellows appealed directly to Laud. Bedell argued that the forbearance of election was a suspension of the fellows' privileges and urged Laud to preserve their rights.[53] Laud, meanwhile, vowed to uphold the fellows' privileges, cited his 'love' for Trinity's freedoms, and claimed that he had no designs on the provostship.[54] This was a lie. In

---

[48] *Ussher Works*, XV, p. 433.
[49] *Ibid.*; *Ussher Correspondence*, II, p. 451, n. 1.
[50] *Ussher Works*, XV, pp. 433–5.
[51] S.R. Gardiner (ed.), *The Constitutional Documents of the Puritan Revolution, 1625–1660* (Oxford, 1906), pp. 75–6, 82–3.
[52] TCD, MUN/V/5/1, pp. 21–2.
[53] TNA, SP 63/248, fols 224r, 229r; *CSPI 1625-33*, pp. 452–3; Shuckburgh, *Bedell*, p. 299.
[54] *Laud Works*, VI, pp. 260–1; *Ussher Works*, XV, pp. 443–4. On Ussher and Laud's

March 1634, Laud revealed to Wentworth that he had planned to install William Chappell, a fellow of Christ's College, Cambridge, as provost had Chappell not declined.[55] Hamilton was correct to assume that there were Laudian designs on Trinity. These actions reveal how both royal authorities and their opponents in Ireland appreciated Trinity's strategic standing to engineer religious transformation. Subsequent clashes over rights and privileges intensified the more existential debates about the types of religious norms into which Trinity's students were to be socialised.

To head off such incursion, in summer 1629, two Trinity fellows travelled to London to petition the king directly to observe their right of free election, but they were met with a cascading scheme that resulted in further control being ceded to royal authorities.[56] Secretary of State Dudley Carleton advised the fellows that they were required to advance to the king their choice.[57] The fellows proposed both Mede and Robert Ussher as potential candidates, settling upon the latter; Mede had once again refused.[58] Laud thought it best that Charles advise Falkland to order an election, but only after he consulted Archbishop Ussher.[59] This suggests that Laud sought an additional layer of legitimacy to the crown's control of appointments. Laud wrote to Ussher requesting his judgement of his nephew's 'worth and fitness' and told Ussher that Carleton had recommended the fellows think of another 'that was known unto us'.[60] Ussher wrote that, beyond being his kinsman and a respected alumnus, of Robert's 'learning, honesty, and conformity of our church, no man, I suppose, will take exception'.[61] The reference to 'our' church suggests that Ussher thought his nephew was an acceptable candidate for Trinity's provostship as it operated within the Irish church under the 1615 articles. This was perhaps a cautious away of safeguarding the Irish church from the controversies plaguing England.[62] Charles assented to Robert's nomination and permitted the fellows to 'proceed to an election'.[63] Bedell relinquished his post in September and in January 1630 Robert assumed the provostship.[64]

The monarchy now exercised its authority decisively in electing Trinity's provost. Yet Ussher proved a poor steward of Ireland's only university, as he

---

correspondence, see Alan Ford, 'Correspondence between Archbishops Ussher and Laud', *Archivium Hibernicum*, 46 (1992), 5–21; Amanda L. Capern, 'The Caroline Church: James Ussher and the Irish Dimension', *Historical Journal*, 39:1 (1996), 57–85.

[55] *Laud Works*, VI, pp. 355–6. Chappell served briefly as Trinity's catechist in 1613. On Chappell, see Alan Ford, 'Chappell, William (1582–1649)', *ODNB*.
[56] TCD, MUN/V/5/1, p. 22.
[57] BL, Egerton MS 2553, fol. 37v; TCD, MUN/P/1/216.
[58] *Ussher Works*, XVI, pp. 494–7.
[59] TCD, MUN/P/1/216.
[60] *Laud Works*, VI, pp. 262–3; *Ussher Works*, XV, pp. 445–6.
[61] *Ussher Works*, XV, pp. 449–50.
[62] Capern, 'Caroline Church', pp. 67–9.
[63] BL, Egerton MS 2553, fols 50v–51r; TCD, MUN/P/1/217, 218.
[64] TCD, MUN/V/5/1, pp. 25–6.

was unable to exert authority over the fellows. He did little to stem crown interference into Trinity's affairs and disarray under his leadership led one fellowship nominee, William Newman, to appeal directly to the king, securing a letter ordering his election in 1633.[65] When Ussher wrote to Laud regarding Trinity's chancellorship in 1633, he lamented that the fellows were 'so factious, that nothing could please them which came from their superiors'. Of Robert, he wrote that he was 'too soft and gentle a disposition to rule so heady a company'.[66] Wentworth expressed similar misgivings.[67] Laud remarked that he was not at fault for the situation, for he had intended to install William Chappell.[68]

At this point, Ussher appears to have put aside any reservations he had about Laud to secure his energies to repair Trinity's constitution.[69] Therefore, by the time Laud became Trinity's chancellor, he was already well acquainted with the college. To transform the college into both a model of order and obedience and a machine to engineer conformity to an Irish church reforming along Laudian lines, Trinity needed both a strong provost and a new constitution. As Wentworth and Bramhall pursued Irish ecclesiastical reform, Laud began his project at Trinity. The 1634 Convocation had resulted in a measure of agreement between the Irish and English churches. As the English church was also undergoing reform along Laudian lines, there was no monolithic English model to impose on the Irish church. The same was true for the universities. Laud had assumed Oxford's chancellorship in 1630, and between 1633 and 1636 he led the reworking of Oxford's constitution.[70] He also began work on a new constitution for Trinity in 1634. Laudian Oxford was certainly an ideal, but Trinity's reform did not mirror Oxford's completely; it did, however, highlight the crucial role that Trinity would play in acculturating future ministers into the new norms of the Irish church.

As Laud began work on Trinity's statutes, royal officials conspired to plant a Laudian client in the provostship.[71] In July 1634, Laud wrote to Wentworth to have his man, Chappell, then dean of Cashel, installed.[72] In August, Wentworth reported that 'I went to the College myself, recommended the Dean to the Place, told them I must direct them to chuse the Dean, or else to stay until they should understand His Majesty's Pleasure, and in no case

---

[65] TCD, MUN/P/1/232; TCD, MUN/V/5/1, pp. 37–8.
[66] *Ussher Works*, XV, pp. 574–5.
[67] TCD, MS 1038, fol. 107r; *Strafford Letters*, I, p. 188.
[68] *Laud Works*, VI, p. 356.
[69] Though Ussher was openly hostile to Laudian reforms in the Irish church, he was nevertheless a firm supporter of Stuart absolutism and ceded authority to royal officials, like Laud. See Ian W.S. Campbell, 'Calvinist Absolutism: Archbishop James Ussher and Royal Power', *Journal of British Studies*, 53:3 (2014), 588–610.
[70] Sharpe, 'Archbishop Laud and the University of Oxford', pp. 147–8.
[71] TNA, SP 63/255, fol. 67; *CSPI 1633–47*, p. 103; *Laud Works*, VI, pp. 355–6, 374.
[72] *Laud Works*, VI, p. 385.

chuse any other.'⁷³ This brazen approach had the intended effect: Chappell was duly 'elected', while Robert Ussher was translated to the archdeaconry of Meath.⁷⁴ In the elections of Bedell and Robert Ussher, Trinity's fellows had at least identified their own nominees and elected them after Charles approved. Chappell, however, was imposed without the fellows' consent. Chappell also assumed his new post without taking the customary provost's oath.⁷⁵ Laud noted that Chappell took exception to portions of the oath.⁷⁶ Chappell, therefore, was not wedded to Trinity's constitution and could thus better support Laud's schemes.

One such scheme was to infuse Trinity with amenable fellows who would cooperate with Chappell. The new provost personified Trinity's reality as a contested space as the college began to transform through Laud's machinations. Chappell projected Laudian authority as it intruded into what had been a largely autonomous, Reformed space. He clashed immediately with Trinity's fellows, the rivals who represented the New English's waning power at Trinity.⁷⁷ In August 1634, Wentworth first suggested 'that we might have half a Dozen good Scholars to be sent us over to be made Fellows'.⁷⁸ For Laud, the solution was to plant Trinity with Englishmen: 'I think some towardly English men, might be sent out of our universityes, to begin a good example, and settlement in that College for the Irish to follow.'⁷⁹ Laud's comment was another reminder of the fact that he viewed the universities as models of order for the realm to emulate – and in this case, the 'Irish' behaviour of the New English scholars and fellows was in need of a proper 'English' example.⁸⁰ By planting fellows sympathetic to Chappell, Laud and Wentworth could exercise greater control over Trinity's governance and teaching.⁸¹

Remaking Trinity into the machine to support Laudian religious reforms required replacing key parts. Thus, between 1635 and 1639, several graduates of Christ's College, Cambridge were installed at the college.⁸² Christ's had been Chappell's home for three decades: he matriculated there in 1600 and served as a fellow until 1633. When he first entered, Christ's was cadre of militant puritans. But, following the election of Valentine Carey as master in 1609, the college developed an Arminian identity with which Chappell

---

⁷³ *Strafford Letters*, I, p. 299.
⁷⁴ TCD, MUN/V/5/1, p. 47.
⁷⁵ *Laud Works*, VI, pp. 398–9.
⁷⁶ HL, HA 15155.
⁷⁷ *Strafford Letters*, I, p. 381; *Laud Works*, VII, pp. 115–16; *CSPI 1633–47*, p. 88. See also Mackenzie, 'Contested Space', pp. 68–9.
⁷⁸ *Strafford Letters*, I, p. 299.
⁷⁹ HL, HA 15156.
⁸⁰ Ford, 'That Bugbear Arminianism', p. 159.
⁸¹ See Stubbs, *History of the University of Dublin*, pp. 20–1, 27, 29, 41; Boran, 'Ramism in Trinity', pp. 177–81; Peter Fox, *Trinity College Library Dublin: A History* (Cambridge, 2014), pp. 16–18.
⁸² See especially Ford, 'That Bugbear Arminianism', pp. 142–7.

identified.[83] It was with former members of this anti-puritan milieu that Laud infused Trinity. Alexander Hatfield was the first Christ's import elected to a senior fellowship, in June 1635.[84] Two years later, in April 1637, Wentworth ordered the election of John Harding. Wentworth acknowledged that Harding's election controverted Trinity's existing constitution: 'onely the Statutes, formerly composed by your fellows, & now ready to expire, doe hinder'.[85] A month later, he issued a similar order for Thomas Marshall's election to a senior fellowship.[86] Christ's graduates were also found among Trinity's scholars and junior fellows during this period.[87]

These actions bred discontent and sparked clashes between the Laudians and their opponents. In January 1636 a dispute erupted when Chappell attempted to nominate one of his former students at Christ's College, Arthur Ware, to a senior fellowship over three junior fellows: Nathaniel Hoyle, Thomas Feasant, and Charles Cullen. Ware, a junior fellow, had been admitted to his place at the same time as Hoyle, Feasant, and Cullen, though his name appears last in the college register, indicating his rank.[88] His promotion was thus out of turn. The dispute that followed, however, was not only about precedence. It involved Trinity's visitors, the lord deputy, and Laud; it amplified the fault lines that had been growing between Trinity's masters and royal authorities; and it underscored the extent to which Trinity's New English establishment perceived the root and branch transformation of the college. At the centre of the debate was the fellowship made vacant by the death of senior fellow William Ince, which left only three of the customary seven senior fellow spots filled. Elections for the remaining vacancies were scheduled for summer 1636. Bedell's statutes stipulated that at least four senior fellows had to be present for elections. But Chappell, with the support of seniors William Newman and Robert Conway, removed this clause and forced through Ware's election.[89] This prompted Hoyle, Feasant, and Cullen to petition Trinity's visitors.[90] Chappell argued that the three were scheming to wrest authority from the provost and drew attention to the fellows'

---

[83] See Tyacke, *Anti-Calvinists*, pp. 36–57, 195; Stephen A. Bondos-Greene, 'The End of an Era: Cambridge Puritanism and the Christ's College Election of 1609', *Historical Journal*, 25:1 (1982), 197–208; David Hoyle, *Reformation and Religious Identity in Cambridge, 1590–1644* (Woodbridge, 2007), pp. 100–30.

[84] TCD, MUN/V/5/1, p. 48.

[85] *Ibid.*, pp. 56, 60.

[86] *Ibid.*, p. 57.

[87] These included William Clopton, Robert Cock, and John Garthwaite. See Ford, 'That Bugbear Arminianism', p. 146; John Peile, *Biographical Register of Christ's College, 1505–1905, and of the Earlier Foundation, God's House, 1448–1505* (Cambridge, 1910), pp. 310, 318, 427.

[88] TCD, MUN/V/5/1, p. 35; TNA, SP 63/256, fol. 27r.

[89] Mahaffy, *Epoch in Irish History*, p. 242.

[90] TCD, MUN/V/5/1, p. 51.

disobedience.[91] Ussher, a vocal opponent of Chappell, threatened to have him removed. The provost responded in turn, noting that if Ussher pursued such an action he could appeal to 'my Lord Canterbury', making clear his fidelity to Laud and the divided loyalties in Trinity's governance.[92] Despite Chappell's threats, the visitors eventually ruled in favour of the petitioners in May 1636.[93]

Chappell insisted that he was acting legally in electing Ware, for Ware was the only candidate to produce a written claim 'for precedencie'.[94] Thus when the visitors ruled in favour of Hoyle, Feasant, and Cullen, Chappell was stunned. He refused to acknowledge Hoyle, remarking petulantly 'Why should I?'[95] He wrote to Bedell that 'the manner of our Visitors in England was always to looke to maintayne the authority of the Governors, & if they had done amisse, some way must bee found to bring them fairely off, & that young mens complaints had neede be just & necessary if they would bring their Governors before Visitors'.[96] The ordeal was an affront to Chappell's authority. He was a true Laudian: he expected deference to his office, and was perplexed that the visitors, who were tasked with supporting, not undermining, Trinity's governance, would rule in favour of those who had presented questionable accusations against their superiors.[97]

The affair provided a space for Trinity and its visitors to air their grievances and highlighted the college's contested nature. Laud understood that he was a target in this dispute, especially because the Irish ecclesiastical establishment was still displeased with the 'altering & ordering' of the canons.[98] Many also took exception to Laud's work on Trinity's statutes, with Theophilus Buckworth, bishop of Dromore, fearing that Laud would 'overthrow, or at least spoil the College' and use his authority to 'maintain Arminianism'.[99] Trinity's visitors, including Ussher and Anthony Martin, bishop of Meath and a Trinity alumnus, directed the most ire at Chappell.[100] Opponents saw Trinity being transformed along Arminian lines; Laud, however, lamented that a minor constitutional squabble had escalated into a major disruption.[101] For Laud, the 'prime prelates' of the kingdom and the provost of Ireland's only university should be working together instead of being 'at such an eager difference in the open face of the state'.[102] For Laud, the welfare of the Irish

---

[91] TNA, SP 63/256, fols 12r–12v.
[92] Ibid., fols 12r, 18r, 23v.
[93] Ibid., fol. 13r.
[94] Ibid., 12r–12v, 14r, 19v; TCD, MUN/V/5/1, pp. 52–3.
[95] TNA, SP 63/256, fol. 13r.
[96] Ibid., fols 14v–15r.
[97] Mahaffy, Epoch in Irish History, p. 241.
[98] TNA, SP 63/255, fols 369v–370v.
[99] Ibid.; Laud Works, VII, pp. 94–5; Cotton, Fasti, III, pp. 280–1.
[100] Laud Works, VII, p. 275; Ford, 'That Bugbear Arminianism', pp. 154–8.
[101] TNA, SP 63/255, fols 375r–377v; Laud Works, VI, pp. 466–8; Ussher Works, XVI, pp. 22–3.
[102] Laud Works, VI, p. 467.

commonwealth depended on Trinity. Irish authorities, and especially the college's visitors, needed to undergird, and not undermine, the college, from which 'religion and civility in that kingdom' was to flow.[103] Laud's opponents, however, harboured a competing understanding of what defined 'religion' and 'civility' in Ireland.

By mid-1637, Hoyle, Ware, and Cullen had been admitted senior fellows, Hoyle the senior and Ware senior to Cullen. Feasant was expelled, though it is unclear why, while Chappell promised not to question the visitors' authority.[104] At first glance, the resolution appears to have been a victory for Laud's opponents, but in truth the episode preceded the overhaul of Trinity's constitution that was to strengthen Laudian hegemony. Bramhall remarked that Ussher had agreed to 'disingage himself' from the controversy, leaving Chappell to deal with 'refractory fellowes', a transfer of power to the provost that would be reflected in the new statutes.[105] Laud and Wentworth conspired to install the Christ's alumni Harding and Marshall as senior fellows in order to guarantee the passage of the new charter and statutes. It was expedient to install these men into senior fellowships before the fellowships transformed into permanent offices under the new statutes.[106] Laud completed the new constitution in early spring 1637 and subsequently sent copies to authorities in Dublin. Trinity adopted the new constitution in June.[107]

Table 1.1 Trinity College, Dublin Staff during Laud's Chancellorship, c. 1633–40.

Provosts
Robert Ussher, 1629–34
William Chappell, 1634–40
Richard Washington, 1640–c. 1641

Fellows and Associated Offices Where Known
Richard Jordan (1626), Vice Provost (1631)
Thomas Price (1626), Catechist (1631)
Randal Ince (1627), Dean (1631), Bursar (1632), Catechist (1633)

---

[103] Ibid., VII, p. 248.
[104] TNA, SP 63/256, fol. 132; Laud Works, VI, pp. 499–500; Ussher Works, XVI, pp. 29–31; Mahaffy, Epoch in Irish History, p. 244; Ford, 'That Bugbear Arminianism', p. 146. Cullen does not seem to have assumed his fellowship. A letter to Ussher references Cullen's stay in Paris. See Ussher Works, XVI, pp. 29–31. In 1661 Cullen assumed the deanery of Kilkenny. HL, HA 15175; Cotton, Fasti, II, p. 294.
[105] HL, HA 14039; CSPI 1633–47, p. 160
[106] Laud Works, VII, pp. 324–5, 333.
[107] Ibid., VI, pp. 487–8. TCD, MUN/V/5/1, p. 58; TNA, SP 63/256 fol. 143; CSPI 1633–47, p. 172.

Table 1.1 (*continued*)

Fellows and Associated Offices Where Known
William Floyd (1627)
George Cottingham (1627)
Dudley Boswell (1628), Bursar (1633)
Ithiel Walker (1628), Senior Lecturer (1631), Catechist (1632)
William Ince (1629), Senior Lecturer (1632), Proctor
Garrett Meade (162?), Dean (1632), Registrar (1633)
John Watson (1631), Registrar (1632), Senior Lecturer (1633)
John Kerdiff (1631)
Robert Conway (1631), Lecturer (1637)
Nathaniel Hoyle (1631), Senior Dean (1637), Vice Provost (1641–c.1646)
Thomas Feasant (1631)
Charles Cullen (1631)
Arthur Ware (1631)
William Newman (1632), Dean (1633)
George Baker (1634)
Christopher David (1634)
Thomas Seele (c. 1634/5), Junior Dean (1637)
Alexander Hatfield (1635)
John Harding (1637), Vice Provost (1637)
Thomas Marshall (1637), Bursar (1637)
Christopher Beckwith (1637)
William Clopton (1637)
Robert Cock (1637)
Gilbert Pepper (1637)
John Garthwaite (1637)
James Bishop (1637), Library Keeper (?) (1637)
Richard Nichols (1638)
Thomas Ginnings (1638)
John Fubbings (1639)
Thomas Perceval (1639)
William Raymond (1640)
George Lovelock (1640)

Sources: Fry, *Dublin University Calendar*; TCD, MUN/V/5/1; Mahaffy, *Epoch in Irish History*; *Alumni Dublinenses*.

Laud's constitution emphasised order and discipline and paved the way for the infusion of the college with his ideals.[108] In the new charter, the power to elect the provost was entrusted exclusively to the king, an inevitable conclusion to the decade-long transfer of power away from the fellows.[109] Laud's charter also decreased the number of the college's visitors from seven – the archbishop of Dublin, bishop of Meath, mayor of Dublin, and several members of the Dublin aristocracy – to two: the chancellor and the archbishop of Dublin. Only on the chancellor's 'absence' would the vice chancellor serve in his stead, but the chancellor held the ultimate authority to arbitrate disagreements.[110] In this way, Laud neutralised Ussher's influence as vice chancellor. Sole power to nominate fellows was granted to the chancellor, and the fellowships themselves were made into lifetime positions; both decisions would guard against disruptions that had long plagued Trinity and allow Laud to choose fellows of his liking.[111] The provost's authority was also extended, as Laud's statutes imbued governing power solely to the provost.[112] This included the power to expel students for misbehaviour.[113] The provost, then, was granted real authority as governor and disciplinarian.

Governing reforms were combined with religious and educational changes, which brought the college further into the Laudian orbit. The Irish canons of 1634 were a compromise that preserved a semblance of the Church of Ireland's autonomy. Laud's new statutes for Trinity, however, ensured that at Trinity the Irish church's clerical estate was exposed to an ecclesiology of a Laudian hue. The Laudian emphasis on order and ceremony is found in the setting of academic exercises, including theses and disputations, while the statutes added the study of the higher faculties of law and medicine to the study of divinity. This suggests that Laud viewed Trinity as an institution capable of functioning as a collegiate-university. Concerning the curriculum, Trinity's Ramism was replaced by a traditional Aristotelian course.[114] Bedell's statutes were clearly beholden to Ramist pedagogy, particularly in the teaching of logic.[115] Laud's statutes removed this Ramist tinge, re-establishing the primacy of the Aristotelian syllogism and forbidding 'all previous Positions or Suppositions'.[116] Laud's revisions were emblematic of learning as practised in larger universities, like Oxford, which supported a hierarchical and

---

[108] See Ford, 'That Bugbear Arminianism', pp. 147–51. See also Stubbs, *History of the University of Dublin*, pp. 76–8; Mahaffy, *Epoch in Irish History*, pp. 255–63; Murphy, *History of Trinity College Dublin*, pp. 96–9.
[109] MacDonnell, *Chartæ et Statuta*, pp. 18–19; Robert Bolton (ed.), *A Translation of the Charter and Statutes of Trinity College, Dublin* (Dublin, 1749), pp. 13–14.
[110] MacDonnell, *Chartæ et Statuta*, pp. 26–7; Bolton, *Statutes*, pp. 21–2.
[111] MacDonnell, *Chartæ et Statuta*, pp. 84–7; Bolton, *Statutes*, pp. 91–5.
[112] MacDonnell, *Chartæ et Statuta*, pp. 35–6; Bolton, *Statutes*, pp. 31–3.
[113] MacDonnell, *Chartæ et Statuta*, pp. 91–3; Bolton, *Statutes*, pp. 99–102.
[114] Ford, 'That Bugbear Arminianism', pp. 148–9.
[115] Boran, 'Ramism in Trinity', pp. 178–9; Mahaffy, *Epoch in Irish History*, pp. 351–2.
[116] MacDonnell, *Chartæ et Statuta*, pp. 65–8; Bolton, *Statutes*, pp. 69–73.

sacramental national church.[117] This was connected to Laudian ceremonialism, as the statutes ordered the use of the Church of England liturgy in services, while proper deference was to be given to ceremony and dress. Trinity's strict sabbatarianism was tempered, while observance was given to feast days. Laud also dropped overt references to the primacy of the Word in Trinity's oaths. The statutes were, lastly, moderate towards Catholicism, where reference to Catholicism's 'heretical' label was rescinded.[118]

Despite his concurrent work on Oxford's constitution, Laud did not foist the Oxford model on Trinity. There were similarities, to be sure, the most evident being the solidification of hierarchical authority and the regulation of discipline and dress.[119] Crucially, Laud's precise religious and educational orders for Trinity, combined with the packing of the college with amenable fellows, suggests that whatever reform that had been attained in the Irish Convocation of 1634 was not final. Trinity was to be the ideal for Ireland: a seminary where 'liberty never descended to license, where order imposed on anarchy, beauty upon dilapidation, learning upon ignorance, unity upon faction'.[120] Through Trinity's reform, Laud had sought to ensure that Trinity's students would be socialised into a Laudian vision of the church and thus better equipped to bring the Church of Ireland into unity with the Church of England. The reforms came at a cost to Trinity's autonomy and Reformed ethos, as opponents fought in vain to prevent the changes. As a contested space, Trinity in the 1630s exemplified how power structures clashed in a university to control the socialisation of future clerical elites. Beyond Ireland, contests for control of higher education, as a dynamic of the process of state formation, were paralleled in Scotland and among expatriates in European and Atlantic spaces.

The Scottish Universities

The Laudian tenor of Charles I's Scottish coronation in June 1633 foregrounded the confessional dynamic that the monarchy wished to impose on Scotland. The Coronation Parliament upheld the Five Articles of Perth, the unpopular liturgical reforms that, among other things, mandated kneeling at communion.[121] Charles and Laud reinvigorated Scotland's episcopal

---

[117] Hotson, 'A Generall Reformation', pp. 204–5.
[118] MacDonnell, *Chartæ et Statuta*, pp. 41–50; Bolton, *Statutes*, pp. 43–51; Ford, 'That Bugbear Arminianism', pp. 149–51.
[119] Sharpe, 'Archbishop Laud and the University of Oxford', pp. 148–50; Fincham, 'Oxford and the Early Stuart Polity', pp. 201–2.
[120] *Laud Works*, V, p. 130.
[121] John Spalding, *Memorialls of the Trubles in Scotland and in England, A.D. 1624–A.D. 1645*, ed. John Stuart (2 vols, Aberdeen, 1850–1), II, pp. 36–7; John R. Young, 'Charles I and the 1633 Parliament', in Keith M. Brown and Alaistar J. Mann (eds), *Parliament and*

bench, with the ecclesiastical hierarchy strengthened via the reinstitution of the Scottish High Commission and the creation of a new episcopal see at Edinburgh, filled by the Arminian William Forbes.[122] But nonconformity had also been on full display at the coronation. A faction of bishops refused to don surplices, while petitions that outlined the Kirk's grievances circulated.[123] It is unsurprising that, on his return to England, Charles ordered a Scottish edition of the Book of Common Prayer, subsequently published in October 1633, to be utilised in the Kirk, whose liturgy and episcopal-in-Presbyterian polity was incompatible with his vision of a well-ordered church and state.[124]

Charles' move to intrude the Prayer Book on Scotland, combined with the propagation of new canons for the Kirk, provided the spark that ignited revolution in Scotland and subsequent civil wars throughout Britain and Ireland. The initial impetus behind mandating the new liturgy, however, also stemmed from the perceived disorder and disobedience that Charles and Laud observed in Scotland's universities. From the time of Charles' Scottish coronation, the Scottish universities figured prominently into the monarchy's plans to overhaul worship in the Kirk. Like the situation in Ireland, Scottish university reform was pursued in parallel, and in some cases pre-empted, the Laudian reform of the Scottish church. A new generation of Scottish ministers had to be socialised into Laudian practices in order to engineer wider social change.

There was precedent for the monarchy's targeting of the universities. In 1616–17, James VI/I had ordered the reintroduction of the doctorate to create a domestic pipeline to the episcopate. He further mandated ceremonies and rites in the Scottish universities be practised as they were 'in the Universities of Cambridge, [and] Oxenforde'.[125] Laud had been present at James' Scottish visit in 1617, where he would have welcomed the English academic ceremonies held in the king's honour at St Andrews. Sixteen years later, it is likely that Laud influenced policy towards Scotland's universities, especially given his concurrent work at Oxford and Trinity. But whereas Laud had intervened directly in the affairs of Trinity and Oxford – occupying

---

Politics in Scotland, 1567–1707 (Edinburgh, 2005), pp. 101–37; Allan I. Macinnes, *Charles I and the Making of the Covenanting Movement 1625–1641* (Edinburgh, 1991), pp. 128–41.
[122] James, *This Great Firebrand*, pp. 43–63; Alan R. MacDonald, *The Jacobean Kirk, 1567–1625: Sovereignty, Polity, and Liturgy* (Aldershot, 1998), pp. 119–21, 143.
[123] NLS, Wod.Fol.XLIII, fol. 255; Spalding, *Memorialls*, p. I, 37; John Row, *The History of the Kirk of Scotland, from the Year 1558 to August 1637*, ed. David Laing (Edinburgh, 1842), pp. 357–66, 375–81.
[124] Joong-Lak Kim, 'The Scottish-English-Romish Book: The Character of the Scottish Prayer Book of 1637', in Michael Braddick and David L. Smith (eds), *The Experience of Revolution in Stuart Britain and Ireland: Essays for John Morrill* (Cambridge, 2011), pp. 14–32, at 19–20.
[125] Beriah Botfield (ed.), *Original Letters Relating to the Ecclesiastical Affairs of Scotland, 1603–1625* (2 vols, Edinburgh, 1851), II, pp. 805–9; Reid, *Humanism and Calvinism*, pp. 243–9.

the chancellorships of both institutions – in Scotland, evidence suggests university reform flowed largely from the king.[126] Just as James had done in 1617, upon his visit to Scotland Charles pursued a range of reforms in the universities as an integral part of a broader policy of realigning the Kirk with the Laudian Church of England.

The process began once Charles returned to England. Between October 1633 and May 1634, he wrote a series of letters to Scotland's bishops concerning the universities.[127] The first letter was sent to Archbishop John Spottiswoode of St Andrews, chancellor of the University of St Andrews, in October 1633.[128] In May, similar letters followed to Archbishop Patrick Lindsay of Glasgow and Bishop Patrick Forbes of Aberdeen, each chancellor of their respective universities. Charles also wrote to Bishop Forbes of Edinburgh and the Edinburgh town council regarding Edinburgh University.[129] Charles linked the nonconformity he witnessed during his visit to disorders in the universities. He concluded that 'No one thing appeareth to us more necessarie then the well setling of our universities both for the service of God and good education of you there.'[130]

One of the central issues that Charles highlighted was the intermixing of university masters and students with commoners during church services, which were held outside of the universities' jurisdictions. Masters and students 'go to the ordinarie parish church to service and sermone, and ther sitt promiscuouslie with the rest of the auditorie which looses much of the honour and dignitie of the universitie'. This was 'qyte contrarie to the course held in other well governed places of the like nature'.[131] Oxford and Cambridge staff and students, by comparison, were enjoined to worship within the universities' confines.[132] To rectify this, and to emulate the English universities, Charles ordered St Andrews to hold morning and evening prayers on Sundays and holy days in the chapel of St Salvator's College. Glasgow's staff and students were to repair to the cathedral adjacent to the university. Members of both King's and Marischal colleges in Aberdeen were commanded to go to 'fitt and convenient places within the quires of the severall churches of these townes as ar most eminent'. Edinburgh's staff and students were to attend a new space in St Giles Cathedral. Finally, all masters and students were required to wear

---

[126] James, *This Great Firebrand*, p. 67.
[127] For an overview of these directives, see also *ibid.*, pp. 64–7.
[128] StAUL, UYSS 110/C/4.23; BL, Add MSS 23111, fol. 128; Charles Rogers (ed.), *The Earl of Stirling's Register of Royal Letters Relative to the Affairs of Scotland and Nova Scotia from 1615 to 1635* (2 vols, Edinburgh, 1885), II, pp. 677–9.
[129] *Laud Works*, VI, p. 318.
[130] MAUG, I, pp. 248–9; *Fasti Aberdonenses*, pp. 393–4; Rogers, *Stirling Register*, II, pp. 745–52.
[131] StAUL, UYSS 110/C/4.23; MAUG, I, p. 249; *Fasti Aberdonenses*, p. 393; Rogers, *Stirling Register*, II, p. 752.
[132] Curtis, *Oxford and Cambridge in Transition*, p. 185.

the proper dress while attending service, 'with their gownes according to their severall degrees'.[133] Additionally, Charles' first set of orders in October 1633, sent to Archbishop Spottiswoode, were made at the same time that he ordered all Scottish clergy to use the English liturgy and wear proper dress during services.[134] Indeed, in each letter, the king insisted on strict town/gown separation. But in his letter to Spottiswoode, Charles wrote that 'Neither will wee have one scholar of quhat rank and degree soever, at the tyme aforesaid, go to the common parish churches, nor anie of the inhabitants of the toune leave ther parish church mixe themselves with the universitie.'[135] Charles, echoing Laud, conceived of the universities as the fountainheads of order and conformity. The Scottish universities needed to be examples for 'the whole bodie of that kingdom' and avoid corruption by Calvinism and localised devotion.[136] University men ran the risk of heterodoxy by intermixing with parishioners, which would poison the kingdom's fountains and perpetuate disorder. The monarchy's specific vision for university worship in Scotland thus underlined the idea of the universities as both models of good order and upholders of the social hierarchy. As future ministers, students especially had to observe proper decorum and deference to authorised norms free from the corruption of common parishioners, to whom they would eventually inculcate such norms in the exercise of social control.

The king's letters to Spottiswoode and St Andrews are also particularly telling because Charles expounded upon what he envisioned intramural worship to entail. His directives to Aberdeen, Glasgow, and Edinburgh make no mention of the form of worship, only that university members should be separated from common parishioners. For St Andrews, however, Charles made clear his intention that 'the service ther read shall be the English liturgy untill such tyme as ane uther be made and published by the authoritie in that Church, and they sall have ane communione under that forme, and kneeling'.[137] Charles commanded St Andrews' staff and students to worship according to the English liturgy and to perform the controversial act of kneeling at communion. These orders had also been encoded in Laud's Trinity statutes. Indeed, though widespread opposition to the Perth Articles existed, it was the king's intention that Scotland's future ministers be conditioned to the ritual at university.

It is likely that Charles issued these liturgical commands for St Andrews

---

[133] StAUL, UYSS 110/C/4.23, 4.23; MAUG, I, p. 249; *Fasti Aberdonenses*, p. 394; Rogers, *Stirling Register*, II, p. 752.
[134] Baillie, *L&J*, I, pp. 421–2; James, *This Great Firebrand*, pp. 68, 80–2; Gordon Donaldson, *The Making of the Scottish Prayer Book of 1637* (Edinburgh, 1954), pp. 42–3.
[135] StAUL, UYSS 110/C/4.23.
[136] StAUL, UYSS 110/C/4.24. On Scottish nonconformity and local religious practice, see Todd, *Culture of Protestantism*, pp. 402–12; Hall, *Puritans*, pp. 167–9, 190–6, 242–4.
[137] StAUL, UYSS, 110/C/4.23.

due to its status as Scotland's principal university and because of his familiarity with the institution. With Laud in his entourage, Charles visited St Andrews in July 1633, and there he would have observed first-hand any perceived errors in worship.[138] Charles' actions also drew on his father's initiatives. James VI/I had endeavoured to transform St Andrews into a Scottish Oxford, introducing a range of reforms to break Andrew Melville's influence and bring St Andrews into synergy with the English universities. In addition to reintroducing the doctorate, in 1623 James ordered the English liturgy to be used at St Mary's College, which Melville had moulded into Scotland's chief seminary.[139] James sought to ensure that students there would be exposed to English-style worship, and thus socialised into the religious norms that he found more agreeable to his royal pretensions.[140] A decade later, his son extended this order to the whole university to ensure that students would be conditioned to the English liturgy; upon laureation and later ordination they could spread these mores in their ministries.[141]

Laud's liturgical reforms for the Kirk also influenced the king's orders for the Scottish universities. Scottish liturgical reform had been in the works since 1629, and the king and Laud wished to import English service wholesale; at the very least, they desired that a Scottish liturgy be compiled 'as near that of England as might be'.[142] Charles alluded to the creation of a new liturgy in his letter to St Andrews in October 1633. The following May, however, Scottish bishops argued against imposing the English service. Laud nevertheless continued ahead and took an active role in creating the liturgy.[143] On the same day that Charles sent his orders to the universities, he proceeded to give the Scottish bishops his formal orders for a new liturgy, which should 'be kept alsweill in the colledges [and] universities'.[144]

David Stevenson notes that 'the only matter concerning the Scottish universities [Charles] took a personal interest in as a result of his 1633 visit was a trifle of ceremony'.[145] This trivialises the extent to which Charles incorporated the universities into his vision of three well-ordered kingdoms. The king had confronted problems at Oxford and Cambridge at the beginning of his reign, where in clear terms he connected broader societal disorders to

---

[138] *Laud Works*, III, p. 218; Cant, *St Andrews*, p. 66.
[139] David Calderwood, *The History of the Kirk of Scotland*, ed. David Laing and Thomas Thomson (7 vols, Edinburgh, 1842–5), VII, p. 569. On Melville and St Mary's, see Reid, *Humanism and Calvinism*, pp. 185–93.
[140] Alan R. MacDonald, 'James VI and I, the Church of Scotland, and British Ecclesiastical Convergence', *Historical Journal*, 48:4 (2005), 885–903.
[141] StAUL, UYSS 110/C/4.23.
[142] *Laud Works*, III, p. 278; Donaldson, *Making of the Scottish Prayer Book*, pp. 27–44.
[143] *Laud Works*, III, pp. 427–78; Kim, 'Scottish-English-Romish Book', pp. 19–21; James, *This Great Firebrand*, pp. 81–92.
[144] Rogers, *Stirling Register*, II, pp. 752–3.
[145] Stevenson, *King's College*, p. 73.

instability in the universities.[146] There was precedent for Charles to link extramural volatility to issues in the universities. In Scotland, he pinned this on the unregulated nature of religious worship. 'Trifles of ceremony' were, for the king, symptomatic of greater issues pertaining to social order. By regulating worship in the universities, Charles could ensure that a form of English liturgy would remain in use at St Andrews. And, when the time came, the new canons and prayer book could be introduced to universities in Aberdeen, Edinburgh, and Glasgow. Similarly to Ireland, the forging of uniformity between the Scottish and English churches was contingent on reforming the Scottish universities, where conformity to Laudianism could germinate.

A ceremonial but no less significant part of reforming the universities was Charles' ratification of the universities' constitutions at the Coronation Parliament. Charles confirmed the rights, privileges, and charters of St Andrews, Glasgow, and King's College.[147] This was an important affirmation of the Jacobean reform of the Scottish universities. James' crusade against Andrew Melville's educational reforms included the revocation in 1621 of the streamlined 'New Foundation' of St Andrews in favour of a return to the university's original foundation.[148] Charles wrote to St Mary's in May 1634 that he had power 'to add to these acts and reforme them in such manner and at what time we in our princelie judgment shall think fitt'.[149] The king confirmed St Andrews' constitution, but he also reserved the right to reform the university outright. In 1619, Bishop Patrick Forbes of Aberdeen, chancellor of King's College, also restored King's original constitution, which had for the previous three decades existed in a beleaguered state between its original foundation and Melvillian reform.[150] Charles cemented the overthrow of the Melvillian higher education project. The king's actions in Scotland paralleled reform at Trinity. In each kingdom, university constitutions that had bred Calvinism, utilised Ramist pedagogy, and allowed for a degree of autonomy from external interference had been eliminated in favour of a return to original foundations, as was the case in Scotland, or new foundations of a Laudian bent, as was the case in Dublin. The perceived chaos of overtly Reformed constitutions had been eradicated and replaced by hierarchical governance under royal authority in order to sustain the wider social order.

---

[146] Curtis, *Oxford and Cambridge in Transition*, pp. 175–7; Fincham, 'Oxford and the Early Stuart Polity', pp. 199–204.

[147] *RPS*, 1633/6/87, 88, 89; *Fasti Aberdonenses*, pp. 145–9a; MAUG, I, pp. 241–4.

[148] *RPS*, 1621/6/117.

[149] Rogers, *Stirling Register*, II, p. 745.

[150] Stevenson, *King's College*, pp. 39–40, 63–7. Unlike St Andrews and King's, Glasgow's Melvillian *Nova Erectio* of 1577 was maintained, for the reworked constitution saved the university from dissolution. See MAUG, I, pp. 215–17; Steven J. Reid, 'The Parish of Govan and the Principals of the University of Glasgow, 1577–1621', *The Society of Friends of Govan Old* (2012), 1–23; idem, *Humanism and Calvinism*, pp. 255–6, 265–71.

At King's College, when Charles' orders for worship were read during a visitation in 1634, King's masters duly agreed to them.[151] Subsequently, when college authorities sought to extend King's jurisdiction, rights, and privileges in Old Aberdeen, they appealed directly to Charles, dispatching professor of medicine William Gordon to London in September 1634. Gordon revealed that King's wished to extend its authority over neighbouring Marischal College.[152] Bringing Marischal under the chancellor's purview was a long-term goal of Bishop Forbes, who, despite his status as the local metropolitan, had been denied authority at Marischal by its founder, George Keith, fifth earl Marischal. The extension of the chancellor's authority over Marischal was a key way to gain control of an institution that was organised according to a Melvillian constitution founded strategically outside King's jurisdiction in a separate burgh.[153] Together with the petition that was sent to London in September 1634 were letters written by Bishop Forbes and his son, John, then rector at King's, to Laud, 'requesting his grace to assist that so pious and laudable ane earand'.[154] This is another parallel with events in Dublin: Laud's recognisable position as a strategic point of contact in university affairs beyond England. Just as Trinity's staff had appealed to Laud in a misguided attempt to protect their privileges, King's authorities appealed to Laud seeking royal approbation to increase their privileges. In both cases, Laud sought to expand royal power. Laud replied that he consulted with the king as to the university's intentions and remarked that Charles would be unfamiliar with many of the specifics of their requests.[155] Charles instead turned to his Scottish bishops, and ordered the archbishops of St Andrews and Glasgow and the bishops of Aberdeen, Moray, and Ross to review King's privileges and ensure that they be 're-established according to the laudable intention of the founder'. He also ordered the bishops to 'repress such abuses and setle such good ordour thairin'.[156] Bishop Forbes' reform of King's was carried out under royal auspices, but they came to a halt with his death in March 1635, leaving the college divided between advocates of the original foundation and proponents of the Melvillian constitution.[157]

---

[151] *Fasti Aberdonenses*, p. 394; Stevenson, *King's College*, pp. 75–9.
[152] *Fasti Aberdonenses*, pp. 304–10.
[153] On Marischal's foundation and constitution and its muddled relationship with King's, see Kerr-Peterson, *Protestant Lord*, pp. 168–85; Stevenson, *King's College*, p. 76. On the authority of the chancellor, see *FAM*, II, pp. 3–10; Reid, 'Aberdeen's Toun College', pp. 174–85. On Aberdeen's dual foundation, see David Ditchburn, 'Educating the Elite: Aberdeen and Its Universities', in E. Patricia Dennison, David Ditchburn, and Michael Lynch (eds), *Aberdeen Before 1800: A New History* (East Linton, 2002), pp. 327–46.
[154] *Fasti Aberdonenses*, pp. 399–400.
[155] *Ibid.*, pp. 400–1.
[156] Rogers, *Stirling Register*, II, pp. 779–80.
[157] Stevenson, *King's College*, p. 79.

The promulgation of new canons for the Kirk in January 1636 represented another area in which the monarchy sought to incorporate the Scottish universities into its ecclesiastical program. The Scottish canons were primarily the work of Scottish bishops in concert with Laud and William Juxon, bishop of London.[158] Like the Irish canons, the Scottish code afforded an elevated place to higher education. Charles' orders of October 1633 and March 1634 to the Scottish universities already signalled his intention to have universities worship like their English counterparts. The Scottish canons make clear that the universities were vital to cultivating a clergy who could foster closer uniformity and identified the universities, specifically, as the institutions to uphold the authority of the monarch. The first canon stated that 'all readers of divinity lectures, all masters, principals, primars, regents fellows, and all whosoever have charge of schools, colleges, and universities' were required to observe and uphold the crown's jurisdiction over Scotland's religious estate.[159] No man was permitted to enter the ministry, to catechise, or to read divinity in the universities unless he first pledged his obedience to the canons, while 'non shall be permitted to teach in any college or schools, either as primar, regent, or fellow, except he take first the oath of allegiance and supremacy'. To further reinforce the royal supremacy, masters were enjoined to promote Richard Mocket's tract *Deus et Rex*, a work that upheld allegiance to the divine right of kings.[160] Mocket produced the text in 1615 as a way to foster obedience to the royal supremacy, and the specific order in the Scottish canons represented another extension of the policies of James VI/I, who in 1616 ordered the General Assembly to ensure the text's use in Scottish schools.[161] This inclusion cohered with the broader tenor of the canons to advance the royal supremacy in the Kirk.[162]

It was essential to build this allegiance in the universities, the nurseries of the ministry. The canons stated that ministers had to have been 'bred' in a 'university or college' and produce verification of their degree and good standing.[163] As with the Irish canons, the requirement that ministers be educated in the universities and in good standing was not unique. But in regard to both the Scottish and Irish canons, it is important to remember that these orders were intended to bring to fruition an ecclesiastical program that inculcated a specific confessional vision. Furthermore, the crown sought

---

[158] James, *This Great Firebrand*, pp. 86–92. On the canons, see especially Joong-Lak Kim, 'Firing in Unison? The Scottish Canons of 1636 and the English Canons of 1640', *Records of the Scottish Church History Society*, 28 (1998), 55–76

[159] *Laud Works*, V, p. 586; *Canons and Constitutions Ecclesiasticall Gathered and Put in Forme, for the Government of the Church of Scotland* (Aberdeen, 1636), p. 7.

[160] *Laud Works*, V, pp. 588, 597–98; *Scottish Canons*, pp. 11, 28.

[161] Botfield, *Original Letters*, II, p. 482; J.P. Sommerville, *Politics and Ideology in England, 1603–1640* (London, 1986), p. 12.

[162] James, *This Great Firebrand*, pp. 89–90.

[163] *Laud Works*, V, p. 587; *Scottish Canons*, p. 9.

to ensure that the universities would be able to do so from a firm economic base, for in October 1636 Charles initiated in an inquiry into the estate of the universities' finances in order to rectify their 'decayed' state.[164] With the concurrent reform of Trinity – and Oxford – these endeavours represented the extension of a 'British' policy of university reform that sought to employ the Scottish universities as structures of power that would prepare the way for a new liturgy and align the Kirk's approach to university-trained clergy with that of England. These exertions of royal power in the universities were also exported to nonconforming communities of English, and Scottish, subjects overseas.

Overseas Communities

Laud's conception of a social order built on loyalty to the monarchy and conformity to the Church of England extended beyond the British Isles. In his reflections on his trial for treason in June 1644, Laud noted that he was confronted about a remark he had made about the puritan minister John Davenport, who several years earlier had fled the Netherlands for New England. Laud, through his network of informants in the Dutch Republic, blocked Davenport from becoming pastor of the English church in Amsterdam. On Davenport's flight across the Atlantic, Laud supposedly claimed 'when I heard he was gone into New-England, I should say my arm should reach him there… I cannot think it fit that any plantation should secure any offender against the Church of England.'[165] Davenport's journey to the Netherlands, and then to New England, was emblematic of the peripatetic existence of puritans who believed that the religious situation, among other concerns, had become untenable under Charles. Such sentiments eventually sparked a 'Great Migration' to New England during the 1630s of some 20,000 migrants of varying puritan beliefs.[166] Ireland, the Netherlands, and thereafter New England were magnets for divines who sought to practise, and advance, 'true religion' in more welcoming religious and intellectual settings.[167] But Laud sought to pursue the cause of uniformity beyond the three kingdoms to expat

---

[164] AUL, MSM 91/1; MAUG, I, pp. 264, 266–70; P. Hume Brown (ed.), *The Register of the Privy Council of Scotland, 1635–1637*, 2nd series, 6 (Edinburgh, 1905), p. 364.
[165] *Laud Works*, IV, p. 260.
[166] Alison Games, *Migration and the Origins of the English Atlantic World* (Cambridge, MA, 1999), pp. 132–4; Bernard Bailyn, *The Barbarous Years: The Peopling of British North America: The Conflict of Civilizations, 1600–1675* (New York, 2012), pp. 365–72; Virginia DeJohn Anderson, 'Migrants and Motives: Religion and the Settlement of New England, 1630–1640', *New England Quarterly*, 58:3 (1985), 339–83.
[167] Hall, *Puritans*, pp. 196–204. See also Keith L. Sprunger, *Dutch Puritanism: A History of English and Scottish Churches of the Netherlands in the Sixteenth and Seventeenth Centuries* (Leiden, 1982).

communities abroad.[168] It was within this crucible of imperial Laudianism and transatlantic migration that Harvard College was founded in New England. The irony is that, at a time when Trinity and the Scottish universities were being reformed along Laudian lines, the university project in America would be pursued almost entirely beyond the bounds of royal control to foster a social order diametrically opposed to the Laudian program.

By the time Laud acceded to the see of Canterbury in 1633, there was a growing puritan presence in the Dutch Republic. Royal authorities wished to compel use of the Book of Common Prayer in these communities to better entrench the authority of the Church of England.[169] In March 1633, Laud drafted proposals for engendering conformity among English and Scottish subjects in the Netherlands. He proposed that none be permitted to 'entertain' a minister that did not conform to the Church of England, while all ministers and preachers, English or Scottish, would be required to preach, administer sacraments, and teach the catechisms according to the Book of Common Prayer 'maintained in the Church of England'. Laud also underlined the implications of nonconformists harbouring in the Netherlands and argued that none should be allowed to organise into a classis, or synod, which the States General had permitted in 1621.[170] To make his point, Laud employed the language of higher learning: 'I conceive it no way fit, that the ministers which are his Majesty's subjects in Holland, should have any classical meetings allowed them... for then it will be a perpetual seminary to breed and transplant men ill affected to the Government into this kingdom.'[171]

Those 'ill affected' puritans in this Dutch 'seminary' found welcoming spaces in Dutch universities. The universities of Franeker, Utrecht, and Leiden were landing spots for English and Scottish scholars, with the arch-puritan William Ames, divinity professor at Franeker from 1622–33, exercising particular influence over his students while occupying much of the crown authorities' attention.[172] Ames was also among the puritan alumni and fellows of Christ's College, Cambridge who were ousted in the wake of

---

[168] Hugh Trevor-Roper, *Archbishop Laud, 1573–1645*, 3rd edn (London, 1988), chap. 7; Keith L. Sprunger, 'Archbishop Laud's Campaign Against Puritanism at the Hague', *Church History*, 44:3 (1975), 308–20; Arthur Lyon Cross, *The Anglican Episcopate and the American Colonies* (New York, 1902), pp. 12–23.

[169] TNA, SP 84/146, fols 66v–67r.

[170] Sprunger, *Dutch Puritanism*, pp. 290–1; Hall, *Puritans*, p. 200.

[171] *Laud Works*, VI, pp. 22–5. See also Peter Heylyn, *Cyprianus Anglicus* (London, 1671), pp. 218–20.

[172] Daniela Prögler, *English Students at Leiden University, 1575–1650: 'Advancing Your Abilities in Learning and Bettering Your Understanding of the World and State Affairs'* (Burlington, 2013), pp. 32–5, 39–40, 53–4, 63–6, 91–2; Keith L. Sprunger, 'William Ames and the Franeker Link to English and American Puritanism', in G.T. Jensma, F. Smit, and F. Westra (eds), *Universiteit Te Franeker, 1585–1811: Bijdragen Tot de Geschiedenis van de Friese Hogeschool* (Leeuwarden, 1985), pp. 264–74.

the Arminian takeover in 1609.[173] While Ames' *alma mater* morphed into an anti-Calvinist bastion, one that would provide amenable men for Laudian Trinity, Ames absconded to the Netherlands. In the aftermath of the Synod of Dort, Ames, a vocal defender of the Reformed position, was nominated for a divinity professorship at Leiden. But royal authorities led by Archbishop Abbott and then-ambassador Dudley Carleton blocked his move, despite the overtures of Leiden's faculty.[174] Franeker next applied for Ames' services in 1622, and once again Leiden's theology faculty appealed on his behalf. Not only had Ames been 'peacefully behaved', but he was also better positioned at Franeker to work 'against the Arminians and Vorstians who break with and trouble our churches'.[175] Dutch Calvinists viewed Ames as a vital opponent against the supporters of Jacobus Arminius and his successor Conrad Vorstius, and his energies would be best employed in the university. During Ames' tenure, Franeker in many ways became the foil to the type of institution that English authorities detested: a bulwark against Arminianism, steeped in Ramism, where all were required by statute to subscribe to the Belgic Confession and the Reformed Heidelberg Catechism.[176] Franeker, like the Scottish universities and Trinity, was both a model and machine, but in an anti-Laudian mould: an exemplar of Reformed orthodoxy and a technology that produced ministers to defend it.

English puritans also championed Ames. Part of the early designs for the settlement of Massachusetts Bay in the late 1620s included enticing Ames to join the company of John Winthrop.[177] Though Ames seemed keen to move, he remained at Franeker, which, like other Dutch universities, remained havens for English and Scottish Calvinists.[178] Hugh Peter's joining with Ames proved especially consequential and aggravated English authorities further. Imprisoned for slandering Queen Henrietta Maria for her 'idolatry', the Cambridge-educated Peter fled to the Netherlands in 1628. A letter of introduction from Ames' Franeker colleague, the logic professor Johannes Hachting, suggests that Peter sought to take up a position as a schoolmaster in Friesland, close to the university.[179] Hachting's letter made clear Peter's connection to Ames at Franeker, and later that year he joined Franeker's staff

---

[173] Bondos-Greene, 'End of an Era', p. 207.
[174] Keith L. Sprunger, *The Learned Doctor William Ames: Dutch Backgrounds of English and American Puritanism* (Urbana, IL, 1972), pp. 65–70.
[175] TNA, SP 84/106, fols 131–3.
[176] Sprunger, *Learned Doctor*, pp. 71–80.
[177] *Winthrop Papers*, II, p. 180; Sprunger, *Learned Doctor*, pp. 90–1. See also *idem*, 'William Ames and the Settlement of Massachusetts Bay', *New England Quarterly*, 39:1 (1966), 66–79.
[178] Prögler, *English Students at Leiden*, pp. 38–44.
[179] 'February Meeting. William Pynchon, Founder of Springfield; Hugh Peter in the Netherlands', *Proceedings of the Massachusetts Historical Society*, 3rd series, 64 (1931), 66–111, at 109–11.

as proctor under Ames' supervision.[180] By early 1633, royal agents reported that Peter had become pastor at Rotterdam and requested that Ames join him.[181] Crucially, Peter's designs for Rotterdam involved not only moulding the Rotterdam church along congregational lines, it also included founding a college.[182] Peter and his associates appealed directly to Dutch authorities and to the Leiden theology faculty to support their Rotterdam project.[183] The Dutch Council of State moved in Peter's favour, stating that 'the English, and Scotch Preachers shall hence forward follow such Classical order, as is held and followed… in this Country'.[184] Dutch authorities provided a window – however fleeting – for Peter's cadre to create a congregational, godly expat community in Rotterdam, for which subscription to a covenant was required for membership.[185]

That a college was part of the equation signals that the Rotterdam community required higher learning to sustain its existence – healthy societies required functional educational institutions. That Peter wished to establish an educational alternative for English puritans also had precedent. Three years earlier, the polymath Samuel Hartlib, the centripetal force of Reformed intellectuals, attempted to establish a breakaway and ultimately abortive academy at Chichester due to increasing pressure on puritans in the English universities.[186] In the Netherlands, Peter would pursue a similar project. Early accounts of the college's planning suggest that it was to be a Latin school or *gymnasium*.[187] In mid-1633, Ames accepted a call to be minister and master of the college for the 'educating & fitting of some studious youths, that should be sent him out of England, for ye holy ministery, & so keep up ye Orthodox Truths, & power of Godlyness, wch were in very declineing condition in his native Country'.[188] According to the Rotterdam city council, Ames was to teach logic and ethics, and he was urged to bring with him his own English students from Franeker, in addition to educating members of the 'English nation' in the city.[189] Peter may have also had in mind the Cambridge-educated Ipswich minister, Samuel Ward, for this project.[190] From this

---

[180] Carla Gardina Pestana, 'Peter [Peters], Hugh (bap. 1598, d. 1660)', ODNB; Sprunger, *Learned Doctor*, p. 86.
[181] TNA, SP 16/223, fols 7–8; Raymond P. Stearns (ed.), 'Letters and Documents by or Relating to Hugh Peter', *Essex Institute Historical Collections*, 72:1 (1936), 43–72, at 43.
[182] Sprunger, *Dutch Puritanism*, 166; Raymond P. Stearns, *The Strenuous Puritan: Hugh Peters, 1598–1660* (Urbana, IL, 1954), pp. 74–5.
[183] Stearns, 'Letters and Documents', pp. 44–5; idem, *Strenuous Puritan*, p. 74.
[184] TNA, SP 84/146, fol. 85.
[185] *CSPD 1633–34*, p. 318.
[186] Charles Webster, *The Great Instauration: Science, Medicine, and Reform, 1626–1660*, 2nd edn (New York, 2002), p. 37.
[187] Sprunger, *Learned Doctor*, pp. 92, 241.
[188] Quoted in *ibid.*, p. 242.
[189] Hugo Visscher, *Guilielmus Amesius: Zihn Leven En Werken* (Haarlem, 1894), pp. 74–5.
[190] TNA, SP 16/241, fol. 96; Stearns, 'Letters and Documents', pp. 45–6.

evidence, the proposed college had the trappings of a Protestant academy. It was to offer Latin instruction in ethics and logic; it found support from local authorities; and it was to maintain the local community by educating future ministers. Furthermore, Ames was a professor whose pedagogy was steeped in Ramism, and he was required to bring English university students. This suggests that the institution would be flexible in its promotion of secondary- and university-level training and rooted in Reformed methodology, again all hallmarks of the academies.[191] That the college was to educate English students explicitly, if not exclusively, is also telling, and resembles the nature of Catholic seminaries that had been founded to educate English, Scottish, and Irish exiles. The Rotterdam project was a puritan seminary for expatriates and exiles, a hybridised educational institution established beyond the reach of hostile authorities. The plan, however, ultimately proved unsuccessful. Ames' death in November 1633 and the planting of Laudian ministers into English garrisons in the Netherlands saw the decline of nonconformity there.[192] But, the proposed Rotterdam college did set an important precedent, as it would not be the last time that puritan expatriates sought to found a university to support a community abroad.

Laud understood the implications of these endeavours, and he disapproved of the Dutch universities' Reformed turn following the Synod of Dort. In a 1631 letter to the Leiden scholar Gerardus Vossius, Laud commented that 'I hear not without pain of the failing education of your universities. These are the seeds of all evils in the church and then civil sphere.'[193] However, Laud and the crown's attention was focused more specifically on frustrating the designs of puritans in the Netherlands than on intervening in the Dutch universities. After all, unlike Trinity or the Scottish universities, he had no authority, real or imagined, to intervene in these institutions' affairs. Nevertheless, Laud was ultimately successful in suppressing nonconformity in the Netherlands.[194] His initial March 1633 proposals were by October actualised in an order of the Privy Council, which barred Merchant Adventurers from receiving any ministers without the king's approval, mandated the use of the 'liturgy and discipline' of the Church of England, and extended the authority of the bishop of London over English communities in the Netherlands.[195]

Nevertheless, the experience of puritan communities in the Netherlands, and the Rotterdam project specifically, underscores the vital place that institutions of higher learning had to support the existence of godly communities, including expat communities abroad. Prior to the Laudian intrusion, Trinity

---

[191] Maag, 'Reformation and Higher Education', pp. 125–8.
[192] TNA, SP 16/250, fol. 129.
[193] *Laud Works*, VI, p. 294. I am thankful to Christopher Rose for assistance on this translation.
[194] Trevor-Roper, *Archbishop Laud*, pp. 252–7; Sprunger, 'Archbishop Laud's Campaign Against Puritanism', pp. 308–9.
[195] TNA, SP 16/247, fols 2–5; *CSPD 1633–34*, p. 225.

was one such institution, a Reformed stronghold that welcomed nonconformists. Trinity's Reformed milieu and Ramist curriculum prompted John Winthrop, the architect of the New England enterprise, to send his son, John Jr, there in the early 1620s.[196] But, the situation in Ireland, like that in the Netherlands, ultimately became tenuous once Laud's attention turned to reforming the Irish church and university. By December 1634, John Jr's tutor at Trinity, Joshua Hoyle, was warning his former student to 'keepe sufficient privacy' on his visit to Dublin.[197] Facing hostile authorities in England, Ireland, and the Netherlands, many English puritans ultimately looked further abroad to New England to form a godly society that would be supported by the requisite educational institutions.[198]

It is perhaps fitting that one of the final decisions to migrate across the Atlantic was made during the 1629 Cambridge commencement, as a majority of the key players who facilitated and led the transatlantic exodus – Winthrop, Emmanuel Downing, Thomas Hooker, John Cotton, and Richard Saltonstall, among many others – constituted 'a phalanx' of Cambridge puritans.[199] As Harry Stout's demographic research has made clear, the New England settlement would be singular in its high concentration of university men.[200] Beyond the intellectual might of its leaders, the Great Migration was also unique in its focus on transplanting traditional English society.[201] Such a society would require the institutions, including schools, to maintain social order and ultimately to survive. Winthrop and Francis Higginson emphasised this point in their 'General Observations for the Plantation of New England' of May 1629. They noted that schools and universities, 'fountaines of learning' that had come under duress in England, would be key institutions to support a peaceful society and to 'carry the gospell into those parts of the world, and to raise a bulwarke against the kingdom of Antichrist'.[202] Crucially, the migrants also brought with them the governance of the Massachusetts Bay Colony, thus relocating governing authority away from England.[203]

The transatlantic migration did not, however, stop royal authorities from attempting to exert control over nonconforming subjects. In respect to New England, there would be no canons and no interventions in educational

---

[196] *Alumni Dublinenses*, p. 890; Francis J. Bremer, *John Winthrop: America's Forgotten Founding Father* (New York, 2003), pp. 138–40; *Winthrop Papers*, I, pp. 271–2, 275–84, 288–9, 311, 313–14; Robert H. Murray, *Dublin University and the New World* (London, 1921), p. 64.

[197] *Winthrop Papers*, III, pp. 179–80.

[198] Alan Ford, 'The Church of Ireland: Power and Distance in the Early-Seventeenth-Century Atlantic', *The Seventeenth Century* (2023), 1–22, at 16–17.

[199] *Ibid.*, II, pp. 102–3; Bremer, *John Winthrop*, pp. 147–8; Bailyn, *Barbarous Years*, p. 381.

[200] Harry S. Stout, 'University Men in New England 1620–1660: A Demographic Analysis', *Journal of Interdisciplinary History*, 4:3 (1974), 375–400.

[201] Bailyn, *Barbarous Years*, pp. 370–1.

[202] *Winthrop Papers*, II, pp. 111–21.

[203] Bremer, *Puritan Experiment*, p. 41; Staloff, *American Thinking Class*, pp. 4–10.

institutions, as had been the case in Ireland and Scotland. Laud, nevertheless, was positioned to intervene in New England's affairs.[204] In April 1634 Charles appointed Laud to lead a Committee for Foreign Plantations that was granted expansive powers, including imposing penalties on religious offences.[205] As the committee's head, Laud received a steady stream of intelligence regarding the colonies in New England and elsewhere.[206] The committee received petitions, arbitrated disputes, and addressed disorders, with its attention focused increasingly on New England following reports of nonconformity and disloyalty. Because the charter and the governance of Massachusetts was located in New England, Laud's committee also actively sought to intervene in the colony's affairs, though with little consequence.[207] Despite the committee's limited reach, the minister Henry Dunster, later Harvard College's first president, still thought it necessary to include a copy of the committee's charge in his notebook, together with a copy of the Massachusetts charter.[208]

But of course, prior to 1636, there was no university for the committee to inspect. Yet there was an important precedent for understanding how English royal authorities administered a university abroad. In 1617, James VI/I commanded the archbishops of Canterbury and York to take up collections to support planting churches and schools in Virginia for 'the education of the children of those Barbarians' for the 'encrease of Christian Religion'.[209] This prompted a donation campaign in England for the erection of a college at Henrico in Virginia.[210] The college at Henrico was meant to convert Native Americans to Christianity, conversion being a key, if subordinate, organising principle of the Virginia Company.[211] Conversion was also a key strategy in which to compete in the imperial arena with Spain.[212] In some ways, too, the Henrico project was an extension of the policies being pursued in Britain

---

[204] See e.g., TNA, SP 16/260, fols 34–35; TNA, PC 2/43, p. 519; CSPC, p. 174; CSPD 1633–34, pp. 450–1.
[205] CSPC, pp. 177, 232; *Winthrop Papers*, III, pp. 180–1; Ken MacMillan, *The Atlantic Imperial Constitution: Center and Periphery in the English Atlantic World* (New York, 2011), pp. 156–7.
[206] See e.g., CSPC, pp. 218, 239, 258–9, 266, 273, 283–5.
[207] MacMillan, *Atlantic Imperial Constitution*, pp. 158–62.
[208] MHS, MS N-1143, pp. 1–23.
[209] CSPC, p. 49; Susan M. Kingsbury (ed.), *The Records of the Virginia Company of London* (4 vols, Washington, DC, 1906–35), IV, pp. 1–2.
[210] VCA, FP 72; Kingsbury, *Records of the Virginia Company*, I, pp. 421–3, 3: 117, 575–7, 642–3; Peter Walne, 'The Collections for Henrico College, 1616–1618', *Virginia Magazine of History and Biography*, 80:3 (1972), 259–66.
[211] VCA, FP 92; CSPC, p. 22; Kingsbury, *Records of the Virginia Company*, III, pp. 70–2. On Henrico, see W. Gordon McCabe, 'The First University in America, 1619–1622', *Virginia Magazine of History and Biography*, 30:2 (1922), 133–56; Robert Hunt Land, 'Henrico and Its College', *William and Mary Quarterly*, 18:4 (1938), 453–98.
[212] Margaret Connell Szasz, *Indian Education in the American Colonies, 1607–1783*, 2nd edn (Lincoln, NE, 2007), pp. 46–63; Pestana, *Protestant Empire*, pp. 66–74.

and Ireland. Nothing suggests that James wished to found an Oxford in the Chesapeake, but the composition of the committee established in June 1619 to supervise the college is telling. It was dominated by Oxford men educated at Brasenose, Corpus Christi, and University colleges, all of which buttressed the monarchy and the high-church wing of the Church of England.[213] Political and religious sympathies of Henrico's college authorities – located in England – cohered with the crown's vision to cultivate institutions that bred orderly societies, not only to convert Native Americans, but also to abet imperial state formation through maintaining orthodoxy among settlers.[214]

The Henrico project also reflected Irish university policy. Both Henrico and Trinity were tied to the enterprise of plantation in economic and religious terms. Just as Trinity was supported both by donations and lands in the Ulster plantation, so too was Henrico's founding rooted in the twin scheme of donation and plantation.[215] In November 1618 the Virginia Company set aside 10,000 acres to endow 'the said University and College with convenient possessions'.[216] Though Trinity largely ignored its founding mission, Henrico's purpose was to convert Native Americans, who, having not wilfully adhered to Catholicism, were considered more worthy of salvation.[217] The college never materialised, however, as the 1622 Powhatan uprising destroyed Henrico and led James to revoke the Virginia Company's charter.[218]

The Henrico project highlighted the imperial nature of early Stuart university policy. It also intimated how crown authorities would administer a colonial university: through erecting a committee within the company whose governing authorities resided in the metropole; by ensuring that pliant officials staffed the committee; and by funding the project through the hierarchy of the established church. Laud, of course, had pursued similar strategies to great effect at Trinity. But for Laud, New England represented a unique challenge, as the Massachusetts charter and government resided much farther away, across the Atlantic. Decisions regarding education, therefore, could be made

---

[213] Kingsbury, *Records of the Virginia Company*, I, p. 231; Robin Darwall-Smith, *A History of University College, Oxford* (Oxford, 2008), pp. 120–31; J. Mordaunt Crook, *Brasenose: The Biography of an Oxford College* (Oxford, 2008), pp. 43–4.

[214] Craig Steven Wilder, *Ebony and Ivy: Race, Slavery, and the Troubled History of America's Universities* (New York, 2013), pp. 21–2.

[215] TCD, MS 571, fols 1v–3r.

[216] CSPC, pp. 22–23; Kingsbury, *Records of the Virginia Company*, I, pp. 234, III, pp. 102–3; Land, 'Henrico and Its College', pp. 475–6, 490–1.

[217] Szasz, *Indian Education*, p. 50; Jorge Cañizares-Esguerra, *Puritan Conquistadors: Iberianizing the Atlantic, 1550–1700* (Stanford, CA, 2006), pp. 5, 9–14, 205–14; Audrey Horning, *Ireland in the Virginian Sea: Colonialism in the British Atlantic* (Chapel Hill, NC, 2013), pp. 285–6.

[218] Wilder, *Ebony and Ivy*, p. 22. A university in Virginia would not be founded until the 1690s. See Jurgen Herbst, *From Crisis to Crisis: American College Government, 1636–1819* (Cambridge, MA, 1982), p. 2, chap. 3.

free of hostile authorities. Indeed, in May 1636, John Endecott, the leader of the Bay Company's first foray into New England, set aside land in Marblehead near Salem for the 'building of a Colledge'.[219] Several months later, the Massachusetts General Court – the colony's resident governing body – founded a college in 'Newtown', soon renamed Cambridge, which would later be named for John Harvard, the Emmanuel graduate who donated his library and portions of his land to the institution.[220] The significance of Harvard's founding was clear to Emmanuel Downing, who noted to Winthrop that

> The name of a Colledge in your plantation would much advantage given that considering the present distast against our universityes. You need not stay till you have Colledges to lodge schollars, for if you could make a combination of some few able men, ministers, or others to read certeyne lectures, and that that were knowne here amongst honest men, you would soone have students, hence, and Incouradgement to proceed further therein.[221]

Downing emphasised how Harvard's founding was a direct reaction to the Laudian campaign against the universities at home. What is more, his insistence that the college proceed with operations quickly with lectures from 'able men' recalled the Rotterdam college project.

On a fundamental level Trinity, Henrico, and Harvard were all imperial apparatuses – bodies of order in culturally unfamiliar spaces.[222] These colonial educational endeavours were exemplars of the early modern process of *translatio studii*, the 'transfer of knowledge' to imperial outposts throughout the Atlantic. Together with the symbolic and physical occupation of native space via the importation of European customs, institutions, and place names, the universities protected and promoted a known body of Christian knowledge on which the survival of orderly, godly societies in the colonies rested.[223] For puritans seeking a purer form of worship, Trinity's promise as a Reformed bulwark amongst the reprobate dissipated with the Laudian intrusion. Harvard represented another opportunity to found such a seminary, this time in the imagined 'tabula rasa' of New England. Through a university to sustain their norms and values, puritan settlers, disregarding the peoples already inhabiting the land, would order the 'chaos' and bring light to the 'darkness' of the American wilderness.[224]

---

[219] Morison, *Founding*, pp. 162–3, 169.
[220] HCR, I, p. 171; *Massachusetts Records*, I, pp. 183, 253.
[221] *Winthrop Papers*, III, pp. 369–71.
[222] Wilder, *Ebony and Ivy*, pp. 33–4.
[223] Jurgen Herbst, '*Translatio Studii*: The Transfer of Learning from the Old World to the New', *History of Higher Education Annual*, 12 (1992), 85–99; J.H. Elliott, *Empires of the Atlantic World: Britain and Spain in America 1492–1830* (New Haven, CT, 2006), chap. 2.
[224] Roderick Frazier Nash, *Wilderness and the American Mind*, 5th edn (New Haven, CT, 2014), pp. 24–6, 38–9.

Harvard had a clear connection to Cambridge, and Emmanuel College especially.[225] The disruptions that embroiled early Massachusetts, highlighted by the Antinomian Controversy, also necessitated founding a university in order to promote correct knowledge so to maintain the wider social order, even without the pressures of Laudian authorities.[226] Still, it is necessary to recognise the context of imperial Laudianism within which the university was founded. Just as Laud and his clients were reforming Trinity, the Scottish universities, and Oxford, and threatening to visit Cambridge, and as royal authorities stamped out nonconformity in the Netherlands, a college was founded in Massachusetts. It makes sense as to why Downing noted that there was little time to waste.[227] If Harvard would eventually be organised similarly to a Cambridge college, its founding and initial operations recalled the precedent set by the Rotterdam project, when just three years prior Hugh Peter called William Ames to lead a college for an English community abroad. But whereas that project deteriorated, in New England, beyond the reach of antagonistic authorities, the educational endeavour was restored. The idea of a college to support a godly society was thus highly mobile.

The Massachusetts General Court appointed Nathaniel Eaton, Ames' former student at Franeker, as master of the nascent seminary.[228] In his confessions to minister Thomas Shepard, Eaton cited Ames' influence.[229] Later, in November 1637, the General Court established for Harvard a Board of Overseers, which included a litany of Cambridge-educated puritans, including many with Dutch experience: John Winthrop, John Davenport, John Cotton, Thomas Shepard, and Hugh Peter.[230] This external board was formed under the aegis of the colonial government within the colony itself. The college may have also made use of Ames' library, which his family had brought with them to Massachusetts under Peter's care.[231] Combined with the library of John Harvard, the college's early curriculum bore the Reformed humanist marks of Ames, Ramus, and other leading Reformed intellectuals who had influenced learning at Trinity, the Scottish universities, and Protestant academies on the continent.[232]

---

[225] Morison, *Founding*, pp. 40–116; Bendall, Brooke, and Collinson, *Emmanuel College*, chap. 7.

[226] Staloff, *American Thinking Class*, p. 91.

[227] *Winthrop Papers*, III, p. 371.

[228] HCR, I, p. 172; Sprunger, 'William Ames and the Franeker Link', p. 273. On Ames' influence, see Clifford B. Clapp, 'Christo et Ecclesiae', PCSM, 25 (1922), 59–83; Miller, *New England Mind*, chap. 6.

[229] George Selement and Bruce C. Woolley (eds), 'Thomas Shepard's Confessions', PCSM, 58 (Boston, MA, 1981), 55–6.

[230] *Massachusetts Records*, I, p. 217.

[231] *Winthrop Papers*, IV, p. 109; Julius H. Tuttle, 'The Library of Dr. William Ames', PCSM, 14 (1911), 63–6.

[232] HCR, I, pp. 158–66; Hotson, 'A Generall Reformation', pp. 201–2; Sprunger, 'William

The education of Native Americans, the primary driver of the Henrico project, was left unmentioned. This was despite the millenarian attitudes of puritan intellectuals who viewed the conversion of Native Americans as precipitating the apocalypse.[233] Indeed, in 1634 the Emmanuel-educated minister John Stoughton, a close associate of the Massachusetts Bay Company, proposed that a college be erected in New England 'where Some may be maintained for learning the language and instructing heathen and our owne and breeding up as many of the Indians children as providence shall bringe unto our hands'.[234] But the express conversion of Native Americans did not appear to motivate Harvard's founding.[235] Rather, its purpose was to educate an English community abroad, one that faced repression at home and whose institutions were increasingly under pressure from hostile authorities. In that respect, the Rotterdam project was, in a way, a forerunner to the educational project in New England. At the same time Laudian authorities were reforming institutions deemed too autonomous in governance and too Ramist in instruction as part of a wider exertion of power to build uniformity to the English church, a college was founded among a breakaway community across the Atlantic that encapsulated each of these features. Harvard was an unintended consequence of the wider pressures exerted upon universities in England, Scotland, and Ireland during the Personal Rule.

Conclusion

This chapter has contended that, as both models of an idealised and ordered society and as the machinery by which authorities could craft their visions of a healthy commonwealth, the universities figured prominently into royal policies to stamp out nonconformity and construct uniformity to a Laudian church in both the British Isles and among communities overseas. The policies that Laud and his acolytes implemented in Ireland and Scotland, and attempted to implement among puritans abroad, were built upon the idea that universities ensured the cultivation of younger generations of churchmen and statesmen to their ideals. These students could more assuredly propagate the uniformity – not merely congruity – predicated on the Laudianism the monarchy craved, as they would be socialised to these norms through their

---

Ames and the Franeker Link', p. 273; Alfred C. Potter, 'Catalogue of John Harvard's Library', *PCSM*, 21 (1919), 190–230; Henry J. Cadbury, 'John Harvard's Library', *PCSM*, 34 (1940), 353–77.
[233] See e.g., Webster, *Great Instauration*, chap. 1, pp. 35–6.
[234] TNA, CO 1/8, fol. 115r; *CSPC*, p. 195.
[235] Though this would not be the case for long, as Harvard's 'Indian College' was founded after the university was chartered in 1650. See Chapter 6.

education, devoid of the Ramist curricula and Reformed constitutions and practices that had predominated.

This chapter has also endeavoured to demonstrate that, prior to the outbreak of the Civil Wars, higher educational spaces in Ireland, Scotland, and among puritan communities abroad emerged as key venues where rival power structures clashed. The Irish and Scottish universities, especially, were contested spaces: not only were they tapped as the machinery by which to engineer social order, they were venues where Stuart royal power, through Laud's interventions, was exerted. Such broader exertion of state power, and the contests for authority and control in educational spaces that they created, fuelled oppositional movements that were most immediately evident among puritans in the Netherlands and New England. Those opposed to the Laudian reforms founded universities in response to religious suppression at home and the pursuit of uniformity abroad. Whether as instruments of royal power or resistance, universities played vital roles in these spheres.

The monarchy's university policies were indeed met with resistance in spaces in Ireland, Scotland, and New England. In the Scottish and Irish cases, the universities were theatres in the longer-term offensive, a strategy that opponents recognised clearly. When the Laudian Prayer Book was introduced in Scotland in 1637, the Tables, the Scots' revolutionary provisional government, prohibited its use in the universities immediately. Similarly, in March 1641, the Irish Commons ordered an inquiry into the Laudian reform of Trinity and the disruptions it caused. Across the Atlantic, meanwhile, Harvard evolved into a seminary that, amidst the Civil Wars, became both a sanctuary for nonconformists and an apparatus that produced partisans for the Parliamentary cause. In the ensuing period, the role of Scotland, Ireland, and New England's universities as politicised, contested seminaries, where competing visions of social order could be realised, was intensified by the Civil Wars and its reverberations throughout the Atlantic.

2
The Scottish Universities, c. 1638–50

Whereas Reformed communities in Ireland, New England, and the Netherlands sought to wield higher learning to support godly communities in inhospitable spaces, in Scotland, the universities would be utilised to construct a kingdom in covenant with God. Scale was perhaps the greatest difference between the seventeenth-century Scottish universities and Trinity and Harvard colleges, and in many ways the former resembled similar developments among the French Huguenot community. Indeed, in Scotland, a unique multitude of smaller colleges, augmented by a seminary devoted to divinity training, would be used to support a specific confessional vision on a national scale. As part of a wider process of state formation, the Scottish universities emerged as essential institutions to socialise a new generation of ministers into the authorised mores of Covenanted Scotland. But first, they had to be made Covenanted.

The introduction of the Laudian Prayer Book in July 1637 sparked a rebellion in Scotland that inaugurated civil war in all three kingdoms. Scottish opposition to Charles' religious policies coalesced in the National Covenant, first promulgated in Edinburgh in February 1638.[1] As the Covenanters seized power, the reform of higher education emerged as a key part of the restructuring of the political system and the Kirk.[2] This chapter examines the process by which the Covenanters moulded Scotland's universities into the institutions to promote true religion and learning. This, in turn, would legitimise and secure the long-term endurance of the confessional state through the production of future generations of Covenanted ministers.[3] This process involved first breaking the universities' previous adherence to royalism and episcopacy. The Covenanters' campaign to reform higher learning underlines the universities' strategic place as contested spaces: of utility to both the Stuart monarchy and to the nascent Covenanting regime, the universities were not only spaces where power was projected, but also effective instruments where political and religious power was perpetuated for future generations.

---

[1] Gordon Donaldson (ed.), *Scottish Historical Documents* (Glasgow, 1999), pp. 194–201.
[2] Julian Goodare, 'The Scottish Revolution', in Sharon Adams and Julian Goodare (eds), *Scotland in the Age of Two Revolutions* (Woodbridge, 2014), pp. 79–96, at 85–7.
[3] Braddick, *State Formation*, p. 287.

This chapter analyses the Covenanters' reform of Scottish higher education during their period of hegemony in Scotland during the late 1630s and much of the 1640s. Recent scholarship has done much to revise long-standing tropes about early modern Scottish intellectual culture and teaching and learning in the universities. Thankfully, our conception of Scottish academe is no longer dominated by a teleological vision of a stagnate intellectual culture paralysed under an austere Calvinist regime in the era before the Enlightenment. Scottish academics engaged with ideas on the vanguard of the Reformed international and employed novel pedagogies and philosophies to varying degrees within Scotland.[4] What we lack, however, is an analysis of how the universities were integrated into the mechanisms of the Reformed Scottish state in the post-Reformation era, and especially after the reign of James VI/I. This chapter thus focuses on how the Covenanters wielded secular and ecclesiastical machinery to promote their vision of social order in the universities. It complements the burgeoning literature that has illuminated Scottish intellectual life and adds to the wider historiography that has advanced our understanding of secular and ecclesiastical governance and social order through their systematic analyses of the workings of the early modern Scottish church and state.[5] As a process of state formation, the Covenanted reform of higher education was contingent and idiosyncratic to the needs of the Covenanted state. Ultimately, the Covenanted reform of higher learning was itself a contested process, marked by internecine conflict; as powerful clerical factions within the Covenanted hierarchy defined and redefined what constituted social order, they pursued requisite changes in the universities.

The first part of what follows examines how the Covenanters broke the universities' initial opposition to the National Covenant and repurposed these institutions into the refineries that engineered adherence to the Covenanted social order. The second and third parts then examine systematically how the General Assembly and Parliament shaped the universities into pillars of the Covenanted state. Here, this chapter analyses the General Assembly's supervision of university affairs, focusing on how the Covenanting regime recast the universities by commissioning visitations, planting new professors, and deposing antithetical staff. A key theme that emerges in these sections is the importance of the people themselves – ministers, regents, and principals – who were tasked with educating Scotland's future ministers. This chapter concludes with an analysis of the Covenanters' 'national' university policies, with a particular

---

[4] For a recent summary of this scholarship, see also Schultz, 'Protestant Intellectual Culture', pp. 43–5.

[5] Important recent examples include Laura A.M. Stewart, *Rethinking the Scottish Revolution: Covenanted Scotland, 1637–1651* (Oxford, 2016); eadem, 'The "Rise" of the State?', in T.M. Devine and Jenny Wormald (eds), *The Oxford Handbook of Modern Scottish History* (Oxford, 2012), pp. 220–35. Chris R. Langley, *Worship, Civil War and Community, 1638–1660* (London, 2016); idem, *Cultures of Care: Domestic Welfare, Discipline and the Church of Scotland, c. 1600–1689* (Leiden, 2020).

focus on the efforts to create a unified curriculum, one of the few aspects of Covenanter university policy that scholars have previously examined. The way the Covenanting regime pursued university reforms was indicative not of the arbitrary policies of some uniquely zealous Calvinist regime, but rather illustrative of a wider process of early modern state formation that paralleled similar situations throughout the Reformed world.

Contested Universities and the Glasgow Assembly

The revolutionary impulse that gave rise to the formation of the Covenanted confessional state was centred on Scottish opposition to the Prayer Book and related crown policies, which mounted throughout the second half of 1637. In Edinburgh, supplicants inundated the Privy Council with petitions that called for the new liturgy's abrogation and the meeting of a 'free' General Assembly and Parliament. Against the better advice of his Privy Councillors, Charles I remained steadfast in his insistence on the Prayer Book's usage, and issued a proclamation, read in Edinburgh on 22 February 1638, in which he reiterated his intention that the new liturgy be used. A week later, the National Covenant, the work of Alexander Henderson, minister of Leuchars in Fife, and Archibald Johnston of Wariston, the firebrand Edinburgh advocate, was proclaimed at Greyfriars.[6] The Covenanters embarked on a widespread subscription campaign to stimulate backing for the movement, garnering widespread but by no means universal support.[7]

Scotland's universities were quickly incorporated into this campaign. Far from being educational institutions primed to build ideological conformity and a sufficient level of societal homogeneity to a Covenanted social order, leaders of the Covenanting movement confronted a heterogenous mix of political and religious opinions that ran counter to Covenanter views.[8] Jacobean and later Caroline religious policy measures were relatively well received in the

---

[6] John Leslie, *A Relation of Proceedings Concerning the Affairs of the Kirk of Scotland, from August 1637 to July 1638* (Edinburgh, 1830), pp. 87–8; David Stevenson, *The Scottish Revolution 1637–1644: The Triumph of the Covenanters* (Newton Abbot, 1973), pp. 56–87; Macinnes, *Covenanting Movement*, pp. 158–72.

[7] Stevenson, *Scottish Revolution*, pp. 86–7; Laura A.M. Stewart, 'Authority, Agency and the Reception of the Scottish National Covenant of 1638', in Robert Armstrong and Tadhg Ó hAnnracháin (eds), *Insular Christianity: Alternative Models of the Church in Britain and Ireland, c. 1570–c. 1700* (Manchester, 2012), pp. 88–106; Julian Goodare, 'The Rise of the Covenanters, 1637-1644', in Michael J. Braddick (ed.), *The Oxford Handbook of the English Revolution* (Oxford, 2015), pp. 43–59; Nathan C.J. Hood, 'Corporate Conversion Ceremonies: The Presentation and Reception of the National Covenant', in Chris R. Langley (ed.), *The National Covenant in Scotland, 1638–1689* (Woodbridge, 2020), pp. 21–38; Jamie McDougall, 'Allegiance, Confession and Covenanting Identities, 1638-51', *ibid.*, pp. 71–87.

[8] See Durkheim, *Education and Sociology*, pp. 62–3; Tilly, 'Reflections', pp. 28, 40.

universities. Writing in late 1637, the Fife minister George Gillespie lamented that 'the rotten dregs of Popery, which were never purged away from England and Ireland, and having been spued out with detestation, are lick up again in Scotland'. This impacted the universities directly: 'the seminaries of learning are so corrupted, that few or no good plants can come forth from thence'.[9] The Laudian liturgy would only corrupt the universities further. Thus, well before the Covenant was promulgated in February 1638, the Tables – the revolutionary provisional government established in Edinburgh – issued a declaration against the use of the Prayer Book in the universities, 'lest parents should be forced to remove their children'.[10] The Scottish revolution came to education, the bedrock of what would become the Covenanted confessional state, immediately.

A week after the Covenant's promulgation, the Tables sent commissioners to each university to collect subscriptions.[11] Between March and November, the Covenanters were reminded that, while the cause for the Covenant had generated substantial support across Scotland, members of the academic elite – those tasked with training the next generation of ministers – were not immediately persuaded. Only Edinburgh proved mostly receptive from the outset.[12] Two regents – Robert Ranken and John Broun – refused to subscribe, and the Edinburgh town council dealt with them swiftly, deposing the regents and installing replacements by October.[13] Edinburgh's case was exceptional for the speed by which authorities dealt with obstinate regents, and for the quickness with which academic staff supported the Covenant. Elsewhere, however, principals and professors came out against the Covenant.

Table 2.1. The Scottish Professoriate on the Eve of the Covenanting Revolution, c. 1638.

University of St Andrews		
St Salvator's College	St Leonard's College	St Mary's College
George Martine, Provost (1624)	Andrew Bruce, Principal (1630)	Robert Howie, Principal (1607)
John Baron, Dean (1628)	Alexander Scott, Humanity (1626)	Patrick Panter, Divinity (1627)
David Forret, Regent (1632)	George Wemyss, Regent (c. 1626)	

---

[9] W.M. Hetherington (ed.), *The Works of Mr. George Gillespie, Minister of Edinburgh* (2 vols, Edinburgh, 1846), I, p. viii.
[10] Baillie, *L&J*, I, pp. 26–7; Rothes, *Relation*, p. 43.
[11] Rothes, *Relation*, p. 82.
[12] Craufard, *History of the University of Edinburgh*, pp. 132–3.
[13] EUL, Dc.5.5, pp. 28–9; Marguerite Wood (ed.), *Extracts from the Records of the Burgh of Edinburgh, 1626 to 1641* (Edinburgh, 1936), pp. 207–10.

Table 2.1 (*continued*)

St Salvator's College	St Leonard's College
John Armour, Regent (1633)	James Mercer, Regent (1630)
James Wood, Regent (1633)	John MacKenzie, Regent (c. 1630/32)
James Wright (1634)	James Guthrie, Regent (1635)
George Martine Jr, Regent (1637)	

University of Glasgow	Marischal College, Aberdeen
John Strang, Principal (1626)	Patrick Dun, Principal (1621)
Robert Maine, Medicine (1637)	Robert Baron, Divinity (1625)
John Rae, Regent (1623)	William Johnston, Mathematics (1626)
William Wilkie, Regent (1628)	William Aidie, Regent (163?)
Patrick Maxwell, Regent (1635)	William Blackhall, Regent (163?)
David Munro, Regent (1637)	John Ray, Regent (163?)
William Hamilton, Regent (1638)	James Hay, Regent (163?)
	John Menzies, Regent (1638?)

King's College, Aberdeen	University of Edinburgh
William Leslie, Principal (1632)	John Adamson, Principal (1623)
Robert Ogilvie, Sub-Principal (1638)	John Sharp, Divinity (1630)
John Forbes of Corse, Divinity (1635)	John Broun, Regent (1626)
James Sandilands, Canonist (1633)	Andrew Hepburn, Regent (1632)
William Gordon, Medicine (1632)	Robert Ranken, Regent (1625)
John Lundie, Grammarian (1629)	Andrew Stevenson, Regent (1611)
Gilbert Ross, Cantor (1634)	
Patrick Innes, Sacrist (c. 1638)	
James Sibbald, Dean (c. 1639)	
Alexander Middleton, Regent (1634)	
William Strachan, Regent (1634)	
Alexander Gardyne, Regent (1635)	
Alexander Scroggie, Regent (1638)	

Sources: Scott, *Fasti*; Laing, *Catalogue*; MAUG, vol. 3; *Fasti Aberdonenses*; Anderson, *Officers and Graduates*; FAM, vol. 2; Smart, *Alphabetical Register*; StAUL, UYUY 412.

The universities' initial opposition to the Covenant was much more widespread than previously thought.[14] Scholarly focus on academic resistance to the Covenant has mostly focused on the famous opposition of the Aberdeen Doctors: John Forbes of Corse, son of Bishop Forbes, divinity professor at King's; Robert Baron, divinity professor at Marischal; Alexander Scroggie, minister at St Machar's in Old Aberdeen; Alexander Ross, minister of Aberdeen and rector of King's; James Sibbald; minister of St Nicholas' Kirk; William Leslie, principal of King's; and, briefly, William Guild, chaplain to Charles I.[15] The writings that underpinned their opposition to the Covenant are well known, beginning with Forbes' *Peaceable Warning to the Subjects in Scotland*, published in April, and the *Generall Demands Concerning the late Covenant*, published in July.[16] But St Andrews also joined the Doctors in opposing the Covenant, highlighted by the university's leadership: Robert Howie, principal of St Mary's; Andrew Bruce, principal of St Leonard's; George Martine, provost of St Salvator's; John Baron, dean of faculty; and Patrick Panter, divinity professor at St Mary's.[17] St Andrews' masters wrote the first response against the Covenant on 20 March, about a month before *Peaceable Warning* appeared.[18] Hostility to the Covenant was also rife among Glasgow University's staff, who, in the presence of the Tables' commission, celebrated Easter in Glasgow Cathedral by taking communion kneeling, a sign of their adherence to the Perth Articles.[19] Principal John Strang also

---

[14] Salvatore Cipriano, 'The Scottish Universities and Opposition to the National Covenant, 1638', *Scottish Historical Review*, 97:1 (2018), 12–37; Russell Newton, 'United Opposition? The Aberdeen Doctors and the National Covenant', *National Covenant in Scotland*, pp. 53–70.

[15] Scott, *Fasti*, VII, pp. 361–9; Anderson, *Officers and Graduates*, pp. 97–8; Newton, 'United Opposition', pp. 54–7; Stevenson, *King's College*, p. 110.

[16] On the Doctors and their anti-Covenanting writings, see Donald MacMillan, *The Aberdeen Doctors* (London, 1909); J.D. Ogilvie, 'The Aberdeen Doctors and the National Covenant', *Papers of the Edinburgh Bibliographical Society*, 11 (1912), 73–86; G.D. Henderson, 'The Aberdeen Doctors', in *The Burning Bush: Studies in Scottish Church History* (Edinburgh, 1957), pp. 5–93; David Stewart, 'The "Aberdeen Doctors" and the Covenanters', *Records of the Scottish Church History Society*, 22 (1986), 35–44; Gordon DesBrisay, '"The Civill Warrs Did Overrun All:" Aberdeen, 1630–1690', *Aberdeen Before 1800*, pp. 238–66, at 240–7; Robert H. Landrum, 'Convincing Aberdeen, 1638: The Nation's Reluctant Converts', *Aberdeen University Review*, 60:210 (2003), 80–95; Aaron Clay Denlinger, '"Men of Gallio's Naughty Faith?": The Aberdeen Doctors on Reformed and Lutheran Concord', *Church History and Religious Culture*, 92:1 (2012), 57–83; Steven J. Reid, 'Reformed Scholasticism'. On the idea of Scotland's conservative north, see Gordon Donaldson, *Scottish Church History* (Edinburgh, 1985), pp. 191–203. For a reassessment of this thesis, see Barry Robertson, 'The Covenanting North of Scotland, 1638–1647', *Innes Review*, 61:1 (2010), 24–51.

[17] Scott, *Fasti*, VII, pp. 411–13, 418, 428.

[18] NLS, Wod.Fol.XLIII, fols 273–4, reproduced in C.J. Lyon, *History of St Andrews, Episcopal, Monastic, Academic, and Civil* (2 vols, Edinburgh, 1843), II, pp. 372–6.

[19] Baillie, *L&J*, I, p. 63; Rothes, *Relation*, p. 82.

penned a treatise for the marquis of Hamilton outlining his misgivings about the National Covenant and his support for the King's Covenant, a rival bond introduced in September.[20] Strang's tract, which garnered the praise of the king and Walter Balcanquhall, the dean of Rochester, remained unknown until 1646.[21] While there is no evidence of coordination between the universities, the correspondence of Glasgow regent William Wilkie reveals that Glasgow's staff read the Doctors' writings.[22] Overall, the universities' opposition illustrates the professoriate's disagreement with a number of Covenanting ideas. The Covenant was widely contested in Scotland's universities.

Aberdeen, Glasgow, and St Andrews' opposition underlined how competing conceptions of royal authority, church government, and true religion – vital elements that underscored the wider early modern social order – clashed in the universities. The universities' arguments against the Covenant highlighted three main grievances: the Covenant was illegal, and made loyalty to the king conditional; the Covenanters' actions, including the formation of a provisional governing body, had seriously injured royal authority; and 'true religion' included episcopal government and other Stuart-backed practices, including kneeling at communion, and not the 'innovations' found within the National Covenant.[23] The Covenant did, of course, precisely what its detractors claimed: it made loyalty to the king conditional by articulating a contractual form of kingship, and its conception of true religion did not include episcopacy, the Perth Articles, or the Laudian reforms.[24] Alexander Henderson spearheaded the response to both St Andrews, his *alma mater*, and to Aberdeen, arguing that the Covenant was lawful because it was a 'public' band that bound all subscribers to uphold the king and Kirk.[25] The polemicist David Calderwood also argued that the Covenant was legal because it was partly a verbatim reproduction of the Negative Confession, which the king had approved in 1581.[26] Henderson, the Irvine minister David Dickson, and the Aberdeen minister Andrew Cant made this point in their *Answeres* to

---

[20] NLS, Wod.Fol.XXXI, fols 7–24, reproduced in Salvatore Cipriano (ed.), 'The Principal of Glasgow Against the Covenant (1638)', in *Miscellany of the Scottish History Society, Volume XVI*, 6th series (Woodbridge, 2020), pp. 95–142.

[21] Baillie, *L&J*, I, pp. 479–91; Cipriano, 'Principal of Glasgow', pp. 102–3.

[22] See especially Paul Goatman and Andrew Lind, 'Glasgow and the National Covenant in 1638: Revolution, Royalism and Civic Reform', *National Covenant in Scotland*, pp. 39–52, at 39–40.

[23] Cipriano, 'Scottish Universities', pp. 17–35.

[24] Macinnes, *Covenanting Movement*, pp. 173–5; idem, 'The Scottish Constitution, 1638–51: The Rise and Fall of Oligarchic Centralism', in John Morrill (ed.), *The Scottish National Covenant in Its British Context* (Edinburgh, 1990), pp. 106–33, at 107–8.

[25] NLS, Wod.Qu.XXVI, fol. 129v; John Aiton, *The Life and Times of Alexander Henderson* (Edinburgh, 1836), p. 216; Stevenson, *Scottish Revolution*, p. 86.

[26] NLS, Wod.Qu.LXXVI, fol. 56r. It is likely that these responses formed the basis of another manuscript included in Baillie's letters and journals. See Baillie, *L&J*, I, 407. For the answers, see NCL, Baill 4/1, fols 67–70; NLS, Wod.Qu.CVI, pp. 155–61.

the Aberdeen Doctors.[27] Henderson argued that obedience to the church was paramount: the Scots were obliged to defend 'true religion' with or without the king.[28] As the Covenant rehashed the Negative Confession, subscribers were obliged to maintain this lawful mandate and oppose innovation, taken to mean any post-1581 changes imposed on the Kirk.[29] Removing these unlawful innovations would be a 'benefite to this Kirke and Kingdome'.[30]

Covenanting leadership took its campaign to the universities. Henderson and his allies had the most luck in convincing the staff at St Andrews, for following Henderson's visit there in March, Robert Baillie wrote to his cousin William Spang that, save for divinity professor Patrick Panter, 'the rest of St Andrewes Doctors, Howie, Bruce, Martine, Baron, hes all subscryved'.[31] Glasgow's masters also subscribed by year's end, but their subscriptions were likely of a conditional nature. Principal Strang signed only after protracted overtures.[32] Strang required a separate declaration that the Covenant did not diminish royal authority, that episcopacy would be maintained, and that religious innovation would be resisted. Wariston was incensed, while Baillie and Edinburgh principal John Adamson reasoned that the Covenant already expressed these conditions.[33] In Aberdeen, beyond William Guild's subscription, the Covenanters were unsuccessful.

Henderson was dismayed that the professors tasked with educating the next generation of ministers would be susceptible to such errors.[34] He assigned a significant role to the divinity professor based on his Reformed understanding of the 'doctor' of divinity, defined in the *Second Book of Discipline*.[35] If the minister was the messenger of God's word, the doctor had the vital task of interpreting it, so that 'sound doctrine be teachit and the puritie of the Gospell not corruptid throw ignorance of evill opinionis'.[36] The chief authors of opposition to the Covenant had failed in this role, and beyond their corrupted views, they also bore the marks of earlier infringements upon the Kirk's autonomy. They were all doctors of divinity in the episcopal sense. James VI/I reintroduced the doctorate in 1616 as part of his campaign to remake the Scottish universities in the image of Oxford and Cambridge.

---

[27] *General Demands, Answers, and Replies*, pp. 4–5, 10, 28. NCL, Baill 4/1, fol. 70r.
[28] NLS, Wod.Qu.XXVI, fol. 129r; Cipriano, 'Scottish Universities', p. 22.
[29] NLS, Wod.Qu.XXVI, fols 129r, 130r.
[30] NLS, Wod.Qu.LXXVI, fol. 56r; *General Demands, Answers, and Replies*, pp. 13, 15.
[31] Baillie, *L&J*, I, pp. 64, 98; R. Thomson Martin (ed.), *Sermons, Prayers, and Pulpit Addresses by Alexander Henderson, 1638* (Edinburgh, 1867), pp. 2, 21–30.
[32] Baillie, *L&J*, I, pp. 66–9; Archibald Johnston of Wariston, *Diary of Sir Archibald Johnston of Wariston, Volume I 1632–1639*, ed. George Morison Paul (Edinburgh, 1911), pp. 367–8; Goatman and Lind, 'Glasgow and the National Covenant', pp. 45–51.
[33] Baillie, *L&J*, I, p. 67; Johnston, *Diary, 1632–1639*, pp. 368–9.
[34] NLS, Wod.Qu.XXVI, fol. 129r.
[35] James Kirk (ed.), *The Second Book of Discipline: With Introduction and Commentary* (Edinburgh, 1980), pp. 176–7.
[36] NLS, Wod.Qu.XXVI, fols 129r, 131r.

Crucially, the degree was a necessary credential to ascend the episcopal hierarchy.[37] The doctoral degree was a key projection of royal power in the Scottish universities and symbolised the monarchy's vision of the universities as tools to construct and legitimise a social order rooted in a hierarchical and sacramental church.[38]

Through their campaigns against the universities throughout 1638 and with the opening of the Glasgow Assembly in November, the Covenanters aimed to root out these symbolic and ideological vestiges of Stuart power and assert their dominance.[39] The Aberdeen Doctors recognised the Covenanters' intentions. Despite the favour they enjoyed from the king, who commended their written polemics, and from the marquis of Hamilton, the king's commissioner in Scotland, the Doctors pled to be exempted from the Assembly, fearing they would experience 'much evill' if they travelled to Glasgow.[40] These misgivings were confirmed when Robert Baron and James Sibbald's commission to attend was rejected in favour of a rival Aberdonian commission of William Guild and David Lindsay.[41] Moreover, King's College's representative was not Principal Leslie, but instead the grammarian John Lundie, who together with the King's sacrist Patrick Innes had subscribed to the Covenant, unlike the majority of their colleagues.[42]

Hamilton's efforts to curtail the Covenanters' domination of the Assembly failed, and he ultimately departed in protest.[43] The Assembly thereafter repudiated the High Commission, Canons, and Prayer Book, and abjured the Perth Articles. The Covenanters abolished episcopacy and condemned and deposed bishops – all actions that had been foreshadowed in the universities' protests. They also revived legislation for the regular visitation of parishes, schools, and universities.[44] The Glasgow Assembly extirpated the 'innovations' of the previous forty years to draw direct continuity with, and restore the imagined purity of, the Reformation-era Kirk.[45] Furthermore, on the Assembly's

---

[37] Row, *History*, pp. 260–1; Calderwood, *History*, VII, p. 222.
[38] On real and symbolic power, see Jones, *Introduction to Political Geography*, pp. 107–8.
[39] NCL, Baill 4/1, fol. 70r.
[40] NRS, GD 406/1/446, 665, 666; AUL, MS 635, pp. 141, 152. On Charles' support for the Doctors' writings, see NRS, GD 406/1/664, 667, 697, 724; Spalding, *Memorialls*, I, pp. 98–9.
[41] Baillie, *L&J*, I, p. 97; *Records of the Kirk*, p. 110; James Gordon, *History of Scots Affairs, from 1637 to 1641*, ed. Joseph Robertson and George Grub (3 vols, Aberdeen, 1841), I, pp. 154–5.
[42] Baillie, *L&J*, I, p. 97; Gordon, *Scots Affairs*, I, pp. 84–6; Spalding, *Memorialls*, I, pp. 68–70; Anderson, *Officers and Graduates*, pp. 26, 47; Stevenson, *King's College*, pp. 110, 117.
[43] On Hamilton's attempt to disband the Assembly and his ultimate departure in protest, see Andrew Lind, 'Battle in the Burgh: Glasgow during the British Civil Wars, c. 1638–1651', *Journal of the Northern Renaissance*, 12 (2021).
[44] *Records of the Kirk*, pp. 21–48.
[45] See e.g., Chris R. Langley, 'Reading John Knox in the Scottish Revolution, 1638–50',

final day, commissioners sanctioned two interrelated acts with important implications for the universities. The first act declared that 'all Ministers, Masters of Universities, Colledges, and Schooles and all others who have not already subscribed the said Confession, shall subscribe the same', with a new oath, the Glasgow Declaration, attached.[46] Anti-episcopal in tenor, the declaration made both episcopacy and the Perth Articles antithetical to the Negative Confession.[47] Accordingly, the second act asserted the General Assembly's authority to censure any 'member of this Kirk' who refused to 'subscribe the confession of Faith, renewed in Februar, with the Declaration of the Assembly set down in the former Act'.[48]

This was a comprehensive reworking of the Scottish church and state that required the concurrent reform of the universities in order to perpetuate this Covenanted social order for future generations. To enforce these strictures, the Assembly revived three acts for the visitation of universities. Two acts, from 1565 and 1567, outlined the particulars for examining principals, professors, and regents to evaluate 'the soundnesse of their judgment in matters of Religion, their abilitie for discharge of their calling, and the honesty of their conversation'. A third, from 1595, granted the General Assembly authority to order visitations, thereby giving the Covenanters real power to control the instruction and socialisation of university students.[49] To further realise this, the universities' ideological diversity, which had been on full display throughout 1638, as well as their relative autonomy, had to be addressed. Among the series of complaints that different presbyteries brought against ministers for various misdeeds were those targeting professors. The Glasgow Assembly seized upon these to enact policies to control the professoriate. Most notably, St Andrews brought a complaint against Patrick Panter, the St Mary's professor of divinity who had refused to sign the Covenant, who was also accused of Arminianism and 'many erroneous Papisticall poynts of doctrine'.[50] One commentator remarked that Panter 'did mantaine justificatioune by works and sundrie other grosse papisticall errours which he publictlie taught in this theological annotations'.[51]

Panter's case was emblematic of the wider existential threat that the Covenanters assigned to the Scottish universities' failure to support the Covenanting movement from the outset. Henderson lamented the 'schism'

National Covenant in Scotland, pp. 89–104, at 91–6.
[46] *Records of the Kirk*, 40. On the Glasgow Declaration, see also Jamie McDougall, 'Covenants and Covenanters in Scotland 1638–1679' (unpublished PhD thesis, University of Glasgow, 2018), pp. 48–52.
[47] *Records of the Kirk*, p. 208; Stewart, *Rethinking the Scottish Revolution*, p. 145.
[48] *Records of the Kirk*, p. 40.
[49] Ibid., p. 34; StAUL, UYSL 156, p. 228.
[50] *Records of the Kirk*, p. 155; Gordon, *Scots Affairs*, II, pp. 45.
[51] EUL, La.III.207, p. 91.

between truth and error within the 'Schooles of Divinitie'.[52] Baillie was similarly disheartened: '[Panter] was never diligent', he wrote, 'but he had not sooner settled himself in his chair while he began to recommend the Englishe method of studie to our youth, to begin with the Popish schoolmen and Fathers, and to close with Protestant neotericks; a most unhappie and dangerous order.'[53] Baillie faulted Panter's teaching of the Church Fathers and Scholastics, subjects that had experienced a resurgence at Oxford through the intervention of Archbishop Laud and his allies.[54] This brand of divinity, taught to impressionable students in the universities, was dangerous and ran counter to the Reformed theology at the heart of the Covenanted social order. Yet though it was in the Assembly's opinion that although Panter's transgressions merited removal, the matter was deferred to the presbytery of St Andrews to 'restore the presbitries to their ancient liberties'.[55] Panter's case came up again at the 1639 General Assembly, where Henderson delivered a scathing sermon on the importance of rooting out ignorance through proper teaching. Henderson emphasised to his fellow Covenanters the importance of a 'wise, peaceablie disposed, and learned' ministry. He connected the ministry's defects to schooling under 'ignorant' masters and emphasised the role of the divinity professor in training a godly ministry: 'as was the schollar, so was his master'.[56] It was thus during this meeting the Assembly deposed Panter and replaced him with Samuel Rutherford.[57]

Panter's case also evinced the Covenanters' readiness to circumvent university privileges, an issue that lay at the heart of Glasgow's contested commission to the Glasgow Assembly.[58] Universities were typically afforded one commissioner at General Assemblies and were included in the rolls with their corresponding presbytery. At the Glasgow Assembly, Principal John Adamson represented Edinburgh, John Lundie, the King's College grammarian, represented Aberdeen, and John Baron, dean of faculty, represented St

---

[52] *Records of the Kirk*, p. 155.
[53] Baillie, *L&J*, I, p. 149.
[54] Nicholas Tyacke, 'Religious Controversy', *History of the University of Oxford*, pp. 569–619, at 581–2.
[55] EUL, La.III.207, p. 279; *Records of the Kirk*, p. 183.
[56] *Records of the Kirk*, pp. 238–9; NRS, GD112/39/73/19. On clerical sufficiency in Scotland, see Chris R. Langley, '"Diligence in His Ministrie": Languages of Clerical Sufficiency in Mid-Seventeenth-Century Scotland', *Archiv Für Reformationsgeschichte*, 104:1 (2013), 272–96.
[57] *Records of the Kirk*, pp. 254, 260.
[58] NLS, MS 3430, fol. 63.

Andrews.[59] Glasgow, however, arrived with four commissioners.[60] Strang had already caused controversy by voicing his opposition to the attendance of lay elders at the General Assembly.[61] Glasgow's commission further compounded Strang's fortunes, and it was during the fifth session that a 'long disputation' unfolded over the issue.[62] Strang was the target of rebukes, including those from Adamson, 'who did somewhat petulantlie reproach him'.[63] But Strang argued that unless any law could be produced that explicitly restricted a university's representation to one, the Glasgow commission should maintain its representation of four. An act was introduced quickly. There 'wes found extract to the act of ane assemblie giving answer for one onlie commissioner from each universities, & so thre wer rejected & one onlie retained according to the use of the rest of the universities ther present'.[64] While rejected initially, Glasgow was encouraged to renew its commission. Baillie noted, however, that Strang refused, and 'resolved to be absent'.[65] Strang and his Glasgow colleagues chose to depart the Glasgow Assembly alongside Hamilton, raising further suspicions about Strang's allegiances.[66]

The dispute over the commissions had important implications. In rejecting Glasgow's commission, the Assembly found 'that Colledges have no privileges above a Kirk'.[67] The invalidation of Glasgow's commission signified a key alteration in university–Kirk relations. The General Assembly gave the Covenanters legal backing to embark on an unprecedented regulation of university affairs. It was unprecedented because although these acts had first been passed in the years after 1560, the General Assembly had rarely intervened in university affairs.[68] The actions of the Glasgow Assembly marked a transition in the nature of intervention into the Scottish universities, reflecting more broadly the move towards external supervision by ministers

---

[59] *Records of the Kirk*, pp. 110–11, 135–7; Andrew Stevenson, *The History of the Church and State of Scotland, from the Accession of King Charles I to the Year 1649* (3 vols, Edinburgh, 1840), I, pp. 275n–7n. John Baron does not appear in the rolls reproduced in Peterkin and Stevenson's histories, but Robert Baillie does mention him as being the 'commissioner for St. Andrewes'. Baillie, *L&J*, I, p. 145.

[60] *Records of the Kirk*, pp. 135, 138; Baillie, *L&J*, I, pp. 133–4. See also Florence N. McCoy, *Robert Baillie and the Second Scots Reformation* (Berkeley, CA, 1974), p. 53.

[61] Baillie, *L&J*, I, p. 135.

[62] MAUG, III, pp. 378–81; *Records of the Kirk*, p. 110.

[63] EUL, La.III.207, p. 34; Baillie, *L&J*, I, p. 134.

[64] EUL, La.III.207, p. 35.

[65] Baillie, *L&J*, I, p 135.

[66] Lind, 'Battle in the Burgh'; *idem*, '"Bad and Evill Patriotts?" Royalism in Scotland during the British Civil Wars, c. 1638–1651' (unpublished PhD thesis, University of Glasgow, 2020), pp. 208–10.

[67] *Records of the Kirk*, pp. 137–8.

[68] Reid, *Humanism and Calvinism*, pp. 11, 27; Duncan Shaw, *The General Assemblies of the Church of Scotland, 1560–1600: Their Origins and Development* (Edinburgh, 1964), pp. 184–91.

and elders that was emblematic of Reformed institutions of higher learning in the early modern period. It also marked a key step in Scottish state formation and the manifestation of the Covenanters' wider system of confessionalised governance, as the power of the General Assembly was extended over the universities to build political and religious conformity that would prove crucial to the survival of the Covenanted project.

Before the Glasgow Assembly closed, it issued visitation commissions for Glasgow and Aberdeen to begin the work of reshaping the universities.[69] Interestingly, Aberdeen and its Doctors had opposed the Covenant, though it was through John Lundie's urging that a visitation was called to rectify the King's College constitutional dispute in favour of the New Foundation.[70] Glasgow had proven to be stubborn and uncooperative, with its principal under suspicion. Panter's case aside, St Andrews appeared for the time amenable to the Covenanting cause, while Edinburgh's only two detractors, regents Robert Ranken and John Broun, were deposed and replaced with James Wiseman and James Wright after a trial overseen by Principal Adamson and Edinburgh town council.[71] The text of the commissions outlined the authority vested to the visitors, and would appear more or less unchanged in commissions issued throughout the 1640s. It stated that the General Assembly,

> Give & grantand unto thame [the commissioners] the full power & commissioun of the Assemblie... To summond & conveine befoir thame all the members thereof, To try & examine the qualities of the members thereof iff they be correspondant to the other of their errectionis, To consider how the doctrine is usit be their Masters & Regents, & if the same be correspondant to the Confession of Faith, & Acts of this Kirk, & how the order is keiped amongst students, how their rents and liveings are bestowit, and all other things, to try & examine whilk anie Commissioners from the Assembly had power to try, or whilk the Generall Assemblie itselff might have tried in her Visitatioun, an efter due tryell of the members and orders theirin, if they be agriable to their Errectioun, and the Acts of this Church; To remove all members superflouous, unqualifiet, or corrupt, & to plant their roumes with moir sufficient & sound masters; To remeid all disorders, rectifie all abuses, and to doe all other things necessarie for the preservatioun of Religion & learning, whilk the Generall Assemblie themselffes might have done, or anie Commissioners from thame in their Visitatiounes haiff done.[72]

---

[69] *Records of the Kirk*, p. 184; EUL, La.III.207, pp. 367–8.
[70] Stevenson, *King's College*, pp. 114–15.
[71] Cant claims that St Andrews avoided a visitation because of Henderson's intervention. Cant, *St Andrews*, p. 67. On Edinburgh's regents, see EUL, Dc.5.5, p. 29; Craufurd, *History of the University of Edinburgh*, pp. 133–5; Wood, *Edinburgh Burgh Records 1626–1641*, pp. 209–10.
[72] Baillie, *L&J*, I, pp. 491–2.

Visitors were endowed with the power to evaluate all staff in accordance with the university's established laws. They were tasked with evaluating professors' orthodoxy and their adherence to the Covenanted Kirk's strictures. The Glasgow Assembly had already passed an act mandating the Covenant's subscription by all university staff and students. But the most decisive power was the ability to eject and replace professors, a power traditionally vested in chancellors and rectors.[73] In employing the power of translation, the General Assembly would manage the universities as it saw fit.

Little time was wasted. The ill will generated by Glasgow's contested commission led to calls to add David Dickson as a 'conjunct' professor of divinity.[74] That scheme was put on hold until the following year, and both Dickson and Baillie instead served on the commission to visit Glasgow. Baillie noted that the visitation was entrusted with the power to establish an additional divinity professorship if the university consented, a post for which both Dickson and Rutherford were recommended.[75] Clearly, planting leading Covenanters at universities was a key way to rectify doctrinal error. Elsewhere, the presbytery of St Andrews called Robert Blair from his parish in Ayr to St Andrews, 'for the good of the Universitie'.[76] By his presence in the 'seminarie toun', the university would benefit. Henderson subsequently recommended his translation.[77] Finally, Aberdeen's commissioners requested that Samuel Rutherford take a divinity post at Marischal. Rutherford also refused: he did not wish to be removed to Aberdeen, where the High Commission had exiled him in 1636.[78] Ministers, so attentive to the needs of the Kirk, viewed translation as aiding the common good so long as their names were not called.

The Glasgow Assembly, which closed on 20 December, reduced the authority of the monarch drastically and restructured the Kirk, which 'returned' to a Presbyterian system.[79] It also redefined the Kirk's relationship with the universities and set the tone, and agenda, for the Covenanters' subsequent supervision of university affairs throughout the 1640s, which sought to remake the universities into both the models and machinery of the nascent Covenanted state.

---

[73] Coutts, *Glasgow*, pp. 12–14; Cant, *St Andrews*, pp. 8–9; Reid, *Humanism and Calvinism*, pp. 103–5, 117–20, 164–78.
[74] EUL, La.III.207, p. 360.
[75] Baillie, *L&J*, I, pp. 135, 171–2.
[76] *Records of the Kirk*, p. 187; Baillie, *L&J*, I, p. 174; Thomas McCrie, *The Life of Mr Robert Blair, Minister of St Andrews* (Edinburgh, 1848), p. 156.
[77] *Records of the Kirk*, pp. 187, 189; McCrie, *Robert Blair*, pp. viii–ix, 156–7; David Stevenson, 'Blair, Robert (1593–1666)', ODNB.
[78] *Records of the Kirk*, p. 189; Andrew A. Bonar (ed.), *Letters of Samuel Rutherford* (Edinburgh, 1891), pp. 163–4, 189, 268, 271, 273–5, 300; John Coffey, *Politics, Religion and the British Revolutions: The Mind of Samuel Rutherford* (Cambridge, 1997), pp. 45–9.
[79] Stevenson, *Scottish Revolution*, p. 125; Stewart, *Rethinking the Scottish Revolution*, p. 145; Trevor-Roper, *Archbishop Laud*, p. 368.

Charles I, Scottish Parliament, and the Universities

For Charles I, the universities' resistance to the Covenant was further evidence of the Covenant's illegality. The king made this clear in the *Large Declaration*, an account of the Scottish troubles composed largely by Walter Balcanquhall and published in England in 1639.[80] Charles extolled Aberdeen and St Andrews' opposition and decried the Covenanters' replies as 'poorely and pitifully... answered'. Likewise, Glasgow's coerced subscription and the expulsion of Edinburgh's regents were evidence of the Covenanters' sedition. 'Now one would thinke', Charles concluded, 'that in any Kingdome the judgement of the learned Professors in Universities and Colledges, in a point of conscience, should weigh downe the groundlesse opinions of their Tables, consisting of Noblemen, Gentlemen, Ministers and Tradesmen.'[81] For the king, adherence to the universities' message would have prevented calamity. The resistance also underscored the ways in which the monarchy had successfully projected its power in the universities and the ways in which university academics legitimised the Stuart conception of the wider social order.

Two years later, Charles was forced to acknowledge the reality of the Covenanters' control of the universities – and the kingdom at large. The Bishops' Wars (1639–40) delayed the opening of Parliament, originally scheduled for May 1639.[82] In the interim, the General Assembly reaffirmed the Glasgow Assembly's acts and prepared overtures for Parliament.[83] In addition to increasing stipends and suppressing heterodoxy, the General Assembly proposed using the rents of vacated bishoprics to support churches, universities, and schools, a measure first recommended in the *First Book of Discipline*.[84] In June 1640 Parliament reconvened and sanctioned these acts.[85] Facing severe pressures in two kingdoms, Charles recalled Parliament in England and assented to many Covenanter demands in the Treaty of London of June 1641.[86]

Charles arrived in Scotland in August 1641 defeated. In Parliament, he would be party to the Covenanting settlement. The 1641 General

---

[80] Peter Donald, *An Uncounselled King: Charles I and the Scottish Troubles, 1637–1644* (Cambridge, 1990), pp. 132–3. On Covenanting responses to the *Large Declaration*, see EUL, La.I.306; *Records of the Kirk*, pp. 265–70.

[81] [Charles I], *A Large Declaration Concerning the Late Tumults in Scotland* (London, 1639), pp. 72–3.

[82] David Stevenson (ed.), *The Government of Scotland under the Covenanters, 1637–1651* (Edinburgh, 1982), pp. xi–xxv; Kirsty F. McAlister and Roland J. Tanner, 'The First Estate: Parliament and the Church', in Keith M. Brown and Alan R. MacDonald (eds), *Parliament in Context, 1235–1707* (Edinburgh, 2010), pp. 31–66.

[83] *Records of the Kirk*, pp. 204–8; Stevenson, *Scottish Revolution*, p. 163.

[84] NLS, Wod.Fol.LXIV, fols 71–2; *Records of the Kirk*, pp. 208–9; Cameron, *First Book of Discipline*, pp. 60, 161–2.

[85] RPS, 1640/6/5, 1640/6/27, 1640/6/33, 1640/6/36, 1640/6/37, 1640/6/38, 1640/6/42.

[86] Harris, *Rebellion*, pp. 374–7.

Assembly produced three key overtures for the universities, which impacted Parliament's subsequent legislation. One called for professorships to be filled with the 'ablest' and 'best affected' divines. Another proposed that there be annual meetings of commissioners from each university to maintain good order. Regarding vacant rents, a third recommended that,

> Because the good estate both of the Kirk and Commonwealth, dependeth mainly upon the flourishing of Universities and Colledges, as the Seminaries of both, which cannot be expected, unlesse the poore meanes which they have, be helped, and sufficient revenues be provided for them and the same well imployed: Therefore that out of the rents of Prelacies… or such like, a sufficient maintenance be provided for a competent number of Professors, Teachers, and Bursars in all faculties, and especially in Divinitie, and upholding, repairing, and enlarging the Fabrick of the Colledges, furnishing Libraries, and suchlike good uses in every Universitie and Colledge.[87]

These proposals, together with the 1639 overtures, were presented to Parliament on 20 August.[88] Charles granted the universities the rents of the 'late bishops', so that the universities 'may be the more able to breed men in the way of knowledge and virtue, fit for the service of church and state'.[89] Inquiries into St Andrews and Glasgow's finances also recommended increasing university resources: St Andrews fell over £800 short of its expenses, while Glasgow was deficient by nearly £500.[90] Parliament agreed to transfer the rents of bishoprics – as well as the house of the bishop of Aberdeen to the principal of King's[91] – to the universities. On 3 November, the archbishopric and priory rents of St Andrews were granted to the university.[92] Two weeks later, the rents of the bishopric of Aberdeen were conveyed to King's and Marischal, which were nominally joined into 'King Charles University'.[93] Glasgow received the rents of the bishopric of Galloway, while the rents of the bishoprics of Orkney and Edinburgh were granted to Edinburgh.[94] The universities' increased finances were born out of the vestiges of the episcopal sees that Charles had leaned on to pursue religious reform in Scotland.

---

[87] EUL, La.I.305/2, fols Av–Br; StAUL, UYSL 156, pp. 228–9; *Records of the Kirk*, pp. 293–4.
[88] RPS, M1641/8/4, A1641/8/7, A1641/8/6; Baillie, *L&J*, I, p. 387.
[89] RPS, 1641/7/5.
[90] Baillie supplicated on Glasgow's behalf. See Baillie, *L&J*, I, pp. 399–400; MAUG, II, pp. 457–62. GUA, 26754, fols 3–6.
[91] *Evidence*, IV, p. 157; *Fasti Aberdonenses*, pp. 149–50.
[92] RPS, 1641/8/137, 1641/8/525; StAUL, UYUY 152/3, fol. 141; StAUL, UYSM 110/B18/P2/5, 61–3. For St Andrews' letter of thanks to Charles, see NRS, GD45/1/65.
[93] RPS, 1641/8/327; *Fasti Aberdonenses*, 150–7. The rents were divided unevenly: two-thirds went to King's and a third to Marischal. See *A Collection of all the Papers Relating to the Proposal for Uniting the King's and Marischal Colleges of Aberdeen* (London, 1787), pp. 68–9.
[94] RPS, 1641/8/329, 1641/8/502; MAUG, I, 285–6. For Edinburgh's grants, see RPS, 1641/8/383; Wood, *Edinburgh Burgh Records 1626–1641*, pp. xxiv, xl, 335–41.

Charles' concessions were partly expedient, for afterward he would direct his attention to the conflict in England.[95] Historians contend that the Covenanters' achievements saw Scotland occupy a unique position to 'set the political agenda' in Britain and Ireland. This 'Scottish moment' was 'consummated' by the Solemn League and Covenant of 1643, the pact between the Covenanters and English Parliament that would establish Presbyterianism in all three kingdoms through a confederation rooted in the Covenant.[96] Exporting the revolution was a security measure, a way to guard Covenanting gains against threats beyond Scotland.[97] Within Scotland, the Covenanted state was taking form, and Parliament, the Committee of Estates, and the General Assembly were the machinery by which Covenanted Scotland would be governed. This left the universities as the institutions to provide the men to operate this machinery. Transforming the universities into the seminaries of the Covenanted state was meant to secure the long-term viability of the Covenanting movement.

The General Assembly and the Universities

General Assembly governance of the universities in the 1640s underlined their key place as a vital infrastructure of power in the emergent Covenanted state. The Covenanters' comprehensive reform program focussed on fashioning the universities into microcosms of the Covenanted state and the machinery that churned out churchmen and statesmen who would go on to govern Scotland and maintain the Covenanted social order in perpetuity. Much of this project was initiated and completed via visitations, and the General Assembly issued dozens of visitation commissions throughout the 1640s.[98] Visitors assessed instruction, reviewed finances, and measured conformity. In doing so, the Covenanters sought to remould the universities to fit Scotland's new confessional paradigm. The Covenanters drew their authority to visit the universities from General Assembly acts passed in 1565, 1567, and 1595, all renewed at the Glasgow Assembly. Commissions included around ten elders and ten ministers, from which a 'quorum' of about half was deemed sufficient

---

[95] Stevenson, *Scottish Revolution*, p. 241.
[96] Allan I. Macinnes, *The British Revolution, 1629–1660* (Basingstoke, 2005), pp. 148–58; idem, 'The "Scottish Moment", 1638–45', in John Adamson (ed.), *The English Civil War: Conflict and Contexts, 1640–49* (Basingstoke, 2009), pp. 125–52. See also Kirsteen M. MacKenzie, *The Solemn League and Covenant of the Three Kingdoms and the Cromwellian Union, 1643–1663* (London, 2017).
[97] Stevenson, *Scottish Revolution*, pp. 283–93, 310–15; idem, 'The Early Covenanters and the Federal Union of Britain', in Roger A. Mason (ed.), *Scotland and England, 1286–1815* (Edinburgh, 1987), pp. 163–81.
[98] See the General Assembly's lists of unprinted acts in *Records of the Kirk*, pp. 46–7, 187, 208, 262–3, 279, 297, 327, 345, 360–1, 407, 432–3, 453, 482, 519, 555–7. See also StAUL, UYSL 156, p. 231.

to carry out the visitation. Commissioners, normally drawn from nearby presbyteries, were empowered to examine 'how the doctrine is used be their Masters and Regents, and if the same be correspondent to the Confession of Faith and Acts of this Kirk'.[99] This order was strengthened by an act of 1639, which ordered all students 'at the passing of their degrees' to subscribe to the Covenant with the Glasgow Declaration attached; of 1640, which prohibited divinity students from teaching or preaching if they refused the Covenant; and of 1641, which barred expectants who were educated in a 'Colledge that was corrupt'.[100] To ensure conformity, visitors were authorised to 'remove all members superfluous, unqualified or corrupt, and to plant their roumes with more sufficient and sound masters'.[101]

The underpinnings of the General Assembly's approach to university reform can be attributed to Robert Baillie's proposals for the reform of Glasgow, submitted in advance of the visitation of January 1640.[102] Separated into three main sections, Baillie's text proposed a comprehensive university reform project that addressed four main areas. The first, 'For Piety', proposed that days begin and end with prayer and the reading of Scripture, that students should listen to and discuss sermons with their masters, and that they defend 'theologick theses' at graduation. The works of the Reformed theologian and Heidelberg divinity professor David Pareus loomed large in these proposals. Students were to read Pareus' commentary on the Heidelberg Catechism and study sections on 'Poperie, Arminianism, and Lutheranism' in Pareus' *Miscellanea*.[103] The Dort-endorsed Heidelberg Catechism and Pareus' commentary were key didactic texts within the Reformed international and, as historians have already identified, found use in the Scottish universities.[104] But recommending the use of Pareus' work also had clear political overtones. Pareus advocated resistance to overmighty monarchs, and eighteen years earlier, James VI/I ordered all of Pareus' works at Oxford burned.[105] Baillie,

---

[99] For extant commissions of visitation for Aberdeen, see Baillie, *L&J*, I, pp. 491–2. For extant commissions for Glasgow visitations from 1639, 1640 and 1643 see MAUG, II, pp. 451, 457, 462–3, 470–2; *Evidence*, II, pp. 256, 258–9, 261; GUA, 26621, 331–2, 336, 342. For extant commissions for St Andrews' visitations from 1642, 1648 and 1649, see *Evidence*, III, pp. 203–4; StAUL, UYUY 812, pp. 79–80, 142–5.
[100] *Records of the Kirk*, pp. 208, 279, 294–5.
[101] Baillie, *L&J*, I, p. 492; MAUG, II, pp. 450–2, 456–7, 460–2; *Evidence*, III, pp. 203–4.
[102] Baillie, *L&J*, II, pp. 463–7; NCL, Baill 4/1, fols 243v–245r, Baill 2/2, pp. 1008–14. See especially Reid, 'Ane Uniformitie', pp. 23–7. See also Kearney, *Scholars and Gentlemen*, pp. 129–33.
[103] Baillie, *L&J*, II, 464.
[104] Reid, 'Reformed Scholasticism'; Hotson, 'A Generall Reformation', pp. 197–8; Daniel Tröhler, 'The Knowledge of Science and the Knowledge of the Classroom: Using the Heidelberg Catechism (1563) to Examine Overlooked Connections', in Emidio Campi *et al.* (eds), *Scholarly Knowledge: Textbooks in Early Modern Europe* (Geneva, 2008), pp. 75–85.
[105] See Richard Serjeantson, 'Preaching Regicide in Jacobean England: John Knight and David Pareus', *English Historical Review*, 134:568 (2019), 553–88.

witness to the controversy that saw Patrick Panter deposed for supporting Arminianism and teaching a highly Scholastic course, proposed ensconcing a decidedly Reformed theological curriculum through polarising texts steeped in Calvinist resistance theory.

Still, the proposed philosophy course was conventional. Scottish pedagogy and philosophy had admirers among Huguenot and Dutch intellectuals, many with whom Baillie was conversant, and thus it is likely that his proposals were influenced by their correspondence.[106] In the second section, 'For Learning', Baillie mapped out a four-year arts course.[107] To this Baillie added the study of Greek and history in the first year; Hebrew, mathematics, and geometry in the third; and astronomy, geography, and anatomy in the fourth.[108] In the third section, 'For Discipline and Manners', he proposed that students remain within the university's bounds to guard against 'debauchery'.[109] For teachers, Baillie recommended increasing stipends and urged that regents not be admitted to teach without proper trial. Finally, he recommended a uniform curriculum and regular communication between the universities.[110] The last two initiatives would be pursued at the end of the 1640s.

Baillie's proposals bore the influence of practices employed at Geneva, Heidelberg, and the Huguenot academies, where divinity and arts teaching were similarly systematised.[111] In Scotland, the proposals influenced the General Assembly's visitations, which ordered student life and required subscription to the Covenant in order to socialise students to the new Covenanted social order.[112] Students were required to converse in Latin, own an English Bible, and obtain the requisite academic dress.[113] The 1643 St Andrews visitation additionally prohibited students from moving between the universities to avoid punishment.[114] The visitations also regulated staff and arts

---

[106] Mijers, 'Addicted to Puritanism'; Marie-Claude Tucker, 'Scottish Philosophy Teachers at the French Protestant Academies in the Seventeenth Century', *Scottish Philosophy in the Seventeenth Century*, pp. 50–72, at 52–3, 65–6.

[107] Reid, 'Ane Uniformitie', p. 24; Cant, 'Scottish Universities in the Seventeenth Century', pp. 230–1.

[108] Baillie, *L&J*, II, pp. 464–5.

[109] Reid, 'Ane Uniformitie', p. 25.

[110] Baillie, *L&J*, II, pp. 465–7.

[111] See e.g., Maag, *Seminary or University*; eadem, 'Huguenot Academies', pp. 148–9; Notker Hammerstein, 'The University of Heidelberg in the Early Modern Period: Aspects of Its History as a Contribution to Its Sexcentennary', *History of Universities*, 6 (1986), 105–33. On interpersonal links, see Marie-Claude Tucker, 'Scottish Masters in Huguenot Academies', *History of Universities*, 29:2 (2016), pp. 42–68.

[112] AUL, MSM 91/2; MAUG, II, p. 456; *Evidence*, II, p. 258; GUA, 26621, p. 335.

[113] For Glasgow, see MAUG, II, pp. 464–5; *Evidence*, II, pp. 259–60; GUA, 26621, pp. 338–9. For St Andrews, see *Evidence* III, p. 205; StAUL, UYUY 812, pp. 2–5; StAUL, UYSM 110/B18/P2/6, pp. 65–7; StAUL, UYSS 110/AG/2d.

[114] *Evidence*, III, p. 209; StAUL, UYUY 812, p. 68. For copies of the 1643 visitation, see StAUL, UYSS 110/AG/2e; StAUL, UYSS 110/AG/2f.

teaching. The 1640 Marischal visitation evaluated Principal Patrick Dun and the regents. By this time, Marischal was devoid of anti-Covenanters – divinity professor and Aberdeen Doctor Robert Baron died in 1639 – and the visitors urged the college to be an example 'in all manners'.[115] The 1643 visitation of St Andrews, meanwhile, mandated that professors at St Leonard's and St Salvator's be provided with competent livings. It also formalised the election of regents: when a post became vacant, replacements from Aberdeen, Edinburgh, and Glasgow were to come to St Andrews with 'testimonial of there good conversation and affection to the reformation of religion, and government of the kirk presently establish in this kingdom'. Candidates would expound on Aristotle's *Organon* and then dispute with St Andrews' masters.[116] At Glasgow, visitors resurrected regenting, a practice that Andrew Melville had abolished. This indicated that the Covenanters desired uniformity across the universities, where regenting continued to be employed.[117] In respect to teaching, the 1640 Glasgow visitation confirmed the Aristotelian course, while the principal and regents were to teach Hebrew as they saw fit.[118] Glasgow was also directed to ensure that regents be 'short in their nots', that Aristotle be instructed in Greek, and that disputations continued.[119] A course that mirrored Baillie's scheme was also established at St Andrews, while at Glasgow and St Andrews regents were warned against 'dyting', in which students took notes through repetition.[120] To augment learning, the Glasgow and St Andrews visitations also called for the construction of libraries. St Andrews received £1,000 Scots from Alexander Henderson for this purpose.[121] Lacking a generous benefactor, Glasgow's visitors recommended to the staff that money be sought 'with diligence' for building a library.[122]

Most importantly, Covenanting visitations aimed to establish a system for divinity instruction. The attention to divinity instruction – in addition to philosophy – underscored the link between theological knowledge and the early modern state, as 'true' doctrine, and the ability to articulate and defend it, legitimised political power.[123] In a nascent confessional state vying for survival amidst the upheavals of the civil war, producing partisans who

---

[115] AUL, MSM 91/2; On Marischal's masters, see *FAM*, III, pp. 28, 34.

[116] *Evidence*, III, pp. 209–10; StAUL, UYUY 812, pp. 69–77.

[117] The visitation also abolished the medical professorship, which had been held by Robert Maine. See *MAUG*, II, pp. 467–8; *Evidence*, II, pp. 260–1; GUA, 26621, pp. 340–2. Professorial specialisation had developed during Melville's tenure. See Reid, *Humanism and Calvinism*, pp. 79–81.

[118] *MAUG*, II, pp. 454–5; *Evidence*, II, p. 257; GUA, 26621, pp. 334–5.

[119] *MAUG*, II, p. 465; *Evidence*, II, p. 259; GUA, 26621, p. 338.

[120] *Evidence*, III, pp. 205–6; StAUL, UYUY 812, pp. 4–6; Baillie, *L&J*, II, pp. 71–2; Reid, 'Ane Uniformitie', p. 25.

[121] *Evidence*, III, pp. 204–5; StAUL, UYUY 812, p. 2.

[122] *MAUG*, II, p. 468; *Evidence*, II, p. 260; GUA, 26621, p. 338.

[123] Braddick, *State Formation*, pp. 289–90; Mann, *Sources of Social Power*, p. 22. On theological knowledge, the state, and political authority, see also Rivka Feldhay, 'Authority,

were trained well and steeped in authorised norms was of the utmost importance. At Glasgow, shoring up divinity training required dividing instruction between Principal Strang, David Dickson, who was translated to Glasgow in 1640, and Robert Baillie, translated in 1642. This division was partly to relieve Strang of his extensive duties, which included overseeing finances.[124] But it also meant that divinity instruction at Glasgow was now the responsibility of two avowed Covenanters, as suspicion remained concerning Strang's orthodoxy.[125] It was also telling that the 1642 Glasgow visitation entreated Strang to continue with his non-teaching duties as the concurrent visitation of St Andrews had ordered each college to establish a separate *œconomus* to oversee finances, as it was 'no way expedient' for a principal to be distracted from teaching.[126] The visitation sought to relieve St Andrews' principals of their administrative burdens to focus on instruction. Perhaps due to the tensions still simmering from the Glasgow Assembly, the Covenanters were clearly content with the limits of Strang's teaching responsibilities. The 1642 St Andrews visitation also envisaged the division of divinity teaching between four masters. The principal would teach theological controversy; a second master would focus on the New Testament; a third would teach the Old Testament; and a fourth would teach the Psalms, Hebrew, Chaldaic, and Syriac. Such a division of labour had previously been proposed for Huguenot academies in 1620 and was employed at other Reformed colleges.[127] In 1642, however, St Mary's had only two masters, whom visitors ordered to 'prosecute this whole course of the study Divinity'. Owing to these vacancies, the visitors encouraged the General Assembly to fill posts at the college.[128] At a base level, these visitations provide evidence of the Covenanters' comprehensive supervision of higher learning.[129] But they also highlighted the Covenanters' pragmatic approach to state formation, as it was realised in the universities: students had to be well versed in rhetoric, argumentation, and divinity in order to serve Covenanted Scotland. Their teachers, therefore, played a crucial role: students who went on to the ministry had to be able to preach well, which meant being able to divide sermons logically and rhetorically into heads of exegesis, doctrine, and application for effective evangelisation to serve the Covenanted state.[130]

Political Theology, and the Politics of Knowledge in the Transition from Medieval to Early Modern Catholicism', *Social Research* 73:4 (2006), 1065–92.

[124] Baillie, *L&J*, II, p. 71. See also H.M.B. Reid, *The Divinity Principals in the University of Glasgow 1545–1654* (Glasgow, 1917), pp. 267–9.

[125] MAUG, II, p. 466; *Evidence*, II, pp. 259–60; GUA, 26621, pp. 339–40.

[126] *Evidence*, III, p. 207; StAUL, UYUY 812, p. 10.

[127] Jean Aymon (ed.), *Tous les Synodes Nationaux des Églises Réformées de France* (2 vols, The Hague, 1710), II, p. 210; Brockliss, 'Curricula', pp. 594–7.

[128] *Evidence*, III, pp. 206–7; StAUL, UYUY 812, pp. 5–7; Reid, 'Ane Uniformitie', pp. 29–30.

[129] This point is underscored in in Reid, 'On the Edge of Reason'.

[130] Schultz, 'Protestant Intellectual Culture', pp. 60–1; Reid, 'Ane Uniformitie', pp. 30–2;

The concern with what was being taught in the universities meant that the Covenanters also devoted immense energy to controlling who was doing the teaching. The control of the professoriate as a facet of Covenanting rule especially demonstrates the extent to which the Covenanters prioritised university reform within the broader construction of the Covenanted state. In a letter to Spang in May 1641, Baillie wrote that 'the General Assemblie had given to the Universities almost a Soveraigne power to call to their profession any Minister of the Land'. The 1641 General Assembly ordered that 'special care be had that the places of the Professors, especially the Professor of Divinity in every University and Colledge, be filled with the ablest men, and best affected to the Reformation and order of this Kirk'.[131] Between 1639 and 1642, there was a flurry of activity that saw several prominent Covenanters fixed in university posts. Only after these moves was a process for the translation of academic staff and ministers formalised at the 1642 General Assembly. There, commissioners decided that the burgh of Edinburgh would have first access to ministers and that St Mary's would be 'first to be served' with professors. The universities were also permitted to 'send abroad' for new staff. St Mary's called Alexander Colville, the Scots professor of theology at Sedan, in 1641, and Edinburgh called Julius Conradus Otto to the Hebrew professorship in 1642.[132] St Mary's position as the principal college recalled a proposal in the *First Book of Discipline*.[133] Scotland's main seminary would be furnished with the brightest minds in order to exert the greatest influence.

David Dickson's translation from his Irvine ministry to Glasgow University is indicative of the Covenanters' process of translating professors. Dickson, a leading Covenanter, was an alumnus and former regent at Glasgow.[134] In July 1639, the burgh of Glasgow called Dickson to the vacant ministry at

---

Langley, 'Diligence in His Ministrie', pp. 276–7. On the manner of preaching, see Crawford Gribben, 'Preaching the Scottish Reformation, 1560–1707', in Peter McCullough and Hugh Adlington (eds), *The Oxford Handbook of the Early Modern Sermon* (Oxford, 2011), pp. 271–86.

[131] *Records of the Kirk*, pp. 293–4.

[132] *Records of the Kirk*, p. 326. The town council referred to Otto as a learned 'Jew', while later historians identified Otto as the Viennese scholar Naphtali Margolioth, a convert to Christianity. Otto held the chair until 1656. See Marguerite Wood (ed.), *Extracts from the Records of the Burgh of Edinburgh, 1642 to 1655* (Edinburgh, 1938), p. 2; George F. Black, 'The Beginnings of the Study of Hebrew in Scotland', in Louis Ginsburg (ed.), *Studies in Jewish Bibliography and Related Subjects* (New York, 1929), pp. 463–78; Morris Zamick, 'Julius Conradus Otto: Manuscripts Remains in the University Library', *University of Edinburgh Journal*, 4 (1931), 229–35. Colville was called to St Mary's in 1641, though he likely did not arrive until 1647. See *Evidence*, III, p. 206; Marie-Claude Tucker, 'Colville, Alexander, de Jure Third Lord Colville of Culross (1595/6–1666)', ODNB.

[133] Cameron, *First Book of Discipline*, 137. St Mary's had previously supplicated for the liberty to call any man to be a professor, but this was opposed by Edinburgh and Glasgow. *Records of the Kirk*, p. 262.

[134] K.D. Holfelder, 'Dickson, David (c. 1583–1662)', ODNB.

Glasgow Cathedral, which sparked a dispute between the presbytery of Irvine and Glasgow's commissioners.[135] Baillie was against his friend's translation and noted that Dickson would be 'degraded from first minister of Irvine to be third minister... in Glasgow', and argued that if the Assembly moved Dickson against his wishes, it would amount to a 'new tyrannie, much worse then that episcopall oppression'.[136] Likewise, Irvine protested that the Assembly was overreaching.[137] Glasgow's commissioners countered by emphasising the cathedral's proximity to the university. Dickson's presence would benefit western Scotland and 'manie uther shyres in this kingdome inland and... lyekways to manie in Ingland and Ireland, [whereas] children and friends resorts hither, and manie mo will do if Mr David be their'. Though the Glasgow burgh council sought to fill a church vacancy, it saw the charge as compatible with teaching divinity. Irvine disputed this: 'Seeing he [is] called to be a paster to their high Church & not a professor in the Colledg any one of them being sufficient to tak up the whole man that argument is an farce for he cannot be both.'[138] The General Assembly agreed, and Dickson remained in Irvine.[139] But Glasgow University presented its own petition for Dickson.[140] This prompted a visitation with authority to invite a new professor, which ultimately compelled Dickson's translation to the university, which he completed in March 1641.[141] Baillie, for his part, supported this translation because he thought Dickson could neutralise Glasgow's remaining hostility to the Covenant and mollify the Covenanters' doubts about Strang.[142]

The 1639 General Assembly's endeavour to translate Samuel Rutherford evinced the Covenanters' commitment to fortifying the universities with leading Covenanters. Both the burgh of Edinburgh and St Andrews University sought Rutherford's services. He had previously received overtures from Marischal College, which he declined, but the burgh of Edinburgh renewed calls for him to join its ministry, while St Andrews called him to the St Mary's divinity post.[143] Would his abilities be put to the best use in Scotland's capital or its chief seminary? Having only recently returned to his parish of Anwoth, Rutherford was unenthusiastic about another move.[144] Yet the Assembly

---

[135] J.D. Marwick (ed.), *Extracts from the Records of the Burgh of Glasgow, A.D. 1573–1642* (Glasgow, 1876), p. 403; McCoy, *Robert Baillie*, p. 64.
[136] NLS, MS 1908, pp. 280–1.
[137] NLS, Wod.Fol.LXII, fol. 143r.
[138] *Ibid.*, fols 141r–145r.
[139] *Records of the Kirk*, pp. 253–4.
[140] *Ibid.*, p. 262; MAUG, II, pp. 450–1; *Evidence*, II, p. 256.
[141] *Records of the Kirk*, p. 279; *Evidence*, II, p. 258; MAUG, II, pp. 452, 456, III, pp. 381–2; GUA, 26621, p. 335.
[142] Baillie, *L&J*, I, pp. 135, 243, II, p. 21; *Evidence* II, p. 256; Reid, *Divinity Principals*, pp. 271–2.
[143] *Records of the Kirk*, pp. 189, 254; Bonar, *Letters*, pp. 15–16.
[144] Bonar, *Letters*, pp. 564–5, 575; David G. Mullan, *Scottish Puritanism 1590–1638* (Oxford, 2000), pp. 39–41.

decided his fate: he would be transferred to St Andrews.[145] Rutherford did not assume the principalship, but instead replaced Patrick Panter, who was then formally deposed. Robert Howie remained principal until 1641. Rutherford moved to St Andrews with Robert Blair, who had been translated to the St Andrews ministry a year earlier.[146]

The General Assembly had declined to move Dickson and Rutherford to new ministries – and Rutherford to Edinburgh, no less – and instead preferred their translations to universities. Covenanting ideologues were being repurposed as divinity professors. By the time Glasgow University called for Baillie's services in 1642, the General Assembly's preference for planting universities was well known. Baillie's own translation to Glasgow resembled that of Dickson's: after Dickson avoided moving to the charge at Glasgow Cathedral, the burgh of Glasgow next called on Baillie.[147] Baillie, however, produced a list of reasons against his translation, in which he argued that his departure would leave his parish destitute; that the General Assembly would be exceeding its authority; and that the burgh had no lawful warrant to compel his move. The Assembly thereafter commanded Baillie to remain in Kilwinning.[148] But, in early 1642, Glasgow University attempted to convince Baillie to take the second professorship of divinity.[149] Baillie had close ties to Glasgow, where he graduated MA in 1620 and served as a regent beginning in 1626, the same year Strang became principal.[150] Glasgow brought the matter before the synod of Ayr, seeking Baillie's services in order 'to erect a sufficient number of Professors of Theologie for the publick good of the Ministrie and common benefit of this Western part of this kingdome'.[151] The synod agreed, and voted unanimously for Baillie's translation. However, Baillie maintained his resistance. He hoped that his parish's petition would convince the Assembly to override a regional ruling.[152] Baillie was too optimistic. As he reached out to his brethren for advice, it became clear that his future lay within the academy.

In April, Robert Ramsay, minister of Glasgow's Blackfriars Kirk, urged Baillie to accept the university post.[153] Ramsay wrote that,

> yow shall be made the instrument to breed manie youths who shall be Leaders of sundrie congregations, (I mean gentlemen in the countrie,) and

---

[145] *Records of the Kirk*, pp. 254, 260.
[146] Blair was not a professor, but a minister in the town. See [Charles I], *Large Declaration*, p. 324; Lyon, *St Andrews*, II, pp. 10–11; *Records of the Kirk*, pp. 187, 189, 251; McCrie, *Robert Blair*, pp. 156–9; Scott, *Fasti*, VII, pp. 418–20, 428.
[147] NLS, Wod.Fol.LXIII, fol. 219r; *Records of the Kirk*, p. 260; Marwick, *Glasgow Burgh Records 1573–1642*, pp. 406–7.
[148] Baillie, *L&J*, II, pp. 11–13, 444–9; McCoy, *Robert Baillie*, pp. 64–5.
[149] For an overview of this affair, see also McCoy, *Robert Baillie*, pp. 79–82.
[150] MAUG, III, pp. 367–8.
[151] Baillie, *L&J*, II, p. 15.
[152] *Ibid.*, II, pp. 14–16.
[153] Scott, *Fasti*, III, pp. 35, 398, 456, 460.

ministers for the Church, more able than yourself, before the private charge of one congregation onlie, and find yourself obliedged to employ your talents there where yow most may be serviceable; and that such ane occasion will represent to yow sundrie characters of a vocation ordered from above.

It was within the university, Ramsay argued, that Baillie would have the greatest impact on the kingdom and Kirk, where he would be charged with educating 'sundrie' future ministers for the good of the Covenanted state. Ramsay also noted that if Baillie did not move to Glasgow, he risked being translated out of the west of Scotland entirely, a point that Dickson, Alexander Henderson, and Robert Blair also emphasised.[154] Dickson was especially exasperated with his friend's obstinacy, and he was confident that the Assembly would 'settle this man in some Universitie, for there will be no rest till it be done'.[155] Baillie would do well to heed Glasgow's call or risk being sent farther afield.[156] He expressed as much in a letter to Kilwinning, and in June 1642 Baillie notified Glasgow of his intention to take up the post.[157] He entered the university the following April, receiving a stipend made available out of the rents of the bishopric of Galloway.[158] Thus by the General Assembly of 1642, a concerted effort had been made to install leading Covenanters into divinity posts. When the 1642 Assembly passed an act for the translation of professors, it was a formality, for the practice had by then been established. The examples of Dickson, Rutherford, and Baillie's translations highlight the protracted, contingent nature of Covenanting state formation as it played out in the universities. Capable intellectuals were not always willing to take on teaching roles themselves. What is clear, however, is that there was widespread recognition of the importance of universities to promote the health of the kingdom through the education and socialisation of students.

Edinburgh, interestingly, was not planted with a leading Covenanter in the early 1640s, but in June 1640 Alexander Henderson became rector.[159] In addition to securing funds for the university, under Henderson's aegis Edinburgh received the vacated rents of the bishoprics of Edinburgh and Orkney and established a Hebrew professorship. The General Assembly allowed universities to look abroad for augmenting their faculties, and competency in Hebrew was essential to equip graduates for careers in the ministry. Henderson, who had railed against clerical insufficiency, considered tuition in Hebrew crucial to cultivating a learned ministry.[160] Producing learned

---

[154] Baillie, *L&J*, II, pp. 19–20, 28.
[155] *Ibid.*, II, pp. 21, 23–4.
[156] Baillie wrote to Henderson, Blair, and Wariston for advice on the matter. See *ibid.*, II, pp. 24–31.
[157] *Ibid.*, II, pp. 32, 37–8; MAUG, III, pp. 383–4.
[158] MAUG, III, pp. 384–5; EUL, La.IV.25/34, fols 24–25, 50.
[159] *Records of the Kirk*, p. 47; Wood, *Edinburgh Burgh Records 1626–1641*, p. 230.
[160] Robert L. Orr, *Alexander Henderson: Churchman and Statesman* (London, 1919), pp. 389–90; John Coffey, 'Henderson, Alexander (c. 1583–1646)', *ODNB*.

ministers also required libraries. In addition to donating £1,000 Scots of his own money to St Andrews, Henderson began securing books for a library at Edinburgh, and construction began in 1644.[161] Henderson's tenure did not go unnoticed. Several letters written to Edinburgh suggest that the university was viewed as a viable option for Englishmen to attend as England devolved into civil war. One letter of October 1642 from a Londoner, John Pemberton, requested that the university find a place for his son, Samuel, formerly of St Catharine's College, Cambridge. 'We in England are in sad distractions', John wrote: 'Our universityes have need of reformation.' It was to Edinburgh that Pemberton wished to send his son, where he hoped 'the most reverend Mr Hinderson' would 'shew your special favours to my child'.[162] Other letters on behalf of English students made similar requests: that scholars would be admitted to continue where their studies had been disrupted.[163] These letters suggest that, by the early 1640s, Scotland's Covenanted universities, like colleges in the Netherlands and other academies abroad, were viewed as viable options for beleaguered Englishmen to send their sons.

Parish clergy ministered to a congregation; professors educated the clergy. The state benefited from authorised clerical education to maintain the wider social order. In Scotland, the manner of planting faculty demonstrated how Henderson's vision of a learned ministry, trained in the universities by accomplished masters, was beginning to take shape. But employing leading Covenanters in the universities was paralleled by the concurrent deposition of antithetical academics. The period 1638–51 witnessed the deposition of over 200 ministers deemed immoral or insufficient.[164] The Covenanters' removal of hostile elements from the universities lends more weight to David Stevenson's claim that Covenanting rule saw the first successful attempt to exclude the 'episcopal' component from the Kirk.[165] But it also highlights the contested nature of the universities, where rival conceptions of political and religious authority clashed, and where the processes illustrative of early modern state formation – such as building towards a homogenised confessional identity through the inculcation of authorised norms – could be resisted. In these situations, authorities resorted to methods to coerce the universities into effective instruments of the state by manipulating the professoriate.[166]

---

[161] Craufurd, *History of the University of Edinburgh*, pp. 144, 153; Grant, *Story of the University of Edinburgh*, I, p. 208; Wood, *Edinburgh Burgh Records 1642-1655*, pp. 6, 58–9.
[162] EUL, Dc.1.4/1, fols 11–12.
[163] *Ibid.*, fols 9, 10, 12–13.
[164] David Stevenson, 'Deposition of Ministers in the Church of Scotland under the Covenanters, 1638–1651', *Church History*, 44:3 (1975), 321–35. See also Todd, *Culture of Protestantism*, pp. 364–5.
[165] Stevenson, 'Deposition of Ministers', p. 334; Reid, 'Ane Uniformitie', pp. 16–23.
[166] Tilly, 'Reflections', p. 24. On state control and the purging of the Scottish professoriate, see Salvatore Cipriano, 'Ejected Academics: Marginalised Scottish University Professors between the Reformation and Revolution', in *Deviance and Marginality in Early Modern Scotland*, ed. Allan Kennedy (Woodbridge, forthcoming).

Table 2.2. The Scottish Professoriate under the Covenanters, c. 1642–7.

University of St Andrews		
St Salvator's College	St Leonard's College	St Mary's College
John Baron, Provost (1646)	Andrew Bruce, Principal (1630)	Samuel Rutherford, Principal (from 1647)
George Martine Jr, Second Master (from 1645)	George Wemyss, Principal (from 1647)	Samuel Rutherford, Divinity (1639)
George Martine Jr, Regent (until 1645)	Alexander Scott, Humanity (1626)	Alexander Colville, Divinity (1647)
Robert Keith, Regent (1642)	David Nevay, Regent (1640)	James Wood, Ecclesiastical History (1645)
Robert Honeyman, Regent (1644)	Robert Norie, Regent (1642)	
William Tweedie, Regent (before 1644)	James Sharp, Regent (1642)	
James Wood, Regent (before 1645)	John Sinclair, Regent (c. 1642)	
Thomas Gleg, Regent (1645)		
William Campbell, Regent (1646)		
Alexander Edward, Regent (1648)		

University of Glasgow	Marischal College, Aberdeen
John Strang, Principal (1626)	Patrick Dun, Principal (1621)
David Dickson, Divinity (1640)	William Muir, Mathematics (1641)
Robert Baillie, Divinity (1642)	John Ray, Regent (163?)
Robert Maine, Medicine (until c. 1646)	Andrew Youngson, Regent (before 1644)
David Munro, Regent (1637)	Patrick Sandilands, Regent (before 1646)
William Hamilton, Regent (1638)	James Hay, Regent (163?)
David Forsyth, Regent (1640)	John Menzies, Regent (1638?)
James Dalrymple, Regent (1641)	Robert Forbes, Regent (164?)
William Semple, Regent (1641)	
John Young, Regent (1645)	
Hugh Binning, Regent (1646)	

Table 2.2 (*continued*)

King's College, Aberdeen	University of Edinburgh
William Guild, Principal (1640)	John Adamson, Principal (1623)
Alexander Middleton, Sub-Principal (1641)	John Sharp, Divinity (1630)
William Douglas, Divinity (1643)	Julius Conradus Otto, Hebrew (1642)
John Lundie, Grammarian (1629)	Thomas Craufurd, Mathematics, Regent (1640)
Patrick Innes, Sacrist (until 1643)	James Wright, Regent (c. 1638)
Patrick Gordon, Regent (1640)	James Wiseman, Regent (c. 1638)
Alexander Gardyne, Regent (1635)	Duncan Forrester, Regent (1639)
William Rait, Regent (1641)	William Tweedie, Regent (1644)
George Middleton, Regent (1642)	James Pillans, Regent (1644)
Andrew Youngson, Regent (1644)	
Patrick Sandilands, Regent (c. 1646)	

Sources: *ODNB*; Scott, *Fasti*; Laing, *Catalogue*; MAUG, vol. 3; *Fasti Aberdonenses*; Anderson, *Officers and Graduates*; FAM, vol. 2; Smart, *Alphabetical Register*; StAUL, UYUY 412.

While the General Assembly oversaw most of the purges between 1638 and 1651, non-ecclesiastical courts had had a hand in purging, evidenced by the Edinburgh town council's removal of John Broun and Robert Ranken for refusing the Covenant. The bulk of the purges under the Covenanters mainly took place at Aberdeen amidst the Bishops' Wars (1639–40), and a university visitation commission accompanied Alexander Leslie's army as it descended upon Aberdeen in spring 1639.[167] Operating under the pretence of settling the dispute between proponents of King's College's new and old foundations, the visitors were instead intent on bringing the intransigent university into line.[168] Aberdeen's masters and students fled the burgh, with many making way to England where 'they were supported by the King's expense'.[169] In

---

[167] Steve Murdoch and Alexia Grosjean, *Alexander Leslie and the Scottish Generals of the Thirty Years' War, 1618–1648* (London, 2016), pp. 93–118.
[168] Stevenson, *King's College*, pp. 115–19.
[169] Stockholm, Riksarkivet, E 748. I am thankful to Steve Murdoch for this reference and translation.

early April the visitors summoned the staff back to Aberdeen.[170] The masters present were forced to subscribe to the Covenant: Lundie and Patrick Innes, who had already subscribed to the Covenant; sub-principal Robert Ogilvie; cantor Gilbert Ross; canonist James Sandilands; professor of medicine William Gordon; and regents Alexander Middleton and Alexander Gardyne.[171] Having subscribed, none were deposed, though the visitors abolished the posts of the cantor and canonist, Catholic remnants of King's medieval foundation; Sandilands later angled to remain as professor of civil law.[172]

The visitors next addressed the absent Principal William Leslie and regent Alexander Scroggie and deposed both.[173] The charges against Leslie included his failure to sign the Covenant, his refusal to acknowledge the authority of the Glasgow Assembly, and his communication with the deposed bishop of Aberdeen.[174] The university filled Scroggie's vacant post in the fall, while William Guild, the once-Doctor who had subscribed to the Covenant in 1638, assumed the principalship.[175] Guild's subscription was at first conditional: he refused to condemn episcopacy and swore only to 'disregard' the Perth Articles.[176] The issue of conditional subscription resurfaced the following year, for another visitation returned in October 1639 intent on making Guild 'subscrive the covenant absolutlie' and installing him as principal.[177] He was instead elected rector.[178] But the following summer, Guild, who had now re-subscribed to the Covenant without any conditions, was made principal.[179] According to one commentator, 'This was done authoritatively, for the electione was not canonicalle, according to the foundatione of that universitye; yet ther was none for to questione it, so it past for current.'[180]

The April 1639 visitation also commanded that 'the absentis wes dischargeit of thair offices'.[181] This would have included John Forbes of Corse, King's divinity professor, and the leading Aberdeen Doctor. Forbes, however, remained active at the college despite the visitation's order. In July, he noted that he had 'concluded my school lectures of divinity in the Kings Colledge for this summer'.[182] Thus if Forbes had been absent from Aberdeen

[170] Spalding, *Memorialls*, I, pp. 150–2, 158–9.
[171] *Ibid.*, I, p. 166.
[172] AUL, MSK 36, p. 57.
[173] Spalding, *Memorialls*, I, p. 166.
[174] *Records of the Kirk*, p. 262. NLS, Wod.Fol.LXIII, fol. 215r.
[175] AUL, MSK 36, pp. 52–3; *Fasti Aberdonenses*, p. 414.
[176] Newton, 'United Opposition', pp. 62–3.
[177] Spalding, *Memorialls*, I, p. 233.
[178] AUL, MSK 36, pp. 52, 53; Anderson, *Officers and Graduates*, p. 10; Spalding, *Memorialls*, I, pp. 231–3.
[179] Newton, 'United Opposition', p. 63; AUL, MSK 36, pp. 58–60; *Fasti Aberdonenses*, p. 417; Anderson, *Officers and Graduates*, p. 26; Spalding, *Memorialls*, I, pp. 233–4.
[180] Gordon, *Scots Affairs*, III, pp. 256–7.
[181] Spalding, *Memorialls*, I, p. 166.
[182] AUL, MS 635, p. 183.

during the visitation, he returned for the remainder of the academic year, disobeying the commission's order. That October, he was also listed among the King's masters.[183]

Forbes was to confront the Covenanters' visitation in October 1639. According to his diary, the meeting and pressure to subscribe drove him into hysterical fits.[184] Summoned before the commission on 17 October, he was supposed to subscribe to the Covenant, state his obedience to the acts of the General Assembly, and account for his divinity teaching. Yet he ultimately did not meet his opponents until July 1640, in advance of the General Assembly at Aberdeen.[185] Forbes insisted that he would only subscribe with limitations in the interest of maintaining peace.[186] The moderator noted that in refusing unconditional subscription Forbes was disobeying the Assembly.[187] But Forbes was not persuaded, and he was charged to 'forbear the exercise of my profession of Divinitie'.[188] With the General Assembly meeting in Aberdeen, Forbes referred to himself and his colleagues as 'lambs in the midst of wolves'.[189] In a week, the Assembly proceeded against ministers, university staff, divinity students, and expectants.[190] The urgency of reforming divinity education, to ensure that conformity to the Covenant was paramount, was also highlighted. King's divinity students exhibited their teachers' influence: one student, Robert Mercer, refused to subscribe to the Covenant, while four others – Alexander White, Robert Rait, William Forbes, and Walter Urquhart – refused to show entirely. The Assembly censured these students and barred all divinity students who refused subscription from 'Pedagogie, teaching of a School, reading at a Kirk, preaching within a Presbyterie' and from 'residing within a Burgh, Universitie, or Colledge'.[191]

The Assembly next deposed James Sibbald, who was charged with refusing to subscribe to the Covenant, preaching 'Arminian poyntes', and circulating the irenic works of William Forbes. The Covenanters installed Andrew Cant to replace Sibbald, who departed Scotland and lived out his days in Dublin.[192] With nearly all of the Aberdeen Doctors deposed or deceased, the final step for the Covenanters to assert their dominance over the Aberdeen colleges was the

---

[183] AUL, MSK 36, p. 52; Gordon, *Scots Affairs*, II, p. 225; Spalding, *Memorialls*, I, pp. 150–2.
[184] AUL, MS 635, p. 219.
[185] *Ibid.*, pp. 224, 228–9, 248; Spalding, *Memorialls*, I, pp. 232n–3n.
[186] AUL, MS 635, pp. 264–5.
[187] *Records of the Kirk*, pp. 237–8.
[188] AUL, MS 635, pp. 350–2; Stevenson, *King's College*, p. 118.
[189] AUL, MS 635, p. 375.
[190] NLS, Wod.Qu.XXVI, fols 91v, 99r; Gordon, *Scots Affairs*, III, p. 231; Stevenson, *King's College*, pp. 118–19.
[191] NLS, Wod.Qu.XXVI, fols 101r–101v, 102v–103r; *Records of the Kirk*, p. 279.
[192] AUL, MSK 36, p. 53; NLS, Wod.Qu.XXVI, fols 85r–88v, 99v, 103; Baillie, *L&J*, I, p. 248; Gordon, *Scots Affairs*, III, pp. 228–30; Spalding, *Memorialls*, I, pp. 311–13.

deposition of John Forbes. Questioning began on 1 August.[193] The Covenanters admired Forbes for his piety and erudition, and the visitation committee reported that 'no man can chalenge him off errours in doctrine', notwithstanding 'scruples concerning the Covenant'.[194] The Assembly allotted Forbes more time to consider, and he was ordered to appear in Edinburgh for a final review.[195] Though he remained barred from teaching, Forbes wrote that he was at first relieved by the decision, spending what seems like several days weeping. But in the time before his appearance in Edinburgh in March, his outlook changed.[196] He prayed for his son George's university education, which he hoped would proceed free of Covenanting constraints.[197] When Forbes came to Edinburgh in March 1641, he refused to subscribe. Knowing he would be expelled, he hoped a 'peaceable' divine would replace him. On 20 April he was formally deposed and his professorship was declared vacant in the Aberdeen synod the next day, 'to the gryte greif of the youth and young studentis of theologie, who were weill instructit and teachit by this lerned doctor'. Forbes was forced from his home and absconded to the Netherlands in 1643; he returned to Corse in 1646 and lived in relative seclusion until his death in 1649.[198]

The highest profile depositions occurred at Aberdeen, but there were also removals at other universities. St Mary's Principal Howie, for instance, departed for financial misconduct. Samuel Rutherford complained that Howie had transferred funds out of the college rents to his son, Panter, and others. Howie supplicated to the 1641 General Assembly, but he ultimately chose to demit his place.[199] Meanwhile, Glasgow emerged as a key centre of activity in the later 1640s. There, the affair prompted by the discovery of John Strang and William Wilkie's correspondence with Walter Balcanquhall in 1638, together with Strang's treatise on the King's Covenant, unfolded in the wake of the Engagement of 1647, the Scots' highly contentious military pact with the king.[200] Strang and Wilkie's documents were discovered following the Battle of Naseby and came into the possession of the Scots commissioners at

---

[193] On Forbes' questioning, see also Aaron Clay Denlinger, 'Swimming with the Reformed Tide: John Forbes of Corse (1593–1648) on Double Predestination and Particular Redemption', *Journal of Ecclesiastical History*, 66:1 (2015), 67–89.
[194] AUL, MS 635, p. 381.
[195] *Ibid.*, pp. 382–3; NLS, Wod.Qu.XXVI, fol. 104r; Baillie, *L&J*, I, p. 248; Gordon, *Scots Affairs*, III, p. 233.
[196] AUL, MS 635, pp. 391–4.
[197] *Ibid.*, p. 441.
[198] *Ibid.*, pp. 454–5, 464–6; Gordon, *Scots Affairs*, III, pp. 233–4; Spalding, *Memorialls*, II, p. 57.
[199] Baillie, *L&J*, I, p. 361.
[200] David Stevenson, *Revolution and Counter-Revolution in Scotland, 1644–1651* (London, 1977), pp. 98–122; Frances D. Dow, *Cromwellian Scotland 1651–1660* (Edinburgh, 1979), pp. 5–9.

the Westminster Assembly.[201] The General Assembly deposed Wilkie, then minister of Govan, in 1649 for failing to oppose the Engagement.[202]

The uncovering of Strang's treatise called into question his capacity to teach divinity to future generations of ministers. The Assembly subsequently ordered Robert Blair and the St Mary's masters Alexander Colville and James Wood to review Strang's dictates.[203] Colville and Wood, professors of divinity and church history, had both recently translated to the college.[204] Strang's dictates were also copied and sent to Henderson, Rutherford, Dickson, and Baillie.[205] Strang argued that it was impossible that his colleagues review his dictates and not find points of disagreement: 'Never any man protestant, or papist, did or shall wryt on that subject without contradiction.' The review was instead a 'hinderance of him to doe good in his calling'.[206] Baillie thought the entire matter unnecessary and dangerous; save for minor discrepancies, the committee had only praise for Strang. There was no evidence of heterodoxy, only minor disagreements; given the intellectual might assembled, that academic dispute arose is unsurprising.[207] Strang was exonerated at the 1647 Assembly, but his days as principal were numbered.[208] He had ceased lecturing given his advanced age.[209] In April 1650 the Assembly accepted Strang's resignation, allowed him to maintain his stipend, and approved a statement of his orthodoxy.[210] Whereas the Doctors were deposed as the Covenanters' rose to power, Strang's resignation came under the theocratic rule of the anti-Engagers, who reigned over a divided Kirk in the aftermath of the Engagement. Even a leading light like Baillie had fallen under suspicion for defending Strang.[211] But as these examples demonstrate, depositions illustrated the extent to which the Covenanting movement began to fracture in the latter 1640s, a topic which will be explored further in Chapter 4.[212]

v

---

[201] Baillie, *L&J*, I, p. 480; Cipriano, 'Principal of Glasgow', p. 103.
[202] Scott, *Fasti*, III, p. 411; *Records of the Kirk*, p. 558.
[203] NLS, MS 3430, fol. 75.
[204] Scott, *Fasti*, VII, 428; *Records of the Kirk*, 432; K.D. Holfelder, 'Wood, James (c. 1609–1664)', *ODNB*.
[205] RCGA, I, 191, 192–3; Reid, *Divinity Principals*, 284.
[206] NLS, MS 3430, fol. 75.
[207] Baillie, *L&J*, II, 404–5, 3: 5–6; Reid, *Divinity Principals*, 285–6.
[208] For the General Assembly's report, see *Ad Lectorem de Vita Autoris*, written by Robert Baillie, which prefaces John Strang, *De Interpretatione & Perfectione Scripturæ* (Rotterdam, 1663); *Records of the Kirk*, p. 482.
[209] Baillie, *L&J*, III, pp. 32, 327; McCoy, *Robert Baillie*, p. 131.
[210] Reid, *Divinity Principals*, pp. 286–7; GUL, MS Gen 1769/1/21.
[211] Baillie, *L&J*, III, p. 105.
[212] See also Salvatore Cipriano, 'The Engagement, the Universities and the Fracturing of the Covenanter Movement, 1647–51', *National Covenant in Scotland*, pp. 145–60.

Table 2.3. Scottish University Staff Removals under the Covenanters, c. 1638–47.

University of St Andrews	King's College, Aberdeen
Robert Howie, Principal, St Mary's College	William Leslie, Principal
Removed, 1641	Deposed, 1639
Patrick Panter, Divinity, St Mary's College	James Sandilands, Canonist
Deposed, 1638	Office abolished, 1639 (became Civilist)
	Gilbert Ross, Cantor
University of Glasgow	Office abolished, 1639
John Strang, Principal	Alexander Scroggie, Regent
Forced retirement, 1650	Deposed, 1639
Robert Maine, Medicine	James Sibbald, Dean
Office abolished, c. 1640, though post apparently held until 1646	Deposed, 1640
	John Forbes of Corse, Divinity
	Deposed, 1641
University of Edinburgh	**Marischal College, Aberdeen**
John Broun, Regent	Robert Baron, Divinity
Deposed, 1638	Died, 1639
Robert Ranken	William Blackhall, Regent
Deposed, 1638	Deposed, 1642

Sources: Scott, *Fasti*; Laing, *Catalogue*; MAUG, vol. 3; *Fasti Aberdonenses*; Anderson, *Officers and Graduates*; FAM, vol. 2; Smart, *Alphabetical Register*

The Covenanting General Assembly's reform and supervision of the universities throughout much of the 1640s were built on regular visitations that reformed curricula, built conformity to the Covenant, and remoulded the professoriate. These processes and policies were rooted in engineering the universities into the models of the Covenanted state and the machinery through which to ensure its survival for future generations. The manner in which they were carried out during the period of Covenanter hegemony also underlines the contested nature of the universities during the era of Covenanting state formation. Authorities drew on one key power structure – the General Assembly of the Kirk – to remake Scotland's institutions of higher learning into effective tools to perpetuate state power.

National Schemes and the Unified Curriculum

The most scrutinised of the Covenanters' university policies has been the creation of a unified curriculum.[213] A unified curriculum, in which each of universities taught a uniform arts course to homogenise training across Scottish higher education, was unique in the context of the British Atlantic world. However, the idea of a unified curriculum had continental analogues. The Huguenot church, for instance, exercised strict oversight of the academies, and by 1603, the national synod called for common statutes across academies to standardise training to guarantee the endurance of a confessionally cohesive French Reformed ministry for future generations.[214] The situation in Covenanted Scotland was remarkably similar. Just as Baillie's 1640 overtures and the expansion of divinity teaching at several universities bore continental influence, so too did the Covenanters' curricular policies.

In addition to curricular reform, the Covenanters pursued several other 'blanket' policies to establish processes and structures through which to govern the universities on a national scale. These processes represented the Covenanters' attempts to build out the apparatuses of the state to oversee higher education, thereby further incorporating the universities into the infrastructures of state power.[215] The 1641 General Assembly set the agenda for these policies in two ways. First, it proposed that there should be a 'communion and correspondencie kept' between the universities, with representatives meeting annually.[216] Second, the General Assembly mandated that every presbytery with twelve ministers – those with fewer were to join together – fund a divinity bursar.[217] Bursars were key to Scottish higher education, and provisions for bursars were included in the *First Book of Discipline*.[218] This was meant to ensure that the promising schoolboys would be able to attend university, eventually study divinity, and join the ministry.[219]

There is limited evidence that both proposals were heeded, though the synod of Argyll did decide in October 1642 that, because of the lack of

---

[213] See Cant, *St Andrews*, p. 71; Reid, 'Ane Uniformitie', pp. 33–8; Christine M. Shepherd, 'A National System of University Education in Seventeenth-Century Scotland?', in Jennifer J. Carter and Donald J. Withrington (eds), *Scottish Universities: Distinctiveness and Diversity* (Edinburgh, 1992), pp. 26–33

[214] Aymon, *Synodes Nationaux*, I, p. 275; Maag, 'Huguenot Academies', pp. 140–9; Tucker, 'Scottish Masters in Huguenot Academies', p. 63.

[215] For a recent study that probes these policies in the Scottish Gaidhealtachd, see Salvatore Cipriano, '"Students Who Have the Irish Tongue": The Gaidhealtachd, Education, and State Formation in Covenanted Scotland, 1638–1651', *Journal of British Studies*, 60:1 (2021), 66–87.

[216] *Records of the Kirk*, pp. 293–4.

[217] *Ibid.*, p. 294. EUL, La.I.305/2 fol. Br; *RPS*, A1641/8/7.

[218] Cameron, *First Book of Discipline*, pp. 60–1, 149–50, 151.

[219] Todd, *Culture of Protestantism*, pp. 59–60; John Durkan, *Scottish Schools and Schoolmasters 1560–1633*, ed. Jamie Reid-Baxter (Woodbridge, 2013), pp. 67–74.

churches, 'every two presbyteries' should combine to fund a bursar.[220] At its 1645 meeting the General Assembly outlined overtures for the Advancement of Learning and Good Order in Grammar Schools and Colledges, which presaged the Scottish Parliament's passage of the 'Education Act' in February 1646.[221] These proposals sought to entrench order and orthodoxy, and as will be examined in Chapter 6, the Massachusetts General Court issued similar proposals for Harvard in 1652. The Scottish acts resolved that schools should be visited regularly and that students and schoolmasters be examined for their orthodoxy. University students would only be permitted to advance to the next class after trial, while the graduating class would be subjected to rigorous evaluation to attain the MA. The Assembly again called for commissioners from each university to meet 'at the time of every Generall Assembly' to deliberate over matters of piety and learning and to pursue 'ane Uniformitie in Doctrine and good Order'.[222] Additionally, the Assembly ordained all presbyteries of twelve ministers to fund a bursar, while the bursars themselves were required to bring testimonies from their universities, and if they were found 'deficient', they would be replaced by 'others more hopefull'.[223]

It was in 1647 that these orders began to be realised. Between 1647 and 1649, representatives from each university met at each year's General Assembly to develop a unified course for instruction.[224] The first meeting was held in late August 1647 in Edinburgh. The commissioners included, from Edinburgh, Principal John Adamson and rector Andrew Ramsay, who succeeded Henderson in 1646;[225] from Glasgow, Principal John Strang, Robert Baillie and the benefactor Zachary Boyd; from St Andrews, Alexander Colville and Robert Blair; and, from Aberdeen, William Douglas, who replaced John Forbes in 1643.[226] It is peculiar that, given the tensions surrounding Strang's orthodoxy, he would be included in the meetings of this commission, though Baillie remarked that Strang's business was put 'to a good and fair end'.[227] The commissioners agreed that there should be a unified philosophy course, and each university was tasked with writing specific sections: St Andrews focused on metaphysics, Glasgow on logic, Aberdeen on ethics and mathematics, and Edinburgh on physics.[228] The commissioners also exhorted the General Assembly to see that the presbyteries carried out the requirement to fund

---

[220] Duncan C. MacTavish (ed.), *Minutes of the Synod of Argyll, 1639–1661* (2 vols, Edinburgh, 1943–4), I, p. 47.
[221] Cipriano, 'Students Who Have the Irish Tongue', pp. 78–9.
[222] *Records of the Kirk*, pp. 419–20.
[223] *Ibid.*, p. 421; StAUL, UYSL 156, pp. 228–30.
[224] The commission's minutes are found in GUA, 26790, pp. 1–37. They are partially reproduced in Bower, *History of the University of Edinburgh*, I, pp. 218–53.
[225] Laing, *Catalogue*, p. x.
[226] Anderson, *Officers and Graduates*, pp. 69–70. GUA, 26790, pp. 1–2.
[227] Baillie, *L&J*, III, p. 21.
[228] GUA, 26790, pp. 1–4; Reid, 'Ane Uniformitie', pp. 33–4.

bursars.[229] Baillie's 1640 overtures were influential in deriving this course and setting down rules for student conduct and examination.[230] Possibly to aid in preparing the course, in October 1647 Baillie wrote to his cousin William Spang at Veere, requesting additional works by Dutch scholars, underlining both the symbiotic relationship between Scottish and Dutch intellectuals and continental flavour of Scottish reforms.[231] Due to Baillie's energies, Glasgow took to the task enthusiastically, and the university's instructions for the commission noted that, in addition to cementing a course in philosophy, 'in the whole course there be inserted wholesome antidotes not only against pagane but chiefly popish errors'. Glasgow also requested £100 for books and scribes for those creating the curriculum.[232]

The 1648 meeting convened in July in Edinburgh. Dickson replaced Strang and joined Baillie as Glasgow's commissioners. Aberdeen's commissioners included the rector David Lindsay, the regent Patrick Gordon, and the Marischal mathematics professor William Muir.[233] The representatives of St Andrews included Rutherford, Colville, George Wemyss, principal of St Leonard's, David Nevay, regent of St Leonard's, and James Reid of Pitlethie, conservator of privileges.[234] Edinburgh arrived with Principal Adamson and the regents Thomas Craufurd, James Wiseman, Duncan Forrester, and Andrew Suttie.[235] The commissioners agreed to assist in promoting 'the common-well of all the universities', deliberated on the philosophy course, and ordered each university to bring draft syllabi to the next meeting. Echoing the 1645 General Assembly proposals, the commission mandated that no student be permitted to move universities without written testimony attesting to their abilities.[236]

At the 1649 meeting, the commissioners established a uniform arts course, much of which drew on what was already being taught.[237] The commissioners ordered the course's implementation by April 1650 and required St Andrews' divinity professors to 'put in Latine' the Covenant, catechism, and Westminster Directory of Worship for each university. They also supplicated to the General Assembly to 'interpose their authority' on the universities

---

[229] GUA, 26790, p. 2; *Records of the Kirk*, p. 478.
[230] Reid, 'Ane Uniformitie', pp. 32–3.
[231] Baillie, *L&J*, III, pp. 23–4; Alexander D. Campbell, *The Life and Works of Robert Baillie (1602–1662): Politics, Religion and Record-Keeping in the British Civil Wars* (Woodbridge, 2017), pp. 37–8, 122, 201–3.
[232] NCL, Baill 2/4, pp. 53–5.
[233] Anderson, *Officers and Graduates*, pp. 11, 26, 87; *FAM*, II, pp. 28, 53; Scott, *Fasti*, VII, p. 57.
[234] Scott, *Fasti*, VII, p. 413; Robert N. Smart (ed.), *Alphabetical Register of the Students, Graduates, and Officials of the University of St Andrews, 1579–1747* (St. Andrews, 2012), pp. 455, 514.
[235] GUA, 26790, pp. 4–5.
[236] *Ibid.*, pp. 4–6; StAUL, UYSS, 110/AI/9. See also EUL, Dc.1.4/1, fol. 21r.
[237] For an outline of the course, see also Reid, 'Ane Uniformitie', pp. 36–41.

to 'hasten' the completion of the curriculum. Robert Douglas, moderator of the 1649 General Assembly, sent letters to each university urging them on.[238] Ultimately, the commission attempted to reform the universities to better serve the Kirk – in its final rulings of August 1649, it not only outlined the unified course, but also stated that 'Through the whole course, a care would be had, to refute solidely, but shortly, the philosophick errors of Pagans, Papists, Arminians, & others, as they come by hand.'[239] This demonstrated that the commission sought to equip its students intellectually to serve Covenanted Scotland.

Of these students, the commission again appealed to the General Assembly for provision of bursars. As late as 1649 the commission found that presbyteries had not been funding their bursars adequately.[240] It is not entirely clear the extent to which bursars went unfunded, but from Argyll to Tweeddale there is evidence that presbyteries funded divinity bursars when sufficient funds could be found.[241] The evidence also points to the 'national' scope of these endeavours – they were not focused solely on the Anglophone students of the Lowlands. Indeed, the General Assembly introduced schemes in 1643, 1646, 1648, and 1649 to raise money throughout Scotland to send Gaelophone boys to the universities so that they might evangelise in the Gaidhealtachd.[242] At least four boys from Argyll were sent to each university in 1648.[243] Though money was always scarce, there is evidence that collections were taken in presbyteries throughout Scotland to support the 'hieland bursars' between 1647 and 1652.[244] Constructing a kingdom in covenant with God required incorporating all elements and traversing early modern Scotland's linguistic and cultural divides.

The Covenanters actively drew on the Kirk's matrix of courts to extend the control of the Covenanted state over the universities. The national schemes described in this section point not only to a concern to formalise processes to better socialise students into the authorised norms of the Covenanted state intellectually, but they also highlight the concern with building structures to support higher learning materially as well. Indeed, far from being concerned only with a unified philosophy course, in the latter half of the 1640s the Covenanters were intent on constructing a working, national educational apparatus to cultivate a Covenanted nation.

---

[238] GUA, 26790, pp. 6–10, 24–6; *Records of the Kirk*, p. 558.
[239] GUA, 26790, pp. 27–8.
[240] GUA, 26790, p. 7.
[241] See e.g., MacTavish, *Minutes of the Synod of Argyll*, I, 153; William Cramond (ed.), *Extracts from the Records of the Synod of Moray* (Elgin, 1906), pp. 92–3; Chris R. Langley (ed.), *The Minutes of the Synod of Lothian and Tweeddale, 1648–1659* (Edinburgh, 2016), pp. 19, 55.
[242] Cipriano, 'Students Who Have the Irish Tongue', pp. 76–9.
[243] *Records of the Kirk*, p. 510; MacTavish, *Minutes of the Synod of Argyll*, I, p. 159.
[244] Cipriano, 'Students Who Have the Irish Tongue', pp. 79–86.

Conclusion

Throughout much of the period of Covenanter hegemony in Scotland, the universities were active sites where the processes of early modern state formation played out. The Covenanters marshalled the structures of state power – most notably the General Assembly, newly girded with widespread authority to intervene in university affairs – to transform the universities into the machinery to support the Covenanted nation. This was also a process that highlighted Scottish higher education's contested nature, as the universities' intellectual and doctrinal heterogeneity and their adherence to the confessional mores of the monarchy clashed with Covenanting visions of a Reformed polity with a limited monarchy predicated on Presbyterianism. Beginning with the Glasgow Assembly of 1638, the Covenanters thus inaugurated sweeping reform of Scottish higher education that was rooted in the core vision of building the conditions to acculturate students to the norms of the Covenanted nation and train future ministers to perpetuate the Covenanted social order.

These processes were comprehensive, aggressive, and at various points coercive, but they were not indicative of some uniquely authoritarian regime. As has been suggested throughout this chapter, such policies were emblematic of the supervision of higher learning found in Reformed communities in Europe and across the Atlantic, and they certainly paralleled the policies of the Stuart monarchy. Though the conceptions of 'true religion' differed, they betray governing authorities' acute concern with how piety was kept, on what was being taught, and on who was responsible for training future churchmen and statesmen. As will be examined in the next chapter, these were concerns that were also shared in the higher educational spaces of Ireland and New England.

The Covenanters' university policies, however, were pursued neither in a colonial space like Ireland or New England, nor a cosmopolitan republic like the Netherlands, but instead within a kingdom that in the 1640s, despite the pressures of war, saw the construction of a confessional state. The endurance of the Covenanted kingdom was predicated on the universities, the seminaries that produced Scotland's future governing elite. In 1638, Scotland's universities, as exhibited by their opposition to the Covenant, could not have been viewed as institutions that served the Covenanted interest. By 1643, following a wave of professorial changes, and during the late 1640s, amidst the implementation of various curricular reforms, the universities were, ideologically as well as materially, both the models and machinery of the Covenanted state.

3

Ireland and New England, c. 1637–50

The Scottish case of the late 1630s and 1640s highlighted how a revolutionary regime took control of the universities to engineer student socialisation. The situation in Ireland and Massachusetts, meanwhile, differed in terms of scale and location. Trinity and Harvard were two universities on cultural margins and, in the 1640s especially, they experienced the vicissitudes of war, poverty, and religious controversy. Despite their diverse settings, this era also magnified the contested nature of each university, as governing authorities in each locale focused on higher education to train future elites. Indeed, at Trinity and Harvard, situated as they were in two colonial spaces, this theme was repeatedly negotiated throughout the 1640s, both as the Covenanting project progressed in Scotland and the Civil Wars impacted life in all corners of the British Atlantic world.

There is no shortage of scholarship that has highlighted the parallels between colonialism in early modern Ireland and North America.[1] In particular, historians have underlined the agency of people – ministers, merchants, diplomats, and others – who traversed the early modern empire and their intent on transporting English models from the metropole to colonial spaces. Scholars have emphasised the uniqueness of the New England enterprise especially for the

---

[1] See e.g., David Beers Quinn, 'Ireland and Sixteenth-Century European Expansion', in T.D. Williams (ed.), *Historical Studies I* (London, 1958), pp. 20–32; Nicholas Canny, *Kingdom and Colony: Ireland in the Atlantic World, 1560–1800* (Baltimore, MD, 1988); especially chaps 1–3; Jane H. Ohlmeyer, 'A Laboratory for Empire?: Early Modern Ireland and English Imperialism', in Kevin Kenny (ed.), *Ireland and the British Empire* (Oxford, 2004), pp. 26–60; David Armitage, *The Ideological Origins of the British Empire* (Cambridge, 2000), pp. 24–5; Karen O. Kupperman, 'How to Make a Successful Plantation: Colonial Experiment in America', in Mícheál Ó Siochrú and Jane H. Ohlmeyer (eds), *Ireland, 1641: Contexts and Reactions* (Manchester, 2013), pp. 219–35. For reappraisals of the Irish influence on colonial expansion in the New World, see Horning, *Ireland in the Virginian Sea*, chap. 1; Alison Games, *The Web of Empire: English Cosmopolitans in an Age of Expansion, 1560–1660* (Oxford, 2008), chap. 8. On conceptions of indigenous peoples across the Atlantic world, see e.g., Nicholas Canny, 'The Ideology of English Colonization: From Ireland to America', *William and Mary Quarterly*, 30:4 (1973), 575–98; James E. Doan, '"An Island in the Virginian Sea": Native Americans and the Irish in English Discourse, 1585–1640', *New Hibernia Review*, 1:1 (1997), 79–99; Karen O. Kupperman, *Indians and English: Facing Off in Early America* (Ithaca, NY, 2000), pp. 53–4, chap. 7.

ways in which colonial leaders transferred English society across the Atlantic.[2] Given the attention devoted to the transportation of metropolitan models to colonial spaces, it is interesting that there has been little scholarly attention devoted to examining two of these exports – Trinity and Harvard – in tandem.

As part of his monumental work on the founding and early history of Harvard College, Samuel Eliot Morison identified significant links between Harvard and Trinity: both were conceptualised as 'mothers' of a university and both primarily served settler communities. The high volume of Cambridge graduates that constituted early Trinity and Harvard's teaching and administrative ranks also engendered a 'sisterly' relation of shared institutional heritage.[3] Beyond Morison's brief, nearly century-old analysis, Helga Robinson-Hammerstein and Elizabethanne Boran's 1998 article on Trinity and Harvard remains the main comparative study of the two colleges. Their work tracked approaches to higher education in puritan efforts to bring the 'civilising' qualities of Christian knowledge to the hostile spaces of Catholic Ireland and colonial New England. Drawing on the concept of *translatio studii*, their study highlighted the ideological origins behind the founding of these institutions, and Harvard in particular, as modes to realise the puritan utopia of a 'city of peace', especially with the 'failure' of the Irish project, punctuated by the 1641 Rebellion.[4] Yet the focus on the transfer of knowledge – crucial to understanding the intellectual currents that drove the founding of European institutions in the New World – and essentially concluding the analysis at 1641, when Harvard was in its infancy, overemphasises puritans' civilising impulses and portrays both colleges as idealised institutions. Universities may have been conceived as ideals that modelled the promise of an ordered society, but that was very rarely the case once they began operating. In pursuing a comparative analysis of early Harvard and post-Laudian Trinity, this chapter aims to move beyond the narrow focus on foundations and 'civilisation' to underscore the colleges' contested utility as sites of settler state formation during an era of pronounced upheaval. In both Atlantic locales, the agency and actions of individuals loomed large in the contested nature of the colleges' existence. When we also consider the situation in Scotland alongside Trinity and Harvard, it is telling that many similar themes emerge despite their locations in vastly different contexts in the Civil War-era Atlantic.

This chapter is divided into two parts. The first examines Trinity, beginning with the period immediately preceding the 1641 Rebellion in which two key episodes unfolded: Provost Chappell's elevation to the Irish episcopate and Irish Parliament's attempts to jettison Laud's reforms and renovate

---

[2] Games, 'Beyond the Atlantic' p. 687; *eadem*, *Web of Empire*, pp. 7–11; Ford, 'Power and Distance'. On New England and the transportation of English society writ large, see Bailyn, *Barbarous Years*, pp. 370–1.
[3] Morison, *Founding*, pp. 121–5.
[4] Boran and Hammerstein, 'Promotion of Civility', *passim*, and especially pp. 502–5.

Trinity's privileges. This section will then examine post-Rebellion Trinity. The upheaval, which nearly shuttered the college, also provided an opportunity, as the vacuum created by the flight of Trinity's masters opened an avenue through which the New English could reassert control of the college. If anything, this era accentuated Trinity's status as a strategic centre and contested space, with partisans seeking to exercise control and exert power in the college despite the tumult. Power and control are also essential to understanding early Harvard. The second part examines Harvard's transformation into a viable educational institution that supported a maturing, and religiously rigid, community of the godly. Harvard experienced few of the direct pressures of Trinity, and in many areas, its early history and operations paralleled Covenanting endeavours in the Scottish universities. But, as will be demonstrated, as authorities pursued schemes to support Harvard and build structures of power to exert control, their remained an underlying recognition of the fragile authority that colonial authorities exercised over the college, and thus the contestability of both the higher educational and wider colonial project. Despite the differences in experiences and fortunes in Ireland and New England during the latter 1630s and 1640s, this chapter highlights how Trinity and Harvard, like the Scottish universities, shared a common purpose as vital machinery of socialisation, no matter the authorities who exerted control.

Trinity College, Dublin

Trinity's new statutes, which concentrated power in the chancellor and provost, took effect in June 1637. The college's conversion to Laudianism seemed all but certain, but in fact, the completion of the new statutes in 1637 marked the apogee of Laudianism at Trinity. In the period immediately thereafter the college, again, was thrown into flux due to the machinations of rival political and religious authorities. Between 1637 and the outbreak of the Irish Rebellion of 1641, contests of power in the college, and over the nature of the socialisation of Trinity's students, intensified.

The completion of the new statutes was a significant step in the Laudian reform program and the wider process of aligning the Church of Ireland with the Church of England. Yet much would ultimately hinge on Chappell's ability to implement them.[5] William Bedell spoke favourably of Chappell's endeavours to reform manners, improve rents, and beautify buildings, but he took exception to Chappell's doctrinal preferences and Arminianism: 'In the service of God many account he hath brought in too much ceremony.'[6] Chappell was a doctrinal Arminian – not an 'Arminian' in the way opponents

---

[5] Mahaffy, *Epoch in Irish History*, p. 247.
[6] Shuckburgh, *Bedell*, p. 362.

viewed Laud – who adhered to Jacobus Arminius' Five Remonstrant Articles that were repudiated at the Synod of Dort.[7] Chappell's Arminianism, coupled with his role in the fellows' dispute in 1636, provoked Archbishop Ussher's hostility.[8] Laud was aware that tensions at Trinity were the product of both factional strife and Chappell's beliefs, but he still viewed Chappell as integral to Trinity's government.[9] Nevertheless, having such a polarising figure charged with leading Ireland's only university did not bode well for the advancement of the Laudian reforms, despite the fact that many of his opponents' power had been limited with the implementation of the new statutes.

Laud ultimately decided that the way to settle Trinity's affairs was to move Chappell to a bishopric. 'We must think how to make the Provost a bishope', he wrote to Wentworth in September 1637, 'and of a good successor for I will never trust myself again if the Primate do not seek all occasion to cross with the Provost.'[10] Laud sought to protect Chappell, and Trinity, from Ussher's meddling, but he also did not want Chappell 'to be a perpetuall drudge to the College'. Laud and Wentworth agreed that Chappell should be preferred to a bishopric and continue to hold Trinity's provostship *in commendam*, contravening Laud's statutes, while they sought a successor.[11] Chappell was still too important to Laudian designs to depart without an agreeable successor.[12] To see out his plan, Laud had to convince Charles I of its necessity, as the Laudian statutes codified the king's authority to appoint a new provost. Laud pressed Wentworth to seek out a vacant see that 'not lie too far from the College', so that Chappell could continue as provost.[13] Wentworth remarked that Chappell 'doth as much good [at Trinity], and more than I think he can do in any Diocese of the Whole Kingdom'.[14] Chappell's centrality to Laudian reform meant that Laud and Wentworth would not let him depart Trinity without an agreeable successor.

An opportunity came with the death of Randolph Barlow, archbishop of Tuam, in February 1638.[15] Wentworth's subsequent scheming to replace Barlow did not escape Ussher's attention.[16] In March, Ussher wrote to Samuel Ward that Chappell would be moved to the bishopric of Clonfert, 'yet still retaining his provostship'.[17] A month later, he reported that the bishop of

[7] Ford, 'Chappell, William'.
[8] Ford, *James Ussher*, pp. 199–203.
[9] *Laud Works*, IV, p. 400, VI, pp. 499–500; HMC, *The Manuscripts of the House of Lords Vol. XI: 1514–1714*, ed. Maurice F. Bond, new series (London, 1962), p. 440.
[10] *Laud Works*, VII, p. 368; MacDonnell, *Chartæ et Statuta*, p. 32; Bolton, *Statutes*, p. 27.
[11] *Laud Works*, VI, p. 514, VII, p. 398.
[12] Ford, 'That Bugbear Arminianism', pp. 156–7.
[13] *Laud Works*, VI, p. 514.
[14] *Strafford Letters*, II, p. 138.
[15] Cotton, *Fasti*, II, p. 42, IV, pp. 13–14; Robert Armstrong, 'Barlow, Randolph (Randal)', *DIB*.
[16] McCafferty, *Reconstruction*, pp. 118–19.
[17] *Ussher Works*, XVI, p. 35.

Cork, Cloyne, and Ross was to move to Tuam, with Chappell to assume the vacancy.[18] On 19 June, the king appointed Chappell to the new bishopric of Cork and Ross while continuing to 'hold his Provostship of Trinity College *in commendam*'.[19] Ussher protested, and in a letter to Laud in July, he denounced the decision.[20] 'The eluding of oaths in this manner', Ussher wrote, 'I do conceive to be a matter of post pernicious consequence.'[21] Laud lamented that the see was, indeed, far from Trinity, but he tried to temper Ussher's anger by writing that the king's dispensation came with a limitation, in that Chappell was to hold the posts *in commendam* for only a short period of time.[22] Regardless, with Chappell's preferment came the need to find a new provost as quickly as possible.

The intrigues and manoeuvrings over Chappell's successor demonstrate the crucial importance of the individual actors at the heart of these machinations. While we may identify impersonal 'forces' that explain transformations and the nature of royal and religious power, ultimately it was the agency of men – their religious preferences, their training, their capacity to lead – that was crucial to realising policies that distilled authorised ideologies.[23] In many ways, these endeavours also paralleled the Covenanters' orchestration of the Scottish professoriate in the 1640s, when it was crucial to focus on the men who were tasked with leading universities and educating students in order to operationalise the aims of the regime. Additionally, the affair over Chappell's successor underlined that, despite Laudian and Wentworth having exercised tight control over Trinity, the college endured as a strategic, contested space where Laudian and New English interests clashed.

For his part, Laud immediately had a successor in mind: the provost's younger brother John, who had already been living at Trinity.[24] Laud's reasoning was straightforward: 'he is fully acquainted with the provost's courses, and I doubt not will be guided and ordered by him. So that still his influence may run into the College and the government thereof.'[25] John Chappell's elevation to the provostship would ensure the continuation of the Laudian project at Trinity.[26]

---

[18] *Ussher Correspondence*, II, p. 740.
[19] *CSPI 1633–47*, p. 194; Empey, 'Diary of Sir James Ware', p. 103.
[20] MacDonnell, *Chartæ et Statuta*, pp. 33–4; Bolton, *Statutes*, pp. 29–31.
[21] TNA, SP 63/256, fol. 269; *Ussher Works*, XVI, pp. 36–7.
[22] *Laud Works*, VII, pp. 463–4.
[23] See e.g., Braddick, *State Formation*, pp. 92–3; Mann, *Sources of Social Power*, I, p. 37. The move towards understanding the agency of individuals in the history of early modern diplomacy offers a useful parallel. See Birgit Tremml-Werner and Dorothée Goetze, 'A Multitude of Actors in Early Modern Diplomacy', *Journal of Early Modern History*, 23 (2019), 407–22.
[24] *Laud Works*, VI, pp. 514, 518, VII, pp. 398, 471, 492, 543.
[25] *Ibid.*, VII, p. 471.
[26] Matthew Reynolds, *Godly Reformers and Their Opponents in Early Modern England: Religion in Norwich c. 1560–1643* (Woodbridge, 2005), pp. 180–2.

Wentworth, however, did not share Laud's zeal for the provost's bother.[27] The lord deputy desired that Chappell remain at Trinity despite Laud's insistence that his brother succeed him.[28] Wentworth was more than comfortable flouting Trinity's constitution, especially if it meant preserving control of the college. He had pursued a similar strategy when he secured a royal dispensation for Vice-Provost John Harding, one of Trinity's Christ College imports and tutor of Wentworth's son, which allowed him to remain as a senior fellow and hold a benefice.[29] In September 1639, Harding was installed as chancellor of Christ Church, Dublin. The following February, his name still appeared in the college register as a senior fellow.[30] This was egregious even for Laud, who argued that this would only anger Ussher further.[31] But for Wentworth, it was necessary to sustain authority over Trinity, which required keeping all suitable men, like Chappell and Harding in place.[32]

These events clearly angered Ussher, and Laud commented that he had not heard from the Irish primate since his July 1639 letter denouncing the dispensation.[33] There is little mention of Trinity in Ussher's correspondence from this period, save for a letter to the German linguistic scholar Christian Ravius. Ravius appeared to have sought work as a Hebrew lecturer at Trinity. Ussher, however, was unsure if the creation of a Hebrew chair was forthcoming – one would only be established at Trinity in the later 1650s – and instead financed Ravius, via Samuel Hartlib, to travel to the eastern Mediterranean to search for manuscripts.[34] Ussher's uncertainty about learning at Trinity speaks to the extent to which he had been cut off from the college's affairs. Ussher did, however, propose two names to succeed Chappell, though he clearly thought that his efforts were meaningless. 'Being here your vice-chancellor', Ussher wrote to Laud, 'I could not in duty conceal from you what I conceived fit to be thought upon for the government of that society, the welfare whereof doth wholly depend upon your provident care and circumspection.'[35] The first was familiar: Joseph Mede, the puritan scholar who had been nominated in previous years. The second was Richard Howlett – previously fellow of Sidney Sussex College, where he had tutored John Bramhall – who was then rector of Aghalurgher.[36] Bramhall supported his former tutor, remarking that

---

[27] HL, HA 15166; *Laud Works*, VI, p. 533, VII, pp. 475, 487–8; Kenneth Fincham (ed.), *The Further Correspondence of William Laud*, Church of England Record Society 23 (Woodbridge, 2018), p. xliii.

[28] *Strafford Letters*, II, p. 194; *Laud Works*, VII, pp. 492, 521–2.

[29] TCD, MUN/V/23/1, p. 1; *Strafford Letters*, II, p. 275; *CSPI 1633–1647*, p. 208.

[30] Cotton, *Fasti*, II, p. 56; *Alumni Dublinenses*, p. 369; TCD, MUN/V/5/1, p. 68.

[31] *CSPI 1633–47*, p. 208; *Laud Works*, VII, pp. 521–2, 531.

[32] *Strafford Letters*, II, pp. 194, 249; Mahaffy, *Epoch in Irish History*, pp. 247–8.

[33] *Laud Works*, VI, pp. 551–2.

[34] *Ussher Correspondence*, II, pp. 772–3; G.J. Toomer, *Eastern Wisedome and Learning: The Study of Arabic in Seventeenth-Century England* (Oxford, 1996), pp. 83–5.

[35] TNA, SP 63/256, fol. 269; *CSPI 1633–47*, p. 196; *Ussher Works*, XVI, p. 37.

[36] McCafferty, *Reconstruction*, pp. 29, n. 44.

'I think little of the Provost's brother.'[37] But neither would succeed Chappell: Mede died in October 1638, while Howlett was preferred to the deanery of Cashel in March.[38] Moreover, both Mede and Howlett's Reformed credentials contrasted greatly with the Chappell brothers' Arminian sympathies. Ussher's nominees were more reflective of Trinity's pre-Laudian ethos, keeping with the identity of the college as he conceived of it.

The choices of these major power brokers betrayed their vision for Trinity and the type of institution they wanted it to be, but ultimately, it was the king alone who chose a new provost. On 30 June 1640, Charles appointed Richard Washington, fellow of University College, Oxford, to succeed Chappell.[39] University College was a bastion of support for the crown and the established church under the mastership of Thomas Walker, a Laudian protégé.[40] On 20 July, Chappell formally resigned the provostship, lamenting the 'evill daies' that marked the end of his provostship due to the strained relationship with Ussher.[41] Washington's appointment indicated the continuation of the Laudian project at Trinity and the formation of a seminary to socialise students to a hierarchical, sacramental church. But upheavals in England and Scotland would halt any further reforms. While in England, Wentworth pressed Charles to call parliaments in Ireland and England in order to provide support for the war with the Covenanters.[42] The proceedings of the Irish Parliament that opened in 1640 and sat through 1648 quickly morphed into a referendum on Wentworth's rule in the highly charged months prior to the outbreak of the Irish Rebellion, ultimately compromising both Wentworth and Laud's position in England and heralding their demises.[43] In Ireland, through a series of by-elections, the number of MPs opposed to Wentworth and Laud – Catholic and Protestant, Old and New English – increased, as many had connections to the Long Parliament and were focused on destroying Wentworth.[44] There are intriguing parallels to the

---

[37] TNA, SP 63/256, fol. 271; *CSPI 1633–47*, p. 196.
[38] HL, HA 15973; McCafferty, *Reconstruction*, p. 120.
[39] *CSPI 1633–47*, p. 242; Empey, 'Diary of Sir James Ware', p. 106.
[40] Darwall-Smith, *University College*, pp. 157–63.
[41] TCD, MUN/V/5/1, pp. 2, 70–1; TNA, SP 63/258, fol. 89.
[42] Aidan Clarke, 'The Breakdown of Authority, 1640–41', in T.W. Moody, F.X. Martin, and F.J. Byrne (eds), *A New History of Ireland, Vol. III: Early Modern Ireland 1534–1691* (Oxford, 1976), pp. 270–88, at 270–3; Jane H. Ohlmeyer, *Making Ireland English: The Irish Aristocracy in the Seventeenth Century* (New Haven, CT, 2012), pp. 232–9; Aidan Clarke, *The Old English in Ireland, 1625–42* (Ithaca, NY, 1966), pp. 47–59, 76–91, 238–54.
[43] Coleman Dennehy, *The Irish Parliament, 1613–89: The Evolution of a Colonial Institution* (Manchester, 2019), pp. 3–4; idem, 'The Irish Parliament after the Rebellion, 1642–48', in Patrick Little (ed.), *Ireland in Crisis: War, Politics and Religion, 1641–50* (Manchester, 2020), pp. 100–18; Hugh Kearney, *Strafford in Ireland, 1633–41: A Study in Absolutism* (Manchester, 1959), pp. 198–215.
[44] Bríd McGrath, 'The Irish Elections of 1640–1641', *British Interventions*, pp. 186–206; Ohlmeyer, *Making Ireland English*, pp. 241–3. See also eadem, 'The Irish Peers, Political

situation in Scotland, where, following the Bishops' Wars, the Covenanters struck against Charles' Scottish reforms through parliament. In Ireland, both houses of parliament, while not enacting a constitutional revolution, sought to undo the policies of Wentworth's tenure. Trinity's reforms were no exception. Parliament's campaign against the Laudian reforms highlighted Trinity's contested and strategic place where rival conceptions of Irish society clashed. Once again, at the heart of parliament's endeavours were questions about who Trinity was for, how its students were to be trained, and what type of social order the institution was to serve.

Between March 1640 and November 1641, the Irish Parliament targeted nearly every aspect of the Laudian reform program and dispensed with the individuals, like Wentworth and Bramhall, most involved in its implementation.[45] In addition to the litany of religious grievances, the Irish Commons highlighted longstanding educational issues.[46] Wentworth's opponents in Westminster also seized upon evidence of misrule in the Church of Ireland.[47] Similarly to the Scottish case, the deterioration of affairs in England forced Charles I's hand in Ireland: in July 1641 he conceded to a number of grievances, which included abolishing the Irish High Commission and reforming the clergy.[48] The concurrent assault on the Laudian reform of Trinity began in February 1641.[49]

Irish Parliament's focus on Trinity represented another way to address the church reforms of the 1630s; dismantling Laudian ecclesiastical reforms required overhauling the institution that was to sustain the reconstructed Church of Ireland.[50] On 23 February, the Irish Commons appointed a committee to consider 'all Matters whatsoever concerning the College, and touching the Reformation of the Grievances thereof'.[51] The Trinity committee consisted of forty members, twenty-seven of whom were Protestants of various extractions: New English, English, and Scottish.[52] Several committee

Power and Parliament, 1640–1641', *British Interventions*, pp. 161–85; eadem, 'Power, Politics and Parliament in Seventeenth-Century Ireland', in Maija Jansson (ed.), *Realities of Representation: State Building in Early Modern Europe and European America* (New York, 2007), pp. 113–32, at 116–21.

[45] HL, HA 14061, 14073; McCafferty, *Reconstruction*, pp. 193–222.
[46] *CJI*, pp. 150–1.
[47] Maija Jansson (ed.), *Proceedings in the Opening Session of the Long Parliament, House of Commons Volume 1: 3 November–19 December 1640* (Rochester, NY, 2000), pp. 36–7, 44–5; McCafferty, *Reconstruction*, pp. 200–1, 209–10.
[48] *CSPI 1633–47*, pp. 317–22.
[49] Dennehy, *Irish Parliament*, pp. 40, 51.
[50] See e.g., Ford, 'That Bugbear Arminianism', p. 158; McCafferty, *Reconstruction*, p. 216; Dennehy, *Irish Parliament*, p. 40.
[51] *CJI*, p. 180.
[52] Bríd McGrath, 'A Biographical Dictionary of the Membership of the Irish House of Commons 1640–1641' (2 vols, unpublished PhD thesis, Trinity College, Dublin, 1998), I, pp. 7–14.

members were also Trinity graduates, including the antiquarian James Ware, who served as an MP for Trinity alongside William Gilbert.[53] The Commons tasked the committee with reviewing Trinity's constitution and grievances among the college community. As the committee deliberated, on 25 February Chappell, sitting in the Irish Lords, was 'excused' from attendance because he was 'indisposed' and 'weak in Body'.[54] Two days later, the Trinity committee reported that part of the college's statutes barred 'any Student or Member of that society' from complaining about the 'Mis-government' or other grievances to external authorities. The statutes prohibited students from appealing directly to the college visitors about internal matters. They also stated that no measures could be taken against the provost, fellows, or students without the chancellor's approval.[55] These statutes were meant to curtail the authority of Trinity's visitors and consolidate power with the chancellor and provost. The Commons' committee voided these statutes and allowed members of the college to voice their grievances.[56]

Grievances thereafter flowed into the Commons. They centred on the Laudian statutes and the collapse of Trinity's 'antient' order. The complaints, detailed on 4 March, enumerated how Laud's statutes undercut the powers of the fellows and visitors. The Commons also prosecuted Chappell and deemed him responsible for these corruptions. The committee urged the Lords to recall Chappell 'to answer their Charge'.[57] Chappell was charged with holding the provostship for three years without taking the provost's oath and was indicted with forcing through the new statutes, which bound 'the whole College' to the new government. The Commons also accused Chappell of importing 'strangers' from Cambridge and holding of the provostship *in commendam* with a bishopric.[58] These grievances drove the Commons to conclude that 'the Natives of the Kingdom by such practices have been infinitely grieved, discouraged, and disheartened to follow their Studies and Civility'. To emphasise this point, the committee juxtaposed Trinity's original Elizabethan constitution with the Laudian statutes.[59] The former protected the 'natives' of Ireland, while the latter disrupted Trinity's traditional order. The Commons summoned Chappell to answer for his 'evil Government and Practice' and appealed to Westminster's Irish Committee and to Ussher, then in England, to supplicate to the king 'for the redress of the said Grievances'.[60]

---

[53] TCD, MUN/V/5/1, p. 68; McGrath, 'Biographical Dictionary', I, pp. 28, 39, 170–1, 301–3.
[54] *Journals of the House of Lords of the Kingdom of Ireland, Vol. 1, 1634–1698* (Dublin, 1779), p. 165.
[55] MacDonnell, *Chartæ et Statuta*, pp. 54–5, 104–5; Bolton, *Statutes*, pp. 56, 116–17.
[56] *CJI*, pp. 186–7; TCD, MUN/V/5/2, p. 4.
[57] *Lords Journal Ireland*, p. 177.
[58] *CJI*, pp. 194–7.
[59] Ibid., pp. 196–7.
[60] Ibid., p. 195.

These grievances underscored the regularly contested questions of who early Trinity was for and what ideal the college was to serve. That the grievances clearly highlighted policies that radically altered the composition of the college's student body and staff and the confessional vision they were to serve underline the extent to which the Laudian reforms had taken root in the college. One of the key grievances was the importation of 'strangers' into students and fellows' places – a key strategy of the Laudian reforms – at the expense of the 'Natives of the Kingdom', who were most wronged by Laud's statutes and Chappell's misrule. This term 'native', as it was defined by Trinity's partisans, ostensibly meant anyone born in Ireland, whether native Irish, Old English, or the sons of New English settlers.[61] The Commons stated that 'There is not among the Senior Fellows, who govern all with the Provost, but only one Native there.' And, because the Laudian statutes made fellowships a lifetime appointment, 'the Averseness, settled in those Strangers towards Natives, is not like to be removed in their Life-time, if not extraordinarily redressed'.[62] In its initial findings, the committee raised the alarm for what this meant for the education of future Irish churchmen and statesmen, and thus the wider social order: 'Strangers are like to come in to favour Strangers.'[63] For November 1640, the college register lists seven senior fellows, only one of whom was a 'native' under the aforementioned criteria: the Dublin-born Thomas Seele, a Trinity alumnus who was made senior fellow in January 1638.[64] But also among the senior fellows was Nathaniel Hoyle, vice-provost, one of the fellows at the heart of the dispute over precedence in 1636. Though likely English by birth, Hoyle was a Trinity alumnus who had served as a junior and senior fellow and had defended Trinity's privileges – hardly a 'stranger' to the college.[65] English birth did not preclude one from being amenable to Trinity's pre-Laudian ethos. Nevertheless, to the committee's point, the five remaining senior fellows – Alexander Hatfield, Christopher Pepper, Christopher Beckwith, William Clopton, and Robert Cocke – were all English 'strangers' who had been imported from Christ's College.[66]

In the committee's report, there were no references to the evangelisation of the native, Gaelic Irish. Such an endeavour, which save for Bedell's academic interests had been mostly ignored at Trinity, was also an afterthought for the Commons. This was a reminder that the Commons' conception of the brand of social order that Trinity was to perpetuate the Irish Protestant community,

---

[61] This was, for instance, how Provost William Temple categorised 'native' students c. 1620. See TCD, MUN/P/1/127.
[62] CJI, p. 197.
[63] Ibid., p. 195.
[64] TCD, MUN/V/5/2, p. 2, MUN/V/5/1, p. 61; Alumni Dublinenses, p. 741; Cotton, Fasti, II, pp. 52, 100.
[65] Alumni Dublinenses, pp. 413–14.
[66] TCD, MUN/V/5/2, p. 2; M.W.J. Fry (ed.), The Dublin University Calendar, Vol. III. Being a Special Supplemental Volume for the Year 1912–1913 (Dublin, 1913), p. 574.

mainly of New English extraction, who adhered to a Reformed version of the Irish church. Trinity, indeed, helped to define the limits of a community that was consolidating power, and thus the reality of its existence in the 1640s paralleled the situation at early Harvard College. The Commons committee's brief, tantalising reference to learning also underscored this idea. It noted that, under Chappell, 'The Mathematick Lectures and Hebrew Lectures were by the said Provost put down, and other Exercises of Learning.'[67] While no formal chairs for mathematics and Hebrew would be established until the following decade, the committee's indictment of learning under Chappell is a fleeting reference to the pre-Laudian Ramist course, which made great use of Trinity library's mathematical textbooks authored by Ramist intellectuals.[68] Hebrew, moreover, was essential for educating godly clerics in Reformed communities.[69] Both were anathema to the Aristotelian course that Laud introduced and Chappell oversaw. This highlights the competing conceptions of who Trinity was for and the social order it was to buttress: the traditional Aristotelian course was advantageous to a territorial and hierarchical established church, while the Ramist course was conducive to a small godly community in a confessionally contested territory.[70] The report's conclusions also accentuated the charged confessional nature of the committee itself. Seven committee members were listed as having submitted the 4 March report, including two Trinity graduates of the 1620s, John Bysse and Archibald Hamilton, the latter of whom had warned Ussher about Arminian designs on the college several years earlier.[71] To Trinity's alumni, Laud's statutes and Chappell's tenure were viewed as a concentrated assault on the college's traditional order.

The committee thereafter focused on impeaching Chappell and charging others who had colluded in the Laudian project.[72] Chappell's impeachment proceedings do not appear in the surviving manuscript records of the Lords, but the Commons' proceedings highlight a systematic effort to redress a wide array of grievances concerning Trinity.[73] The committee received complaints from Chappell's opponents, including petitions from Charles Cullen and Thomas Feasant.[74] By May 1641, Chappell had been imprisoned as the Commons drew up charges of impeachment.[75] The committee summoned at least two former

---

[67] *CJI*, p. 195.
[68] Boran, 'Ramism in Trinity', pp. 184–5.
[69] Morgan, *Godly Learning*, pp. 113–18, 178.
[70] Hotson, *Reformation of Common Learning*, pp. 4–9.
[71] *CJI*, p. 197; McGrath, 'Biographical Dictionary', I, pp. 7–14, 96–7, 173.
[72] Coleman Dennehy, 'Some Manuscript Alternatives to the Printed Irish Parliamentary Journals', *Parliaments, Estates and Representation*, 30:2 (2010), 129–43, at 135–9; Empey, 'Diary of Sir James Ware', p. 108.
[73] See e.g., National Library of Ireland, Dublin, MS 9607, pp. 107, 117, 122–30. I am grateful to Coleman Dennehy for providing these and other references concerning the Irish Lords.
[74] *CJI*, pp. 203, 210; Ford, 'That Bugbear Arminianism', p. 158.
[75] *CJI*, pp. 204, 221.

senior fellows who had been imported from England, Alexander Hatfield and John Harding.[76] The committee also examined Christopher Kerdiff, a former student who graduated in 1629.[77] It was presumably building a case against Chappell, but it is unclear what the committee uncovered. At the same time, however, the Commons selected thirteen members, including Hamilton and Ware, to deliberate on Trinity's affairs and prosecute Chappell.[78]

In June 1641, the Commons voted unanimously that 'all and every the Proceedings' of the college under Chappell's provostship constituted 'great Grievances' and were 'fit to receive redress'.[79] According to James Ware, the committee member Robert Bysse 'made a severe Speech against [Chappell], upon the delivery of the Articles of his Charge'. In prosecuting Chappell, Bysse and the committee drew on the testimony of Archbishop Ussher and Anthony Martin, bishop of Meath, a Trinity alumnus, former fellow, and former visitor who sat in the Lords.[80] The committee cited all acts and proceedings at Trinity during Chappell's tenure as requiring remedy and delivered articles of impeachment against the provost.[81] The surviving evidence is scarce on the details of the charges, save that they were first read in June and that Chappell was unable to provide satisfactory answers.[82] It is likely that Ussher testified against Chappell's doctrinal preferences, though much of the reaction against his tenure seems to have stemmed from distaste for his arbitrary rule. We can surmise that the charges mirrored the initial list of grievances reported on 4 March, which indicted the entire scope of Chappell's provostship.[83] With Chappell's tenure officially repudiated, the Commons could begin the process of renovating Trinity in earnest.

One of the only actions that the Commons took prior to October 1641 and the outbreak of the Irish Rebellion concerned Trinity's elections, a crucial and equally contested constitutional mechanism that royal authorities had seized upon to control the college. In June, the Commons ordered Provost Washington and the fellows to cease electing scholars and fellows 'until this House give further Direction therein'.[84] Controlling elections was

---

[76] *Ibid.*, pp. 218, 222. At this time, Hatfield and Harding were, respectively, rector of Cloghran in County Dublin and dean of Christ Church, Dublin. See Cotton, *Fasti*, II, p. 56; Francis Elrington Ball, *A History of the County Dublin: The People, Parishes and Antiquities from the Earliest Times to the Close of the Eighteenth Century. Part Second* (Dublin, 1903), p. 496.

[77] *CJI*, p. 226; *Alumni Dublinenses*, p. 464.

[78] *CJI*, p. 222; McGrath, 'Biographical Dictionary', I, pp. 110–11, 173, 301–3.

[79] *CJI*, p. 228.

[80] Walter Harris (ed.), *The Whole Works of Sir James Ware Concerning Ireland* (2 vols, Dublin, 1739–45), I, p. 567.

[81] McCafferty, *Reconstruction*, p. 218.

[82] *CJI*, pp. 243, 254, 259; Harris, *Ware Works*, I, p. 567.

[83] The Commons also received complaints about Chappell's mishandling of revenues in August. *CJI*, p. 286.

[84] *Ibid.*, p. 228; TCD, MUN/V/5/2, p. 5.

a way to curb the influx of English students and fellows into Trinity. But the moratorium did not last long. In August, the Commons allowed elections of new scholars after learning that several 'Natives of the Kingdom' had applied for scholarships. The Commons barred the provost and fellows from refusing scholars' places to 'the natives' and mandated that they prefer 'those Natives, bred in the Schools of Dublin before other Natives'.[85] The college register lists the election of twenty-one scholars on 20 August.[86] Save for two students for whom there is no information, each scholar is listed in *Alumni Dublinenses* has having been born in Ireland. Three were recognisably native Irish: James Fyeagh, Malachy Horgan, of Limerick, and John Lysaght, of Dublin.[87] Two were also identifiably Old English: John Briscoe and Paul Prendergast, the latter having been born in Wexford and educated in Dublin.[88] The others were nearly all from Dublin or farther afield in Leinster, with several from Munster and Ulster, origins that mirror the British patterns of plantation and the dense New English settlement of Dublin and its environs.[89] Irish birth and Protestant religion were again the core criteria to be counted as a 'native'. Moreover, almost all students had been educated in a Dublin grammar school. The insistence that Trinity prefer Dublin-educated students highlights the inclination towards repopulating the college's student body with New English 'natives'. Three scholars are listed has having been educated at the Protestant St Patrick's grammar school.[90] The rest of the Dublin scholars were likely either taught by tutors or attended the Dublin Free School, which had been founded in the sixteenth century and regularly sent scholars, including James Ussher, to Trinity.[91] The Commons' concern with who should be attending the college and the assertion that Trinity students attend Dublin schools highlighted its intention to return the college its original function: a

---

[85] *CJI*, p. 279.
[86] TCD, MUN/V/5/2, p. 5.
[87] *Alumni Dublinenses*, pp. 312, 411, 520. Ford identifies these three surnames as included in the small contingent of twelve native Irish students at Trinity between 1638 and 1641. See Ford, 'Who Went to Trinity?', pp. 70, 74.
[88] *Alumni Dublinenses*, pp. 98, 681. Prendergast and Briscoe were two of the twelve Old English students at Trinity from 1638–41. See Ford, 'Who Went to Trinity?', pp. 70, 74.
[89] *Alumni Dublinenses*, pp. 4, 9, 43, 68, 101, 355, 356, 366, 616, 655, 681, 777, 824, 863, 887. On the New English settlement of Leinster and Munster and the plantation of Ulster, see Colm Lennon, *Sixteenth-Century Ireland: The Incomplete Conquest* (New York, 1995), pp. 178, 199–202, 229–36; Canny, *Making Ireland British*, pp. 187–242.
[90] William Addis, George Haggis, and John Wilson. *Alumni Dublinenses*, pp. 4, 355, 887; Murray, 'St Patrick's Cathedral', pp. 3–5.
[91] Ford, *Protestant Reformation*, pp. 92–3; Michael Quane, 'City of Dublin Free School', *Journal of the Royal Society of Antiquaries of Ireland*, 90:2 (1960), 163–89. From 1625 to 1643 two Trinity alumni, Leonard Shortall and Gilbert Booth, oversaw the school. See *Alumni Dublinenses*, pp. 81, 751; Quane, 'City of Dublin Free School', pp. 179–80.

Pale-based institution that defined the limits of and served the local settler population narrowly defined as 'natives'.[92]

The Irish Parliament's attempts to undo the Laudian reforms were part of a wider process of dismantling the structures of Wentworth's Ireland and reassert 'native' New English power in the college. Trinity had never been an institution that served the broad swath of Ireland's multi-confessional and multi-ethnic population. That did not change with Parliament's policies. But despite the highly charged political atmosphere and Trinity's centrality as a political and religiously contested institution, the Commons' efforts across 1641 were moderate when compared with the purging that had taken place in the 1640s at the Scottish universities. It seemed that the Commons was intent on rebuilding the college from the ground up, first by ensuring that the types of students who had traditionally attended Trinity continued to do so. The Commons did not depose any fellows, several of whom were holdovers from Chappell's tenure, nor did it remove Provost Washington, the Oxford import. Of course, the Commons did not necessarily have, nor did it assume, the authority to do so. But given the list of grievances, one might assume that the Commons would have pursued further reforms at Trinity if not for the outbreak of the Irish Rebellion.

The Rebellion that began in October 1641 inaugurated a decade of war in Ireland and introduced a new theatre to the wider conflict that had begun in Scotland. The reasons for the irruption in 1641 and the course of the subsequent Confederate Wars has been a subject of continuous debate, but the long-term social, political, and economic dislocation of Catholic native Irish and Old English stemming from the plantations and, more immediately, Wentworth's rule, were core causes.[93] There was, of course, the sectarian dimension to the rising, and the eventual joining of the native Irish and Old English in the Catholic Confederation of Kilkenny reinforced the extent of the fissure in Irish politics, especially after some Confederate leaders had collaborated with their Protestant counterparts in the Parliamentary session of 1640–1.[94]

Catholic grievances highlighted the extent to which Catholics had been excluded from public life and the exercise of political power in Ireland, while a series of complaints underscored the educational gulfs between Catholics and Protestants. One such petition noted that Ireland's Catholics were 'debarred of publicke Catholick free schooles, Colledges and universities for

---

[92] Ford, *Protestant Reformation*, pp. 79–80.
[93] See e.g., Canny, *Making Ireland British*, pp. 461–550; Clarke, *Old English*, pp. 156–61; Russell, *Fall of the British Monarchies*, pp. pp. 373–83; Michael Perceval-Maxwell, *The Outbreak of the Irish Rebellion of 1641* (Montréal, 1994), pp. 192–239.
[94] Micheál Ó Siochrú, *Confederate Ireland: A Constitutional and Political Analysis* (Dublin, 1999), pp. 256–7; Bríd McGrath, 'Parliament Men and the Confederate Association', in Micheál Ó Siochrú (ed.), *Kingdoms in Crisis: Ireland in the 1640s: Essays in Honour of Dónal Cregan* (Dublin, 2001), pp. 90–105.

education of their Children', while a similar remonstrance to the king stated that 'the one only University of Ireland doth exclude Catholicks, thereby to make us utterly ignorant of literature and civil breeding'.[95] Catholics rarely, if ever, sent their children to Trinity, whose pre-Laudian statutes equated Catholicism to heresy. But despite the Laudian relaxation of anti-Catholic language, native Irish Catholics still travelled to the continent for schooling.[96] In December 1641, the Catholic priest Patrick Roch sent a letter to Provost Washington that implicated Trinity in the 'affronts' against Catholics and labelled Washington as an 'ill disposed Governor, and enemy to that true Church, whereof you ought to be a prime Member'. Trinity was characterised as a 'den of Theeves' that robbed 'the Natives of this Kingdome of their priviledges (yea their Birth-rites) and extirpating those, whose lights would so shine forth to this Kingdome'.[97] Roch's grievances, and those of other Catholics, underlined the fact that Trinity was an institution that perpetuated the control of a settler class that continued to suppress Catholic rights and privileges. Trinity's insularity would only be reinforced in the ensuing decade.

In the Rebellion's aftermath, the attention of the now all-Protestant Irish Parliament understandably turned away from Trinity. The renovation of Trinity did not come to a halt, though during the early years of the 1640s the members of the college were concerned primarily with surviving. Provost Washington fled Ireland a week after the Rebellion's outbreak, never to return, and Chappell absconded to England in December 1641, thus eluding further prosecution.[98] At that early juncture, Trinity assumed a role as an English military outpost in Ireland and housed troops for the defence of Dublin.[99] The presence of troops drained the college financially. In December 1641, Vice-Provost Nathaniel Hoyle and the fellows petitioned the lords justices of Ireland for repayment, citing the 'great necessities now fallen on this whole Society'.[100] The lords justices then petitioned Wentworth's successor, the earl of Leicester, for aid in order to prevent the 'dissolution of so royall a foundation'.[101] Lords justices John Borlase and William Parsons provided some relief: in June 1642 they ordered the removal of 'all soldiers that pretend to be billeted on the Colledge', though this did little to improve Trinity's fortunes.[102] In a subsequent petition, Trinity's students noted that they had

---

[95] TCD, MS 840, fols 25r–26v; Corcoran, *State Policy in Irish Education*, pp. 68–9; Thomas Carte, *The Life of James Duke of Ormond*, new edn (6 vols, Oxford, 1851), II, p. 364.
[96] Ford, 'Who Went to Trinity?', pp. 55, 64–8.
[97] Patrick Roch, *A True Copie of a Letter Sent from Patrick Roch, a Romish Priest in Ireland, to Doctor Washington, Provost of the College of Dublin, and to the Whole Society* (London, 1641).
[98] TCD, MUN/V/5/2, p. 7; Harris, *Ware Works*, I, p. 567.
[99] TCD, MS 833, fols 1, 86; *CSPI 1633–47*, p. 447.
[100] TCD, MUN/P/1/329.
[101] TCD, MUN/P/1/331; HMC, *Calendar of the Manuscripts of the Marquess of Ormonde*, new series (8 vols, London, 1902–20), II, pp. 106–7.
[102] TCD, MUN/P/1/332.

been keeping a 'constant & carefull night watch for the safetie of the College' since 12 March, and were 'now brought to the lowest ebb of extremity & want of all necessaries, having no meanes to subsist', save for a daily ration of bread.[103] James Ware and several other committee members proposed seizing rebel lands and rents and transferring them to the support of the college.[104] It is likely that nothing came of this scheme, for soon after Trinity's governors began 'to live' on the college plate in an attempt to stay solvent, and would continue to do so at least until 1647.[105]

Shortly after the outbreak of the Rebellion, the Irish Privy Council appointed Faithful Teate 'to take the government of the colledge upon him, until it shall please his Majesty, to make a choise of a new Provost'. Teate and Dudley Loftus, the later lord chancellor, were to serve as temporary 'sub-rectors'.[106] Loftus does not appear to have assumed any role in the college, but Teate served as a virtual provost for several years, and he was allowed to occupy the provost's lodgings.[107] Teate was likely born in England and moved to Ireland at a young age during the plantation of Wexford; he studied at Trinity in the late 1610s and 1620s. It is probable that during this time Teate developed puritan sympathies, and during the 1630s he held a number of church offices in Cavan.[108] After the Rebellion, he fled Cavan for Dublin but was beaten, stripped, and robbed en route.[109] Teate's puritanism seemed agreeable to the college's ethos. But his selection likely had more to do with the virulent anti-Catholicism of Borlase and Parsons.[110] Teate shared their anti-Catholic disposition, and in May 1642 he preached an anti-Irish sermon at Christ Church at the invitation of the former Trinity fellow, John Harding.[111]

Teate's short tenure was marked by disaffection and destitution. Despite the Commons' criticism of learning under Chappell, instruction seems to have come to halt altogether, with student matriculations having ceased by late 1641. The Trinity matriculation album for this period simply notes 'chasm', with no matriculations recorded until following the Cromwellian

---

[103] TCD, MUN/P/1/334.
[104] CJI, p. 307.
[105] John Pentland Mahaffy (ed.), *The Plate in Trinity College, Dublin: A History and a Catalogue* (London, 1918), pp. 12–18.
[106] TCD, MUN/V/5/1, p. 2, MUN/V/5/2, p. 7.
[107] Stubbs, *History of the University of Dublin*, p. 84; Empey, 'Diary of Sir James Ware', p. 109.
[108] *Alumni Dublinenses*, p. 803; Terry Clavin, 'Teate, Faithful', *DIB*.
[109] TCD, MS 833, fols 61r–62v. It appears Teate received recompense in 1643. See BL, Add. MS 46927, fol. 55.
[110] See e.g. Terry Clavin, 'Parsons, Sir William', *DIB*; Patrick Little, 'The Irish 'Independents' and Viscount Lisle's Lieutenancy of Ireland', *Historical Journal*, 44:4 (2001), 941–61.
[111] *CSPI 1633–47*, p. 384; Raymond Gillespie, 'The Crisis of Reform, 1625–60', in Kenneth Milne (ed.), *Christ Church Cathedral, Dublin: A History* (Dublin, 2000), pp. 195–217, at 204.

conquest.[112] In spring 1642, the remaining fellows and scholars – consisting of a small 'native' nucleus devoid of imports – petitioned the Dublin authorities concerning the great 'distempers… through the defect of government and all collegiate discipline for the space of these seven moths past'. The petitioners noted that the college lacked a true provost and full complement of fellows and would 'return to its former chaos unless sustained by a governor whose extraordinary abilities may recover the same'. They proposed that Anthony Martin, bishop of Meath, assume control.[113] Martin was a meaningful choice. He was a Galway-born prelate who had attended Trinity before taking his MA at Emmanuel College. He was a fellow in 1610–11 under Provost Temple and likely served alongside Ussher; he received his doctorate from Trinity in 1625. During the contentious Convocation of 1634, he opposed imposing the English articles on Ireland, and during the fellows' dispute at Trinity in 1636 he ruled against Provost Chappell.[114] More recently, Martin had been an active participant in the Lords, conversed regularly with the Commons, and sat on the committee of grievances, which made him privy to the prosecutions against Chappell.[115] In many respects, the choice of Martin reflected the continued drive to return Trinity to its pre-Laudian character.

The lords justice thereafter summoned Teate for questioning in June 1642. The following March, Charles I directed the justices to install Martin in the college. The Irish Privy Council noted that Teate 'hath in many ways manifested himself to be ill affected unto the present established Government under his Majesty's subjection, and is thereby lyable to a further inquiry to be made unto his life and conversation'.[116] Teate's puritanism, parliamentarian sympathies, and anti-Catholicism led to his indictment. But Borlase and Parsons, with whom Teate shared religious and political sympathies, disregarded the king's order and kept Teate at Trinity until at least May 1644. By this time, Ireland's governance had been transformed with the appointment of James Butler, marquis and later duke of Ormond, as the king's lord lieutenant.[117] Writing in May 1644 from his base in Oxford, Charles ordered Ormond to commit Bishop Martin to 'the care and charge of the College in as full and ample a manner as any Provost has had it'.[118] Charles then appointed two former students, Thomas Locke and John Kerdiff, to fellowships.[119] The king concluded that 'these regulations are not to be used as precedent, but are made upon serious consideration of the present great exigencies of that house and

---

[112] TCD, MUN/V/23/1, pp. 13–17. See also Mahaffy, *Epoch in Irish History*, p. 290.
[113] Stubbs, *History of the University of Dublin*, p. 411.
[114] Cotton, *Fasti*, III, p. 118; *Alumni Dublinenses*, p. 557; Mahaffy, *Particular Book*, fols 118v–119r; TNA, SP 63/256, fols 11v–13r; McCafferty, *Reconstruction*, p. 83.
[115] *Lords Journal, Ireland*, pp. 152–3, 159–61.
[116] Stubbs, *History of the University of Dublin*, pp. 411–13.
[117] Toby Barnard, 'Butler, James, First Duke of Ormond (1610–1688)', *ODNB*.
[118] *CSPI 1633–47*, p. 394.
[119] *Ibid.*, p. 395; TCD, MUN/P/1/351, MUNV/5/2, p. 29; *Alumni Dublinenses*, pp. 464, 508.

the means to prevent the ruin thereof and the dissolution of that Society'.[120] Despite the Rebellion and the Commons' assault on Laud's reforms, Trinity remained governed by the Laudian statutes. Charles ensured their continued enforcement, but keeping Trinity operating, and wresting influence away from malcontents like Teate, Borlase, and Parsons, was more pressing. Martin effectively assumed the provostship while also holding a bishopric, while the elections of fellows would proceed without Laud's consent as chancellor, who was confined in the Tower of London.

Authorities therefore continued to jostle for control of the college as Trinity's fellows and students continued to press for support.[121] They implored the Dublin government for aid in an early 1644 petition likely authored by Nathaniel Hoyle, which emphasised the 'likely Ruin of the College (the mother of the University in this Kingdom)' without additional assistance.[122] Hoyle's supplication linked Trinity's welfare to that of Ireland as a whole. He stressed that the kingdom risked losing 'the Foundation from whence it should hereafter be supplied and served with all Professions'.[123] Trinity, by Hoyle's reasoning, was the institution from which the church and state's future ministers and magistrates would be trained. Of course, any assistance for Trinity would ultimately serve the wider purpose of preparing and placing godly ministers in Ireland, which Westminster's Irish Committee had highlighted as a key issue.[124] But in a time of great extremity, Hoyle linked Trinity's plight to that of the entire kingdom. A college that served an insular community was, during a time of hardship, reimagined as a territorial university in the service of the wider realm. As discussed below, a similar situation would arise in New England. In Ireland, Ormond ordered troops based in Dublin to pay a weekly sum to Trinity's bursar. It is unclear how long these payments lasted, but they did continue in some form under governor Michael Jones, even after the fall of Dublin in summer 1647.[125] Ormond was subsequently chosen as Trinity's chancellor, replacing Laud in 1645.[126] The exigencies of war, however, meant that Ormond would not devote the same energy to Trinity as his predecessor.

In the period immediately preceding the surrender of Dublin to English Parliamentarians in 1647, securing an amenable, and able, provost was an important step for Trinity's survival; the college register notes that by September 1646, Martin was in the college.[127] Fellows' elections continued

---

[120] *CSPI 1633–47*, p. 395.
[121] See e.g. TCD, MUN/P/1/340; TCD, MUN/V/5/2, p. 31.
[122] TCD, MUN/V/5/2, p. 24, MUN/P/1/348.
[123] TCD, MUN/P/1/348; Stubbs, *History of the University of Dublin*, p. 410.
[124] BL, Add MS 4771, fol. 6v.
[125] Patrick Little, 'Michael Jones and the Survival of the Church of Ireland, 1647–9', *Irish Historical Studies*, 43:163 (2019), 12–26, at 19–21.
[126] TCD, MUN/P/1/359.
[127] TCD, MUN/V/5/2, p. 2

in an *ad hoc* manner, with a shortage necessitating that their formal election, as outlined in the Laudian statutes, be ignored. What is evident, however, is the complete co-option of senior fellowships formerly held by Chappell's imports, who were either dead or had long been absent from the college.[128] Additionally, Hoyle, probably the longest tenured Trinity academic, left Trinity for Brasenose College, Oxford, in 1646.[129] Hoyle's departure, according to one 1647 petition, left only one senior fellow in the college: Thomas Seele. This led three junior fellows – John Kerdiff, James Bishop, and William Raymond – to petition Ormond for senior places. All three were elevated on Ormond's order.[130] Kerdiff had previously resigned his place as a fellow in the 1630s rather than accept Laud's statutes.[131] In 1648, the senior fellowship of Robert Cocke, another English import who had been absent 'these seven yeares last past', was assumed by Thomas Vale, who had previously been chosen as a junior fellow alongside three former 'native' scholars: Richard Coughlan, Roger Boyle, later bishop of Clogher, and Daniel Neyland, later dean of Ossory.[132] Coughlan proved to be a nuisance in the college, as he was charged with abusing fellows and calling Provost Martin a 'fool & knave & swore he would kick him'. He was expelled in October 1647.[133]

Table 3.1. Trinity College, Dublin Staff in the 1640s.

Provosts
Richard Washington, 1640–c. 1641
Faithful Teate, 1641–c. 1644, temporary 'sub-rector'
Dudley Loftus, c. 1641, temporary 'sub-rector'
Anthony Martin, 1645–50

Fellows and Associated Offices Where Known
Nathaniel Hoyle (1631), Vice Provost (1641–c.1646), Catechist (1643)
John Kerdiff (1631), made senior fellow, c. 1647
Thomas Seele (c. 1634/5), Senior Dean (1641), Catechist (1642), Bursar (1643)
James Bishop (1637), Lecturer (1643), made senior fellow, c. 1647
Gilbert Pepper (1637), Bursar (1641, 1642), Senior Dean and Registrar (1643)
Christopher Beckwith (1637)
Thomas Perceval (1639), Junior Dean (1641)

---

[128] *Ibid.*, p. 41; TCD, MUN/P/1/371.
[129] He would return to Trinity in 1652. Urwick, *Trinity College Dublin*, p. 60.
[130] TCD, MUN/P/1/369, 370, 371.
[131] Mahaffy, *Epoch in Irish History*, p. 289; TCD, MUN/V/5/1, p. 41 *Alumni Dublinenses*, pp. 464, 694.
[132] TCD, MUN/V/5/1, p. 72, MUN/V/5/2, p. 41; *Alumni Dublinenses*, pp. 89, 162, 618, 835.
[133] TCD, MUN/V/5/1, p. 73.

Table 3.1 (*continued*)

Fellows and Associated Offices Where Known
Christopher Pepper (1639), Senior Lecturer (1641)
William Raymond (1640), Lecturer (1641), Junior Dean and Lecturer (1643), made senior fellow, *c.* 1647
Thomas Locke (*c.* 1643), Junior Philosophy Lecturer (1643)
Richard Coughlan (*c.* 1643), Logic Lecturer (1643)
Roger Boyle (*c.* 1643), Grammar Lecturer (1643)
Nicholas Welsh (*c.* 1643), Librarian (1643)
Daniel Neyland (1646)
Thomas Vale (1646)

Sources: Fry, *Dublin University Calendar*; TCD, MUN/V/5/1, MUN/V/5/2; Mahaffy, *Epoch in Irish History*; *Alumni Dublinenses*

Thus by 1648, Trinity very nearly had a complete complement of fellows, many of whom had been educated at the college prior to the Laudian intrusion, in addition to a provost, himself a Trinity alumnus and former fellow and visitor, who had opposed the Laudian reforms. These machinations, in a time of pronounced hardship, evinces the significance placed on individuals who occupied places of influence in the universities. In spring 1647, when the Irish Commons asked Trinity's provost and fellows as to whether the house should reopen its prosecution of William Chappell, they readily assented.[134] And that fall, despite the fall of Dublin to English Parliamentarians, Church of Ireland services had resumed at Trinity.[135] With Governor Jones' support, Provost Martin refused Parliament's order banning the Irish liturgy.[136] Trinity's governors, it seems, were equally as hostile to the Parliamentarians as to the Laudians. This did not make up for the fact that during this period the college held no public commencements and saw few, if any, new matriculates.[137] Indeed, the narrative of Trinity's history from the completion of the Laudian statutes and the fall of Dublin to Parliamentarian forces has typically been marked by an emphasis on the college's destitution and its struggle to

---

[134] *CJI*, 367, pp. 369, 371, 373.
[135] Little, 'Michael Jones', pp. 18, 21. See also Martyn Bennett, 'God's Wall of Brass: Cromwell's Generals in Ireland, 1649–1650', in Martyn Bennett, Raymond Gillespie, and R. Scott Spurlock (eds), *Cromwell and Ireland: New Perspectives* (Liverpool, 2021), pp. 135–56, at 142.
[136] Harris, *Ware Works*, I, p. 158; Carte, *Ormond*, III, pp. 308–9; Barry Robertson, *Royalists at War in Scotland and Ireland, 1638–1650* (Burlington, VT, 2014), pp. 117–20. On the prohibition of the liturgy, see HMC, *Report on the Manuscripts of the Earl of Egmont Volume I: 1573–1661* (London, 1905), p. 425; St John D. Seymour, *The Puritans in Ireland, 1647–1661*, 2nd edn (Oxford, 1969), pp. 2–4.
[137] Mahaffy, *Epoch in Irish History*, pp. 288–90.

survive, and rightly so. But this section has endeavoured to demonstrate that during this period the college remained a strategic centre of power where rival authorities sought to exercise control to maintain, dismantle, or reconstruct conditions that fostered competing social orders. In this era the ebb and flow of royal and localised control, the irruptions of war, and the politics of individual influence and state power were all felt and negotiated at Trinity.

Harvard College

Writing in his memoir, the Cambridge, Massachusetts minister Thomas Shepard noted, with great relief, the suppression of two threats to Massachusetts society: the Antinomian Controversy and the Pequot War. For Shepard, the twin defeat of heresy and heathens led Massachusetts magistrates 'to think of erecting a School or College, and that speedily, to be a nursery of knowledge in these deserts, and to supply for posterity'. Shepard noted with delight that the General Court chose his home of Cambridge, then called Newtown, which had been 'kept spotless from the contagion of [Antinomian] opinions', as the site of the college.[138] In Ireland, the Rebellion's devastation drove Trinity to the brink of collapse, but there nevertheless remained an acute focus on higher education's importance in maintaining social order. In Massachusetts, the cessation of the plantation's early difficulties fostered the conditions to found a university.[139] Such conclusions of New England elites reinforced the notion that the perceived American wilderness represented a 'blank slate' upon which to construct a godly society whose endurance was all but guaranteed by a college that would, as highlighted in *New Englands First Fruits*, 'advance *Learning*, and perpetuate it to Posterity; dreading to leave an illiterate Ministry to the Churches, when our present Ministers shall lie in the Dust'.[140] In Cotton Mather's estimation, without Harvard the New England project would have 'been less than a *business of one age*, and soon have come to nothing'.[141]

Massachusetts' authorities experienced the pressures of Laudianism in England, Ireland, and the Netherlands, but the Laudian reforms themselves did not make their way to America. This saw the swift construction of a civil state and religious polity, which bolstered a 'New England Way' of

---

[138] Alexander Young (ed.), *Chronicles of the First Planters of the Colony of Massachusetts Bay, from 1623–1636* (Boston, MA, 1846), pp. 550–1; Staloff, *American Thinking Class*, p. 93.
[139] Mark A. Peterson, 'The Practice of Piety in Puritan New England: Contexts and Consequences', in Francis J. Bremer and Lynn A. Botelho (eds), *The World of John Winthrop: Essays on England and New England, 1588–1649* (Boston, MA, 2005), pp. 75–110, at 89–90.
[140] *New Englands First Fruits* (London, 1643), p. 23.
[141] Cotton Mather, *Magnalia Christi Americana*, ed. Thomas Robbins and Lucius F. Robinson (2 vols, Hartford, CT, 1853), II, p. 8.

uncompromising puritan orthodoxy.[142] Certainly, New England stands apart for the rapidity in which a durable colonial society was constructed, with the founding of a college the exemplar of this rapid pace, especially when compared to Ireland. But New England was hardly disconnected from events unfolding in the metropole. On the contrary, the colonies were alive to the deterioration of affairs in Britain and Ireland, and while clerics and magistrates in Massachusetts initially shared affinities with Parliament, they were also concerned with protecting their privileges, having already migrated across the Atlantic with the colony's governance.[143] New England settlers sought the construction of a godly society, underpinned by Reformed higher learning, while also seeking to safeguard their privileges, ensconced in the Massachusetts charter. This paralleled the experiences of the New English in Ireland and the Covenanters in Scotland.

Harvard's function, then, was twofold, and analogous to Trinity and the Scottish universities: it was to be both model and machinery. It had to both model the privileges and ethos of a settler population regularly at odds with the metropole and engineer and nurture the religious and intellectual orthodoxy of fledgling New England society. But despite the conclusion of the Pequot War and Antinomian Controversy, Harvard's embryonic years were marked by controversy and poverty. The first master, Nathaniel Eaton, was in keeping with Harvard's heritage as an anti-Laudian bastion established in the fashion of expatriate puritan cells. Backed by an external advisory board – the Overseers – consisting of leading ministers and magistrates, the nascent college seemed primed to replicate the successes of the Dutch academies.[144] But Eaton turned out to be a terrible choice, and his short-lived tenure was a disaster.[145] He physically abused his students and beat his assistant teacher, Nathaniel Briscoe, over a minor dispute. Eaton's wife was also implicated for mistreating Harvard's first students, and she admitted that she and her staff served students expired meat, though she denied knowingly serving the infamous 'hasty pudding' laced with goat faeces.[146] Appointed only a year earlier, the General Court dismissed Eaton in September 1639.[147] Eaton had prime intellectual credentials, having been educated at Franeker under William Ames, and he had been welcomed into Cambridge's godly community. But, as had been the case at Trinity in the 1630s under Robert Ussher, amenability to local authorities did not make up for ineffectual leadership.

---

[142] See e.g., Peterson, 'Practice of Piety', p. 85. See also Philip F. Gura, *A Glimpse of Sion's Glory: Puritan Radicalism in New England, 1620–1660* (Middletown, CT, 1984).
[143] Pestana, *English*, pp. 15–21, 29–31, 40–2; Agnès Delahaye, *Settling the Good Land: Governance and Promotion in John Winthrop's New England (1620–1650)* (Leiden, 2020), pp. 111–14.
[144] *Massachusetts Records*, I, p. 217.
[145] Mather, *Magnalia*, II, p. 10; Morison, *Founding*, chap. 17.
[146] *Winthrop Journal*, pp. 301–5; Morison, *Founding*, pp. 228–33.
[147] *HCR*, I, p. 173; *Massachusetts Records*, I, pp. 275, 277; *Winthrop Papers*, IV, pp. 142–3.

Nearly a year lapsed before Massachusetts' magistrates invited Henry Dunster to assume the position of Harvard president in August 1640.[148] Dunster, who had proceeded BA and MA from Magdalene College, Cambridge, served as a schoolmaster in England before migrating to New England shortly before his election.[149] Dunster later noted that he was chosen by a group of ten magistrates and sixteen elders, more than twice the size of the original twelve officials appointed to be Overseers in November 1637. In a memorandum written in 1653, Dunster stated that when he was initially elected, he was assured that he would only be responsible for teaching students, for he was called 'to undertake the instructing of the youth of riper years and literature after they came from grammer schools… No further care or distraction was imposed on mee or expected from mee but to instruct.'[150] Morison notes that such confusion may have been due to the use of the term 'president', not commonly used at Cambridge and not suggestive of the administrative duties that came with being 'master'.[151] Dunster's apparent misunderstanding of his role has fuelled the legend that authorities had hoped to lure the Bohemian educational reformer John Amos Comenius to Harvard at this early juncture.[152] Nevertheless, the fact that Dunster was chosen from among a large group of Massachusetts ministers and magistrates stresses the magnitude of the decision to select Eaton's successor. As it was at Trinity and the Scottish universities, Dunster's selection also highlighted the importance of individual actors – in the form of their training, their theological acumen, their conformability to the authorised norms of society, and, perhaps, their pliability to ruling authorities and capacity to mould institutions – in assuming positions of authority in higher education.[153]

If Harvard was to be a pillar of orthodoxy, it also had to be well maintained. Following the Bishops' Wars, the Covenanters had sought to strengthen the Scottish universities, which were to provide the foundation for a renewed godly state. Without access to vacated rents, Massachusetts officials instead drew on the charity of their neighbours and the rents of the ferry between

---

[148] *HCR*, I, p. 173.

[149] Morison, *Founding*, pp. 241–3; Francis J. Bremer, 'Dunster, Henry (Bap. 1609, d. 1659)', *ODNB*.

[150] Morison, *Founding*, p. 448; HUA, UAI 15.850, Box 1, Folder 16.

[151] See also Richard G. Durnin, 'The Role of Presidents in the American Colleges of the Colonial Period', *History of Education Quarterly*, 1:2 (1961), 23–31.

[152] Morison, *Founding*, pp. 244–5; Mather, *Magnalia*, II, p. 14; Albert Matthews, 'Comenius and Harvard College', *PCSM*, 21 (1919), pp. 146–90; Zachary McLeod Hutchins, 'Building Bensalem at Massachusetts Bay: Francis Bacon and the Wisdom of Eden in Early Modern New England', *New England Quarterly*, 83:4 (2010), 577–606, at 598–9.

[153] On the influence of cosmopolitan individual actors in imperial spaces, such as the New England of the early English empire, see e.g., Jennifer Wells, 'Prelude to Empire: State Building in the British Archipelago and Its Global Repercussions, 1620–1688' (unpublished PhD thesis, Brown University, 2016), pp. 241–2.

Boston and Charlestown to support the higher education project.[154] But the poverty of the college was also linked to New England's troubled economy, a product of dwindling immigration, failing credit, and shipping restraints, among other factors.[155] The plight eventually led the General Court to appeal to Parliament, though some feared that this would come at a price. Having already sparred with royal authorities concerning their charter, Massachusetts magistrates, including John Endecott, feared that by appealing to England, the colony risked relinquishing its autonomy to Parliament.[156] Nonetheless, a commission consisting of Hugh Peter, then minister at Salem, Roxbury minister Thomas Weld, and the Boston merchant William Hibbins arrived in England in September 1641. The trio was tasked with raising funds for the colony, advancing the cause of reformation in England, and soliciting monies for Harvard and the conversion of Native Americans.[157]

Regarding these latter two charges, the mission experienced early, modest success and secured donations for the 'enlargement' of the college and its library. The publication of *New Englands First Fruits* in London in early 1643 further advanced the cause. Unlike Trinity's supplications for assistance following the 1641 Rebellion, *New Englands First Fruits* did not portray a scholarly society on the brink of collapse, but instead a seminary in North America that was fully operational and warranted support. Portions of the pamphlet were likely authored by Dunster, Peter, John Cotton, the missionary John Eliot, and John Winthrop Jr, who had recently arrived in England to support the mission, and, supposedly, recruit prominent staff for the college, including Comenius.[158] *First Fruits* began by showcasing the progress of Native American conversion, a topic that had been a keen interest among eschatological thinkers in England.[159] The pamphlet noted the difficulties confronting missionary activity – unfamiliarity with Christianity, the manoeuvrings of Satan, and ignorance of native languages – but also some promising developments, including the conversion of native children and adults to Christianity. The section concluded with a rallying call, 'to spread the light of [the] blessed

---

[154] See e.g., *Massachusetts Records*, I, p. 304; HCR, I, pp. 173–5; *Winthrop Papers*, IV, p. 207–8.
[155] Bailyn, *Barbarous Years*, pp. 477–80; Morison, *Founding*, pp. 253–7.
[156] *Winthrop Papers*, IV, pp. 314–16.
[157] *Winthrop Journal*, pp. 353–4; Raymond P. Stearns, 'The Welde-Peter Mission to England', PCSM, 32 (1934), 188–246, at 188–97.
[158] On Winthrop Jr's mission, see *Winthrop Journal*, pp. 354, n. 52; Morison, *Founding*, p. 245; Hutchins, 'Building Bensalem', p. 599. On *First Fruits* and the question of authorship, see Morison, *Founding*, pp. 304–5; Worthington C. Ford, 'New Englands First Fruits', *Proceedings of the Massachusetts Historical Society*, 43 (1909), 259–66.
[159] See e.g. HP, 3/2/127A-128B, 13/92A–93B, 27/16/1A–14B. See also Webster, *Great Instauration*, pp. 35–6; Andrew Crome, 'The Jewish Indian Theory and Protestant Use of Catholic Thought in the Early Modern Atlantic', in Crawford Gribben and R. Scott Spurlock (eds), *Puritans and Catholics in the Trans-Atlantic World 1600–1800* (New York, 2016), pp. 112–30.

Gospel, to such as never heard the found of it… Lend us, we beseech you… your prayers, and help in heaven and earth for the furtherance of this great and glorious worke in our hands.'[160] Like Nathaniel Hoyle's appeals to support Trinity, *First Fruits* imagined a colonial setting in which education was crucial to constructing a godly community that incorporated all inhabitants, natives included.

But this was not the case. Like Trinity, Harvard was a college that mainly defined the limits of a community as opposed to incorporating those beyond the bounds of the godly.[161] Save for the energies of John Eliot, Edward Winslow, and others who would be instrumental in the missionary New England Company founded nearly a decade later, most New England puritans were antipathetic to missionary work, despite the stated goals of most English colonial ventures.[162] New Englanders were mainly concerned with fortifying the elect and delineating a division between the godly and 'unregenerate', the latter of whom could be civilised – a prerequisite to Christianisation – by way of the settlers' example, not through intentional missionary work.[163] Indeed, the authors of *First Fruits* were thankful, not dismayed, that God had pre-emptively 'cleared' many natives from Massachusetts through a smallpox epidemic.[164] The authors of *First Fruits*, in an attempt to raise money, may have employed the familiar language of a hellscape, tainted by Satan, calling out for Christianity, but their focus on Harvard communicated that a godly community had been firmly planted, with the university the clearest example for a Christian audience that the mature society was capable of maintaining social order and perpetuating its existence, albeit with additional assistance.[165] Likewise, in Ireland, New English settlers demarcated their community not by evangelising to the native Irish, but by reinforcing their status as a Reformed community among the reprobate through a university. *First Fruits'* authors made this Irish comparison explicit by underscoring the strict discipline of New England society, which, 'as Ireland' did not 'brooke', or tolerate, 'venomous beasts'.[166] This did not stop authorities from forcing native peoples

---

[160] *First Fruits*, pp. 3–21.
[161] J.H. Elliott, 'Religions on the Move', in Stephanie Kirk and Sarah Rivett (eds), *Religious Transformations in the Early Modern Americas* (Philadelphia, PA, 2014), pp. 25–45, at 36–7.
[162] Pestana, *English Atlantic*, p. 80.
[163] See e.g., Pestana, *Protestant Empire*, pp. 69–71; William Kellaway, *The New England Company, 1649–1776: Missionary Society to the American Indians* (London, 1961), pp. 5–8; Alden T. Vaughan, *New England Frontier: Puritans and Indians, 1620–1675*, 3rd edn (Norman, OK, 1995), p. 238; Charles L. Cohen, 'Conversion Among Puritans and Amerindians: A Theological and Cultural Perspective', in Francis J. Bremer (ed.), *Puritanism: Transatlantic Perspectives on a Seventeenth-Century Anglo-American Faith* (Boston, MA, 1993), pp. 233–56, at 244.
[164] *First Fruits*, p. 37.
[165] Cañizares-Esguerra, *Puritan Conquistadors*, pp. 9–12.
[166] *First Fruits*, p. 46.

and African slaves into the service of the new college.[167] Dunster took in two native hostages as servants, and according to a contemporary pamphlet, sought to educate them in their own language.[168] Several years later, however, Dunster found himself incapable of such bilingual instruction, and released them from his service, despite his hope to train his servants for eventual entry as students in the college.[169]

Any interest that Dunster had in educating forced indigenous labourers, however, was subordinate to supporting the college in its purpose of educating the future leaders of New England society. Thus, the second half of *First Fruits* outlined, in detail, the course of learning at Harvard, its operations, and its first commencement. There were, unsurprisingly, no references to the difficulties of Eaton's tenure. The pamphlet instead described the existence of a college 'to advance Learning, and to perpetuate it to Posterity', with a 'faire and comely' edifice, a large library with 'some Bookes', and an attached grammar school under the guidance of Elijah Corlet.[170] It lauded Dunster as an industrious teacher who 'trained up his Pupills in the tongues and Arts, and so seasoned them with the principles of Divinity and Christianity that we have to our great comfort, (and in truth) beyond our hopes, beheld their progresse in Learning and godlinesse also'. Dunster, as foil to Eaton, oversaw a system of education in which 'publique declamations in *Latine* and *Greeke*, and Disputations Logicall and Philosophicall' exhibited robust learning. The second part of the pamphlet devoted to Harvard, 'Rules, and Precepts that are observed in the Colledge', outlined familiar disciplinary strictures and a course of study. The system of learning resembled the course recommended by Robert Baillie for the Scottish universities in 1640, one that bore the Ramist influence of continental academies.[171] But it was also intelligible to a Cambridge- and Oxford-educated audience, with a course rooted in the Aristotelian *Organon*, punctuated by the study of Greek, Hebrew, Aramaic, and other biblical languages. A scholar, 'of godly life & conservation', who was able to produce of a 'summe of *Logick*, Naturall and Morall *Phylosophy*, *Arithmetick*, *Geometry* and *Astronomy*' and defend theses was then able to proceed to a degree.[172] The Harvard library augmented this curriculum. It possessed the works of Ramus, Ames, and Keckermann, the encyclopaedias of Comenius and Johan Heinrich Alsted, and the empirical works of Francis Bacon.[173] For would-be donors, the course of learning in *First Fruits* may have

---

[167] Wilder, *Ebony and Ivy*, pp. 26–33.
[168] Thomas Lechford, *Plaine Dealing: Or, Newes from New-England* (London, 1642), pp. 52–3.
[169] MA, MS 30, fol. 9r.
[170] *First Fruits*, pp. 24–5; Mather, *Magnalia*, I, p. 351.
[171] Morison, HCSC, I, pp. 139–44.
[172] *First Fruits*, pp. 26–30. The course described in *First Fruits* is mapped out in Morison, HCSC, I, p. 141; Norton, 'Harvard Text-Books', p. 362.
[173] Norton, 'Harvard Text-Books', pp. 383–438. Francis Bacon's *Advancement of Learning*

intimated the existence of an institution not unlike Oxford and Cambridge, but, as scholars from Perry Miller to Howard Hotson have emphasised, the library highlighted that the college was also on the vanguard of pedagogy and new learning.[174]

The course of study on its own, however, would not convince potential donors that Harvard existed. In the final section on Harvard, *First Fruits* gave an account of the college's first commencement, held in September 1642. The commencement drew governor John Winthrop and the 'Magistrates, and Ministers from all parts'.[175] The exercises included Latin and Greek orations, declamations, and disputations of 'Logicall, Ethicall, Physicall and Metaphysicall Questions' prior to the conferral of degrees upon the nine initial graduates: Benjamin Woodbridge, George Downing, John Bulkeley, William Hubbard, Samuel Bellingham, John Wilson, Henry Saltonstall, Tobias Barnard, and Nathaniel Brewster.[176] According to *First Fruits*, it was a ceremony according to English university customs – '*pro more Academiarum in Anglia*'.[177] The account of the commencement was the strongest evidence that Harvard existed and was operational – and, moreover, was an established institution that supported a mature society. Early modern commencements were important civic events, where graduates participated in a solemn and public ritual consisting of symbol-laden processions that exhibited a university's ethos and reinforced community stability. They underlined the role that universities played as the nurseries of the church and state and as purveyors of the extramural community's common good.[178] Trinity's lack of commencements in the 1640s highlighted the extent to which the Dublin community had been debased. Across the Atlantic, Harvard's first commencement signalled both the college's vitality, its function as both model and machinery, and the maturity of the commonwealth. For *First Fruits*' authors, and for Peter and Weld, the commencement was their most convincing evidence that their enterprise warranted further provision.

With *First Fruits* to assist their efforts, Peter and Weld experienced modest success. In May 1643, Ann Moulson, widow of the former lord mayor of London, donated £100 to fund poor students, while the mission secured additional donations totalling in excess of £200 for the college and a £20 annual payment from Mary Armine to support preaching to Native

---

was part of the library that John Harvard donated. See Potter, 'Catalogue', p. 198.

[174] See e.g., Miller, *New England Mind*, chap. 5; Morison, HCSC, I, pp. 187–90; Hotson, 'A Generall Reformation', pp. 201–3; Hutchins, 'Building Bensalem', pp. 596–9.

[175] *First Fruits*, p. 31; *Winthrop Journal*, pp. 416–17; Morison, HCSC, II, p. 582.

[176] HCR, I, p. 82; HUA, UAI 5.120, First Series, Box 1, Folder 2; Morison, *Founding*, pp. 257–62.

[177] *First Fruits*, pp. 31–6.

[178] See e.g. Frijhoff, 'Graduation and Careers', pp. 355–62; Helga Robinson-Hammerstein, 'Commencement Ceremonies and the Public Profile of a University: Trinity College, Dublin, the First One Hundred Years', *Università in Europa*, pp. 239–55.

Americans. Additionally, 'some Gentlemen of Amsterdam' donated £49 for a 'Printing-Press with Letters'.[179] And the funds were important, as Dunster made clear in a letter sent to the Massachusetts colonial treasurer in September 1643, in which he pleaded that the donations not be encumbered by various duties and rates.[180]

What Harvard gained in external funding it did not necessarily lose in control. An argument against the mission to England had been that it would cost the colony its autonomy. This betrays the idea that partisans viewed the nascent college as a space in which state power and control were tenuous and thus contestable. Early Harvard may have been supplied with English money, but it would continue to operate under Massachusetts' authority. *First Fruits'* authors stressed this point by stating that the Overseers, chosen by the General Court, 'are to promote the best good of [the college], and having a power of influence into all persons in it are to see that every one be diligent and proficient in this proper place'.[181] This is telling, for in September 1642, just before *First Fruits* was published, the General Court reconstituted the Overseers. The board would now consist of the 'all the magistrates of this jurisdiction' and the ministers of Cambridge, Boston, Watertown, Charlestown, Roxbury, and Dorchester – Massachusetts' secular and clerical elite. The General Court granted the Overseers 'full power & authority to make & establish all such orders, statutes, & constitutions as they shall see necessary for the instituting, guiding, & furthering of the said colledge & the severall members thereof from time to time in piety, morality, & learning'.[182] At one of its first recorded meetings, in December 1643, the Overseers wielded wide authority, appointing a treasurer, Herbert Pelham, to oversee Harvard's finances, and ordering two of Harvard's first graduates – George Downing and John Bulkeley – to serve as tutors under Dunster.[183] Moreover, the Overseers, acting in concert with President Dunster, also approved the college laws and lent legitimacy to the first commencement, both recounted in *First Fruits*.[184] Harvard was not an institution in need of royal (or Parliamentarian) intervention to correct internal difficulties, as was the case with Trinity in the 1630s. It was an educational institution over which an external authority already exercised strict supervision of the college's operations, discipline, and learning.[185] There is a sense that *First Fruits'* authors

---

[179] HCR, I, p. 175; Stearns, 'Weld-Peter Mission', pp. 219–20; Morison, *Founding*, pp. 303–13; Julius H. Tuttle, 'Thomas Weld's Receipts and Disbursements', *PCSM*, 14 (1911), 121–6, at 124.
[180] MA, MS 240, fol. 58r.
[181] *First Fruits*, p. 25.
[182] *Massachusetts Records*, II, p. 30; HCR, I, pp. 173–4.
[183] HCR, I, pp. clvi, 17; *Winthrop Journal*, p. 490.
[184] HCR, I, pp. 24–7.
[185] Staloff, *American Thinking Class*, p. 97.

were at pains to stress how well regulated, and thus well controlled, the college was in order to fend off external intervention.

In emphasising the reality of colonial control of the college, authorities highlighted Harvard's key function in perpetuating New England's social order. In June 1642 the General Court had ordered that 'parents & masters' train 'children in learning' so that they may be 'proffitable to the common wealth', focusing specifically on developing children's 'ability to read & understand the principles of religion & the capitall lawes of this country'.[186] Harvard sat at the top of this educational apparatus, in which youths were socialised into the authorised norms, orthodoxy, and order of New England society.[187] The diversity of opinions that both Weld and Peter encountered in England, where they engaged in the growing disputes between Presbyterians and Independents, also lent further weight to Harvard as a bulwark of Reformed orthodoxy in its New England mould.[188] And, the form and charge of the Overseers in the 1640s was analogous to the General Assembly's visitation commissions for the Scottish universities. Both represented the extension of state power, ideologically and administratively, into higher education to ensure the maintenance of authorised norms.

Table 3.2. Harvard College Staff, c. 1636–50.

Overseers, November 1637	
John Winthrop (Governor)	John Cotton
Thomas Dudley (Deputy Governor)	John Davenport
Richard Bellingham (Treasurer)	Hugh Peter
Roger Harlakenden	Thomas Shepard
John Humphrey	Thomas Weld
Israel Stoughton	John Wilson

First Master
Nathaniel Eaton, c. 1637–9

President
Henry Dunster, 1640

Treasurer
Herbert Pelham, 1643–50

---

[186] *Massachusetts Records*, II, pp. 6–7, 8–9.
[187] Staloff, *American Thinking Class*, p. 91.
[188] Stearns, 'Welde-Peter Mission', p. 236.

Table 3.2 (*continued*)

Tutors/Teachers
Nathaniel Briscoe, c. 1637–9
George Downing, c. 1643–6
John Bulkeley, c. 1643–6
Samuel Danforth, c. 1644–9(?)
Samuel Mather, c. 1646–9(?)
Jonathan Mitchell, c. 1646–50(?)
Comfort Starr, c. 1649–50

Sources: HCR; Sibley, *Biographical Sketches*

The General Court's authority over Harvard, via the Overseers, was crucial. It was also a key step in the broader formation of a 'puritan commonwealth' in North America, for in spring 1643 the colonies of Massachusetts, Plymouth, and New Haven joined in the United Colonies of New England. The confederation, which was underpinned by a shared puritan orthodoxy, strove to promote order, stability, and cohesion among the expanding settlements in New England. It also legitimated the existence of the colonial governments without recourse to metropolitan intervention.[189] Though traditionally viewed as a military alliance against Native Americans, the exclusion of settlements in Rhode Island and Maine reinforced the United Colonies as a highly confessionalised entity that promoted a specific brand of puritan state formation rooted in the congregationalist model.[190] The United Colonies defined the bounds of New England's godly society, including its religious definitions.[191] In September 1643, the same month that the Solemn League and Covenant was agreed, Harvard hosted an assembly of nearly fifty ministers that repudiated Presbyterianism and affirmed the region's congregationalist principles.[192] The following March, the Massachusetts General Court entered into a 'civil agreement' for the maintenance of religion with the United Colonies.[193] Harvard became the educational bedrock that undergirded this

---

[189] See Neal T. Dugre, 'Repairing the Breach: Puritan Expansion, Commonwealth Formation, and the Origins of the United Colonies of New England, 1630–1643', *New England Quarterly*, 91:3 (2018), 382–417.

[190] Pestana, *English Atlantic*, pp. 33, 56; Dugre, 'Repairing the Breach', pp. 409–11; Francis J. Bremer, 'The Puritan Experiment in New England, 1630–1660', *Cambridge Companion to Puritanism*, pp. 127–42, at 137.

[191] *Plymouth Records*, IX, pp. 3–8; *Winthrop Journal*, pp. 432–40. See also Dugre, 'Repairing the Breach', pp. 411–16.

[192] *Winthrop Journal*, p. 476; Williston Walker (ed.), *The Creeds and Platforms of Congregationalism* (New York, 1893), p. 139.

[193] *Winthrop Journal*, p. 503; *Massachusetts Records*, II, p. 61.

confederation and maintained its unique brand of puritan religion, especially as affairs worsened across the Atlantic.

With the coming of the civil war in England, New England was ideologically in Parliament's camp, though most New England authorities pursued a policy of neutrality. Because Massachusetts, in particular, exercised a great deal of autonomy in its governance as an authorised plantation, the colony had much more to lose by entering into the conflict.[194] Parliament had attempted to shore up New England support by lauding the propagation of the gospel in the colony and by removing customs on New England goods in March 1643.[195] Parliament also erected its own Committee for Foreign Plantations under the governorship of the earl of Warwick in November 1643. While analogous to the Laudian committee of the 1630s, the Parliamentary committee represented a power grab that wrested control of the colonies away from the king.[196] Among other charges, the committee was empowered to 'provide... to the Preservation and Advancement of the true Protestant Religion amongst the said Planters and Inhabitants, and the further Enlargement and Spreading of the Gospel of Christ amongst those that yet remaineth there in great and miserable Blindness and Ignorance'.[197] Evidence on the committee's workings is scarce, and scholars have noted that it largely failed to foster colonial backing for the Parliamentary effort.[198] Nevertheless, its existence threatened metropolitan oversight of New England religious affairs. The United Colonies, with its wide governing remit, combined with the reconstitution of the Harvard Overseers, represented a guard against such external intervention, real or imagined, into New England religious life.

That is not to say that New England, or Harvard, would be shuttered from the conflict embroiling Britain and Ireland. As historians have noted, while New England did not export its 'way' wholesale to England, it provided intellectual and spiritual manpower via scholars and ministers to England and Ireland.[199] This included most of Harvard's first graduates, including George Downing, John Bulkeley, and Samuel Mather, who after graduating taught at the college before migrating across the Atlantic.[200] Despite these connections,

---

[194] Pestana, *English Atlantic*, pp. 31, 39–43.

[195] Leo Francis Stock (ed.), *Proceedings and Debates of the British Parliaments Respecting North America, Vol. 1: 1542–1688* (Washington, DC, 1924), pp. 140–2.

[196] MacMillan, *Atlantic Imperial Constitution*, pp. 163–4; L.H. Roper, *Advancing Empire: English Interests and Overseas Expansion, 1613–1688* (Cambridge, 2017), pp. 128–9.

[197] *Acts and Ordinances*, I, pp. 331–3; Stock, *Proceedings and Debates*, pp. 147–9.

[198] Pestana, *English Atlantic*, pp. 48–9.

[199] *Winthrop Journal*, pp. 600–1; William L. Sachse, 'The Migration of New Englanders to England, 1640–1660', *American Historical Review*, 53:2 (1948), 251–78; Harry S. Stout, 'The Morphology of Remigration: New England University Men and Their Return to England, 1640–1660', *Journal of American Studies*, 10:2 (1976), 151–72.

[200] HCR, I, p. clviii. See also John L. Sibley, *Biographical Sketches of Graduates of Harvard University, in Cambridge, Massachusetts* (3 vols, Cambridge, MA, 1873–85), I, pp. 20–73, 78–87.

in religious matters New England and England – and Scotland – diverged radically, and rapidly, in the 1640s. While Scotland was rooted in the Covenant, with Scottish commissioners bent on exporting Presbyterianism to England via the Solemn League and Westminster Assembly, England witnessed the expansion of varying strands of Independency, with toleration, as opposed to confessional cohesion, emerging as a key principle. New England's intolerant puritanism was not a model for Civil War or Cromwellian England.[201]

Harvard, as New England's principal higher educational institution, was still politicised. Its early 'Formula of Admission' for students, while not a formal oath, provides clues into the affinities of those who controlled the university and evidence of its potential as a contested space.[202] In a brief address, the president admitted Harvard students by compelling them to obey the Massachusetts authorities and the college president; requiring them to pursue their studies and follow all college laws; and warning them against ill-discipline and damaging college property.[203] When compared to Scotland, where in the 1640s students were obliged to take the Covenant, and Ireland, where entrance oaths were a crucial point of contention in Trinity's statutes, Harvard's admission formula seems rather general. There were typical emphases on attentive studies and good order, and President Dunster and the Overseers continued to discipline students corporeally, even after Eaton's ouster.[204] But in the formula there was also no reference to upholding the majesty of the king, yet there is the requirement to 'observe all due reverence' to colonial authorities. While this is unsurprising, it is still telling, for in May 1644, the Massachusetts General Court ordered that anyone 'by word, writing, or action, endeavor to disturbe our peace, directly or indirectly, by drawing a party, under pretence that he is for the King of England, & such as adioyne with him, against the Parliament, shalbe accounted as an offender of an high nature against this comon wealth'.[205] Harvard could not admit an avowed royalist, nor would it countenance a detractor of the Massachusetts authorities. It served to bolster the legitimacy of localised governance and power in New England.

And in New England, the focus remained on supporting the institution. Harvard drew students from English settlements in the wider New England region, the Caribbean, and, in a few cases, overseas – the pressures of the Civil Wars seem to have driven aggrieved English scholars not only to the Covenanted universities of Scotland but also across the Atlantic.[206] To

---

[201] Pestana, *English Atlantic*, chap. 2; Hall, *Puritans*, chap. 9.
[202] On 'oaths' at Harvard, see Sletcher, 'Historians and Anachronisms', pp. 190–1; Morison, *Founding*, pp. 339–40.
[203] HCR, I, pp. 177–9; Morison, HCSC, I, pp. 60–1.
[204] *Winthrop Journal*, p. 510; *Plymouth Records*, IX, p. 95.
[205] *Massachusetts Records*, II, p. 69.
[206] Morison, HCSC, I, pp. 74–7; *Massachusetts Records*, II, p. 84.

support these students, in September 1644 Cambridge minister Thomas Shepard sent proposals to the commissioners of the United Colonies for the maintenance of 'poore Schollers' at Harvard. Shepard connected the 'publike benefitt' of all the colonies to the 'comfortable maintenance for that Schoole of the Prophets that now is'. Shepard requested that each plantation 'give yearely but the fourth part of a bushell Corne, or somethinge equivalent thereunto' to support students.[207] The commissioners approved Shepard's motion and ordered the general courts of each colony to begin providing for the college.[208] Between 1646 and 1653, this 'college corn' accounted for almost £50 annually.[209] But in addition to funding, scholars also required intellectual nourishment. In a December 1645 letter to Hugh Peter, Shepard requested that 'You should do very well to helpe our Colledge with a more compleat Library, we have very good wits among us and they grow up mightly, but we want bookes.' Shepard thought that Harvard's library required more Scholastic texts – 'we want schoolmen especially' – perhaps to complement the college's collection of Reformed, humanist works. He had a specific source in mind: 'we were thinking to desire the Archbishop's Library'.[210] Parliament had transferred Laud's library to the possession of Peter, already the custodian of Ames' library, assuming that he would gift the books to Harvard.[211] The library, however, would not cross the Atlantic.[212] Having his library used at a Reformed seminary – the very type of institution he sought to suppress – would have been a final, lasting insult for Laud.

Three years after Shepard's proposals, Dunster sent the confederation queries regarding discipline, scholarships, and additional funding. On the point of which students were eligible for scholarships, the confederation recommended that funding should first go to scholars who come from 'Colonies that doe contribute liberally and consequently' before any students from 'forraine places, as old England, Virginia and the like'.[213] Dunster also requested that the funding scheme be transformed into a tax, though the confederation skirted his appeal.[214] Shepard and Dunster's petitions highlighted how Harvard's operations were tied to New England as a whole, and how college authorities drew upon the institutional framework provided

---

[207] *Plymouth Records*, IX, pp. 19–21.

[208] *Ibid.*, IX, p. 19.

[209] HCR, I, pp. 179–80; *Massachusetts Records*, II, p. 86; *Winthrop Journal*, pp. 568–9; Morison, *Founding*, pp. 315–17.

[210] C.H. Firth (ed.), 'Thomas Shepard to Hugh Peter, 1645', *American Historical Review*, 4:1 (1898), 105–7, at 106.

[211] Morison, *Founding*, pp. 267–8.

[212] Joseph B. Felt, 'Memoir of Hugh Peters', *New England Historical and Genealogical Register*, 5:3 (1851), 275–94, at 278–9.

[213] MA, MS 58, fols 8–9.

[214] Morison, *Founding*, pp. 320–1.

by the United Colonies. The focus was on creating and, through a college, maintaining a godly magistracy and ministry.

The confederation opined that 'those who have benefitt by the contributions of the Collonies should be engaged to attend the service of the country upon tender of imployment & maintenance sutable to their condition & state of the Country'.[215] A year earlier, the confederation had stressed the need to keep Harvard-educated scholars in New England.[216] The Massachusetts General Court ordered that ministers and elders take 'due care' to 'improve & exercise such students, especially in divinity, as, through the good hand of God, may issue forth of the colledges, that so… they be not forced from us'. It mandated that each church 'which hath but one officer' to bear 'the charge of such scholler' to assist church officers.[217] Students funded by the colonies, ideally, would serve New England. Just as the Irish Parliament sought to maintain Trinity as a seminary for the New English 'natives', New England authorities conceived of Harvard as a seminary for New Englanders first and foremost. Though these orders did not necessarily stem migration to England, it did underline Harvard's purpose as a seminary for the burgeoning colony.

Scholarships, funded by contributions from the wider confederation, would support students attending an institution that perpetuated the social order and rigid orthodoxy of New England society. Contemporaneous to Shepard's push to fund students was a series of orders in the Massachusetts General Court that outlawed Anabaptism, which put it at odds with an increasingly tolerant, and religiously experimental, England.[218] The parameters of New England orthodoxy were defined in a synod held over 1646–8 and codified in the Cambridge Platform.[219] While mollifying Parliament by accepting several tenets of the Westminster Confession – and thus heading off external intervention – the Cambridge Platform repudiated Presbyterianism and championed the core aspects of congregationalist church membership as biblically ordained.[220] The platform empowered New England authorities to censure and suppress those who veered from official orthodoxy.[221]

In a newsletter sent to Samuel Hartlib in December 1645, Robert Child contested Harvard's existence and implicated the college in New England's intolerance. Child was among the aggrieved New England 'Remonstrants' who supported transporting the Directory of Worship – and thus the Presbyterian system – across the Atlantic to replace the theocracy then in place.[222] He

---

[215] *Plymouth Records*, IX, p. 96.
[216] MA, MS 240, fol. 125r; *Plymouth Records*, IX, p. 82.
[217] *Massachusetts Records*, II, p. 167.
[218] See e.g., *ibid.*, II, p. 85, III, pp. 18–19, 51.
[219] *Plymouth Records*, IX, pp. 81–2; *Massachusetts Records*, III, pp. 70–3.
[220] Bremer, 'Puritan Experiment', p. 139.
[221] Walker, *Creeds and Platforms*, pp. 157–237; B.R. Burg, 'The Cambridge Platform: A Reassertion of Ecclesiastical Authority', *Church History*, 43:4 (1974), 470–87.
[222] Pestana, *English Atlantic*, pp. 77–8.

observed not an ordered and cohesive commonwealth, but a society that had stagnated under an oppressive regime: 'Truly I suppose all thinges would prosper in this place if they would give libertie of conscience otherwise I expect nothing to thrive.' Harvard was a cog in this intolerant system that 'goes on indifferently well every yeare'.[223] The General Court censured Child and other Remonstrants, while New England's defenders engaged in a pamphlet war in England to defend the colony.[224] Yet despite the ink spilled over the nature of the 'New England Way', one point remained clear: absent of direct intervention from the metropole, Harvard would endure as a bedrock of the embryonic New England social order.

Conclusion

Trinity and Harvard were each vital to the maintenance and endurance of their localised social orders in an era of upheaval and transition. By the end of the 1630s, Trinity had become increasingly Laudian in character. But as the Irish Parliament's policies demonstrated, the college remained a contested space and emerged as an epicentre in the broader fight to undo the Laudian reforms. This was not merely a redress of the violation of Trinity's autonomy, but the attempted renovation of the college to its pre-Laudian ethos as part of a wider recalibration away from the perceived misrule of Wentworth. At root was the control of an institution that had perpetuated the distinctive social order, and identity, of a 'native' settler community, the New English. It is this emphasis on the New English interest, beginning with Parliament's policies in 1641 and continuing throughout the 1640s, that demonstrates the persistence of the notion that Trinity was an institution beholden to a narrow minority that served an autonomous, albeit established church. Harvard was similarly crucial to its settler population, both in supporting the doctrinal orthodoxies of New England puritans and in upholding the legitimacy of the colonial governing elite, who were at regular pains to safeguard their liberties. As *First Fruits* demonstrated and as subsequent actions by the General Court and United Colonies bore out, Harvard served as a legitimating force in a period in which the nature of New England's colonial governance and its inflexible religiosity were regularly contested.

To be sure, Trinity during this time had not been resurrected as a New English seminary, at least not completely, despite an amenable provost and a handful of sympathetic fellows. There were active, if piecemeal, attempts to return Trinity to its pre-Laudian ways, which resulted partly from the power vacuums created by the Rebellion. Harvard, meanwhile, with the support and

---

[223] YUL, OSB MS 16794; HP, 15/5/1A–2B.
[224] *Massachusetts Records*, III, pp. 90–1. On the pamphlet war, see Pestana, *English Atlantic*, pp. 235–40.

strict oversight of local authorities, and from a location far removed from the wars, did evolve, rather quickly, into a seminary for New England, with an emphasis on supporting and training the sons of New England settlers. In both spaces, the actions and agency of individuals, coupled with rival authorities' acute focus on who occupied spaces of authority within higher education – the personnel necessary to distil authorised norms and consolidate political power – were essential. Like the situation in Scotland, political, religious, and social upheaval did not preclude intervention in higher education – it invited it. As will be seen in the following chapter, the dawn of the Cromwellian era would see renewed attention paid to the affairs of Trinity, Harvard, and the Scottish universities, as they were employed as tools to consolidate conquest and advance empire.

4

The Cromwellian Conquest and the Universities

In the British Isles, the Cromwellian conquests of Ireland and Scotland between 1649 and 1653 upended each kingdom's religious, political, and social dynamics. The birth of the English Commonwealth also heralded stricter oversight of English plantations across the Atlantic.[1] The universities of Scotland, Ireland, and New England provided potentially ready-made machinery to extend Cromwellian rule, build up and consolidate the Cromwellian social order, and enlarge the dominion of the Commonwealth state beyond England.[2] There was already important precedent for how the Cromwellian regime would wield higher education to consolidate its rule. In England, Parliamentarians, and thereafter the Cromwellians, abolished political and religious institutions, like the monarchy and established church, antithetical to its conception of an ordered commonwealth. At the same time, they incorporated Cambridge, which Parliament seized in 1644, and Oxford, conquered in 1646, into the bounds of Parliamentarian power in order to turn them into reliable instruments of the emerging republican state.[3] Parliamentarians inaugurated a series of visitations that purged masters and fellows of royalist and Laudian sympathies who refused to conform to Parliamentarian control, subscribe to loyalty oaths, or accept the Westminster's Assembly Directory of Worship, all components of the embryonic, anti-monarchical social order that was under construction in the late 1640s.[4] The Cromwellians drew upon these Parliamentarian antecedents to prosecute further reform, purging Stuart sympathisers and orienting the

---

[1] On the Cromwellian conquests of Ireland and Scotland, see David Stevenson, 'Cromwell, Scotland and Ireland', in John Morrill (ed.), *Oliver Cromwell and the English Revolution* (London, 1990), pp. 149–80; Micheál Ó Siochrú, *God's Executioner: Oliver Cromwell and the Conquest of Ireland* (London, 2009); Canny, *Making Ireland British*, pp. 569–78; Stevenson, *Revolution and Counter-Revolution*, pp. 180–210; Dow, *Cromwellian Scotland*, pp. 13–34. On the Commonwealth and the Atlantic colonies, see Pestana, *English Atlantic*, chap. 3.
[2] Jim Smyth, 'Empire-Building: The English Republic, Scotland and Ireland', in Ariel Hessayon and David Finnegan (eds), *Varieties of Seventeenth- and Early Eighteenth-Century English Radicalism in Context* (Farnham, 2011), pp. 129–44, at 132–3.
[3] Tilly, 'Reflections', p. 24.
[4] For useful analyses of Parliament's reform of Cambridge and Oxford, see Twigg, *Cambridge and the English Revolution*, pp. 92–120; Ian Roy and Dietrich Reinhart, 'Oxford and the Civil Wars', *History of the University of Oxford*, pp. 687–731, at 720–31.

universities towards a monarch-less commonwealth via regular visitations and the installation of sympathetic fellows.[5]

Parliament's victories in the 1640s and the Cromwellian conquests, coupled with the rise of the Commonwealth, unleashed a torrent of literature that called for a range of radical reforms in higher education. Historians of higher learning have highlighted the proliferation of revolutionary ideas regarding education during this period. Calls for reform went beyond curricular improvements to include the adoption of new modes of pansophism and scientific inquiry and the relegation of theology and philosophy. Some thinkers, like the New Model Army chaplain William Dell, wished to secularise Oxford and Cambridge completely, to divorce the universities from their function as machineries of ideological power in the production of churchmen.[6] Many puritan educational reformers were also part of the loose network of empiricists and scientists associated with the Hartlib Circle, a number of whom held positions in the Cromwellian administrations in England and Ireland.[7] But, as several scholars have shown, it was rare that radical educational ideas were actually operationalised in the universities of England, Scotland, Ireland, or New England during the Interregnum, either in the Commonwealth era or during the Protectorate.[8] Indeed, acting in his role as vice-chancellor of Cromwellian Oxford, the eminent Independent theologian John Owen noted that the university had persisted in its primary function with 'greater strength than usual' in providing the land with stability and continuity in a sermon at the Oxford Convocation of 1657. For Owen, well-ordered universities were essential to maintaining the health of the commonwealth.[9]

And yet, despite the precedent of Parliament's reform of Oxford and Cambridge, there was no uniform strategy or policy that governed the Cromwellian approach to the universities in Ireland, New England, and

---

[5] *Acts and Ordinances*, I, pp. 925–7; CJ, VI, p. 200; Twigg, *Cambridge and the English Revolution*, pp. 149–203; Blair Worden, 'Cromwellian Oxford', *History of the University of Oxford*, pp. 733–72, at 733–43.

[6] Christopher Hill, 'The Radical Critics of Oxford and Cambridge in the 1650s', in John W. Baldwin and Richard A. Goldthwaite (eds), *Universities in Politics: Case Studies from the Late Middle Ages and Early Modern Period* (Baltimore, MD, 1972), pp. 107–32, at 131–2.

[7] See e.g., Webster, *Great Instauration*, pp. 48–51, 523–8; idem (ed.), *Samuel Hartlib and the Advancement of Learning* (Cambridge, 1970), pp. 11–64. John Twigg, 'The Limits of 'Reform': Some Aspects of the Debate on University Education during the English Revolution', *History of Universities*, 4 (1984), 99–114; J.J. O'Brien, 'Commonwealth Schemes for the Advancement of Learning', *British Journal of Educational Studies*, 16:1 (1968), 30–42; Elizabethanne Boran, 'Malignancy and the Reform of the University of Oxford in the Mid-Seventeenth Century', *History of Universities*, 17 (2002), 19–46.

[8] Boran, 'Malignancy', p. 41; Toby Barnard, *Cromwellian Ireland: English Government and Reform in Ireland, 1649–1660* (Oxford, 1975), pp. 213–48.

[9] Peter Toon (ed.), *The Oxford Orations of Dr John Owen* (Callington, 1971), pp. 40–5. On Owen and Oxford, see also Crawford Gribben, *John Owen and English Puritanism: Experiences of Defeat* (New York, 2016), pp. 128–30.

Scotland. Rather, as this chapter demonstrates, Cromwellian imperial formation as it was borne out in the universities beyond England was rooted in responding to localised needs and realities.[10] The nascent British republic endeavoured, to varying degrees, to control the universities as part of a wider process of imperial subjugation, the strategies and tenor of which differed across the three spaces under examination. Cromwellian university policy was framed by the vision of a social order rooted in republican and anti-monarchical mores. It was underpinned by a religious ethos in which Independency flourished and a policy of liberty of conscience, which would invite the multiplying of 'sects' in England and beyond, that was extended to most Protestants.[11] The English universities, as Blair Worden has argued, were meant to inculcate a broad puritan orthodoxy, support preaching, and thus 'stabilise' the land after years of upheaval. Radical proposals were not entertained seriously in governing circles, as the universities served too important a function to transform drastically or to eliminate completely.[12] But what did this mean for universities in conquered realms and across the Atlantic? Cromwellian imperialists contended that conquest would transmit reform, freedom, and improvement to the enlarged republican dominion, thereby fostering a more durable union under the Cromwellian aegis.[13] To cultivate the conditions to build a social order rooted in Commonwealth principles, the universities in conquered realms had to be incorporated. Yet in these spaces, the forces of Cromwellian imperial formation clashed with rival forces of state and communal power in the universities, where ideological power could be developed and real authority exerted in the institutions that, during the 1640s, had been crucial to the realisation of competing visions of healthy commonwealths.[14] In Scotland, the universities were the machinery by which the Covenanters began constructing a confessional state; in Ireland, Trinity was the institutional basis for the revitalisation of a communal identity and narrowly puritan social order; and in New England, Harvard was essential to the formation of a godly plantation defined by both its own developing settler identity and by its opposition to what was unfolding in England.

In many ways, Cromwellian approaches echoed the initiatives of royal authorities over a decade earlier, only at this juncture university reform

---

[10] See especially Hindle, *State and Social Change*, pp. 15–16.

[11] John Spurr, *The Post-Reformation: Religion, Politics and Society in Britain 1603–1714* (London, 2006), pp. 103–5; John Morrill, 'The Puritan Revolution', *Cambridge Companion to Puritanism*, pp. 67–88, at 71–9. On Cromwellian liberty of conscience, see e.g., Haefeli, *Accidental Puritanism*, chap. 13; Jeffrey R. Collins, 'The Church Settlement of Oliver Cromwell', *History*, 87:285 (2002), 18–40, at 18–19; Blair Worden, 'Toleration and the Cromwellian Protectorate', in W.J. Sheils (ed.), *Persecution and Toleration*, Studies in Church History vol. 21 (Oxford, 1984), pp. 199–233.

[12] Blair Worden, *God's Instruments: Political Conduct in the England of Oliver Cromwell* (Oxford, 2013), p. 123.

[13] Smyth, 'Empire-Building', pp. 139, 142.

[14] Mann, *Sources of Social Power*, pp. 22, 27–8.

policies came on the heels of military conquest. The first part of this chapter focuses on Ireland and New England, where two corresponding acts for the propagation of the gospel highlighted the regime's varied priorities for, and thus its divergent approach to higher education in, each location. Whereas Parliament exercised systematic control over Trinity to activate its religious policy, it was more concerned with missionary activity in New England. Harvard was left to its own devices, which underlined New England's intent to maintain control over its clerical nursery. The second part examines the breakdown of the Covenanting consensus in Scotland on the eve of the Cromwellian conquest and the subsequent subjugation of the universities. In much the same way that Charles and Laud pursued a British university policy, so too did the Cromwellians, albeit under vastly different circumstances, through different means, and to different ends. Even Harvard was employed, albeit indirectly, by the nascent British republic, as an institution that was already producing partisans to consolidate Cromwellian rule. Amidst the upheavals of the wider political, religious, and social dynamic of the British Atlantic born from the execution of Charles I, and through the crucible of war and conquest, the universities' strategic, and contested, function as of structures of power and purveyors of the wider social order was in many ways amplified.[15]

Harvard, Trinity, and Cromwellian Expansion

In 1649 and 1650, the Rump Parliament passed a series of acts for advancing the gospel in Wales, northern England, Ireland, and New England.[16] This legislation was reflective of the Commonwealth's emphasis on propagating the gospel, a core aspect of the recalibration of the English social order, which also promoted liberty of conscience and Independency. The legislation also attempted to export these visions to Ireland and New England.[17] Each act was rooted in providing maintenance for ministers and schoolmasters, though there were telling differences. The acts for northern England and Wales did not make any mention of provisions for higher education, as neither space possessed universities. Ireland and New England had the collegiate machinery to aid the cause of evangelisation, to potentially reconstruct the social orders of each locale by socialising new partisans according to the vision of the imperial republic. This machinery also provided the possibility of incorporating inhabitants beyond the Protestant settler populations. Yet these were processes that were nevertheless conditioned by localised realities, as evidenced by the ways these acts, and the Cromwellian state's approaches, diverged.

[15] MacKenzie, 'Contested Space', pp. 68–9.
[16] *Acts and Ordinances*, II, pp. 197–200, 342–8, 355–7; CJ, VI, pp. 366, 370, 374, 396.
[17] See e.g., Smyth, 'Empire-Building', pp. 131–2; Elliott, 'Europe of Composite Monarchies', pp. 59–60; Armitage, *Ideological Origins*, pp. 21–3.

The Rump passed the Act for Promoting and Propagating the Gospel of Jesus Christ in New England in July 1649, nearly a year prior to the act for Ireland. The act for New England erected a body in England to oversee the conversion of Native Americans, which had important implications of higher education across the Atlantic. Parliament lauded the progress of the gospel among the 'Heathen Natives of that Countrey' because of the 'pious care and pains of some godly English of this Nation'. But the continued success of this enterprise would not be realised 'unless fit instruments be encouraged and maintained to pursue it, Universities, Schools, and Nurseries of Literature setled for further instructing and civilising them'. The act therefore created the Society for the Propagation of the Gospel in New England. The corporation, also known as the New England Company, consisted of a president, treasurer, and fourteen assistants in charge of fundraising and managing the missionary endeavour in New England. Edward Winslow, the former governor of Plymouth, was one of the few members who had experience across the Atlantic, and the London lawyer William Steele, later lord chancellor of Ireland, served as its first president.[18]

At first glance, the act seemingly evaded the issue of exporting Cromwellian religious policy to New England. There, liberty of conscience was anathema to the orthodox polity that had been constructed in the 1640s.[19] The focus on indigenous conversion also did not necessarily indicate any renewed advances of the Cromwellian regime to wield greater authority over English subjects in the New England plantation in religious matters or otherwise.[20] Carla Pestana posits that the conversion of Native Americans was a key way to repair the relations between the New England authorities and Parliament, which had frayed during the 1640s.[21] In New England, John Eliot was at the forefront of this missionary drive, and by the time Parliament passed its act in July 1649, both the Massachusetts General Court and the commissioners of the United Colonies had granted Eliot money and land in order to proselytise to indigenous peoples.[22] Though Eliot was exceptional among puritans for the zeal with which he pursued missionising, other ministers in 'orthodox' New England – the evangelising energies of Roger Williams and Samuel Gorton notwithstanding – did not share similar sentiments. In a letter of December

---

[18] *Acts and Ordinances*, II, pp. 197–200; CJ, VI, p. 271; Stock, *Proceedings and Debates*, p. 209; Kellaway, *New England Company*, pp. 17–20.
[19] Bremer, *Puritan Experiment*, pp. 126–7, chap. 9; Anderson, 'New England in the Seventeenth Century', pp. 204–8.
[20] Hall, *Puritans*, pp. 327–8. On the act and the relationship between New and Old England, see also Linda Gregerson, 'The Commonwealth of the Word: New England, Old England, and the Praying Indians', in Linda Gregerson and Susan Juster (eds), *Empires of God: Religious Encounters in the Early Modern Atlantic* (Philadelphia, PA, 2011), pp. 70–83.
[21] Pestana, *English Atlantic*, pp. 79–81.
[22] *Massachusetts Records*, II, pp. 166, 178–9, 189, III, pp. 85, 106; *Plymouth Records*, IX, pp. 137–8.

1646, Thomas Shepard noted that 'the poore Indians' had not come to know god 'till now very lately', though 'diverse of them the Lord is now hammering & fitting (we hope) to be vessells of glory'.²³ In February 1648, President Dunster, in a letter to Christian Ravius, also highlighted with enthusiasm the course of learning 'in the woods amongst the Indians in their Savage booths or wigwams'.²⁴ In London, Edward Winslow delivered news of this godly progress to Parliament's attention, with two pamphlets – Shepard's *Clear Sunshine of the Gospel* (1648) and Winslow's *Glorious Progress of the Gospel Amongst the Indians in New England* (1649) – ultimately doing for evangelisation what *First Fruits* had done for Harvard.²⁵ Winslow's news about the New England missions spurred Parliament to support the cause of evangelisation – and recuperate English perceptions of New England.

Evangelisation efforts, ensconced in the act establishing the New England Company, nevertheless had ramifications for New England's autonomy over Harvard. There were some, like Benjamin Worsley, who thought it was essential that Parliament 'assert & take Care' of colonial governance, and in an August 1649 letter to Samuel Hartlib, Worsley thought it important that the Parliament do more to 'promote the higher ends', including the 'Education of Indians'.²⁶ There was no Parliamentary takeover, however, and the July 1649 act in actuality further legitimised colonial governance by imbuing the United Colonies with the power to receive and distribute the funds that the New England Company raised for propagating the gospel and 'maintaining of Schools and Nurseries of Learning, and for the better education of the children of the Natives'.²⁷ Notably absent is any explicit mention of Harvard. Just prior to the legislation's passage, the clause 'shall conduce for the maintaining of the universities of Cambridge in New-England, and other schools and nurseries of learning there, and for the preaching and propagating of the Gospel among the natives' was removed.²⁸ According to Morison, a Suffolk MP, John or Brampton Gurdon – both relatives of Richard Saltonstall whose son, Henry, was among Harvard's first graduates – were responsible for attempting to include the college within the company's responsibilities.²⁹ The focus, and most importantly, the funding, would remain on converting Native Americans, not on educating the children of English settlers at the local college.³⁰

---

[23] BL, Add MS 4276, fol. 138.
[24] MHS, MS N-1143, p. 115.
[25] Thomas Shepard, *The Clear Sunshine of the Gospel Breaking Forth Upon the Indians in New-England* (London, 1648); Edward Winslow, *The Glorious Progress of the Gospel Amongst the Indians in New England* (London, 1649).
[26] HP, 33/2/1A–1B.
[27] *Acts and Ordinances*, II, p. 199.
[28] CJ, VI, p. 246; Stock, *Proceedings and Debates*, p. 209.
[29] Morison, *Founding*, pp. 321–2, 321 n. 3.
[30] Kellaway, *New England Company*, pp. 14–15.

This proved to be a momentary blow to President Dunster's drive to raise more money for Harvard, and he would continue to press the United Colonies for continued assistance through the end of his presidency. Formal assistance, which led to the founding of the Indian College, would not come for four more years, as the focus remained on supporting the missionary efforts of Eliot, Thomas Mayhew, and others prior to 1653.[31] Dunster's own academic interests in converting Native Americans and seeing them schooled at Harvard persisted, however. In his letter to Ravius, he spoke at length about his observations on the Massachusett language, though he remarked that 'We doe not trouble the Indians to learn our English, But onely such as for their own behoof doe it of their owne accord', though he highlighted Eliot's efforts 'to bring their tongue under the Skill of Rules of Grammar'.[32] Literacy was a 'civilising', and thereby destructive force to indigenous ways of life, and Eliot's attempt to teach natives to read was an essential precondition to understanding scriptural languages in university study, where students would be immersed in the liberal arts that buttressed ordered, Christian societies.[33] At Harvard, moreover, any natives would also be taught Hebrew, where they would utilise Ravius' grammars.[34] Ravius, having previously been in contact with James Ussher about teaching at Trinity, seems to have now been interested in a position at Harvard, though Dunster noted that 'Our Infant Colledge compared with the Academyes in Europe' was unworthy of his talents.[35] Yet in 1649, neither Ravius' services nor formal university instruction for Native Americans would be forthcoming.

On the heels of Charles I's execution, the birth of the Commonwealth, and the seismic impact it had on the political, religious, and social order in the British Isles, higher education in New England remained notably *uncontested*. Despite the plantation's drive to maintain its autonomy, there was general amenability to the new republican regime, especially when compared to the Stuart monarchy; indeed, New Englanders found favour in England, Ireland, and Scotland, and Harvard graduates assumed various posts in the ministry and civil administration throughout the British Isles under the Cromwellian regime.[36] Harvard, the unintended offspring of imperial Laudianism, had spawned partisans and administrators to aid in the construction of a new republican social order in the metropole. In New England, control over higher learning was thereafter consolidated. Dunster, in addition to petitioning for

---

[31] See e.g., Morison, *HCSC*, I, pp. 26–7, 340–2; *Plymouth Records*, IX, pp. 162–5, 167, 192–9, 205–6, 216–17.

[32] MHS, MS N-1143, p. 115; Jeremiah Chaplin, *Life of Henry Dunster: First President of Harvard College* (Boston, MA, 1872), pp. 273–4.

[33] Edward G. Gray, *New World Babel: Languages and Nations in Early America* (Princeton, NJ, 1999), pp. 49–54, 62–73.

[34] Morison, *HCSC*, I, pp. 200–3.

[35] MHS, MS N-1143, p. 116; Chaplin, *Dunster*, pp. 274–5.

[36] See Stout, 'Morphology of Remigration'. See also Wells, 'Prelude to Empire', chap. 1.

increased funding, appealed directly to the General Court for a 'graunt of a corporation for the well ordring & managinge the affayre belonginge to the colledge'.[37] He likely also brought this to the attention of the Overseers at a meeting in spring 1650, when new rules were issued regarding student discipline.[38] The General Court was willing to grant to Harvard a charter of incorporation, doing so without remit to any royal or parliamentary authorities. The charter of May 1650 established a corporation consisting of a president, five fellows, and a treasurer, with Dunster named as the first president, Samuel Mather, Samuel Danforth, Jonathan Mitchell, Comfort Starr, and Samuel Eaton the first fellows, and Thomas Danforth the first treasurer. Crucially, the charter empowered the corporation to elect new members and manage finances.[39] Control would thus be largely vested in the corporation acting in concert with the Overseers. The charter underlined the consolidation and exercise of settler authority in the college.

Table 4.1. Harvard College Staff, c. 1650–4.

President
Henry Dunster, 1640–54

Treasurer
Thomas Danforth, 1650–68

Fellows and Tutors*
Samuel Mather, c. 1650
Comfort Starr, c. 1650
Urian Oakes, 1650–3
Samuel Danforth, 1650–c. 1654
Samuel Eaton, 1650–4
Jonathan Mitchell, 1650–68
John Collins, 1651–3
Michael Wigglesworth, 1652–4

* Fellows, created in the 1650 charter, continued to serve as tutors.

Sources: HCR; Sibley, *Biographical Sketches*.

---

[37] *Massachusetts Records*, III, pp. 207–8.
[38] HCR, I, pp. 27–9, 32–5; Morison, HCSC, I, p. 4.
[39] For the charter, see HCR, I, pp. 40–2, 181–3, III, pp. 1–5; CSPC, p. 340; *Massachusetts Records*, III, pp. 195–6, IV.1, pp. 12–14; Morison, HCSC, I, pp. 5–8.

In addition to consolidating power, the creation of fellowships in 1650 realised one of Dunster's goals to use recent graduates as fellows.[40] Each of the initial fellows graduated from Harvard between 1643 and 1649.[41] Samuel Mather would not last long in this role: he soon departed for England, where he served briefly as a chaplain of Magdalen College, Oxford under the presidency of Cromwell's ally Thomas Goodwin, before serving the Cromwellian regime in Scotland and later Ireland, where he became a senior fellow at Trinity. Mather is a clear example of the way New England clerics could move, rather seamlessly, throughout the Reformed Anglophone world. It also underscored the legitimacy of a Harvard degree.[42] Furthermore, the ease with which he found homes at colleges in Ireland and England, in addition to New England, was illustrative of the extent to which the Laudian educational project had been upended.[43] Yet from an institutional standpoint, Harvard's first fellows, having all been former students, also demonstrated how Dunster, the Overseers, and the General Court sought to perpetuate the college ethos by socialising graduates, reared under Dunster and his tutors, who would continue to train future generations of New England ministers and magistrates. The personnel in these roles mattered – their familiarity to authorities, their religious persuasion, and their training under amenable masters.[44] Prior to the Laudian intrusion, Trinity had employed a similar tactic as part of a broader mission to support Ireland's New English settlers. That the Harvard Corporation would work in tandem with the Overseers reinforced the idea that Harvard would continue to support the developing New England social order and provide education to the orthodox settler community, regardless of the New England Company's focus on missionary efforts. The passage of Harvard's charter formalised this practice for the college and was a crucial part of a wider process of societal development in New England.

In Ireland, by contrast, the conquering regime actively controlled Trinity. For the Cromwellians, extending authority over Trinity was part of a wider religious policy that included abolishing the Church of Ireland's hierarchy, forbidding the use of the Book of Common Prayer, and replenishing the number of preaching ministers.[45] Yet beyond doing away with the 'popish' elements of the established church, the conquerors' religious policy was doctrinally incoherent, leading to intra-Protestant dispute in Ireland, which after the conquest witnessed an explosion of sects – Independents, Baptists,

---

[40] *Plymouth Records*, IX, p. 95.
[41] Samuel Mather (1643); Samuel Danforth (1643); Jonathan Mitchell (1647); Comfort Starr (1647); Samuel Eaton (1649). Urian Oakes (1649) replaced Mather after his quick departure in 1650. HCR, I, p. cliv; Morison, HCSC, I, pp. 15–18; Sibley, *Biographical Sketches*, I, pp. xvii–xviii.
[42] Morison, HCSC, I, pp. 298–9.
[43] Sibley, *Biographical Sketches*, I, pp. 78–82; Seymour, *Puritans in Ireland*, p. 217.
[44] Hindle, *State and Social Change*, pp. 18–19; Mann, *Sources of Social Power*, p. 37.
[45] *Ireland under the Commonwealth*, I, pp. 4–5; Barnard, *Cromwellian Ireland*, pp. 136–82.

Quakers, and Presbyterians, in addition to 'Old Protestant' New English adherents to the Church of Ireland – that clashed during the Interregnum.[46] Trinity was a centre of this upheaval.

Whereas the Rump's 1649 act for propagating the gospel in New England focused primarily on indigenous conversion, the March 1650 Act for the Advancement of the Gospel and Leaning in Ireland was concerned mainly with increasing financial provisions for and establishing a commission to supervise Trinity's affairs.[47] This was a stark departure to the approach to higher education in New England, as the conquering regime sought rather immediately to incorporate Ireland's only university into its dominion. The act likely stemmed from the influence of John Owen, who arrived in Dublin as chaplain with the New Model Army in August 1649.[48] After his return to England, he preached before Parliament in February 1650, when he connected the need to propagate the gospel to Ireland's subjugation, noting that Dublin's inhabitants '[cried] out for supply' of God's word.[49] During his time in Dublin, Owen resided at the college and used its library to aid his preaching and writing.[50] While there, Oliver Cromwell also supposedly encouraged Owen to seek ways to 'regulate' Trinity's affairs.[51] Owen was ostensibly to consider Trinity's constitution, which at that point was still codified by Laud's statutes. He was no stranger to Laudian educational strictures: as a student at Queen's College, Oxford in the 1630s, he was witness to the Laudian reforms, which drove him from the university in 1637.[52] At Trinity, Owen was in a position to reform another institution stained by Laudianism. Yet there are few explicit references to Owen's work in respect to Trinity beyond a mention in the preface to one his tracts that he was 'burdened by manifold employments'.[53] Because he stayed at Trinity, he observed its derelict physical and spiritual state, the consequences of which had negatively impacted extramural society. He noted

---

[46] See especially Crawford Gribben, *God's Irishmen: Theological Debates in Cromwellian Ireland* (Oxford, 2007), pp. 3–54. See also Barnard, *Cromwellian Ireland*, p. 94; Phil Kilroy, 'Radical Religion in Ireland, 1641–1660', in Jane H. Ohlmeyer (ed.), *Ireland from Independence to Occupation, 1641–1660* (Cambridge, 1995), pp. 201–17.

[47] *Acts and Ordinances*, II, pp. 355–7; Barnard, *Cromwellian Ireland*, pp. 96–7.

[48] Richard L. Greaves, 'Owen, John (1616–1683)', *ODNB*.

[49] William H. Goold (ed.), *The Works of John Owen* (24 vols, Edinburgh, 1850–5), VIII, pp. 208–41. On the sermon, see also Gribben, *John Owen*, pp. 113–15.

[50] Urwick, *Trinity College Dublin*, p. 55. On Trinity's library, see John Pentland Mahaffy, 'The Library of Trinity College, Dublin: The Growth of a Legend', *Hermathena*, 12:28 (1902), 68–78; Peter Fox, *Trinity College Library Dublin: A History* (Cambridge, 2014), pp. 25–33.

[51] William Orme, *Memoirs of the Life, Writings, and Religious Connexions, of John Owen, D.D.* (London, 1820), p. 113.

[52] Gribben, *John Owen*, pp. 35–6.

[53] Goold, *Owen Works*, X, p. 479; Orme, *Life of Owen*, pp. 118–19; Peter Toon (ed.), *The Correspondence of John Owen (1616–1683): With an Account of His Life and Work* (Cambridge, 1970), pp. 34–5.

that he was unable to find the writings of the Polish Reformed theologian Johannes Maccovius in Trinity's library, which increased his concern about Ireland's spiritual needs.[54] As both model and machinery, Trinity was severely lacking. This experience conditioned Owen's view of Trinity and led to the passage of the March 1650 act.

The chief outcome of the Act for the Advancement of the Gospel and Learning in Ireland was the establishment of a council of fifteen 'trustees' to oversee Trinity's affairs. The act conveyed the revenues of the archbishopric of Dublin, the bishopric of Meath, and the deanery of St Patrick's to the trustees, who were tasked with 'setling the maintenance of… Trinity Colledge, and of a Master, Fellows, Scholars, and Officers there', as well as with erecting a second college in Dublin. The lord lieutenant was to work in concert with the trustees 'to place in the said University, Colledges and Free-Schools' amenable men. The trustees were to also review and 'put in writing such Rules, Directions, Statutes, Ordinances and Instructions, as they in their judgements think fit'. Any reforms would then have to be approved by the English Parliament. The trustees included Owen, Henry Jones, bishop of Clogher and Trinity's existing vice-chancellor, and Henry Cromwell.[55] In the meantime, Parliament sent six ministers to Dublin to begin preaching.[56] This multifaceted act much more closely incorporated Trinity into the bounds of Cromwellian state power and underlined the approaches by which the Irish social order would be transformed: transferring the rents of the established church to Trinity signalled its strategic role in the overhaul of the ecclesiastical hierarchy, while the emphasis on placing agreeable men into positions of academic authority pointed to the potential alteration of Trinity into an institution to steep students in newly authorised religious norms.

Given the recent history of higher educational policy that dated back to Charles I's reign, the Irish act's parameters were not novel. Parliament's measures were concerned with re-establishing the social order within a Cromwellian mould, to which Trinity was closely linked. Trinity's institutional endurance – it had been on the brink of closure throughout much of the 1640s – was central to Cromwellian designs; the college required recuperation, remodelling, and spiritual redirection, but not dismantling.[57] The act also resembled other endeavours for the support of higher education from all sides of the religious and political divide in British and American spaces. A pattern is discernible and speaks to the ways in which universities were incorporated into the contested processes of state and imperial formation. An ascendant power – in this case, the Cromwellians – sought the realisation of its religious and political vision, and thus the extension of its power, in part by strengthening university finances (at times, out of rival ecclesiastical

---

[54] Goold, *Owen Works*, X, pp. 430, 471; Gribben, *John Owen*, p. 113.
[55] *Acts and Ordinances*, I, pp. 355–7.
[56] *CJ*, VI, p. 379.
[57] Barnard, *Cromwellian Ireland*, p. 198.

rents), removing and planting faculty, and reviewing and amending statutes. In Trinity's case, the act also saw the creation of an external board to supervise the college's affairs, which paralleled similar actions in Reformed polities in Scotland and New England in the preceding decade. Assigning the management of university affairs to the spiritual elite was the surest way to guarantee socialisation to authorised norms, via correct instruction and the training of ministers, to better propagate the gospel.

In October 1650, Parliament issued further instructions to the commissioners for Ireland – Edmund Ludlow, Miles Corbett, John Jones, and John Weaver – to cooperate with Henry Ireton, deputy general of Ireland, to enhance preaching, gospel instruction, and 'the training up of youth in piety and literature'.[58] To see out the advancement of learning, the commissioners sought John Owen's advice. In a July 1651 letter, they wrote that in their endeavours to promote religion and learning, they found Trinity 'furnished with very few officers or other members fit to be continued there', especially as plague was then afflicting Dublin.[59] To remedy this, the commissioners requested that Owen consult with his colleague, Magdalen's Thomas Goodwin, to review Trinity's statutes.[60] The commissioners concluded, rather tellingly, that 'educating of youth in the knowledge of God and principles of piety may be in the first place promoted, experience having taught that where learning attained before the work of grace upon the heart, it serves only to make a sharper opposition against the power of godliness'.[61]

Scholars have previously cited this letter to highlight the central role that Owen played in Trinity's affairs in the early days of the Interregnum.[62] Yet the letter also exhibits how the commissioners viewed Trinity as the institution that, while requiring reform, would lead the way in promoting the Cromwellian social order. By referencing the poor state of Trinity's masters, the commissioners signalled the forthcoming overhaul of the staff and students. In writing that 'learning' should not take place 'before the work of grace upon the heart', the commissioners suggested that the college should only accept youths out of the community of the elect.[63] Given the paucity of preachers, this was a restrictive view of who could attend Trinity, which naturally excluded the Catholic native Irish and, perhaps, adherents to the now disestablished Church of Ireland.[64] Cromwellian authorities thus focused on the composition of Trinity's staff and student body in order to re-engineer

---

[58] BL, Egerton MS 1761, fols 18v–19r, 42; *Ireland under the Commonwealth*, I, pp. 1–2.
[59] Mahaffy, *Epoch in Irish History*, p. 295; *Ireland under the Commonwealth*, I, p. 112.
[60] Gribben, *John Owen*, pp. 127–8; Worden, *God's Instruments*, pp. 174–5.
[61] *Ireland under the Commonwealth*, I, pp. 10–11; Corcoran, *State Policy in Irish Education*, p. 75.
[62] See e.g., Mahaffy, *Epoch in Irish History*, p. 295; Murphy, *History of Trinity College Dublin*, pp. 115–16; Barnard, *Cromwellian Ireland*, p. 200; Gribben, *John Owen*, p. 127.
[63] Gribben, *God's Irishmen*, p. 68.
[64] *Ireland under the Commonwealth*, I, pp. 60–1.

the institution into machinery to distil the values of the new regime and cultivate broader social formation.

It is unclear if Owen responded to this letter, though it is likely that he suggested the man to take the reins as Trinity's provost. Provost Anthony Martin, who shepherded Trinity through the latter 1640s, died in mid-1650 and he was succeeded by Samuel Winter, an English Independent minister.[65] Winter's credentials and training made him potentially well placed to support Cromwellian aims. He had been educated at Emmanuel under the tutelage of John Preston before gaining experience under two later puritan settlers of Massachusetts, John Cotton and Ezekiel Rogers. He came to Dublin in 1650 as the Parliamentarians' chaplain and subsequently ministered to a congregation of government and army officials.[66] The precise date that Winter assumed Trinity's provostship is unclear, though in April 1651 the Irish commissioners wrote to his parish in Yorkshire that Winter would be unable to return.[67] It is likely that soon after this date Winter assumed the provostship. On 22 August, the commissioners pressed Winter and Dublin alderman Daniel Hutchinson to 'consider of those Scholars and under graduates in the College of Dublin who are hopefull and fit to be provided for there and to certify the same to the Commissioners'.[68] On 3 September, the commissioners ordered the keys of Trinity delivered to Winter and commanded Trinity's trustees to remedy the college's 'ruinous' condition. The commissioners then authorised Hutchinson to allocate funds for repairing the college buildings and maintaining fellows and scholars.[69] In November, Winter was granted a bachelor of divinity – the minimum degree required for the provostship – when he was referred to as the 'provost of the Colledge'.[70] Finally, in June 1652, Cromwell formally appointed Winter provost by the virtue of the authority granted to him by Parliament's March 1650 act.[71] Even before this official appointment, Winter had taken to reviewing Trinity's accounts.[72] With a notebook that contained an abstract of James VI/I's land grants to Trinity, he embarked on a survey of college lands in Ulster and Munster in August 1653, repeating the journey several times

---

[65] TCD, MUN/V/5/1, p. 2; Harris, *Ware Works*, I, pp. 157–8.
[66] On Winter, see BL, Add MS 4460, fols 34–5; Gribben, *God's Irishmen*, pp. 129–32, 144–6; Toby Barnard, 'Winter, Samuel (1603–1666)', *ODNB*; Seymour, *Puritans in Ireland*, pp. 26–39.
[67] *Ireland under the Commonwealth*, I, p. 172.
[68] BL, Egerton MS 1762, fol. 1r. On Hutchinson, see Barnard, *Cromwellian Ireland*, pp. 81–3.
[69] BL, Egerton MS 1762, fol. 4r; Urwick, *Trinity College Dublin*, p. 58.
[70] TCD, MUN/V/5/2, p. 45.
[71] TCD, MUN/V/5/1, p. 2, 74; *Cromwell Writings*, II, p. 555, IV, pp. 947–8; J[ohn] W[eaver], *The Life and Death, of the Eminently Learned, Pious, and Painful Minister of the Gospel, Dr. Samuel Winter, Sometime Provost of Trinity Colledge near Dublin in Ireland* (London, 1671), pp. 9–11.
[72] Urwick, *Trinity College Dublin*, p. 58; Gribben, *God's Irishmen*, p. 146.

through 1657.[73] Working through Trinity's trustees, who appealed directly to Parliament's commissioners, Winter's efforts saw Trinity recover its rents and increase its revenues in Ulster.[74] According to his brother-in-law John Weaver, Winter also oversaw 'the return of divers Fellows, and Students to the Colledge'. He took 'great pains' in instructing them in 'Humane and Divine learning, Preaching, and expounding the Sacred Scriptures', thus stimulating the 'flourishing of that Seminary in Learning, and Piety'.[75]

The Cromwellian regime had therefore placed a capable leader and thoroughgoing Independent at the helm of Ireland's university, and Winter certainly paralleled Harvard's President Dunster in his care for the intellectual and material well-being of the college. But whereas Dunster had advocated for a group of fellows who had been educated under his tutelage to better govern Harvard's intellectual and religious direction, Winter's first group of fellows represented a curious diversity of confessional and political allegiances. As has been evidenced at the Scottish universities and Harvard, the composition of college masters was integral to seeing through the schemes of those who held power. More specifically at Trinity, it was crucial to support the provost's authority, who worked in tandem with Dublin and London authorities.

The same could not necessarily be said for Trinity's fellows of the early 1650s.[76] Given the importance of these individuals to the socialisation of future partisans of state power, it is worth investigating the composition of Trinity's masters as the college was being incorporated into the bounds of Cromwellian power and considering their potential utility. The first entry in the college register following Winter's appointment lists five names: John Stearne, Joseph Travers, Nathaniel Hoyle, Adam Cusack, and Caesar Williamson.[77] Previously, in December 1652, Miles Symner was appointed to a professorship of mathematics and made a fellow by Parliament's commissioners and not by Trinity's trustees, who had been empowered to appoint ministers. Symner's appointment seemed tied directly to the consolidation of the Cromwellian conquest of Ireland. He was a Trinity alumnus and former minister in the Church of Ireland, but by the late 1640s he had assumed roles as major and engineer in the army in Dublin.[78] Symner was appointed to the mathematics professorship because, according to the commissioners, 'there

---

[73] TCD, MS 805, fols 20r–25r.
[74] BL, Egerton MS 1762, fols 97v, 101; Murphy, *History of Trinity College Dublin*, pp. 117–18; Hugh J. Lawlor (ed.), *The Registers of Provost Winter (Trinity College, Dublin): 1650 to 1660* (Exeter, 1907), pp. 3–4.
[75] W[eaver], *Life of Winter*, pp. 10–11.
[76] Fry, *Dublin University Calendar*, p. 575.
[77] TCD, MUN/V/5/1, p. 75.
[78] Webster, *Great Instauration*, pp. 226–7; Toby Barnard, 'Miles Symner and the New Learning in Seventeenth-Century Ireland', *Journal of the Royal Society of Antiquaries of Ireland*, 102:2 (1972), 129–42.

is a greate occasion for surveing of lands in this country'.⁷⁹ In addition to teaching, Symner was to instruct soldiers and administrators in surveying to support plantation efforts. While the nature of the role might suggest a turn towards science and new learning, especially given Symner's own affinity for 'experimentall learning', in reality the professorship did not represent the advancement of new learning at the college.⁸⁰ William Petty lamented the state of learning in Ireland and the nature of Symner's position in two letters to Samuel Hartlib, writing that 'there is no course that I know taken to advance any kind of learning by' the mathematics post.⁸¹ Symner's professorship certainly served a practical utility in consolidating conquest. The position was linked to the broader land revolution in Cromwellian Ireland, as the professorship would aid the technical aspects of the surveys of Ireland, which would in turn fuel the transfer of lands from Catholics. By virtue of its establishment by Parliament's commissioners, Symner's professorship was wedded explicitly to the aims of the regime, but it did not herald the wholesale introduction of experimental learning at Trinity.

But the utility of Trinity's other fellows is not as clear. The Parliamentary commissioners appeared to have had the final say in selecting the fellows, regardless of the powers granted to Trinity's trustees. Between August 1651 and December 1652, the commissioners appointed John Stearne, Joseph Travers, and Matthew Wootton to fellowships at Trinity.⁸² Stearne, the nephew of Archbishop Ussher who had matriculated at Trinity in 1639 but was forced to flee after the Rebellion, completed his studies at Sidney Sussex College under the mastership of Samuel Ward.⁸³ Travers was also a Trinity alumnus who had previously served as a fellow in the 1620s.⁸⁴ Nathaniel Hoyle, the former vice provost and one of Chappell's opponents, was evidently amenable to Parliament, and was translated back to Trinity from Brasenose College.⁸⁵ Adam Cusack, appointed in 1654, was also a Trinity alumnus and the son of the former mayor of Dublin, though he would soon enter Lincoln's Inn in 1655.⁸⁶ Finally, Caesar Williamson had been educated at Trinity College,

---

⁷⁹ TCD, MUN/V/5/1, p. 95.
⁸⁰ BL, Sloane MS 427, fol. 85.
⁸¹ YUL, OSB MS 16799, 16807. On Petty and the Hartlib Circle, see Webster, *Great Instauration*, pp. 436–44; Toby Barnard, *Improving Ireland? Projectors, Prophets and Profiteers, 1641–1786* (Dublin, 2008), pp. 41–72.
⁸² BL, Egerton MS 1762, fols 11v, 54v. It is unlikely Wootton that assumed his position as his name never appears in the college registers.
⁸³ TCD, MUN/V/5/1, p. 67; *Alumni Dublinenses*, p. 777; T.W. Belcher, *Memoir of John Stearne, M. & J.U.D., S.F.T.C.D., Founder and First President of the College of Physicians* (Dublin, 1865), pp. 10–13.
⁸⁴ TCD, MUN/V/5/1, p. 75; *Alumni Dublinenses*, p. 821; Urwick, *Trinity College Dublin*, p. 58.
⁸⁵ *Alumni Dublinenses*, pp. 413–14; Barnard, *Cromwellian Ireland*, pp. 202–3.
⁸⁶ Fry, *Dublin University Calendar*, p. 575; Ball, *History of the County Dublin*, pp. 145–6.

Cambridge, but had previously served as a fellow of the Dublin college in 1644 before his reappointment in 1654.[87]

Table 4.2 Trinity College, Dublin Staff, c. 1651–5

Provosts
Samuel Winter, c. 1651–60

Fellows and Associated Offices Where Known
Nathaniel Hoyle (1631)
Miles Symner (1652), Mathematics (1652)
Joseph Travers (c. 1651–2), Vice Provost (1654–5)
John Stearne (c. 1651–2), Registrar (1652–8), Physic (c. 1654)
Matthew Wootton (c. 1651–2), likely declined
Caesar Williamson (c. 1654)
Adam Cusack (c. 1654)
Edward Veele (c. 1654)

Sources: Fry, *Dublin University Calendar*; BL, Egerton MS 1762; TCD, MUN/V/5/1; *Alumni Dublinenses*.

J.P. Mahaffy wrote that Cromwellian authorities' policy of keeping older fellows was prudent, in that these fellows were agreeable to the 'Puritan spirit' of the conquering regime. This certainly speaks to the imperial authorities' responsiveness to localised realities.[88] But Mahaffy was conflating Trinity's Reformed ethos with the Cromwellians' 'puritanism', writing that 'the College had hardly change its views on religion'.[89] This oversimplifies the nature of New English religious identity and the fissiparous state of the Irish religious climate at the outset of the Interregnum.[90] The initial crop of Cromwellian fellows were likely puritan inclined, but none seemed to have shared the Independent fervour of Provost Winter. Winter was also the only Englishman without any prior association with Trinity, as the fellows were either former students or former fellows. Winter's attempt to revive Irish language instruction at Trinity is telling in this regard.[91] His enthusiasm for

[87] Harris, *Ware Works*, II, p. 343; Fry, *Dublin University Calendar*, p. 575; Barnard, *Cromwellian Ireland*, p. 202.
[88] Hindle, *State and Social Change*, p. 16.
[89] Mahaffy, *Epoch in Irish History*, pp. 296–7.
[90] Barnard, *Cromwellian Ireland*, pp. 98–100.
[91] Among Winter's belongings on his travels in Ulster and Munster was an Irish catechism, though it is unclear the extent to which he learned Irish. See TCD, MS 805, fol. 39r. On Winter's Irish language interests and conversion, see W[eaver], *Life of Winter*, pp. 13–14; Barnard, 'Winter, Samuel'; Gribben, *God's Irishmen*, p. 32.

evangelising to the native population was not shared among the fellows, nor was it among the known Protestant ministers in Ireland in this period.[92] While the first Cromwellian fellows thought highly enough of Winter's diligence to award him a doctorate in August 1654, the failure to recommence Irish language instruction indicated that there was little support for such a program among other Dublin intellectuals.[93] Like Bedell before him, Winter scheme's was anathema to a godly community disinterested in proselytising.[94] As will be discussed in Chapter 6, tensions in the college would result in clashes between Winter and the fellows throughout the 1650s. Such tensions were indicative of the heterogeneity of Trinity's masters and foregrounded the shortcomings of the actions of the Cromwellian regime in restructuring the Irish social order.

Ireland and New England represented two imperial spaces in which Cromwellian authorities sought to assert control over higher education. While measures to promote the propagation of the gospel were pursued in each space, approaches varied, and the way Harvard and Trinity were impacted differed greatly. In Ireland, Cromwellian authorities clearly envisaged a prominent place for Trinity in establishing control over a conquered Ireland, and in doing so, the regime took its cue from the vision of John Owen: the college would endure, and it would play a traditional but no less important role in socialising ministers to propagate the gospel in Ireland. Financial amelioration and the creation of trustees to oversee the college's affairs, however, amounted to little more than institutional scaffolding. Imperial state formation, built on creating the conditions to cultivate societal homogeneity, foundered in the college. Once the men were installed in their posts to operate Trinity's machinery, tensions became apparent.[95] Provost Winter's Independency did not sync with the New English ethos of the fellows, resulting in internecine difficulties that underscored Trinity's contested nature and the ways in which the conflicts endemic to conquest Ireland reverberated in the academy. In New England, meanwhile, the Cromwellian regime's direct intervention into the religious affairs of the colony through the creation of the New England Company had little initial bearing on Harvard. Instead, Dunster, the General Court, and Overseers took matters into their own hands by chartering the college and establishing a corporation that reinforced Harvard's autonomy, insofar as it would function to support the rigidly homogenised orthodoxy of the New England social order. The twin extremes of sectarianism and orthodoxy, and the ways in which they challenged and buttressed competing understandings of healthy commonwealths in Ireland and New England, would continue to foment tensions at both Trinity and Harvard into the 1650s.

---

[92] Barnard, *Cromwellian Ireland*, pp. 174–5.
[93] Urwick, *Trinity College Dublin*, pp. 59–60; W[eaver], *Life of Winter*, pp. 11–13.
[94] See e.g., *Ireland under the Commonwealth*, II, pp. 412–14.
[95] Durkheim, *Education and Sociology*, p. 62; Tilly, 'Reflection', p. 40.

The Scottish Universities, Schism, and Conquest

The Cromwellian regime confronted a much different situation in Scotland. There, throughout much of the 1640s, the Covenanting regime had incorporated the universities into bounds of state power by remaking and controlling the Scottish professoriate, pursuing curricular reforms, and mandating fidelity to the Covenant in order to mould conformity to the Covenanted social order. Yet mounting divisions within the Covenanting movement in the period immediately preceding the Cromwellian conquest broke whatever consensus may have existed among political and religious authorities in Scotland, and the turmoil born from this rising ideological conflict reverberated in the universities. Scottish higher education reignited as a contested space as internecine disputes among rival Covenanting groups manifested. Competing conceptions of how the Covenanted nation should be defined led to new, conflicting policies for the Scottish universities that focused on entrenching the power of clerical factions. Following the conquest, the Cromwellian regime would exploit this conflict to control Scotland's universities.

The undoing of the Covenanting movement was rooted in the Engagement controversy. To safeguard Presbyterian interests in the three kingdoms, the Scots signed the Engagement, a military pact with Charles I, in December 1647.[96] Charles agreed to authorise the Solemn League and Covenant and establish Presbyterianism for a three-year period, but, crucially, he would not take the Covenant himself. This scandalised many in the Kirk. When Cromwell defeated the Engager army at Preston in August 1648, hard-line opponents of the pact – anti-Engagers – assumed control of the church and state. Anti-Engagers drew most of their support from the southwest, the epicentre of radical opposition to the Engagement and from which the Whiggamore Raid, the rising that ousted 'Engagers' from power after Preston, originated.[97] The southwest was also home to the Western Association, an army of radicals who saw themselves as the true defenders of the Covenants. The anti-Engagers' grip on power was solidified in January 1649, when the Scottish Parliament passed the Act of Classes, which barred and purged all 'malignants' – Engagers and royalist sympathisers – from temporal and spiritual office.[98]

With the Covenanted state under anti-Engager control, the movement to expunge 'malignants' came to the universities, where unambiguous opposition

---

[96] Gardiner, *Constitutional Documents*, pp. 347–53.
[97] See e.g., Sharon Adams, 'The Making of the Radical South-West: Charles I and His Scottish Kingdom, 1625–1649', in John R. Young (ed.), *Celtic Dimensions of the British Civil Wars* (Edinburgh, 1997), pp. 53–74.
[98] *RPS*, 1648/3/19, 1649/1/43. On the Engagement, see Stevenson, *Revolution and Counter-Revolution*, pp. 94–154; Stewart, *Rethinking the Scottish Revolution*, pp. 219–21; MacKenzie, *Solemn League and Covenant*, pp. 68–71.

to the Engagement was expected.[99] The 1648 General Assembly armed the Kirk's commissioners with the ability to root out 'malignant' ministers, and in August it commissioned a visitation of St Andrews with a wide remit to intervene in the university's affairs.[100] The visitors were empowered to inspect whether all staff and students were 'correspondent with the confession of faith and acts of this kirk' and remove any staff 'superfluous, unqualiefied or corrupt'.[101] The commission, which included the hard-line anti-Engagers Robert Douglas, James Guthrie, and the marquis of Argyll, targeted university staff who had either supported or failed to oppose the Engagement publicly. At St Andrews, this initially included John Baron, provost of St Salvator's, the regents Thomas Gleg of St Salvator's and David Nevay of St Leonard's, and the St Leonard's *oeconomus* Patrick Murray. All were cited for either failing to preach against the Engagement or for demonstrating 'malignancie'. By early 1649, the St Salvator's dean George Martine, regent Alexander Edward, and *oeconomus* Robert Yule were also under investigation for not conforming to anti-Engager principles. Only Martine and Edward seemed to have been spared – the rest were either expelled or forced to demit.[102] The purging also came to King's College, where a visitation deposed King's principal William Guild, sub-principal Alexander Middleton, and two regents for their 'malignancy'.[103] The commission intended to replace Guild with the Marischal divinity professor John Menzies, a radical Covenanter who later emerged as a leading Independent, but he refused the post. Guild thus remained as principal until he was removed by the Cromwellians.[104]

Table 4.3. Anti-Engager Purges at the Scottish Universities, c. 1647–51.

University of St Andrews	University of Glasgow
John Baron, Provost, St Salvator's College	John Strang, Principal
Forced to demit, 1649	Forced retirement, 1650
Thomas Gleg, Regent, St Salvator's College	
Forced to demit, 1649	*King's College, Aberdeen*
David Nevay, Regent, St Leonard's College	William Guild, Principal
Deposed, 1649	Deposed, but kept office, 1649

[99] For a more detailed account of what follows, see Cipriano, 'Engagement', pp. 147–52.
[100] *Records of the Kirk*, pp. 510, 517, 519.
[101] StAUL, UYUY 812, fols 79–81.
[102] Cipriano, 'Engagement', pp. 148–9; *Records of the Kirk*, p. 519; RCGA, II, pp. 286–7; StAUL, UYUY 812, fols 94–95, 98, 108–9, 113v–120v, 134; George R. Kinloch (ed.), *Selections from the Minutes of the Presbyteries of St. Andrews and Cupar, 1641–1698* (Edinburgh, 1837), pp. 44–5.
[103] *Records of the Kirk*, pp. 557, 559; RCGA, II, p. 303; Anderson, *Officers and Graduates*, p. 26.
[104] Cipriano, 'Engagement', pp. 150–1.

Table 4.3 (continued)

University of St Andrews	King's College, Aberdeen
Robert Yule, Treasurer, St Salvator's College	Alexander Middleton, Sub-Principal
Deposed, 1649	Deposed, 1649
Patrick Murray, Treasurer, St Leonard's College	Patrick Gordon, Regent
Investigated	Deposed, 1650
George Martine, Dean, St Salvator's College	
Investigated	
Alexander Edward, Regent, St Salvator's College	
Investigated	

Sources: ODNB; Scott, Fasti; MAUG, vol. 3; Fasti Aberdonenses; Anderson, Officers and Graduates; StAUL, UYUY 812; RCGA; Cipriano, 'Engagement'.

The reactive nature of these purges suggests that even the slightest suspicion of 'malignancy' invited scrutiny, for anti-Engagers could not risk younger generations of students being tainted with stain of the uncovenanted alliance and thus further debasing the Covenanted state. These purges highlighted the exertion of anti-Engager power in the universities and the aim to entrench it for future generations. Thus, in addition to purges, anti-Engagers crafted requirements for replacement academics, who had to be amenable to this newly redefined Covenanted Scotland. The abilities and, most important, conformability of those tasked with socialising future churchmen and statesmen to a specific set of authorised norms was again brought to the forefront. Both anti-Engager visitations to St Andrews and Aberdeen established new rules for electing principals and regents, who had to be 'men of good affection to the publick cause of religion'.[105] The regime deployed the mechanisms of state power, which the Covenanters had reconstituted in the early 1640s, to effect change in the universities. Similarly to university reform earlier in the decade, authorities sought to block 'malignants' from university posts and ensure that only ardent anti-Engagers moulded the minds of Scotland's future ministers.

While the purging of public officials accelerated in the wake of the Engagement, the universities remained contested spaces at the heart of a burgeoning dispute that emerged in the Covenanting movement.[106] Anti-Engager hegemony crumbled following the execution of Charles I and

[105] For St Andrews, see StAUL, UYUY 812, fols 103–104. For Aberdeen, see AUL, MSM 91/4 and NCL, Baill 2/4, pp. 124–7. Observers at Glasgow noted that these new rules were punishments for university master's 'gross and publick offence'. See NCL, Baill 2/4, p. 127.
[106] Stevenson, 'Deposition of Ministers', pp. 329–33; Cipriano, 'Engagement', pp. 152–3; MacKenzie, 'Contested Space', p. 74.

the proclamation of his son as King Charles II, who by the Treaty of Breda agreed to take the Covenant but refused to export Presbyterianism to England and Ireland. This provoked a backlash among the most radical anti-Engagers, who responded by purging all supposed 'malignants' from the Scottish army, leaving a depleted force that Cromwell soundly defeated at Dunbar in September 1650. This defeat exacerbated divisions in the Kirk. In October, the Glasgow radical Patrick Gillespie authored the Western Remonstrance, which claimed that Dunbar was God's retribution for the Scot's association with Charles II. His solution was additional purges, thus further restricting membership in the Covenanted community. Gillespie's opponents in the Commission of the Kirk, the standing committee that met between General Assemblies, refused to endorse the Remonstrance.[107] The English defeat of the Remonstrant army in December prompted the Commission to issue Public Resolutions that readmitted Engagers and royalists into the army and wider community.[108] 'Resolutioners' were among the moderate majority who supported the king in the face of an invading English republican army. Even after the Scots' defeat at Worcester in September 1651, the Kirk remained divided among these Resolutioners and Remonstrants, later named Protesters.[109]

The universities emerged as critical venues where the quarrel between Protesters and Resolutioners manifested prior to the Cromwellian conquest. Such events not only underscore the extent to which the Covenanting movement had turned on itself, but also how the universities were clearly marked as highly politicised, contested institutions caught in the interplay between rival factions.[110] Resolutioners immediately neutralised what they could of Protester opposition at the 1651 General Assembly, where, in addition to reproaching Protesters and deposing Gillespie, they censured all expectants and university students who opposed the Resolutions.[111] In 1651, the only Protester to hold a university post of considerable authority was Samuel Rutherford, the principal of St Mary's. Resolutioners at St Andrews, which included James Wood, who had occupied the chair of ecclesiastical history at St Mary's since 1645, outnumbered Rutherford.[112] At Glasgow, Robert Baillie emphasised that the health of the commonwealth was in the

---

[107] *RCGA*, III, pp. 130–2; Baillie, *L&J*, III, pp. 123–4.

[108] Robert H. Landrum, 'Vast Visions and Intransigent Realities: The Anglo-Scottish Union of 1651–60' (unpublished PhD thesis, University of Wisconsin, Madison, 1999), pp. 4–5.

[109] R. Scott Spurlock, *Cromwell and Scotland: Conquest and Religion, 1650–1660* (Edinburgh, 2007), pp. 104–6.

[110] Cipriano, 'Engagement', pp. 153–5.

[111] *Records of the Kirk*, p. 636; *RCGA*, III, p. xii; Baillie, *L&J*, III, p. 140; McCrie, *Robert Blair*, p. 278.

[112] Baillie, *L&J*, III, p. 121; Bonar, *Letters*, pp. 668–71; Coffey, *Politics, Religion and the British Revolutions*, p. 59.

balance: it was essential that the university preserve the 'Nationall Church' and protect it from both sectaries and 'treacherous radicals'.[113]

But Glasgow was a site of substantial contestation prior to the Cromwellian conquest because of two vacancies that emerged in early 1650.[114] In February 1650 the Commission of the Kirk translated David Dickson, Glasgow's first professor of divinity and a staunch Resolutioner, to the vacant divinity post at Edinburgh.[115] The second vacancy came with Principal Strang's retirement in April.[116] Baillie devoted considerable energy to countering the Protesters' designs on the vacancies.[117] The ensuing contest over Glasgow's vacancies centred upon James Durham, a Glasgow alumnus and minister of Glasgow's Blackfriars Church.[118] Following Dickson's translation, both the Commission of the Kirk and the Glasgow burgh council called Durham to the open professorship. By January 1651 Baillie had been promoted to the first professorship, while Glasgow's moderators chose Robert Ramsay, the minister of Glasgow's High Church, to assume the second divinity professorship. The burgh council, which had fallen under the influence of Gillespie's Protester faction, blocked Ramsay's move.[119] Durham's allegiances were not easily defined, and he has been described as a 'centrist'.[120] Baillie was determined to keep him away from the university, for he recognised that his willingness to conciliate with the Protesters was valuable for their designs, noting that Durham would 'strengthen much the faction that professe difference from the Public Resolutions, though he as yet professe none'. He was also at pains to keep Gillespie out of the university's affairs: 'if Mr. Patrick get his will of us in this our Universitie, he will be their owne to sow what seed in it they like'.[121] In Baillie's eyes, if the Protesters gained influence in the universities, they would have free rein to defile the Covenanted state.

---

[113] Baillie, L&J, III, pp. 466–8, 474–5.
[114] On Glasgow, the Protester-Resolutioner controversy, and the Cromwellian conquest, see Lind, 'Battle in the Burgh'; MacKenzie, 'Contested Space', pp. 71–5.
[115] RCGA, II, pp. 360–1; John Nicoll, *A Diary of Public Transactions and Other Occurrences, Chiefly in Scotland from January 1650 to January 1667* (Edinburgh, 1836), p. 3; Wood, *Edinburgh Burgh Records 1642–1655*, p. 228.
[116] Cipriano, 'Engagement', p. 156.
[117] EUL, La.IV.25/34, fols 28, 50; MAUG, III, pp. 388–9.
[118] George Christie, 'James Durham as Courtier and Preacher', *Records of the Scottish Church History Society*, 4 (1930), 66–80, at 68–72.
[119] MacKenzie, 'Contested Space', pp. 76–8; RCGA, III, pp. 44, 69, 117–18, 133–4; J.D. Marwick (ed.), *Extracts from the Records of the Burgh of Glasgow, A.D. 1630–1662* (Glasgow, 1881), p. 198.
[120] Baillie, L&J, III, pp. 185–6. On Durham's allegiances and the wider conflict between the Protesters and Resolutioners, see K.D. Holfelder, 'Factionalism in the Kirk during the Cromwellian Invasion and Occupation of Scotland, 1650 to 1660: The Protester–Resolutioner Controversy' (unpublished PhD thesis, University of Edinburgh, 1998), pp. 19, 84, 97, 115, 124, 137–8, 163–4.
[121] RCGA, III, p. 335; Baillie, L&J, III, pp. 146–7, 149–53, 158–9, 557–8.

Baillie ultimately succeeded in blocking Durham's appointment, but the Protesters nonetheless turned their attention to an arguably bigger prize, the vacant principalship, which Gillespie eyed for himself. To counter this new push, Glasgow's masters sought to encourage Robert Blair, Baillie's mentor and the leading Resolutioner at St Andrews, to take the principalship.[122] But Blair declined, and Robert Ramsay was ultimately elected as principal. After receiving approval from the Resolutioner-controlled Commission, Ramsay was installed in July 1651.[123] At this time, Glasgow also adopted a resolution prohibiting the principal and divinity professors from holding benefices in the burgh and declared their freedom to elect principals and divinity professors – all attempts to fortify the university against Protester machinations.[124] But Robert Ramsay died on 4 September 1651, a day after Cromwell's victory at Worcester, which left a vacant principalship and divinity post at Glasgow in the balance as the Cromwellian regime conquered Scotland.

Unlike Ireland, which was declared part of the Commonwealth after monarchy was abolished, and New England, whose government remained mostly unchanged by the revolution, defining Scotland's relationship in the new political system was more complex, though it was a conquered domain over which the Cromwellian state sought to expand power.[125] In October 1651, Parliament issued plans for incorporative union in the Tender of Union in February 1652.[126] English agents negotiated with the Scots at Dalkeith and London, though there was only a veneer of dialogue.[127] The Resolutioners opposed the Tender and what they viewed as the usurpation of monarchy and the violation of the Solemn League and Covenant; they were also wary that the Protesters would wilfully comply with the Cromwellians.[128] The 'negotiations' resulted in an archipelagic union dominated by England, declared at the Barebones Parliament through the Instrument of Government of December 1653 and proclaimed by Cromwell, as Lord Protector of England, Scotland, and Ireland, via an April 1654 ordinance.[129] Much of what transpired confirmed Baillie's fears, and the regime would go on to exploit the Protester–Resolutioner schism in the universities.

With the union came the possibility that the conquering regime would extend its power and enlarge the dominion of the Cromwellian state via

---

[122] Baillie, *L&J*, III, pp. 237–8; Marwick, *Glasgow Burgh Records 1630–1662*, p. 520.
[123] RCGA, III, p. 462; MAUG, III, p. 368.
[124] MAUG, II, p. 321.
[125] Smyth, 'Empire Building', pp. 138–9.
[126] *Cromwellian Union*, pp. xxi–xxiii; *Scotland and the Protectorate*, pp. 393–8; Nicoll, *Diary of Public Transactions*, p. 86.
[127] *Cromwellian Union*; Robert H. Landrum (ed.), 'Records of the Anglo-Scottish Union Negotiations, 1652–1653', in *Miscellany of the Scottish History Society, Volume XV*, 6th series (Woodbridge, 2014), pp. 153–293.
[128] Baillie, *L&J*, III, pp. 175–80.
[129] *Acts and Ordinances*, II, pp. 813–22, 871–83.

the reform of Scotland's social order. In religious matters, at the heart of many of the conflicts that marked the Civil Wars, the regime's espousal of Independency and liberty of conscience was antithetical to the rigid Presbyterianism of Covenanted Scotland, debased as it was by factional strife.[130] Cromwellian commissioners were nevertheless ordered to encourage all 'godly' Scots, assuring them that they would be protected under the union.[131] Scotland's universities were squarely in the crosshairs of the conquerors and were key institutions to extend Cromwellian power.[132] In December 1651, Parliament instructed commissioners to visit and reform 'the severall Universities, Colledges, and Schools of Learning… and to alter or abolish such statutes, Orders, or Customs in [any] of them as you shall judge not agreeable to the good of this Island or inconsistent with the government of this Commonwealth'.[133] Frances Dow has argued that the Cromwellian regime sought to control the universities, specifically, to weaken the power of Covenanting leaders and so dismantle the authority and influence of the Scottish ministry.[134] When considered alongside analogous policies in Ireland, and to a lesser extent New England, it also represented a key strategy in the imperial formation of the Cromwellian state in Scotland.

To exert control over the universities and project the power of the conquering regime, Parliament established a formal commission to regulate Scotland's universities in June 1652. The commissioners included three army officers – Major-General Richard Deane and colonels George Fenwick and Edmund Syler – and five civilians – George Smyth, Samuel Desborough, Richard Saltonstall Jr, Andrew Owen, John March, and Edward Moseley.[135] Fenwick, Desborough, and Saltonstall were all veterans of the New England enterprise.[136] The commission's duties were much expanded beyond those first enumerated in December 1651. In addition to reforming all university laws inconsistent with the then-Commonwealth, the commissioners were empowered to expel anyone 'found scandalous in their lives and conversations, or that shall oppose the Authority of the Common-wealth of England, exercised in Scotland, and place others more fitly in their rooms'. Like Trinity's trustees, the Scottish commission was granted power to control university masters and examine internal laws and affairs.[137] The commission

---

[130] *Records of the Kirk*, pp. 474, 476.
[131] *Cromwellian Union*, p. xxi; *Scotland and the Protectorate*, p. 394.
[132] Spurlock, *Cromwell and Scotland*, pp. 11–37, 199–203.
[133] *Scotland and the Protectorate*, p. 394.
[134] Dow, *Cromwellian Scotland*, p. 52.
[135] *Cromwellian Union*, pp. 174–5.
[136] Wells, 'Prelude to Empire', pp. 34–5. Richard Saltonstall Jr's brother, Henry, was one of Harvard's first graduates in the class of 1642. Saltonstall Jr was also close with President Dunster, with whom he corresponded about his work in Scotland. See Sibley, *Biographical Sketches*, I, p. 67; 'The Dunster Papers', *Collections of the Massachusetts Historical Society*, 4th series, 2 (Boston, MA, 1854), pp. 191–9, at 194.
[137] *By the Commissioners for Visiting and Regulating the Universities, and Other Affairs, Relating*

would later be empowered to punish any in the universities or the Scottish clergy who either prayed openly for Charles II or publicly condemned the Cromwellian regime.[138] These actions exhibited the regime's desire to curtail the influence of the Kirk's clergy. But the scope of the commission's duties also speaks to how the Cromwellians viewed the universities: as an apparatus of state power closely linked to the preaching ministry. Richard Saltonstall Jr could have potentially conceptualised the universities in this way, as he would have experienced first-hand how Harvard so clearly perpetuated the ministry in New England, while the ministry in turn cultivated the college. More broadly, the Cromwellians' conception of the university-as-seminary underlined their markedly non-radical understanding of the university's function in society as a purveyor of the extramural order. As was the case at Trinity, Cromwellian agents in Scotland did not pursue radical reform of higher education. In Scotland, authorities employed the existing institutions of higher learning to serve the vision of a new power structure.

Baillie recognised the implications of this university commission. In a letter to Francis Rous in August 1652, he wrote that if the commissioners 'be instructed to minister the Tender to us, they must purge out of St Andrewes Mr. Blair, Mr. Rutherfoord, and Mr. Wood; out of Edinburgh Mr. Dickson; and me out of Glasgow; and thereafter multitudes of our most precious ministers'.[139] Scotland's professors – and most of its clergy – opposed the union. The Scots were required to swear an oath to the Commonwealth and assent to the Tender of Union.[140] The Covenanters had been committed to fortifying the universities with their leading lights, but the professoriate was on the verge of collapse following the conquest.

Baillie's vexations and the commission's actions emphasise the crucial importance of personnel to actualising the visions of those who held power. To ensure that the universities did, in fact, undergird the authority of the Commonwealth in Scotland, positions of influence in the universities had to be filled with amenable men. Thus the chief thrust of Cromwellian policy in Scotland was the installation of men in the universities who supported the Commonwealth. Widespread purging of the kind that Baillie feared did not materialise. Rather, the Cromwellian commission drew upon the realities of the Scottish context and took advantage of already-vacant posts. The commissioners began their visitations in September 1652, and in the following months planted new principals at three universities: Glasgow, King's College, Aberdeen, and Edinburgh, all of which had vacant principalships.[141] But before these principalships were filled, the commission first addressed

---

to the Ministry of Scotland (Leith, 1652); Scotland and the Commonwealth, pp. 44–5.
[138] CSPD 1652–53, p. 417; A Declaration of the Commissioners for the Visitation of Universities, and for Placing and Displacing Ministers in Scotland (Leith, 1653).
[139] Baillie, L&J, III, p. 199.
[140] Dow, Cromwellian Scotland, p. 53.
[141] McCrie, Robert Blair, p. 300; Dow, Cromwellian Scotland, pp. 59–60.

the matter of the second divinity chair at Glasgow, which represented the first instance of direct Cromwellian intervention in the universities. John Young, a regent and the son of the dean of faculty, George, was placed in the post in October 1652.[142] As a regent, Young had yet to be ordained. Baillie opposed his election, for beyond his lack of clerical experience, Young was also a Protester. To compound matters for Baillie, George Lockhart, Glasgow's rector, had 'joyned affectionately with the English', and saw to Young's election. Baillie expressed his misgivings that an un-ordained regent 'should immediately turne Divinity Professor without any call from the Church, especially being professedly opposite our Church and Generall Assemblie'.[143]

The commission kept its attention on Glasgow by next focusing on the vacant principalship. In December 1652, Moseley notified Patrick Gillespie that the commission had chosen him to be Glasgow's principal. Cromwell had recently been in contact with Gillespie, exhorting him to appoint the 'godly' to positions of authority in Glasgow.[144] In respect to Glasgow's principalship, he would be the Cromwellians' man. The commissioners did not give Gillespie much of a choice – not that he would have required much convincing – writing that, 'yow can not, yow may not refuse this call'.[145] The following January, Gillespie received a letter of invitation from the university. Only four names are subscribed to the letter: George Lockhart, John Young, and the regents Richard Robertson and James Veitch.[146] Baillie claimed that this invitation came 'after much whispering with the English', and he noted that himself, George Young, Vice-Chancellor Zachary Boyd, and the regent Patrick Young opposed the move.[147]

In February 1653, the Cromwellian commissioners wrote to Glasgow stating that they understood that there were professors who opposed Gillespie and requested their opinions on the matter. They received letters from professors as well as the Glasgow presbytery, which argued that civil authorities should not meddle in religious affairs.[148] Even Thomas Wylie, a Glasgow Protester, expressed in a letter to Gillespie that it was abnormal for civil officers to plant universities, a practice that had been 'annexed by the kirk'.[149] Baillie reasoned similarly, arguing that Gillespie's appointment infringed upon Glasgow's right of free election, which the university had recently asserted. He also wrote that Gillespie was a deposed minister, having been expelled at the 1651 General Assembly. Finally, Baillie contended that Gillespie was 'not furnished with that measure of learning which the place of our Principall

[142] MAUG, II, p. 323, III, p. 390.
[143] Baillie, L&J, III, pp. 238–9.
[144] MacKenzie, *Solemn League and Covenant*, p. 107.
[145] GUL, MS Gen 1769/1/29.
[146] GUL, MS Gen 1769/1/24.
[147] Baillie, L&J, III, p. 239.
[148] *Ibid.*, III, pp. 205–6.
[149] NLS, Wod.Qu.XXXIII, fol. 116v.

does necessary require'.[150] The commissioners sidestepped these accusations, and in response Moseley, Saltonstall, and Smyth reaffirmed their authority to intervene: Parliament had granted to them the authority to plant vacancies, and no presbytery or university could do so without their approbation, 'least ye contract a further trouble upon yourselves'.[151]

Naturally, the situation infuriated Baillie. He argued that Gillespie colluded with the English and warned David Dickson that action must be taken to prevent the 'corrupting of our universities'.[152] To James Wood, Baillie complained that Gillespie held the principalship with his ministry in Glasgow, which the university had forbidden in July 1651.[153] Baillie was furious: 'The matter was totallie new; a Principall in part, not fullie for a time, not finallie, bot till a General Assemblie rightly constitute; a Principall with a full ministrie in the towne; a Principall, upon no invitation from the Colledge, bot some private men, after a Facultie had judiciallie refused all invitation.'[154] He then noted that Gillespie called a meeting to regulate university affairs and replace Glasgow's notary, John Herbertsone, with John Spreule, Gillespie's 'confident on the English interest'.[155] The speed of Gillespie's actions led Baillie to conclude that 'there is more betwixt that partie and the English than we yet know'.[156] Gillespie assumed the principalship in March 1653.[157] The Protester leader and advocate of closer ties with the English had assumed control of one of Scotland's universities.[158]

The situation surrounding Edinburgh's vacant principalship also saw the Cromwellian commission's intervention, and thus its strategy of circumventing established norms, though at first the Edinburgh town council attempted to proceed with filling the vacancy as normal. The principalship had been vacant since the death of John Adamson in 1651. In April 1652 the town council produced a list of candidates that included Alexander Colville, Thomas Craufurd, and William Colville, an Edinburgh minister deposed in 1649 for not disavowing the Engagement.[159] The council decided on William Colville, for 'if he had not bein deposed they thogt him a verie able and weill

---

[150] GUL, MS Gen 1769/1/4; Baillie, *L&J*, III, pp. 207–8.
[151] Baillie, *L&J*, III, p. 209.
[152] Ibid., III, pp. 209–11.
[153] MAUG, II, p. 321; Baillie, *L&J*, III, pp. 213, 239–40.
[154] Baillie, *L&J*, III, p. 213.
[155] Ibid., III, pp. 213, 241; *Cromwellian Union*, p. 35; Marwick, *Glasgow Burgh Records 1630–1662*, p. 218.
[156] Baillie, *L&J*, III, pp. 213–14.
[157] MAUG, III, p. 368.
[158] On the planting of Gillespie, see also Coutts, *Glasgow*, pp. 126–9; Mackie, *Glasgow*, pp. 108–9; McCoy, *Robert Baillie*, pp. 158–60; MacKenzie, *Solemn League and Covenant*, pp. 107–8; eadem, 'Contested Space', pp. 79–80.
[159] Wood, *Edinburgh Burgh Records 1642–1655*, pp. 276–7, 278; Baillie, *L&J*, II, pp. 41, 63–4, 92, 96.

qualified man for that place', and ordered that he be contacted in Utrecht.[160] Shortly thereafter, Edinburgh's regents assented to the decision, and in June 1652 Colville accepted.[161] Yet the next entry in the council register regarding the principalship, for 17 January 1653, notes that, 'thair hes beine divers obstructiouns to [Colville's] admissioun... the counsell for the tyme passes fra the forsaid nominatioun and electioun of the said Mr William Colvin and declares the place vacand'. Robert Leighton, minister of Newbattle, was then elected.[162] The Cromwellian commission had become involved.

Leighton was the son of the English preacher Alexander Leighton, who was steeped in London's puritan underground.[163] The elder Leighton sent his son to university in Edinburgh, where in the late 1620s he was suspended for writing poems against ceremonialism and Arminianism.[164] Leighton later subscribed to the Covenant and was ordained minister at Newbattle in 1642, but in 1648 he was rebuked for failing to pronounce the General Assembly's declaration against the Engagement. He was not deposed, however, for he pleaded that sickness and absence prohibited his public disavowal; he later sided with the Resolutioners. Dickson welcomed Leighton's appointment, for although it came under Cromwellian auspices, he felt that his presence in Edinburgh would counter Protesters there.[165]

Historians have attributed Leighton's election to his moderate disposition.[166] It is also indicative of the Cromwellian commission's ability to navigate local contexts. Evidence is sparse, but it is likely that Leighton's appointment could also be attributed to his own ideological formation that bent towards the visions of the Cromwellian regime. In March 1652, the synod of Lothian and Tweeddale ordered Leighton, who made almost annual trips to visit his father in London, to go south to negotiate the release of ministers captured at Worcester.[167] Leighton remained in London from May through November

---

[160] Wood, *Edinburgh Burgh Records 1642–1655*, p. 278.
[161] *Ibid.*, pp. 279, 283.
[162] *Ibid.*, pp. 304–5; Bower, *History of the University of Edinburgh*, I, pp. 259–60.
[163] David R. Como, 'Predestination and Political Conflict in Laud's London', *Historical Journal*, 46:2 (2003), 263–94, at 290.
[164] Crawford Gribben, 'Robert Leighton, Edinburgh Theology and the Collapse of the Presbyterian Consensus', in Elizabethanne Boran and Crawford Gribben (eds), *Enforcing Reformation in Ireland and Scotland, 1550–1700* (Aldershot, 2006), pp. 159–83, at 159–61; Hugh Ouston, 'Leighton, Robert (bap. 1612, d. 1684)', *ODNB*.
[165] Gribben, 'Robert Leighton', pp. 172–3.
[166] Dugald Butler, *The Life and Letters of Robert Leighton: Restoration Bishop of Dunblane and Archbishop of Glasgow* (London, 1903), p. 246; Spurlock, *Cromwell and Scotland*, p. 139; Dow, *Cromwellian Scotland*, p. 59.
[167] Langley, *Minutes of the Synod of Lothian and Tweeddale*, pp. xx, xxv–xxvi, 36, 40; Butler, *Life and Letters*, pp. 210, 235–36; David Laing (ed.), 'Extracts from the Presbytery Records of Dalkeith, Relating to the Parish of Newbattle, During the Incumbency of Mr Robert Leighton, 1641–1653', in *Proceedings of the Society of Antiquaries of Scotland, Vol. IV Part II* (Edinburgh, 1863), pp. 459–92, at 472–3, 475–6.

1652, during which time he came into contact with the Cromwellian authorities.[168] There is no direct evidence to support claims that Leighton actively pursued the principalship while meeting with the Cromwellians, and the town council had already elected Colville by the time Leighton departed Scotland.[169] But Leighton, it seems, made an impression on the English authorities. In a letter to Patrick Gillespie in December 1652, Moseley requested assistance with moving Leighton to Edinburgh's principalship. He wrote that, 'if he & yow both setled according to our desires I am confident the universities would be as well provided with Principalls as ever they were since theire foundacons'.[170] Moseley's letter suggests that Gillespie, a leading radical, had some association with Leighton that was known to Cromwellian officials. It is also likely that the government in London had, through its meetings with Leighton, decided that Leighton would be the best fit for the post. In December, at about the time Moseley wrote to Gillespie, Leighton submitted two letters to the Dalkeith presbytery resigning his charge.[171] Meanwhile, the Cromwellian commission forced the Edinburgh town council to revoke Colville's election, and by February Leighton was installed as principal.[172] Leighton's theology also offers clues as to why he may have been amenable to Cromwellian authorities. By the end of the 1640s, Leighton's zeal for Covenanting had dissipated. During the 1640s he came to believe that the Covenanters' political program could not achieve true reformation of the heart because 'external' covenants were temporal pacts that had no bearing on salvation.[173] It is, of course, not clear if he recounted these ideas in London. But the Cromwellians would have welcomed his repudiation of the Covenanters' political agenda – and the potential for distilling these ideas among impressionable students. This outlook, promoted from Edinburgh's influential principalship, would further undercut the Covenanters' authority in Scotland and advance the vision and power of the Commonwealth.

The Cromwellian commission's campaign to exert control over the universities also came to Aberdeen. The burgh had become home to a growing Independent movement as the Kirk fractured amidst the Protester–Resolutioner controversy. Many Aberdeen Independents initially sided with the Protesters, but they began to radicalise further by questioning the Kirk's polity and the Covenant's legality – though, unlike the Aberdeen Doctors, through a decidedly anti-episcopal lens. They fell out with mainline Protesters, including Wariston and Rutherford, which highlights how Scotland also

---

[168] Butler, *Life and Letters*, p. 246.
[169] Grant, *Story of the University of Edinburgh*, II, p. 247.
[170] GUL, MS Gen 1769/1/29.
[171] Laing, 'Records of Dalkeith', p. 478; Butler, *Life and Letters*, p. 239.
[172] Wood, *Edinburgh Burgh Records 1642–1655*, p. 305; Grant, *Story of the University of Edinburgh*, II, p. 247.
[173] See Gribben, 'Robert Leighton', pp. 167–9.

witnessed the proliferation of sects that came with the English army.[174] The radicalisation of Alexander Jaffray, provost of Aberdeen, and several Marischal College staff saw Independency's entrenchment in the burgh. Captured at Dunbar, during Jaffray's captivity he converted to Independency under the influence of Cromwell and John Owen, who convinced him of the evil of the Scots' alignment with a malignant.[175] Upon his return to Aberdeen in 1651, Jaffray began considering these matters with Marischal principal William Muir, divinity professor John Menzies, and regent Andrew Birnie, thus forming an Independent cadre at the college.[176] Also included was John Row, minister of New Aberdeen's St Nicholas Kirk, grammarian, and noted Hebraist.[177] After the Engagement Row became a prominent Protester in Aberdeen and joined with the Independents by May 1652.[178]

It was from this radical Aberdonian milieu that the Cromwellian commission chose the new principal of King's College. In September 1652, Fenwick, Moseley, Owen, Desborough, and Smyth visited Aberdeen and replaced Principal Guild with John Row.[179] The commissioners also once again circumvented the Kirk's authority and installed Row, with Gillespie in attendance, as the new principal, despite Row having been suspended by the synod of Aberdeen two months earlier.[180] They also placed Gilbert Rule, an Independent and former Glasgow and King's regent, into the sub-principalship.[181] With Muir and Menzies occupying, respectively, the principalship and divinity professorship at Marischal, both of Aberdeen's colleges took on a strong Independent hue, which aligned comfortably with the vision of the Cromwellian regime.

As historians have noted, St Andrews was the only university to avoid interference in 1652–3, though to this conclusion should be added Marischal,

---

[174] Spurlock, *Cromwell and Scotland*, pp. 121–40.

[175] Alexander Jaffray, *Diary of Alexander Jaffray*, ed. John Barclay, 3rd edn (Aberdeen, 1856), pp. 58–9, 164.

[176] John Stuart (ed.), *Extracts from the Council Register of the Burgh of Aberdeen. 1643–1747* (Edinburgh, 1872), p. 97; Scott, *Fasti*, VII, p. 357; FAM, II, pp. 28, 36, 51; Rait, *Universities of Aberdeen*, p. 151; Spurlock, *Cromwell and Scotland*, pp. 107, 123.

[177] Row, *History*, pp. xliv–xlvi. For Row's praxis of Hebrew grammar of 1651, see EUL, La.III.179.

[178] Row was the son of John Row (1569–1646), author of *The History of the Kirk of Scotland*. The younger Row completed this work in 1650, bringing the history to 1639. On Row the younger, see Row, *History*, pp. xxxvix–liv; K.D. Holfelder, 'Row, John (c. 1598–1672)', ODNB. See also John Stuart (ed.), *Selections from the Records of the Kirk Session, Presbytery, and Synod of Aberdeen* (Aberdeen, 1846), p. 220; Spurlock, *Cromwell and Scotland*, pp. 122–4, 135–7.

[179] McCrie, *Robert Blair*, p. 301.

[180] Lamont, *Diary*, pp. 47–8; Anderson, *Officers and Graduates*, p. 26; Row, *History*, p. xlvii; Stuart, *Synod of Aberdeen*, p. 222; NLS, Wod.Qu.XXIX, fol. 175; Spurlock, *Cromwell and Scotland*, pp. 140, 299, n. 280.

[181] Anderson, *Officers and Graduates*, p. 41; Alexander Du Toit, 'Rule, Gilbert (c. 1629–1701)', ODNB.

which embraced Independency before Worcester.[182] Furthermore, neither university had vacant principalships that the regime could exploit, save for one: the provostship of St Salvator's College. This post had remained vacant since John Baron's resignation in 1649. Baillie wrote that the commissioners offered the provostship to 'Samuell Colville', though he did not enter the college.[183] Colville was a Fife native and graduate of St Leonard's, the son of Elizabeth Melville, Lady Culross, the younger brother of the St Mary's professor Alexander Colville, and, according to the St Andrews presbytery, something of a nuisance.[184] He is best known for his Restoration-era poetry, in which he satirised disputes among Presbyterians, but his antipathy for the Covenanters likely made him a potential candidate in Cromwellian eyes. At about this time he penned a Latin epigram to the English commander in Scotland, Colonel Robert Lilburne, to ingratiate himself to the regime.[185] Despite these intrigues, the provostship was not filled until 1657.

It does seem that the commissioners were initially intent on making changes at St Andrews, where they arrived in September 1652. The commissioners claimed the authority to remove staff found scandalous in their charges or averse to the Commonwealth, and they called before them the masters and reviewed all laws and statutes.[186] The commissioners also sought to examine St Andrews' students, but they were not yet present, which means that the visitation likely took place in early September before Michaelmas term. Beyond these actions, the commission did little else. According to the biography of Robert Blair, the commissioners' 'moderation' towards St Andrews was likely due to Blair's prior association with Fenwick, whom Blair had met during his time in London in the early 1630s before Fenwick departed for New England, a migration that Blair had also contemplated.[187] The commissioners left St Andrews with a warning: no vacancies should be filled in the university until the commission was notified.[188] The commission, while initially making minimal change at St Andrews, still positioned itself as the main arbiter in university affairs.

The Cromwellian regime's control of the Scottish universities was part of the larger process of imperial formation that saw the dismantling of the Kirk's institutional dynamic. Colonel Lilburne disbanded the General Assembly in

---

[182] Dow, *Cromwellian Scotland*, p. 60.
[183] Baillie, *L&J*, III, p. 244.
[184] Kinloch, *Minutes of St. Andrews and Cupar*, pp. 66–7.
[185] On Colville, see David Irving, *The History of Scotish Poetry*, ed. John Aitken Carlyle (Edinburgh, 1861), p. 483; Jamie Reid-Baxter, 'Elizabeth Melville, Lady Culross: Two Letters to Her Son James', in Janay Nugent and Elizabeth Ewan (eds), *Children and Youth in Premodern Scotland* (Woodbridge, 2015), pp. 205–20. For Colville's epigram, see NLS, Adv. MS 19.3.4. I am grateful to Jamie Reid-Baxter for these references and for his lively correspondence on the Colvilles.
[186] Lamont, *Diary*, p. 47.
[187] McCrie, *Robert Blair*, pp. 92–101, 300.
[188] Lamont, *Diary*, p. 47.

July 1653, thus creating a void for the administration of university affairs, which had throughout much of the preceding fifteen years fallen under the purview of the Assembly.[189] The General Assembly would not meet again until 1690. With its suppression, single professors of divinity who opposed the Cromwellian regime – such as Baillie, Dickson, and James Wood – had no institutional apparatus to support them. They were left to complain to each other and to remonstrate to their Cromwellian-backed principals. The Cromwellians eliminated the political and ecclesiastical machinery of Covenanted power in Scotland while incorporating the universities into its emerging infrastructure.

Conclusion

The universities of Ireland, New England, and Scotland were useful organs to extend Cromwellian dominion, consolidate power, and build conformity to a new republican social order. There was precedent for how the universities would be incorporated into this new dynamic, as Parliamentarian and thereafter Cromwellian authorities pursued wholesale reforms at Oxford and Cambridge. But, in practice, the Cromwellian regime's actions towards the universities in these spaces were informed by local needs and realities. At Trinity and the Scottish universities, the Cromwellians installed amenable divines into positions of authority. The only Englishman imported to take a university post was Samuel Winter, at Trinity; in Scotland, Cromwellian authorities exploited infighting to draw upon agreeable Scots. Beyond Winter's presence, there was also no extensive importation of Englishmen into these institutions, while the purging was kept to a minimum. Harvard, meanwhile, was initially left to its own devices. An ocean away, the university was free from direct intervention of the Cromwellian state, even though the institution, and Dunster most of all, would have gladly received additional financial support, like the regime granted to Trinity, as part of a wider drive to propagate the gospel. Harvard, however, proved useful to the republican government regardless of any direct intervention, as it provided personnel who staffed Cromwellian civil and military offices throughout England, Scotland, and Ireland.

As imperial formation and the control of higher education in conquered realms reflected local realities, it nevertheless underscored a thoroughly conventional vision of the universities as structures of state power that socialised future churchmen and statesmen. Radical university reforms, at least in the era of conquest and consolidation, were not pursued in Ireland, New England, or Scotland. In each locale, rather, there was a persistent emphasis on the individuals who staffed these institutions. While the strategies in each

[189] *Scotland and the Commonwealth*, pp. 161–5; Nicoll, *Diary of Public Transactions*, p. 110.

space differed, the universities were employed in the service of the British republic to build, or maintain, conformity and consolidating state power, in much the same way that Charles I and William Laud had sought to use them to shape their own brand of conformity and unity. As will be discussed in the next two chapters, because the universities endured as conventional institutions – and that so many academics who opposed the Cromwellian regime remained in place – conflict and resistance were pervasive in these institutions throughout the Interregnum. As contested spaces, the universities witnessed the persistence of anti-Cromwellian sentiments, for the remnants of both the Covenanting movement and of Ireland's old Protestant interest were tied to the institutional endurance of the universities. Additionally, burgeoning religious radicalism impacted the course of university affairs on either side of the Atlantic. With the conclusion of the conquest, competing conceptions of true religion, Reformed orthodoxy, and the advancement of learning clashed and were repeatedly negotiated in the universities of Scotland, Ireland, and New England.

5

The Scottish Universities, c. 1652–60

In July 1654, Robert Baillie lamented to William Spang that 'All our Colledges are quicklie like to be undone. Our Churches are in great confusion: no intrant getts any stipend till he have petitioned and subscryved some acknowledgment to the English.'[1] Baillie's coupling of the Scottish universities' potential ruin with the Kirk's demise is telling. As key institutions to the formation of Covenanted Scotland, the universities had been reformed to buttress the nascent Covenanted state, where they were to socialise future churchmen into the authorised mores of the Covenanted Kirk. But this project had deteriorated: schism paralysed the Kirk, while Independency strengthened within parts of the Protester faction. Cromwellian sympathisers had been planted at three universities, whose graduates now, by necessity, had to be agreeable to the Cromwellian regime if they desired an adequate living. In Interregnum Scotland, the contested nature of the universities was thrown into sharp relief. On the one hand, they provided venues for Cromwellian authorities to secure long-term allegiance to the British republic; on the other, they remained as one of the key institutional spaces in which to resist the regime.

Scholars have contended that the Cromwellian Protectorate sought the promotion of English, if Cromwellian, republican mores in its conquered realms, with some, including Barry Coward, suggesting that this amounted to a policy of 'Anglicisation'.[2] The seizure of the universities could be interpreted as part of the conquering regime's wider policy to impose a preconceived set of authorised behaviours on a conquered realm as a way to consolidate control and legitimise the new political and religious order. However, as was argued in the previous chapter, Cromwellian authorities did not necessarily impose a blanket policy on the universities, opting rather for an approach that drew upon the realities of local Scottish politics and religion. This saw not the importation of English republican partisans into academic posts, but instead the planting of Scots who were agreeable to the Cromwellian commission

---

[1] Baillie, *L&J*, III, p. 244.
[2] See especially Barry Coward, *The Cromwellian Protectorate* (Manchester, 2002), pp. 36–7, 142–3. See also Stevenson, 'Cromwellian, Scotland and Ireland', pp. 161–5; Smyth, 'Empire-Building', pp. 131–4.

into principalships in the universities.³ What remains unclear is how the universities figured into Cromwellian policies for Scotland beyond this initial flurry of activity in 1653 and, more importantly, how, and the extent to which, Cromwellian power was projected and resisted in these institutions.

By examining these considerations, this chapter aims to provide a clearer sense of how disputes over the nature of the Scottish social order persisted throughout the Interregnum. It will also seek to address something of a gap in our understanding of the history of higher education in early modern Scotland. Writing about the universities and the Interregnum, Ronald Cant claimed that 'these bitter years have little of specialist interest'.⁴ Luckily, there has been a growing historiography that has engaged critically with a range of topics that has enhanced our understanding of Interregnum Scotland. Among these, scholarship that examines the rise and proliferation of Protestant sects, the practice of toleration and its reception in Scotland, the fallout of the Protester–Resolutioner controversy, the nature of the Cromwellian occupation, and the exercise of religious and social discipline, have elucidated the dynamic realities of the incorporative union and its impact on the wider Scottish society in the 1650s.⁵ This chapter attempts to more fully integrate the Scottish universities to these conversations. More critically, this chapter will show that Scotland's universities, in an era of conquest and occupation, remained alive to the febrile political and religious dynamics of the Interregnum. Questions and competitions over what constituted a healthy, functioning commonwealth – even as a constituent entity in a union formed through conquest – persisted throughout this period, and as such, the Scottish universities were directly implicated. What is more, for both Resolutioners and Protesters, the universities took on added importance as one of the remaining institutional embodiments of their competing conceptions of the Covenanted nation. The universities were the chief venues where

---

³ This contrasted with the approach to Scottish law courts, where the Cromwellian regime sought to forcibly remove Scottish jurists with partisans trained in England. See e.g., Jennifer Wells, 'English Law, Irish Trials and Cromwellian State Building in the 1650s', *Past & Present*, 227 (2015), 77–119, at 96–7. See also Dow, *Cromwellian Scotland*, pp. 59–60; MacKenzie, *Solemn League and Covenant*, p. 107.

⁴ Cant, *St Andrews*, p. 72.

⁵ K.D. Holfelder's PhD thesis, 'Factionalism in the Kirk', remains the most comprehensive account of the Protester–Resolutioner controversy. On religion, discipline, toleration, and occupation in Cromwellian Scotland, see also Spurlock, *Cromwell and Scotland*, pp. 100–57; idem, '"Anie Gospell Way": Religious Diversity in Interregnum Scotland', *Records of the Scottish Church History Society*, 37 (2007), 89–119; Patrick Little, *Lord Broghill and the Cromwellian Union with Ireland and Scotland* (Woodbridge, 2004), pp. 94–124; Ryan Burns, 'Unrepentant Papists: Catholic Responses to Cromwellian Toleration in Interregnum Scotland', *History*, 103:355 (2018), 243–61; Michelle Brock, 'Keeping the Covenant in Cromwellian Scotland', *Scottish Historical Review*, 99 (2020), 392–411; eadem, '"The Man Will Shame Me": Women, Sex and Kirk Discipline during the Cromwellian Occupation', *Scottish Historical Review*, 51:2 (2022), 133–56.

these rival understandings of Scottish society were contested. How and to what ends university students were educated was in many respects amplified in this period, especially as Cromwellian authorities sought a religious settlement for Scotland.

This chapter underscores the universities' strategic and contested space between the regime, its supporters, and its opponents during the Interregnum. The first part evaluates the nature of resistance to the regime in the post-conquest universities, highlighting symbolic and actual modes of opposition to the projection and exercise of Cromwellian power in the universities. The second part deals more broadly with the universities' engagement with the Protectorate government, highlighting how it was at times prudent for opponents of the regime to work with the new political order. This section examines the universities' place in the Protesters' proposed settlement, Gillespie's Charter. Finally, the third part examines the scope of Cromwellian university policy in the years leading up to the Restoration. Once again, the Cromwellian regime, like power structures before it, placed utmost importance on the individuals who held university posts, while nevertheless pursuing strategies that were informed by local conditions. But, as will be highlighted in this section, questions can be raised about the efficacy of Cromwellian policies in the universities, and the extent to which the regime effectively wielded the universities as instruments of state power.

Resisting the Cromwellian Regime in the Scottish Universities

The Cromwellian regime's installation of Scottish allies into the principal-ships of Glasgow, Edinburgh, and King's College was not complemented by the concurrent removal of antithetical staff. A fair number of opponents of the new political order maintained their posts, and thus their ability to educate, and influence, students. The universities were spaces where competing projections of power and influence materialised along at least three fronts: Cromwellian, Protester, and Resolutioner.[6] But how was Cromwellian power contested in the universities? Robert Baillie's letters are littered with assertions about Scotland's decline and the universities' deterioration – again underscoring higher education's vital connection to the health of the nation – but there are few examples of direct, outright resistance beyond Glasgow. Even though opponents of the regime like Baillie, David Dickson, and James Wood occupied influential divinity posts, they nevertheless served under Cromwellian appointees and sympathisers. Still, there are indications that university staff and students employed different modes of resistance and disobedience to oppose the Cromwellian regime. These examples represented

---

[6] This parallels the experiences of local government structures, the burgh of Glasgow most of all. See e.g., MacKenzie, 'Contested Space', pp. 71–2.

a type of wider 'counter-conduct' across Scottish higher education that highlighted the limits of Cromwellian power in the universities. The evidence at once centres the agency of university staff and students, who were very much alive to the power dynamics at play, in challenging and ultimately delegitimising Cromwellian power in the very institutions that served to legitimise state power.[7]

An initial example of disobedience comes from the notebook of a student of Edinburgh regent Thomas Craufurd. Student notebooks, alongside graduation theses and lecture notes, provide rich insight into the ways and extent to which political, religious, and ethical ideas were contemplated in the Scottish universities. Notebooks often contain marginalia that provide clues not only about the curriculum, but also student engagement, temperament, and biases.[8] In the margins of Craufurd's student notes on logic from March 1653 is the phrase 'Love live Charles King by the grace of God'. Next to this is an inscription, 'Charles Stewart, Warrior King of Scots and England'.[9]

Craufurd, a Covenanter, was also loyal to Charles I, and he had assisted Principal Adamson in planning the 1633 coronation celebrations. Apparent disloyalty to the Cromwellians did not spell his ouster, however, for he remained at Edinburgh until his death in 1662. It is not known if Craufurd revealed his feelings to students directly, but his student's notes expose his hostility to the Cromwellian regime. One might assume others in his class may have also felt this way.[10]

Laureation, or commencement, ceremonies were another area where the power of the Cromwellian regime was resisted, via more public contestations, and delegitimised. According to the Fife diarist John Lamont, the July 1652 laureations at St Andrews were held in 'private (without examination), about 6 or 7 weikes before the ordinary time; for if publick, they wold beine urged with the Tender by the English, so refusing it, they wold not bein graduat'.[11] Baillie also reports that laureation ceremonies were not held at Glasgow in 1653.[12] Similarly, the graduating class at Edinburgh petitioned the town council in April 1652 to hold its laureation ceremony in private because of the 'paucitie of their number and severall uther serious and grave reasons'.[13]

---

[7] On the exercise of power and counter-conduct, see Michel Foucault, *Security, Territory, Population: Lectures at the Collége de France, 1977–1978*, ed. Michel Senellart, trans. Graham Burchell (New York, 2007), pp. 201–3.
[8] The notes of Zurishaddai Lang are particularly vibrant. See EUL, Gen.1965. On the uses of student notebooks, see especially Schultz, 'Protestant Intellectual Culture', pp. 47–9.
[9] EUL, Dc.5.122, fol. 122v.
[10] Christine M. Shepherd, 'University Life in the Seventeenth Century', *Four Centuries Edinburgh University Life*, pp. 1–15, at 8.
[11] Lamont, *Diary*, pp. 44–5; Dow, *Cromwellian Scotland*, p. 60.
[12] Baillie, *L&J*, III, pp. 253–4.
[13] Wood, *Edinburgh Burgh Records 1642–1655*, p. 276; Dalzel, *History of the University of Edinburgh*, II, pp. 162–3.

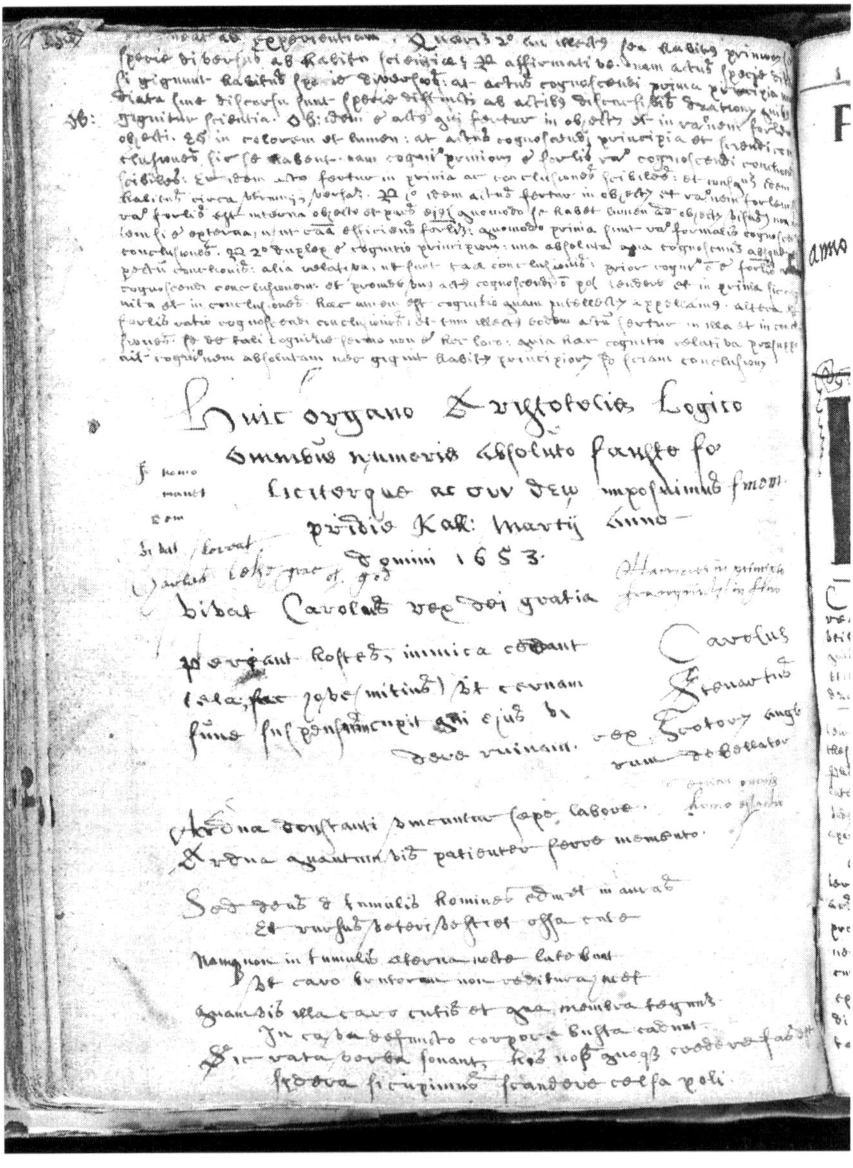

Figure 5.1. Excerpt from the Dictates of Thomas Craufurd, March 1653 (Dc.5.122), Centre for Research Collections, University of Edinburgh.

Beyond external political pressures, Edinburgh's class of 1652 numbered only nineteen graduates out of fifty original entrants.[14] Indeed, according to the Edinburgh town council records, public laureations were not held until 1657.[15] There were clear political undertones to commencing in private: it meant that Scotland's newest graduates, future statesmen and churchmen, would not subscribe publicly to the Tender of Union. Added to this was a ploy pursued by the Edinburgh town council, which withheld the college mace, an instrument typically used at the university's public gatherings and processions, from use in the university's business from the outset of the Cromwellian conquest to at least 1655.[16] Beyond the Edinburgh town council's decision regarding the college mace, the impetus for private laureations seemed to have stemmed from student initiative, which suggests the students and their regents' unwillingness to acknowledge and legitimate the contemporary political reality and the authority of the Cromwellian regime in Scotland.[17]

Private laureations, somewhat paradoxically, were a noticeable mode of resistance. As discussed in Chapter 3, commencements were important public rituals that evoked the university's ethos for the extramural community.[18] The inhabitants of Glasgow, Edinburgh, and St Andrews would have recognised the lack of such a public ritual, as the ceremonies occupied a key place on the civic calendar. While private laureations underscored the extent to which the Cromwellian conquest disrupted public life, they also highlight the meaning assigned to university rituals as a marker of healthy commonwealths. As *New Englands First Fruits* trumpeted Harvard's first commencement to highlight the vitality of New England society, the opposite was apparent in Cromwellian Scotland. The contested nature of these laureations, and the sheer lack of ceremonies, signalled the extent to which the conquest had debased Scottish society – the universities were, in a sense, a microcosm. The absence of laureations can be taken as further evidence of opposition to the Cromwellian regime and an example of a demonstrative form of action in which staff and students assumed roles as agitators against the vectors of state power. This resistance, a type of 'academic secession' of ritual, was part of a longer tradition of academic protest that dates to the Middle Ages.[19] In the

---

[14] EUA, IN1/ADS/STA/2/1, p. 47; Laing, *Catalogue*, p. 73.

[15] Wood, *Edinburgh Burgh Records 1642–1655*, pp. 314–15; eadem (ed.), *Extracts from the Records of the Burgh of Edinburgh, 1655 to 1665* (Edinburgh, 1940), pp. xlvii, 59.

[16] Bower, *History of the University of Edinburgh*, I, p. 264; Dalzel, *History of the University of Edinburgh*, II, pp. 172–3.

[17] Refusals to subscribe the Tender were also seen in Scottish law courts. See e.g., J.D. Ford, *Law and Opinion in Scotland during the Seventeenth Century* (Oxford, 2007), pp. 93–100.

[18] See also Richard Kirwan and Helga Robinson-Hammerstein, 'University Ritual and the Construction of the Scholar', in Per Andersen *et al.* (eds), *Liber Amicorum Ditlev Tamm. Law, History and Culture* (Copenhagen, 2011), pp. 107–20, at 108–9.

[19] Pieter Dhondt and Laura Kolbe, 'Students as Agents of Change?', in Pieter Dhondt and Elizabethanne Boran (eds), *Student Revolt, City, and Society in Europe: From the Middle Ages to the Present* (London, 2018), pp. 1–8; Steffen Hölscher, 'Moving Out! Student

Scottish context, one of the venues of public oath taking to the Cromwellian regime was abandoned. By sidestepping the performative aspect of the Tender, Scottish students and regents, for a brief time at least, contested the public presentation of Cromwellian authority in Scotland.[20]

There is only limited evidence of university students and staff engaging in direct, armed action against the Cromwellian regime. An important flashpoint of military opposition to the new political order was the rising in the Highlands led by the earl of Glencairn from 1653 to mid-1654. Though it failed to restore Charles II, the rebellion did accentuate the level of disaffection to Cromwellian rule.[21] To suppress the rising, Oliver Cromwell gave George Monck, general of the army in Scotland, wide remit to arrest opponents.[22] Though fighting was concentrated in the Highlands, the rising drew support from every facet of Scottish society, including the church and universities.[23] This led to the prohibition of meetings of ministers, whom Cromwellian authorities believed were communicating with the rebels; it also prompted an order prohibiting public prayers for Charles II, which incited opposition to the regime.[24] The rising also magnified the Kirk's internal divisions. Clerical support for the rising came from the Resolutioners, and Colonel Robert Lilburne rationalised his suppression of the 1653 General Assembly by citing Edinburgh professor David Dickson's prayers for the king.[25] Lilburne, furthermore, recognised that the Protester faction, led by Patrick Gillespie, were against the rising. In a letter to Cromwell in October 1653, Lilburne wrote that 'I perceive Galeaspe of this town [Glasgow], who was with mee, and these Westerne people, due much detest' the actions of their Resolutioner counterparts.[26] While it would be a stretch to suggest that Resolutioner professors encouraged their students to partake in armed conflict – especially given the litany of laws and regulations that sought to mitigate student violence within university walls and adjoining towns – it nevertheless appeared that St Andrews' students were particularly fervent for

---

Identity and Symbolic Protest at Eighteenth-Century German Universities', *Student Revolt*, pp. 120–35, at 121–4.

[20] Stewart, *Rethinking the Scottish Revolution*, pp. 87–90. On the representation of political authority, see also Michael J. Braddick, 'Administrative Performance: The Representation of Authority in Early Modern England', in Michael J. Braddick and John Walter (eds), *Negotiating Power in Early Modern Society: Order, Hierarchy and Subordination in Britain and Ireland* (Cambridge, 2001), pp. 166–87.

[21] On Glencairn's Rising, see Dow, *Cromwellian Scotland*, pp. 78–142; Danielle McCormack, 'Highland Lawlessness and the Cromwellian Regime', *Scotland in the Age of Two Revolutions*, pp. 115–33.

[22] *Scotland and the Protectorate*, pp. 76–80; *Cromwell Writings*, III, pp. 246–7.

[23] *Scotland and the Protectorate*, pp. 90–1, 94.

[24] *Scotland and the Commonwealth*, pp. 161–5; Nicoll, *Diary of Public Transactions*, pp. 110–11.

[25] *Records of the Kirk*, pp. 656–7.

[26] *Scotland the Commonwealth*, pp. 241–2.

the cause. In April 1654, Lilburne wrote that 'the country is so false to us… I heare 20 Collegians are gone out of St. Andrewes, and undoubtedly many of the ministers are great promoters of the Rebellion'.[27] These actions were symptomatic of wider hostility to Cromwellian rule and indicative of the extent to which university students opposed the regime.

Within the universities, opposition to Cromwellian clients who occupied university posts paralleled acts of symbolic and direct resistance to the regime. This was certainly the case at Glasgow, where Robert Baillie was seemingly bent on making the tenure of Patrick Gillespie, the main representation of Cromwellian power in the university, as difficult as possible. Baillie was by no means some 'heroic' dissident, but rather an academic who continued to do his duties to the institution and its divinity students while taking opportunities to subvert Gillespie's authority, thus contesting Cromwellian power.[28] At each meeting of university staff, Baillie protested the presence of both Gillespie and John Young, the divinity professor whom the Cromwellian commission for the universities foisted into a divinity chair in October 1652, maintaining that each held their positions illegally.[29] When Baillie signed official university documents, he added 'P.S.S.', or *Protestationibus Salvis*, after his name in order to maintain his constant protest to Gillespie's legitimacy.[30] In addition to these examples of counter-conduct, Baillie also subverted Gillespie's authority through his direct action in ousting the regent Richard Robertson on the grounds of heterodoxy. The Protester faction, according to Baillie, had 'violently… thrust in over all our priviledges' Robertson in December 1649.[31] It was likely that Baillie's son, Henry, a student of Robertson's, alerted his father to the potential heresies, which included anti-trinitarianism.[32] Baillie called Robertson before him to review his dictates, which he found heterodox. Gillespie and his acolytes in the university agreed that they 'mislyked' the tenets, but they thought Robertson to be 'holy', and refused to disgrace him with removal. Baillie, however, told Gillespie that, 'if he keeped in the Colledge one who had taught so blasphemous heresies, and who yet was not sensible, for any purpose, of his sinne, I would let the world know it for my own exoneration, and would charge this connivance on him'. After Archibald Johnston of Wariston and James Guthrie advised Gillespie not to challenge Baillie on this issue, he agreed to Robertson's ouster. Baillie succeeded in removing a purported heretic from Glasgow, but he wrote that 'It grieved my to see no zeale at all against the most grievous errors.'[33] This affair,

---

[27] *Scotland and the Protectorate*, pp. 80–1.
[28] Foucault, *Security, Territory, Population*, p. 202. On Baillie's teaching and administrative responsibilities under Gillespie's principalship, see also McCoy, *Robert Baillie*, p. 164.
[29] Baillie, *L&J*, III, p. 239.
[30] *Ibid.*; GUL, MS Gen 1769/1/6.
[31] Baillie, *L&J*, III, p. 239; MAUG, III, p. 388.
[32] Baillie, *L&J*, III, p. 223–4; McCoy, *Robert Baillie*, p. 163.
[33] Baillie, *L&J*, III, pp. 239–40.

while providing another example of protest, and conflict, in Scottish higher education, also reinforced how Scottish academe was still experiencing the impact of the Protester–Resolutioner controversy, and how representations of factional power clashed in the universities.

Beyond his opposition to what he believed to be the illegality of the authority exercised by Cromwellian allies, Baillie also had personal reasons to protest. According to Baillie, Gillespie 'took all the keys of the little chambers from my schollars, whereof they had long, by my allowance, been in possession, and gave them to whom he liked better'. Gillespie also procured an order from the English government to remove the elderly John Strang, Baillie's friend and father-in-law, from his lodging. Gillespie then changed the locks and invited John Young to take up residence there.[34] Such temperamental actions, coupled with Baillie's persistent protests, appeared to have affected Glasgow's students. Baillie reported that some students contested the authority of university leadership by refusing to pledge their obedience to the lessons of the principal and divinity professor, believing neither Gillespie, nor Young, held their posts legally. Baillie found little fault in the students' behaviour: 'This insolence grieved me, yet I neglected it; only told [Gillespie] at meeting that I could concurre in no such violence.'[35] There also appeared on the university's gates and closes a 'number of most base and scandalous Latine verses' that targeted Gillespie, Young, and the regents. Students took to repeating the slanders, which led Gillespie and Young to interrogate a number of scholars, causing 'such affrightment' that several left the university.[36] The practice of subverting the authority of the Cromwellian regime in the university was not without its consequences.

The extent to which Cromwellian authority was contested in the Scottish universities following the conquest can be viewed as the extension of a longer tradition of both passive and participative protest endemic to Scotland during the Covenanting and Cromwellian eras.[37] In the universities, Cromwellian authority clashed with individuals opposed to the regime, many of whom who aligned with the Resolutioner faction in the Kirk and who thus espoused competing understandings of an orderly Scottish church and state. Flashes of resistance at Glasgow, Edinburgh, and St Andrews reinforced the notion that the universities were contested spaces, but they also scored small, mostly symbolic victories that subverted Cromwellian authorities and their appointees and further delegitimised their standing in Scottish academe.

---

[34] *Ibid.*, III, p. 242.
[35] *Ibid.*, III, p. 243.
[36] *Ibid.*, III, p. 243; McCoy, *Robert Baillie*, p. 168.
[37] See e.g., Karin Bowie, *Public Opinion in Early Modern Scotland, c. 1560–1707* (Cambridge, 2020), pp. 36–45.

Gillespie's Charter and the Scottish Universities

While the fallout of the Cromwellian conquest reverberated in the Scottish universities, higher education in general, as an apparatus of state power, remained bound to the policies that emanated from central authorities. The Instrument of Government, promulgated in 1653, and related legislation, had particular ramifications for the Scottish universities under Cromwellian rule. The Instrument established a new constitution for the archipelagic Protectorate, and of its forty-two articles, the three that concerned religion championed the Cromwellian tenets of liberty of conscience and clerical maintenance.[38] Furthermore, the corresponding Ordinance for Appointing Commissioners for Approbation of Public Preachers established a national scheme for the assessment of candidates for vacant benefices. A central body of thirty-eight 'triers' was to evaluate the orthodoxy of all expectants before they assumed their posts.[39] The triers included Independents, Presbyterians, and Baptists, and the system that they oversaw, which remained in place in England until the Restoration, was responsible for the approval of some 3,500 ministers.[40] Within the context of the archipelagic union, these policies also represented a new type of political and religious order that the universities, in England and beyond, were to buttress.

While an overarching ecclesiastical apparatus like the national system of triers provided a potential model for Scotland, it was not simply imposed upon the conquered kingdom. Rather, the Protectorate government drew upon local conditions to inform its approach to Scotland, leaning heavily on its closest allies. In March 1654 Cromwell summoned Principal Patrick Gillespie of Glasgow and Principal John Menzies of Marischal College to London to establish a concurrent religious settlement for Scotland.[41] Among the Protester faction, Gillespie had previously shown his willingness to work with the regime, and for Cromwell, he was the most obvious candidate to cooperate in setting religious policy.[42] His allies among the Protesters did not share this sentiment. A year earlier, in March 1653, a faction of Protesters that included Wariston, Rutherford, Andrew Cant, and James Guthrie, issued a declaration against Cromwellian encroachment into Scotland's ecclesiastical affairs. In addition to their opposition to English interference, they took

---

[38] Gardiner, *Constitutional Documents*, pp. 406–18.

[39] *Acts and Ordinances*, II, pp. 855–8. The scheme resembled a proposal found in the Humble Proposals, which had been submitted to the Rump in February 1652 by John Owen, Philip Nye, and Thomas Goodwin. See Coward, *Cromwellian Protectorate*, p. 40.

[40] On the triers system and its work, see Ann Hughes, '"The Public Profession of These Nations": The National Church in Interregnum England', in Christopher Durston and Judith Maltby (eds), *Religion in Revolutionary England* (Manchester, 2006), pp. 93–114, at 94–9.

[41] *Cromwell Writings*, III, pp. 210–11; *Scotland and the Protectorate*, pp. 57–8.

[42] *Scotland and the Protectorate*, pp. 40–2.

exception to the regime's breaking of the Covenants and its intention to do away with them entirely, including the 'expresse inhibition to the Colledges and Universities in this land anent taking of the Covenant'.[43] This Protester faction was concerned that prohibiting subscription to the Covenants in the universities would result in their abeyance in the long term, for generations of ministers would not be acculturated to Covenanted mores. This was the price of collusion with Cromwell. When Gillespie attempted to engage his fellow Protesters about the merits of working with Cromwell in late March 1654, he was rejected: they would not countenance an 'Erastian' settlement with a usurping regime.[44] For their part, the Resolutioner faction was also wary that the Cromwellian regime would erect a system similar to England's triers.[45] In May, Cromwell also summoned Robert Douglas, a Resolutioner, Robert Blair, a centrist, and James Guthrie, to review a proposed settlement.[46] A religious settlement that would affect the universities need not have been Gillespie's to monopolise. But attending would have been tantamount to legitimising Cromwellian power, and each of the three men summoned refused to go south, citing their opposition to liberty of conscience.[47]

While in London Gillespie, Menzies, along with John Livingston, minister of Ancrum, devised a settlement with English representatives that was promulgated on 8 August 1654 as An Ordinance for the Better Support of the Universities in Scotland and Encouragement of Public Preachers There.[48] The ordinance, which became known as Gillespie's Charter, was multifaceted. The second half of the Charter resembled the earlier English ordinance. It ordained that adequate provisions be kept for godly ministers and granted authority to the Cromwellian commission for visiting the universities to take 'especiall care that none but the godly and able men be authorised by them to enjoy the livings appointed for the Ministry in Scotland'. Like the English ordinance, any expectant would have to be certified by triers consisting of ministers and elders who oversaw five proposed ecclesiastical provinces: Lothian, Merse, and Teviotdale; Dumfries and Galloway; Glasgow and Ayr; Perth, Fife, and Angus; and 'be-north' Angus. Gillespie's Charter also favoured radical Protesters, who alongside Independents predominated in the fifty-seven potential triers listed.[49]

---

[43] William Stephen (ed.), *Register of the Consultations of the Ministers of Edinburgh and Some Other Brethren of the Ministry, 1652–1660* (2 vols, Edinburgh, 1921–30), I, p. 33.

[44] Johnston, *Diary 1650–1654*, pp. 218–24; Stephen, *Register*, I, pp. 45–56; Holfelder, 'Factionalism in the Kirk', pp. 198–201.

[45] Baillie, *L&J*, III, pp. 243, 253.

[46] *Cromwell Writings*, III, pp. 284–5; *Scotland and the Protectorate*, p. 102; Stephen, *Register*, I, pp. 70–1; Nicoll, *Diary of Public Transactions*, p. 127.

[47] *Scotland and the Protectorate*, pp. 105–6; McCrie, *Robert Blair*, pp. 315–16.

[48] TNA, SP 25/75, p. 425; *Acts and Ordinances*, III, pp. cxii–cxv; Nicoll, *Diary of Public Transactions*, pp. 164–7; *CSPD 1654*, pp. 285, 288, 290.

[49] *Acts and Ordinances*, III, pp. cxiv–cxv. As John Morrill has noted, the Charter gave Gillespie's party 'a greater prominence than its natural strength warranted'. See John

Where Gillespie's Charter diverged from the English antecedent was in its focus on the universities.[50] The Charter began by stating that the universities 'should receive both countenance and encouragement, and be provided for with competent maintenance for the members of the said Universities, for the better training up of youth in piety and good literature'.[51] Though vague on details, this suggests that Gillespie, Menzies, and their Cromwellian collaborators were cognisant of the power of the universities to socialise students into the new religious settlement, an acutely un-Covenanted system that was then being proposed in the Charter. In order to realise this vision, proper maintenance was required. The Charter earmarked provisions for Glasgow and Aberdeen universities that mirrored the grants initially conveyed in 1641. Each university would receive the rents of the dissolved bishoprics of Glasgow and Aberdeen, respectively, and an annual payment of 200 marks sterling for the maintenance of principals, professors, and regents.[52] Tellingly, similar grants were not made for Edinburgh and St Andrews, the two universities that had displayed the most opposition to the Cromwellian regime.

That Glasgow and Aberdeen were the only two universities to receive financial enrichment in Gillespie's Charter was due to Gillespie and Menzies' presence. In late July, both entreated the English for augmentations for their respective universities, which the Council of State granted.[53] It is likely that they went to London with requests for their institutions; Gillespie carried with him a set of instructions from his Glasgow colleagues.[54] A document dated 27 March 1654 and signed by Glasgow's moderators – though, unsurprisingly, not by Robert Baillie – instructed Gillespie to obtain what he could to boost Glasgow's finances and to add funding and resources for the library, the latter having been promised by Charles I. He was also instructed to confirm the university's rights and privileges with the Protector.[55] Gillespie and his allies in the university were willing to deal with the Protectorate to improve their lot; it was a pragmatic calculation that would ultimately bear fruit. And, in urging Gillespie to garner confirmation of promises made by the king, Glasgow's masters did not display any doubts about the Protector's legitimacy. Baillie's continued protest in not signing underlined his refusal

---

Morrill, 'Seventeenth-Century Scotland', *Journal of Ecclesiastical History*, 33:2 (1982), 266–71, at 268.
[50] *Acts and Ordinances*, II, p. 858.
[51] *Ibid.*, III, p. cxii.
[52] *Acts and Ordinances*, III, pp. cxii–cxiv; *Fasti Aberdonenses*, pp. 163–5; *Evidence*, II, p. 250, IV, pp. 159–60.
[53] TNA, SP 25/75, p. 445.
[54] Baillie, *L&J*, III, p. 282.
[55] GUL, MS Gen 1769/1/41. The signatories included the rector Sir George Maxwell of Pollock, divinity professor John Young, and three regents: James Veitch, Patrick Young, and Andrew Burnet.

to recognise the Cromwellian regime as a legitimate governing body that could intervene in university affairs.

The Charter's confirmation and augmentation of the grants made in 1641 exemplified the benefits that came with loyalty to Cromwell.[56] As Gillespie, Menzies, and authorities in London devised the settlement, another apparatus of Cromwellian state power in Scotland – the commission for regulating the universities – continued its work. The commission, which had been responsible for the installation of new principals at the outset of the Interregnum, was initially established as a temporary body, but the work to be done in settling the tumultuous state of the Scottish church saw its renewal in October 1653.[57] With Gillespie's Charter, it was clear that the commission for the universities – still staffed entirely by English officials – was to be a permanent fixture in Scottish religious affairs.[58] This was despite calls from both Resolutioners and Protesters to have the commission abolished.[59] The Protesters issued a declaration immediately upon the commission's formation in June 1652, protesting its 'encroachments… upon the liberties and priviledges of the church of Christ in this land', in which the Kirk 'seemes to be excluded from all interest in visiting of universities which are the seminaries of the church'.[60] And, before departing with Gillespie and Menzies to London, John Livingston maintained that he would attempt to have the commission suspended, as it 'was lyke to plan als many evil as good men'.[61] These protests fell on deaf ears, another reminder of Scotland's conquered status and the strength of Cromwellian political authority. The commission remained, and though the Charter itself did not make specific reference to the planting of university staff, the commission's authority to do so endured under a system of triers dominated by Scottish radicals.[62] While the Church of Scotland's more local courts, like kirk sessions and presbyteries, continued to operate, the abolition of the General Assembly left something of a power vacuum for the control of Scottish higher education.[63] This was a space that could be potentially filled by the commission and triers working in tandem. At the same time, it would solidify the radicals' headway into Glasgow and Aberdeen and open a direct path to increased intervention at Edinburgh and St Andrews. At stake was not only the subversion of the Kirk, but radicals' control of the universities, where they could extend the purges that had

---

[56] Spurlock, *Cromwell and Scotland*, p. 147.
[57] CSPD 1653–54, pp. 202–4; TNA, SP 25/71, pp. 107–12.
[58] The commission also continued to deal with stipends and vacancies throughout the 1650s. See NRS, GD214/214.
[59] NLS, Wod.Fol.XXVI, fols 9–10; Baillie, *L&J*, III, p. 240.
[60] NLS, Wod.Fol.XXX, fols 107–8.
[61] Johnston, *Diary 1650–1654*, p. 217; Holfelder, 'Factionalism in the Kirk', pp. 200–1.
[62] EUL, La.I.321, fol. 12r.
[63] Brock, 'Keeping the Covenant', p. 394.

already begun in Lowland synods.[64] Gillespie's Charter signalled the attempt radically alter the Scottish social order; the universities, as ever, were an essential part of the equation.

Gillespie's Glasgow was a microcosm of what could be pursued on a national scale. His machinations at Glasgow also underlined, again, the importance of the personnel – and their political leanings – who staffed teaching posts in the college. Gillespie had already preferred John Young to a divinity post despite Young's inexperience and lack of ordination. But the principal was also intent on stacking the regents' places with Protesters. The vacancies made by Young's promotion and Robertson's ouster should have resulted in open competitions, a point that Baillie strained to make clear.[65] However, Gillespie instead called Robert McWard, a regent at St Salvator's, and Andrew Burnet, a scholar from Aberdeen, to assume the regents' posts.[66] McWard, an avowed Protester and favourite of Rutherford, was admitted without trial in August 1653.[67] Burnet came to Glasgow with 'the testimonie of all the apostates in the Colledge of Aberdeen', an embodiment of the synergy between Gillespie's Protesters and the Aberdeen Independents; he prevailed in a trial over John Glen, a Glasgow graduate who suspected 'his favour was so little'. Gillespie admitted Burnet in September 1653 without requiring that he subscribe to the Covenant.[68] The following year, Gillespie preferred the St Andrews scholar George Sinclair to a regent's post vacated by McWard's quick departure. Though Sinclair came with the testimony of James Wood, Baillie noted that Sinclair's installation went without trial and once again at Glen's expense.[69] Gillespie sought the preferment of scholars familiar to him, who held Protester affinities, and he did so contrary to the university's practices. Baillie was, understandably, incensed by these actions, and he refused to be present at, and thus provide legitimacy to, their appointments.

While Baillie lamented Glasgow's affairs, his Protester colleagues railed against him and the Resolutioner faction. In a long tirade, the Glasgow regent James Vietch lambasted the Resolutioners, including Dickson, Wood, Douglas, Blair, and Baillie as a 'faction, so great enemies to grace and pietie'. The Resolutioners' persistent, impious opposition to the new political order confounded Vietch. He contended that Baillie and his allies 'count it a pest and ane epidemick disease that God is filling the kirks and the schooles with a generation of young men, whose eminent pietie and great learning does good to soules, which we with our impietie would corrupt'.[70] Vietch

---

[64] Holfelder, 'Factionalism in the Kirk', pp. 203–9.
[65] Baillie, L&J, III, p. 240.
[66] McCoy, *Robert Baillie*, pp. 164–5; Smart, *Alphabetical Register*, p. 383.
[67] MAUG, III, p. 391; Baillie, L&J, III, pp. 240–1; Ginny Gardner, 'McWard, Robert (c.1625–1681)', ODNB; Coffey, *Politics, Religion and the British Revolutions*, pp. 26, 49.
[68] MAUG, III, p. 391; Baillie, L&J, III, p. 242; Spurlock, *Cromwell and Scotland*, p. 140.
[69] MAUG, III, p. 391; Baillie, L&J, III, pp. 285, 314.
[70] Baillie, L&J, III, p. 262.

tied the Resolutioners' opposition in the universities to the health of the commonwealth. He understood that the universities trained the future generations of churchmen who distilled piety and discipline – particular ways of life – in society at large. Vietch, clearly, was supportive of the direction that the Scottish religious and political life was headed under Gillespie's influence. In Vietch's mind, the Resolutioners' intransigence risked corrupting this cycle, and thus debasing the social order.

As the situation at Glasgow evinced, Gillespie's Charter had potentially significant implications for the universities and for the Scottish church and state. But, in reality, the Charter was dead on arrival in Scotland.[71] In November 1654, General Monck wrote to Cromwell that many ministers, both Resolutioners and Protesters, 'are very much dissatisfied with the Instructions brought doune by Mr. Galeaspie, and very few (if any) will act in it'.[72] Protesters in the Wariston-Guthrie-Rutherford camp argued that it was an 'authoritative, arbitrarie and prelaticall' action that undercut the authority of the presbyteries and established examiners who were not themselves subject to any trial.[73] Resolutioners argued similarly: the Charter undermined the Kirk's privileges and afforded the triers a power 'more absolute than any the Prelats ever attained'.[74] Gross disaffection did not stop Cromwell from instructing the Council of Scotland, a body newly assembled in September 1655 to oversee Scottish affairs under the presidency of Roger Boyle, Lord Broghill, to see to the plantation of 'honest and faithful ministers' according to the Charter's strictures.[75] In October, the ordinance was promulgated in Edinburgh.[76] Following this, Protesters and Resolutioners attacked it as reviving the 'high commission off the prelats... in a mor Arbitrarie and tyranicall way then ever' and allowing 'toleration of whatsoever error is ushered' into Scotland. Named triers also refused to act, making the Charter unenforceable.[77] By late summer 1656, the regime scrapped the settlement proposed in Gillespie's Charter.[78] The Charter's failure highlighted the limits of Cromwellian power in Scotland. The regime's favouring of radical Protesters would not lead to a broader acculturation to Cromwellian mores, either in the church or the universities, while large swaths of the Scottish clerical estate remained hostile to the perceived Erastian settlements of a usurping government.

The backlash against Gillespie's Charter, and the failure to implement its system of triers, seemed not to have impacted the Charter's fiscal

[71] *Ibid.*, III, p. 283.
[72] *Scotland and the Protectorate*, pp. 211–12.
[73] MacKenzie, *Solemn League and Covenant*, p. 131.
[74] Stephen, *Register*, I, pp. 57–80.
[75] *Cromwell Writings*, III, pp. 677–8; *Thurloe State Papers*, III, pp. 496–8.
[76] Nicoll, *Diary of Public Transactions*, pp. 163–4.
[77] EUL, La.I.321, fols 6–7, 8, 10; *Thurloe State Papers*, IV, pp. 128–9.
[78] Holfelder, 'Factionalism in the Kirk', pp. 212–27.

support for Aberdeen and Glasgow. In this way, Cromwellian authorities were still positioned to exercise pronounced influence in the universities.[79] In September 1654, the commission of customs in Scotland ordered the payments to Aberdeen, and in November Cromwell ratified the grants to Glasgow in a charter.[80] Each university also saw the fulfilment of the 200 marks yearly payment for university staff.[81] For the remainder of the Interregnum, the regime provided Aberdeen and Glasgow with further support, with Glasgow pursing its interests in the former bishopric of Galloway.[82] And, when Gillespie travelled to London with another Protester delegation in January 1657, he brought additional instructions from Glasgow's masters for increasing the university's fabric – Baillie, again, did not sign.[83] In July 1657, Cromwell confirmed the gifts in Gillespie's Charter and granted the university the deaneries of Glasgow, the stipends of vacant parishes, and the right to print the Bible and theological, legal, philosophical, and medical texts.[84] Both Marischal and King's also received a charter in June 1658 that gave new provisions and confirmed the gifts in Gillespie's Charter.[85] With this windfall, each university pursued building projects. In September 1656 Baillie noted that Gillespie, 'with very great care, industrie, and dexteritie', managed construction at Glasgow. Baillie was almost always at odds with Gillespie, but with these projects he gave the principal credit, even if, according to Baillie, Gillespie had his house razed 'to build up ane another greater show, but farr worse accommodation'.[86] At King's, Principal John Row received donations from Monck and several English officers to construct a new edifice, 'Cromwell's Tower'. Not to be outdone, Principal Muir began building a public school at Marischal with donations from Oxford, Cambridge, and Eton College.[87] Both Aberdeen and Glasgow's economic situations improved during the Interregnum.[88] These actions speak to what came when an institution was in Cromwell's good graces, but it also indicated another avenue through which the regime exercised control over institutions, and thus projected its legitimacy, via the fiscal management of the universities.[89]

[79] MacKenzie, *Solemn League and Covenant*, p. 130.
[80] *Evidence*, IV, p. 160; *Fasti Aberdonenses*, pp. 165–6; *FAM*, I, pp. 278–9; *MAUG*, I, pp. 321–5.
[81] *MAUG*, I, p. 335; *FAM*, I, pp. 279–80.
[82] GUL, MS Gen 1769/1/50; *MAUG*, II, pp. 326–7.
[83] GUL, MS Gen 1769/1/15; *CSPD 1656–57*, p. 277.
[84] *MAUG*, I, pp. 336–43. See also *CSPD 1656–57*, pp. 303–5, 308.
[85] *Evidence*, IV, pp. 160–1; *Fasti Aberdonenses*, pp. 166–9; *FAM*, I, pp. 287–90.
[86] Baillie, *L&J*, III, pp. 285–6, 313, 384, 396. See also GUA, 26627.
[87] *FAM*, I, 280–2, 304. See also Spurlock, *Cromwell and Scotland*, p. 148; Rait, *Universities of Aberdeen*, pp. 160, 241, 286; Colin A. McLaren, 'New Work and Old: Building at the Colleges in the Seventeenth Century', *Aberdeen University Review*, 53:183 (1990), 208–17.
[88] Bulloch, *University of Aberdeen*, pp. 124–5; Mackie, *Glasgow*, pp. 109–10; Coutts, *Glasgow*, pp. 129–38.
[89] See e.g., Charles Tilly, *Coercion, Capital and European States: AD 990–1990* (Oxford,

To varying degrees, Edinburgh and St Andrews also sought aid. In March 1657, Cromwell conferred the vacancies of the archbishopric of St Andrews to the university, confirming the grants of 1641. It is not clear if university masters petitioned for this augmentation, and the only evidence for this gift is a warrant signed by the commissioners for the administration of justice in Scotland held in the St Andrews University Library Special Collections.[90] Even if St Andrews' masters did not appeal directly, the Cromwellian regime did appear willing to support the university, for several months later the government examined as to whether £5,000-worth of rents might be used to benefit the 'church and university'.[91] If extant evidence suggests that St Andrews' masters were somewhat aloof in the budding academic arms race in Scotland, it is more obvious that Edinburgh had clearly observed the favours that could be attained. In July 1657, the Edinburgh town council instructed Principal Leighton to journey to London and entreat for 'ane augmentatioun of the rentall of the Colledge'.[92] The following month, Leighton petitioned Cromwell, claiming that Edinburgh had 'the great number of students… usually beyond any other one Colledge in the nation, and yet… its greater poverty and more need of such help then any of the rest, it being but a late foundation', which he remarked the commissioners for visiting the universities had themselves noticed.[93] The Council decided that £200 sterling out of church lands would be paid to Edinburgh.[94] The exchequer desired that Cromwell authorise this grant in the town council's name and that it should be earmarked for augmenting the stipends, funding six bursars of philosophy, repairing buildings, and enhancing the library.[95] In July 1658, Cromwell issued a yearly grant of £200 to Edinburgh.[96] Almost immediately, however, funding became a problem, for unlike the gifts for Glasgow, Aberdeen, and St Andrews, Edinburgh's grant did not specify vacancies, and in August 1658 assessors for the town council concluded that 'the said Gift might prove ineffectuall be reasone that it wes verie hard to find a localitie upon any such rentis'.[97] Baillie remarked that Edinburgh's grants 'will be als-soone obtained as the flim-flams of Mr. Gillespie's gifts'.[98] Regardless, by early September 1658 Cromwell had died, which ceased any forthcoming financial gifts to Edinburgh.

1990), p. 15.
[90] StAUL, UYUY, 459/2/2.
[91] TNA, SP 25/78, pp. 372–3; *CSPD 1657-58*, p. 233.
[92] Wood, *Edinburgh Burgh Records 1655–1665*, p. 63.
[93] TNA, SP 18/156, fol. 68.
[94] TNA, SP 18/156, fol. 69; *CSPD 1657–58*, p. 78.
[95] Wood, *Edinburgh Burgh Records 1655–1665*, pp. 73, 99–100.
[96] TNA, SP 25/78 pp. 750–2; NRS, RH9/12/4; *CSPD 1657–58*, pp. 95–6; *Cromwell Writings*, IV, pp. 852–3.
[97] Wood, *Edinburgh Burgh Records 1655–1665*, pp. 113–14.
[98] Baillie, *L&J*, III, p. 366.

Fiscal management and economic advancement did not engender loyalty and conformity to the regime. If anything, the Cromwellian regime's actions in Scotland were analogous to the act for propagating the gospel in Ireland, in which the augmentation of Trinity's finances was coupled with the creation of the board of trustees. But, as opposed to imposing legislation over a conquered realm, the situation in Scotland once again demanded the regime draw on the conditions of the locale to inform its approach to controlling higher education. Leaning on Gillespie and his allies among the radical Protesters did not work, but where Gillespie's Charter failed in reshaping Scotland's social order, it succeeded in bringing the universities further under Cromwellian control. While the universities would not be subjected to oversight by a group of handpicked triers, the Protectorate government exercised wider control, and thus advanced its standing as a legitimate governing authority, over Scottish higher education through its fiscal policies.

The Protectorate Government and the Universities

The disputes over Gillespie's Charter and the wider contests for authority in the universities during the Protectorate highlighted the unsettled nature of the Scottish church under Cromwellian rule. The lack of a religious settlement would only further undermine the Protectorate government in Scotland, for it lacked the legitimising capabilities of an ecclesiastical apparatus that reinforced and distilled political power. The Council of Scotland, the new governing body for Scottish affairs established in September 1655 under the presidency of Roger Boyle, Lord Broghill, would potentially change that. In addition to Broghill, the Council included Monck, the New Englander Samuel Desborough, Nathaniel Whetham, Edward Rhodes, and three colonels: Charles Howard, Adrian Scroope, and Thomas Cooper. Two Scots, William Lockhart and John Swinton, were also included.[99] The Council's work, and Broghill's energies specifically, have previously been examined mainly through the prism of the Protester–Resolutioner controversy.[100] Broghill was a shrewd politician with a seemingly acute understanding of local contexts, and like other officials in the English administration, he quickly identified the Protesters as more agreeable.[101] Yet he also exploited the schism to bring as many as he could from both factions under the government's control.[102]

---

[99] CSPD 1655, p. 108; *Scotland and the Protectorate*, p. 306; *Thurloe State Papers*, III, p. 423.
[100] Dow, *Cromwellian Scotland*, pp. 162–228; Little, *Lord Broghill*, pp. 95–121; MacKenzie, *Solemn League and Covenant*, pp. 132–6; Julia M. Buckroyd, 'Lord Broghill and the Scottish Church, 1655–1656', *Journal of Ecclesiastical History*, 27:4 (1976), 359–68.
[101] *Thurloe State Papers*, IV, pp. 48–9.
[102] Baillie, *L&J*, III, p. 315. For a similar judgement, see Nicoll, *Diary of Public Transactions*, p. 183.

Broghill deflected the Protesters' overtures for 'union' between the factions that would have privileged the Protesters' minority position. He was also open to Resolutioner demands to maintain the Kirk's courts. By the end of 1657, the Council of State agreed to a settlement that essentially maintained the Kirk's polity, without the General Assembly, and with religious toleration. The settlement was agreeable to wide swaths of Resolutioners and Protesters, save for the most uncompromising of the latter.[103]

If the broader ecclesiastical settlement arrived at in late 1657 was one that sought to repair the fissure in the Kirk under Cromwellian auspices, English authorities, acting through the Council of Scotland, aimed to exert further control over the Scottish universities in order to stimulate wider socialisation to the Cromwellian rule.[104] Among the orders Cromwell issued to the Council in March 1655 was the authority to 'visit and reform the universities, colleges, and schools of learning, suspend such statutes as they find unfitting, propose others for encouragement of godliness and learning, remove scandalous, insufficient, or disaffected persons, and substitute others godly, learned, and fitting'.[105] Further instructions in July 1655 ordered the Council to plant 'honest and faithful' ministers according to the triers system.[106] In October, a month into the Council's tenure, the Council received additional instructions from London to require the universities commission to plant vacancies only when called to do so, with 'All former orders to the contrary are declared voide.'[107] These latter instructions signalled the abrogation of the triers system in Gillespie's Charter and reaffirmed the commission's authority to place and remove ministers. Overall, these commands mirrored the orders initially given to the universities commission in June 1652, but more broadly, exhibited the tendencies of ruling authorities to wield higher education, particularly via the control of the professoriate, to cultivate allegiance and conformity to support state power. From this, nearly all other actions followed. Once again, the focus of ruling authorities was on who was tasked with educating future generations of churchmen and statesmen. On the one hand, the Council's actions in this regard shed more light on the ways in which English authorities assumed the vacancy left by the General Assembly as the main authority in Scottish university affairs. On the other, it clarifies the extent to which the Cromwellian regime sought to effect social change, via the universities, in the last years of the Protectorate. Several episodes regarding the movement of professors at Edinburgh, St Andrews, and Glasgow are illustrative in this regard.

---

[103] Holfelder, 'Factionalism in the Kirk', pp. 213–44; MacKenzie, *Solemn League and Covenant*, p. 135.
[104] See e.g., Wells, 'Prelude to Empire', pp. 106–7.
[105] *CSPD 1655*, pp. 108–10; *Cromwell Writings*, III, pp. 677–8.
[106] *CSPD 1655*, p. 256; *Thurloe State Papers*, III, pp. 496–8.
[107] *Cromwell Writings*, III, pp. 873–4; *Thurloe State Papers*, IV, pp. 129–30.

As was the case throughout the Interregnum, authorities did not pursue a blanket policy that was applied to each university. In Edinburgh, where the Council of Scotland was headquartered, the body initially did not appear to circumvent the town council's authority in Edinburgh University's affairs.[108] For instance, several regents' places became vacant in 1656 and 1657, and each time the town council filled the posts according to established protocols.[109] Neither the Council nor the Cromwellian universities commission seemed to have played a part in filling these posts. The filling of Edinburgh's vacant Hebrew professorship, however, garnered the Council of Scotland's attention. The post had been established in 1642 and Julius Conradus Otto held it until his death in 1649. David Dickson and his divinity students petitioned for a new Hebraist to aid divinity studies, and in August 1656, several Edinburgh ministers, including Robert Douglas, attested to the election of David's son Alexander. The younger Dickson was admitted on 3 September 1656.[110] Baillie noted that the elder David Dickson and Douglas urged Lord Broghill 'to desire the Toune-Councell to present [Alexander] to the vacant place of the Hebrew Tongue'.[111] From this it appears that the Council was involved in the appointment – in that they impressed upon Broghill and the Council to urge the Edinburgh town council to see through Alexander's appointment. Further, it was done while Principal Leighton was on his annual trip to London; on his return, he disputed the move, but Alexander remained.[112] Lord Broghill, acting on the advice of two Resolutioners – Dickson and Douglas – saw to this selection over the head of a Cromwellian-appointed principal. This was emblematic of the authority that the Council possessed, but it also showed Broghill's readiness to conciliate with Resolutioners and their own capability to work with Cromwellian officials.[113] Alexander Dickson's appointment also highlighted the capacity of the Council of Scotland, while possessing widespread authority over Scottish affairs, to nevertheless work through established governing structures.

---

[108] Wood, *Edinburgh Burgh Records 1642–1655*, p. 379.
[109] Wood, *Edinburgh Burgh Records 1655–1665*, pp. 12, 63–4; Dalzel, *History of the University of Edinburgh*, II, pp. 174, 176–7.
[110] Wood, *Edinburgh Burgh Records 1655–1665*, pp. 33–4; Laing, *Catalogue*, p. xiii; Scott, *Fasti*, I, p. 332.
[111] Baillie, *L&J*, III, pp. 365–6.
[112] *Ibid.*, III, p. 366; Gribben, 'Robert Leighton', p. 174.
[113] Little, *Lord Broghill*, pp. 105–8.

Table 5.1. The Scottish Professoriate, c. 1652–60.

University of St Andrews		
St Salvator's College	St Leonard's College	St Mary's College
James Wood, Provost (1657)	George Wemyss, Principal (1647)	Samuel Rutherford, Principal (1647)
Robert Burnet, Medicine (1658)	James Wemyss, Regent (1647)	Alexander Colville, Divinity (1647)
William Campbell, Regent (1646)	Alexander Jameson, Regent (1649)	James Wood, Ecclesiastical History (until 1657)
Alexander Pitcairn, Regent (1647)	James Allen, Regent (1650)	
Alexander Edward, Regent (c. 1648)	James Blair, Regent (c. 1650)	
William Tullideph, Regent (1649)	William Preston, Regent (1654)	
Robert McWard (until 1653)	Andrew Bruce Jr, Regent (c. 1655)	
David Bruce, Regent (1653)	John Patterson, Regent (1657)	
John Colville, Regent (1655)	James Wemyss, Regent (1657)*	
Patrick Lyon, Regent (c. 1656)	*This is the same James Wemyss who was previously regent at St Salvator's until 1657. There appears to be no relation to the James Wemyss who was a regent at St Leonard's from 1647.	
Laurence Charteris, Regent (1657?)		
Robert Learmonth, Regent (1657)		
James Wemyss, Regent (until 1657)		

University of Glasgow	Marischal College, Aberdeen
Patrick Gillespie, Principal (1653)	William Muir, Principal (1649)
Robert Baillie, Divinity (1642)	John Menzies, Divinity (1649)
John Young, Divinity (1652)	John Thomson, Porter (1652)
Richard Robertson, Regent (1649)	Robert Forbes, Regent (164?)

Table 5.1 (*continued*)

University of Glasgow	Marischal College, Aberdeen
James Veitch, Regent (1650)	Robert Burnet, Regent (164?)
Patrick Young, Regent (1651)	James Chalmers, Regent (164?)
Robert McWard, Regent (1653)	Andrew Cant, Regent (164?)
Andrew Burnet, Regent (1653)	Andrew Birnie, Regent (165?)
George Sinclair, Regent (1654)	Alexander White, Regent (*c.* 1655)
Robert Erskine, Regent (1656)	George Meldrum, Regent (*c.* 1655)

King's College, Aberdeen	University of Edinburgh
John Row, Principal (1652)	Robert Leighton, Principal (1653)
Gilbert Rule, Sub-Principal (1652)	David Dickson, Divinity (1650)
Patrick Sandilands, Sub-Principal (from 1657)	Julius Conradus Otto, Hebrew (until 1656)
William Douglas, Divinity (1643)	Alexander Dickson, Hebrew (1656)
Andrew Moore, Medicine (1649)	Thomas Craufurd, Mathematics, Regent (1640)
John Brodie, Grammarian (1655)	James Wiseman, Regent (*c.* 1638)
John Strachan, Regent (1651)	Duncan Forrester, Regent (1639)
Hugh Anderson, Regent (1652)	William Tweedie, Regent (1644)
Andrew Massie, Regent (1656)	James Pillans, Regent (1644)
William Johnston, Regent (1657)	Andrew Suttie (1647)
George Gordon, Regent (1659)	John Wishart (1653)
	William Forbes (1654)
	James McGowen (1656)
	Hugh Smith (1658)

Sources: ODNB; Scott, *Fasti*; Laing, *Catalogue*; MAUG, vol. 3; *Fasti Aberdonenses*; Anderson, *Officers and Graduates*; FAM, vol. 2; Smart, *Alphabetical Register*; StAUL, UYUY 412.

Events at St Andrews also brought the Council's involvement. By 1656 the animosity between Samuel Rutherford, a Protester, and James Wood, a Resolutioner, had reached a boiling point. Baillie wrote that Rutherford's 'daily bitter contentions…made [Wood] wearie of his place exceedingly'.[114] The vacant provostship of St Salvator's, which had not been filled since John Baron's demission in 1649, portended another potential controversy. St Salvator's masters were divided over whom to call. One regent, William

---

[114] Baillie, *L&J*, III, pp. 316, 376.

Campbell, was a Protester who desired the post.[115] Another, George Martine, claimed the post by stressing his seniority and 'went to the English' to gain favour.[116] Broghill was convinced to accept Wood on the advice of James Sharp, minister of Crail and the Restoration archbishop of St Andrews.[117] Sharp accompanied Broghill to London in August 1656, when he likely persuaded Broghill of Wood's worth.[118] Broghill moved the Council to select Wood, who assumed the provostship in 1657.[119]

Robert Baillie, perhaps owing to his experience having witnessed Gillespie's machinations in Glasgow, was highly aware of the Protester faction's attempts to install its partisans in positions of influence. In a December 1656 letter to James Wood, Baillie wrote that the Protesters sought 'to plant all places in church, state, schooles, families, with men of their own stamp, and no other, say and swear what they will to the contrare. See to your Colledges as you may: they are fully masters of Glasgow, Aberdeen, and almost of Edinburgh.'[120] Thus, both Wood's elevation and Alexander Dickson's appointment went against the tide of Protester domination in the universities. Baillie, however, was nevertheless mindful that Wood's translation had come under English auspices: Broghill and Council of Scotland, even if they were acting in Resolutioner interests, had orchestrated the move. Baillie wrote to William Spang that 'I am not yet satisfied of [Wood] accepting of that place on the English command... I love not that we should justifie or harden the English in their usurpations in our Universities rights.'[121] The manner of Wood's translation was, for Baillie, problematic. Baillie's comment also underlines the way Cromwellian governing apparatuses, like the Council of Scotland, had assumed places of power in Scottish university affairs, and the anxieties it stoked among opponents of the regime who were navigating the new political reality.

English intervention had been one of Baillie's main concerns throughout the Interregnum, which was one aspect of the larger upheaval that the conquest, occupation, and union had caused in Scotland. The instructions that the Resolutioners Dickson, Douglas, and Wood issued to James Sharp on his journey to London in August 1656 emphasised that English rule 'doth overturn the established order and government of this Kirk, especially as to the plantation and calling ministers'.[122] Baillie asserted that the universities' rights and privileges also needed protection. To Wood he wrote that 'It would

---

[115] McCrie, *Robert Blair*, p. 415; Baillie, *L&J*, III, p. 316.
[116] Baillie, *L&J*, III, p. 316.
[117] On Sharp, see Julia M. Buckroyd, *The Life of James Sharp, Archbishop of St Andrews, 1618–1679: A Political Biography* (Edinburgh, 1987).
[118] Holfelder, 'Factionalism in the Kirk', p. 228; Dow, *Cromwellian Scotland*, pp. 207–8.
[119] Baillie, *L&J*, III, p. 316; Scott, *Fasti*, VII, p. 411.
[120] Baillie, *L&J*, III, pp. 326–7.
[121] *Ibid.*, III, p. 316.
[122] Stephen, *Register*, I, pp. 204–10; Baillie, *L&J*, III, pp. 568–72.

be one of Mr. J. Sharp's chief cares to gett a settled order for our Universities, that Independent *ignari's* may no more, by English orders be planted in them, for the corrupting of our youth.'[123] Baillie recognised that, if universities were instruments to socialise youths, they were also equally capable of corruption. He tied this corruption directly to the power the Cromwellian regime exercised in higher education. Baillie thus subsequently wrote to Sharp in London in January 1657 to 'get abolished that very unjust commission for visiting the Universities' and stressed that no Independent or Protester 'should take up our Universities, as they have done Aberdeen'.[124]

Despite the pronounced disaffection with the situation, it was to Cromwellian authorities that the Scots, like Baillie, had to appeal. The anxieties stoked by the illness of Patrick Gillespie is a case in point. In a letter to Sharp in early 1657, Baillie noted with alarm the principal's illness, which ultimately raised questions about the future of the principalship. Baillie, ever Gillespie's opponent, worried that 'we are in hazard to have his place quicklie filled with a worse'. In particular, Baillie was wary that Gillespie's English associates, like John Owen, might encourage the Protector to seek the election of a new, Independent principal. Baillie urged Sharp to press John Thurloe, secretary of state, and Lord Broghill, then in Ireland, to appeal to the Council of Scotland, and to seek the advice of Robert Douglas and David Dickson, in order to identify a nominee acceptable to both Cromwell and to Presbyterians 'in both nations'.[125] Gillespie survived his illness, so nothing came of Baillie's desperation plot. This episode was, however, suggestive of a key fact: the Scots, Resolutioners included, were deferring to an English governing authority. The Council of Scotland, in filling the void left by the elimination of the General Assembly, had emerged as a central, legitimate apparatus through which to supervise university affairs.

In addition to the contests for authority over Scottish higher education that occurred at the administrative level, there are also telling examples for how the Cromwellian regime's policies affected learning and impacted academic life. These examples provide evidence of the extent to which the new political order transformed the education and training, and thus the broader socialisation to authorised norms, of future Scottish churchmen. It will be recalled that, under the Covenanters, General Assembly commissioners sought to establish a curriculum across the universities that would produce effective preachers to serve the Covenanted state. Under Cromwell, it appears that this training was debased. Baillie's letters account for the situation at Glasgow, where students were few and examinations superficial. He remarked that he was happy to bring all of Glasgow's students to his Hebrew and catechism lessons, 'for divinitie students we have very few'.[126] The

---

[123] Baillie, *L&J*, III, p. 327.
[124] *Ibid.*, III, p. 335; Spurlock, *Cromwell and Scotland*, p. 147.
[125] Baillie, *L&J*, III, pp. 343–4.
[126] *Ibid.*, III, pp. 285–6.

lack of divinity students was also indicative of the impact the Cromwellian occupation had on the Scottish ministry. The state was such that Baillie's son, Henry, grew disillusioned with his studies and desired to become a merchant.[127] Glasgow's divinity students were abandoning their studies, especially as students elsewhere 'after their laureation, put in the best places, the exceeding poor sufficiencie, it makes the rest the more to neglect all studie, but only to preach in their popular kind of way, which requires little learning'.[128] This reference to preaching is indicative of a post-conquest phenomenon: the move away from a preaching style marked by its rigid organisation into exegesis, doctrine, and application, a hallmark of the Covenanters and the higher education program they built to support it. It was replaced partly by a 'popular' preaching style in Scotland, less wedded to organisational clarity and more susceptible to innovation.[129] This innovatory form was championed by, among others, Robert Leighton, whom Baillie criticised as promoting a homiletical style that left 'little or nought to the memorie and understanding'.[130] It was also a style that, much to Baillie's dismay, did not seem to necessitate formal divinity study. The Cromwellian regime's preferment of principals, like Leighton, who espoused novel preaching techniques, coupled with the government's policies that debased the Scottish ministry, was having a direct impact on the training of university students. No longer required to abide by the strictures set forth by the Covenanters, a generation of divinity student were being socialised into uncovenanted norms.

Glasgow again provides insights into the transformations in Scotland's academic life. In 1655, the students of Patrick Young, appointed regent of philosophy in 1651, issued a complaint against his truancy, ambivalence to subject matter, failure to administer examinations, and inability to promote piety.[131] This led to students departing Glasgow for other universities, opting for private study in the town, or withdrawing from their studies entirely.[132] Young's shortfalls mirrored Gillespie's missteps as principal. His regular trips to Edinburgh and London meant that he skirted most of his pedagogical responsibilities. Gillespie, it appeared, was most concerned with ingratiating himself to English authorities – he offered Glasgow's chancellorship to Secretary Thurloe in February 1658[133] – overseeing construction, and garnering financial gifts for the university, through which he augmented his own salary.[134] But Gillespie proved to be a poor steward of Glasgow's divinity students. Matters

---

[127] Ibid., III, pp. 252–3.
[128] Ibid., III, p. 313.
[129] Gribben, 'Preaching the Scottish Reformation', pp. 279–81.
[130] Baillie, L&J, III, pp. 258–9; Gribben, 'Robert Leighton', pp. 173–4.
[131] MAUG, III, p. 388.
[132] GUL, MS Gen 1769/1/27.
[133] Thurloe State Papers, VI, p. 777. Baillie opposed this action: 'I was against all English flesh.' Baillie, L&J, III, p. 386.
[134] Baillie, L&J, III, pp. 285, 384–5; Mackie, Glasgow, pp. 110–11.

came to a head following his attempt to bar 'malignants' from Glasgow's burgh elections in early 1658.[135] In response, the burgh council issued a damning report that argued that Gillespie 'ought not to be principal of the Colledge of Glasgow, both for insufficiencie, neglect of duetie, and maladministration of the revenues of the said colledge'. The articles noted that Gillespie neglected his teaching and failed to oversee disputations, advise theses, and examine students of philosophy. This meant that he was ignorant of the teaching of his regents, such as Patrick Young. The council also stated that Gillespie's knowledge of Latin was insufficient.[136] These charges infuriated Gillespie, who called on Glasgow's staff to show its support for him; Baillie, naturally, declined, and noted instead that 'at his entrie, I had protested of his unfitness for the Principall's charge'.[137]

This situation underscores the fact that neither the Council of Scotland, the Cromwellian commission for the universities, nor the administration in London for that matter, interceded in matters concerning the discipline and academic life of the universities. At the very least, central government's actions marked a departure from both the crown's policy in the 1630s and the Covenanters' in the 1640s. In fact, in June 1658, at about the same time Gillespie was on the defensive against the Glasgow burgh council, Cromwell issued a new set of instructions to the Scottish Council, which included empowering the body once again 'to visit all universities, schooles, &c., and suspend any statutes or persons whose action does not promote the good of the State... Also to remove any who are scandalous or insufficient, and appoint godly and learned persons in their place.'[138] This order reiterated commands that had been issued periodically since the Council's creation, and did not stem from any counsel regarding the state of Scotland's universities. But there is no evidence that visitations were carried out.

The General Assembly under the Covenanters had regulated Scottish higher education, exercised strict discipline to perpetuate order, and directed the confessional compass of the universities in the 1640s through annual visitations. Such policies ensured that the universities both modelled an orderly society and produced the ministers and magistrates to one day take the reins of state power. The Council of Scotland and the Cromwellian universities commission had similar, self-appointed authority, but this measure of supervision over higher learning was largely absent in the 1650s, except as it related to the planting of professors and, in some cases, fiscal management. The failure to keep good order at the universities was most apparent at Aberdeen, where tensions between King's and Marischal colleges erupted in violence in late 1659. Though strict laws governed each college's student body – at King's, Principal Row issued a comprehensive and stringent legal

---

[135] NLS, Wod.Fol.L, fols 112–21. See also Nicoll, *Diary of Public Transactions*, p. 211.
[136] NCL, Baill 2/4, pp. 544–8; Baillie, *L&J*, III, pp. 574–7.
[137] Baillie, *L&J*, III, pp. 372–3. See also McCoy, *Robert Baillie*, pp. 198–9.
[138] *Cromwell Writings*, IV, pp. 825–6; *CSPD 1658–59*, pp. 60–1.

code, which included continuing the course of learning inaugurated by the Covenanters – the failure of either institution to control the movement of students between colleges, a regulation that the Covenanters adopted in the 1640s, led to rioting in the burgh.[139] In December 1659 a gang of Marischal students and regents, believing that King's was stealing students, stormed the old town and injured scholars.[140] This was brought to Monck's attention on his return to England; in January 1660 he commissioned local magistrates to review the matter.[141] Patrick Sandilands, the King's sub-principal, urged the commissioners to not only punish the perpetrators but to 'obviate the like dangerous practice for the future, that so our seminaries maye no more bee theaters of bloode, nor Masters disturbed in the civilliane function of their calings'.[142] The commissioners promoted reconciliation between the two institutions.[143] By this point the Cromwellian regime was teetering with the Protector's death in September in 1658, the brief and impotent rule of Richard Cromwell, and the fall of the Protectorate in April 1659, which inhibited authorities in Scotland from governing.[144] But Aberdeen's troubles were symptomatic of the disorder endemic to the Cromwellian administration of the universities. Law codes could do little if unenforced, and the absence of visitations, in Aberdeen's case at least, bred disarray. Witness to the perceived decline of his own university and perhaps aware of the events in Aberdeen, in March 1660 Baillie wrote to Sharp in London that 'I hope yow will get us Visitations for all our Universities, who hes great need of them.'[145]

While the Cromwellian regime sought to undercut the power of the Covenanting ministry, there is no evidence that authorities sought to purposefully impair Scottish higher education. However, while there were numerous pronouncements and policies about the role of universities, the maintenance of their good order, and the importance of ensuring they adhered to the laws and norms of the new political order, questions can be raised about the overall effectiveness of Cromwellian university policy in Scotland. There seems to have been early efforts to put into place the mechanisms to turn the Scottish universities into the machinery of the Cromwellian state, but it would be a stretch to view the universities as models of order and discipline in this era. Earlier generations of scholars have viewed the 1650s as a watershed for the

---

[139] *Fasti Aberdonenses*, pp. 240–55; Shepherd, 'Philosophy and Science', pp. 22, 42. On Row's legal code for the King's College, see Colin A. McLaren, 'Discipline and Decorum: The Law Codes of the Universities of Aberdeen, 1605–86', *Scottish Universities*, pp. 128–137; idem, *Aberdeen Students 1600–1860* (Aberdeen, 2005), pp. 33–65.
[140] AUL, MSK 231/1/1, 231/9/1. For an overview of this violence, see also Colin A. McLaren, 'Affrichment and Riot: Student Violence in Aberdeen, 1659–1669', *Northern Scotland*, 10:1 (1990), 1–17.
[141] AUL, MSK 231/3/1, 2.
[142] AUL, MSK 231/8.
[143] AUL, MSK 231/12; McLaren, 'Affrichment and Riot', p. 8.
[144] Dow, *Cromwellian Scotland*, pp. 231–2, 243–5.
[145] Baillie, *L&J*, III, p. 398.

universities and Scottish intellectual life in general, as Cromwell inaugurated a 'social revolution' that delivered Scotland from the bondage of the austere Covenanters.[146] But as has been highlighted thus far, it is difficult to argue that the Cromwellian conquest cultivated unique conditions in Scotland that spurred intellectual advancement. The era was rife with resistance, disorder, and, in some places, the decline of learning and instruction. Historians have shown that Scottish academics were already engaged with a wide array of new philosophical and scientific ideas and debates, such as the contemporary arguments around Cartesianism, and drew on a wide corpus of authors to complement the Aristotelian course, much of which was channelled through close links with Dutch scholars.[147] Given the extent of the opposition in the universities to the Cromwellian regime, the persistence of pre-existing intellectual networks between Scottish and continental intellectuals, and the continued use of the Covenanters' curricular program, upon which the regime offered no apparent revisions, it could be argued that any intellectual advancements that did occur in this era – an assertion with clear teleological connotations – did so almost in spite of Cromwellian rule, not because of it.

The inefficacy of Cromwellian policy for the Scottish universities was due in some ways to the lack of consistent oversight from an organ of state power. The commission for the universities and the Council of Scotland, as apparatuses and mouthpieces for London, did centre themselves as legitimate authorities in managing staff and finances, but otherwise there appeared to be little review of teaching, learning, discipline, and other items pertinent to well-ordered universities. Beyond Edinburgh, where the town council seems to have continued in its role as a key authority in the university's affairs, the visitations of the universities, whether by town councils or chancellors, were also lacking.[148] Moreover, the ecclesiastical body that the Protesters endorsed, the national system of triers, was a non-starter. For all the authority to intervene in university affairs given to English governing bodies in Scotland, the Cromwellian administration of Scottish higher education was something of a missed opportunity. In the end, the evidence suggests that this did far more to disrupt learning and sow tension than it did socialise students to Cromwellian rule.

At St Andrews, the matter of St Mary's divinity professorship is emblematic of the Cromwellian administration's shortcomings and how the onset of the Restoration reverberated in the universities. Once again, an affair around a

[146] An argument put most forcefully in Trevor-Roper, 'Scotland and the Puritan Revolution', pp. 411–30.

[147] See e.g., Reid, 'On the Edge of Reason', pp. 44–6; Raffe, 'Intellectual Change', pp. 28–37; Giovanni Gellera, 'The Scottish Faculties of Arts and Cartesianism (1650–1700)', *History of Universities*, 29:2 (2016), 166–87; David McOmish, 'The Scientific Revolution in Scotland Revisited: New Sciences in Edinburgh', *History of Universities*, 31:2 (2018), 153–72.

[148] Wood, *Edinburgh Burgh Records 1655–1665*, pp. xlvi–lvi.

vacant professorship, and who should occupy it, loomed large. James Wood's translation to St Salvator's in 1657 left the third divinity professorship at St Mary's vacant. Several parties proposed candidates, which provoked 'great present strife' at St Andrews.[149] Wood and James Sharp initially recommended Patrick Scougal, a Resolutioner minister of Leuchars, though Scougal declined the professorship to take a parish charge.[150] Another candidate was Alexander Jameson, a St Leonard's regent. Jameson was a Protester whom Patrick Gillespie, at Samuel Rutherford's urging, advised Cromwell to move to St Mary's.[151] To this effect, Cromwell issued a proclamation sometime in 1657 that appointed Jameson to the divinity post.[152] It is noteworthy that Cromwell would appoint Jameson directly, and move neither the Council of Scotland nor the universities commission to see his appointment. This typifies the *ad hoc* nature of the regime's supervision of the universities. Jameson nonetheless declined the post, and instead moved to the parish of Govan in 1659.[153]

The matter was not settled in 1657 and it appears to have created more difficulties than Rutherford cared for. 'I am in this college between wind and weather', he wrote to the Protester general Gilbert Kerr, likely sometime in spring 1658 or 1659. 'Dr. Colville is for Mr. James Sharp; I am for Mr. William Rait, but know not the event.'[154] Scougal and Jameson's decision to decline the post led to a divide between Rutherford and Alexander Colville, the second divinity professor, as to who would become their colleague. It has been assumed that by 1657 Colville had returned to the Huguenot academy at Sedan, where he had taught before moving to St Andrews. In truth, Colville was active at St Andrews through the Restoration, and he became principal of St Mary's in 1662.[155] Colville, a Resolutioner, nominated James Sharp. Sharp had a prior connection with St Andrews, having been made a regent at St Leonard's in 1642 at Alexander Henderson's urging.[156] Sharp also opposed the Protesters' dealings with the English, and remarked of Rutherford

---

[149] Baillie, *L&J*, III, p. 365.
[150] *Ibid.*; David G. Mullan, 'Scougal, Patrick (1607–1682)', ODNB.
[151] Baillie, *L&J*, III, p. 365; Robert Wodrow, *Analecta: Or, Materials for a History of Remarkable Providences* (4 vols, Glasgow, 1842–3), III, pp. 75–7; Smart, *Alphabetical Register*, p. 298.
[152] GUL, MS Gen 1769/1/2.
[153] Scott, *Fasti*, III, pp. 411–12.
[154] NLS, Wod.Fol.LIX, fol. 8r; Bonar, *Letters*, pp. 678–9.
[155] See Tucker, 'Scottish Masters in Huguenot Academies', p. 66; *eadem*, 'Colville, Alexander'. Marie-Claude Tucker seems to have premised this argument on the suggestion that Colville returned to Sedan in 1656. See L'Abbé Boulliot, *Biographie Ardennaise, Ou Histoire Des Ardennais, Tome Premier* (Paris, 1830), p. 271. In the nineteenth century Charles Peyran questioned this and reasoned that because of his age, and the fact that he would be installed as St Mary's principal in 1662, Colville likely remained in Scotland. See Charles Peyran, *Histoire de l'Ancienne Académie Réformée de Sedan* (Strasbourg, 1846), p. 50.
[156] Buckroyd, *James Sharp*, pp. 11–15; Smart, *Alphabetical Register*, p. 553.

and Gillespie that 'nothing will satisfie them unless they have all ther will whatever may be the consequents therof'.[157] William Rait, Rutherford's nominee, had been minister of Brechin since 1644.[158] His allegiance in the Protester–Resolutioner divide is not clear, though he was named as one of the triers in Gillespie's Charter.[159] The vexed state of these competing nominations underlines how the universities still figured as a contested space as Protester and Resolutioner factions continued to clash.

The competition between Rutherford and Colville's candidates occurred as the Protectorate fell in spring 1659. No evidence suggests that either party deferred to English authorities, as had occurred in Wood's translation to St Salvator's. This is likely due to the tumultuous political situation in England following Cromwell's death in September 1658. The subsequent decline of the Protectorate and the restoration of the Rump voided the authority of the Council of Scotland.[160] Rutherford and Colville therefore instead took their cases to the local presbytery. Rutherford formally nominated Rait at a meeting of the presbytery of St Andrews in March 1659.[161] Not to be outdone, later that month Colville nominated Sharp.[162] In a letter to Robert Douglas, Colville feared that an impasse in the presbytery would lead to the matter being taken up by the synod of Fife, which 'might prove dangerous for it is not certain who wod be the moderator of the synod and no doubt sum members of the comittee may be courtiators and remonstators... I intend not to divert my self of the interest I have in planting the college.'[163] Tellingly, even as the Protectorate collapsed, Colville was wary of the Protesters. Yet despite Colville's misgivings and Rutherford's vexations in the presbytery, the matter was referred to the synod.[164] In autumn 1659, Rutherford further entreated a group of commissioners gathered at Edinburgh to attempt to unite the two factions to use their authority to call Rait to St Mary's.[165]

The St Mary's vacancy would only be filled after the Restoration, when, after General Monck restored the Long Parliament and the Convention Parliament renovated the monarchy in England, Charles II was proclaimed king – for a second time – in Scotland.[166] In June 1660, Rutherford continued to push Rait's nomination, noting that, with the return of the king, any decision made by the synod of Fife may 'prejudge the full and true consultation

---

[157] Osmund Airy (ed.), *Lauderdale Papers Vol. 1: 1639–1667* (London, 1884), pp. 3–4.
[158] Scott, *Fasti*, V, p. 375.
[159] *Acts and Ordinances*, III, p. cxv.
[160] Dow, *Cromwellian Scotland*, pp. 238–50; Coward, *Cromwellian Protectorate*, pp. 101–12; Ronald Hutton, *The British Republic, 1649–1660*, 2nd edn (New York, 2000), pp. 114–28.
[161] NLS, Wod.Fol.XXVI, fol. 66r; Kinloch, *Minutes of St. Andrews and Cupar*, pp. 74–5.
[162] Kinloch, *Minutes of St. Andrews and Cupar*, p. 75.
[163] NLS, Wod.Fol.XXVI, fol. 70r.
[164] Kinloch, *Minutes of St. Andrews and Cupar*, p. 75.
[165] Bonar, *Letters*, pp. 690–1; Holfelder, 'Factionalism in the Kirk', pp. 287–9.
[166] Clare Jackson, *Restoration Scotland, 1660–1690: Royalist Politics, Religion and Ideas* (Woodbridge, 2003), pp. 14, 18–20.

and determination of a hoped for Generall Assemblie'.[167] This suggests that Rutherford thought that the Restoration would also see the return of the General Assembly. This sentiment was shared by many Scottish divines: that Charles II would return as a covenanted king to uphold the privileges of the Church of Scotland.[168] They hoped that Charles would return, uphold the Covenants, and re-establish the Kirk's authority and institutions, including the General Assembly. Its restoration would return order to the governing of the universities. As institutions that survived the conquest, the universities had been integrated, haphazardly and incompletely, into the machinery of the Cromwellian state; their endurance beyond the fall of the Protectorate would potentially see their reintegration into a Covenanted state. This sentiment proved to be misguided.

The matter was settled in June 1660, when the St Andrews presbytery nominated Sharp, at that point still in London. When Sharp returned north in October 1660, he received additional encouragement to take the post from the synod of Fife.[169] Moreover, in a measure of how the political situation remained fluid, in November, the earls of Rothes and Glencairn, lord chancellor of Scotland, issued a letter to the presbytery desiring Sharp's plantation.[170] Sharp was installed in January 1661.[171] It was significant that Sharp received approval from Scottish nobles in particular, for Sharp, while in London in early 1660, saw out the Resolutioners' plan to release nobles imprisoned in England.[172] But many nobles sought an ecclesiastical settlement for Scotland that jettisoned the Covenants and restored episcopacy. Yet at the time of Sharp's appointment at St Mary's, Scotland's Restoration settlement still remained unclear.[173] Sharp was a proponent of upholding Presbyterianism, and he was at pains to cool the anti-royalist rhetoric of the Protesters so as to not sour opinions of Presbyterianism.[174] By March 1661, however, the nobility saw through the Act of Rescissory in the Scottish Parliament, which nullified all legislation since 1633 and invalidated the Covenant, paving the way for episcopacy's return.[175]

The matter of Sharp's election had begun under the Cromwellian state and would be settled under the monarchy intent on re-establishing episcopacy

[167] Kinloch, *Minutes of St. Andrews and Cupar*, p. 76.
[168] GUL, MS Gen 210, pp. 3, 96; Dow, *Cromwellian Scotland*, pp. 262.
[169] Kinloch, *Minutes of St. Andrews and Cupar*, pp. 76–7; Buckroyd, *James Sharp*, pp. 63–4.
[170] Kinloch, *Minutes of St. Andrews and Cupar*, p. 77; Nicoll, *Diary of Public Transactions*, p. 297.
[171] Buckroyd, *James Sharp*, p. 67.
[172] Airy, *Lauderdale Papers*, pp. 26–8; Julia M. Buckroyd, 'The Resolutioners and the Scottish Nobility in the Early Months of 1660', in Derek Baker (ed.), *Church Society and Politics* (Oxford, 1975), pp. 245–52.
[173] Jackson, *Restoration Scotland*, pp. 105–7.
[174] Buckroyd, *James Sharp*, pp. 63–5.
[175] RPS, 1661/1/158; Buckroyd, *Church and State*, pp. 33–7; Jackson, *Restoration Scotland*, pp. 107–8.

and hierarchical order. The new political and religious order demanded that the universities followed suit. Episcopacy's restoration would require potential office holders to have the proper credentials, as most of the pre-1638 prelates had perished. Beyond socialising students into the (re)authorised norms of the Stuart monarchy, the Scottish universities would now be institutions that legitimised the episcopal hierarchy via training and proper credentialing. Upon taking the professorship at St Mary's, Sharp was granted the doctorate of divinity, which had not been granted at the Scottish universities since before 1638. Sharp's doctorate foreshadowed how the universities would be transformed, again, into the machinery that buttressed the power of the monarchical state. Robert Blair's biographer noted cynically that,

> Mr James Sharp was made Doctor Sharp; and therein lay the knack of the business, for his design was not (as the event proved) to continue any time one of the masters of that College, but to make the doctorate a stirrup to mount him to Prelacy; for, according to the canon law, none can ascend to Prelacy, except first he be a doctor of divinity.[176]

In December 1661, Sharp left St Mary's to assume the archbishopric of St Andrews.[177] Both the Cromwellian and Covenanting revolutions had been reversed.

Conclusion

The experience of the Scottish universities during the Interregnum reinforces the argument that the Cromwellian state drew upon local realities and conditions to drive higher education policies. The attempts to implement Gillespie's Charter, while abortive, are indicative of the ways in which Cromwellian central government played upon political and religious rivalries in Scotland to potentially implement a religious settlement that would impact the universities. However, given the Charter's failure, the extent to which the state effectively wielded the universities to effect widespread socialisation to the new political order can be questioned. Certainly, the impact of the Cromwellian occupation reverberated in the universities, as they endured as contested sites where the legitimacy of English rule was resisted, the factional strife of the Protester–Resolutioner controversy continued to play out, and the education of Scottish university students, and thus the long-term survival of the Scottish state, was repeatedly questioned. Additionally, the regime, in some respects, positioned itself as a legitimate force in university affairs, especially as it pertained to managing the professoriate and supervising finances. But it is difficult to contend that the Cromwellian regime wielded

[176] McCrie, *Robert Blair*, p. 373.
[177] Buckroyd, *James Sharp*, pp. 70–3.

the universities to engineer a long-term transformation in Scotland's social order, especially when compared to the Covenanting and royal policies, and more immediately, to foster allegiance to the Protectorate state.

Many of the underlying themes that marked the experience of Scottish higher education during the Interregnum were also apparent in Ireland and New England. A conquered realm and a colony, the currents of religious and political rivalry, many of which were born from the conquest and occupation, and disputes over religious orthodoxy, sparked tensions that impacted higher education in these spaces. Similarly to the Scottish experience, Cromwellian central government took varying approaches to controlling higher learning. Moreover, the aftershocks of the conquest, and the wider revolution in politics and religion, continued to be felt in these universities. As the next chapter demonstrates, they were negotiated and contested within Trinity and Harvard and led to novel higher educational projects that sought to ensure the effective socialisation of students to ensure the health of the commonwealth.

6

Ireland, New England, and New College Projects, c. 1655–60

In the 1650s, the proliferation of Protestant sects across the British Atlantic challenged Reformed orthodoxies and how power structures conceived of ordered societies. As we have seen, this situation stoked tensions at the Scottish universities, Trinity College, Dublin, and Harvard College, where doctrinal amorphism and heterodoxy tested each institution's ability to sustain coherent, godly communities. In Ireland, especially, the civil wars and Cromwellian conquest severely upended this dynamic and bred much of the doctrinal diversity that rattled Trinity. In contrast, following the conquest, Harvard escaped close government oversight and proved to be a useful fount of personnel that staffed the administrations of the Commonwealth and Protectorate. In both Ireland and New England – in addition to Scotland – there existed persistent challenges to established social orders due to the rise of factions and religious controversies that resounded in the universities. As this chapter aims to demonstrate, the broader impact of these religious tensions gave life to new educational projects in the British Atlantic, projects that sought the founding of new colleges to realise competing visions of social control and the wider political order in each locale.

This chapter contends that ideas that were contested in the colleges, the controversies that reverberated in each institution, and the resultant higher education projects of the 1650s can be viewed as part of wider developments born from the heated political, religious, and intellectual climate of the 1650s.[1] As will be discussed, the attempted founding of new colleges in New England, Dublin, and northern England at points intersected with the wider

---

[1] On studies on the intellectual climate of this era see e.g., Barnard, *Improving Ireland*, chap. 1; Walter W. Woodward, *Prospero's America: John Winthrop, Jr., Alchemy, and the Creation of New England Culture, 1606–1676* (Chapel Hill, NC, 2010); Sarah Rivett, *The Science of the Soul in Colonial New England* (Chapel Hill, NC, 2011); Zachary McLeod Hutchins, *Inventing Eden: Primitivism, Millennialism, and the Making of New England* (Oxford, 2014). For useful overview of 'radical' religion during this period, see Andrew Bradstock, *Radical Religion in Cromwell's England: A Concise History from the English Civil War to the End of the Commonwealth* (London, 2011). On religion, radicalism, and dissent in Ireland, New England, and the wider British Atlantic during this era, see e.g., Kilroy, 'Radical Religion in Ireland' and Gribben, *God's Irishmen*, chap. 4; Pestana, *Protestant*

educational movement promoted by the Hartlib Circle. However, scholarly focus has largely been rooted in examining intellectual developments, and has not necessarily focused on examining these developments in tandem and through a lens that has understood universities as vital institutions to the health of the state.[2] Additionally, this chapter's focus on Harvard and Trinity will also permit for a further investigation of how these two 'sister' institutions navigated the vicissitudes of the Interregnum and the extent to which they addressed the persistent question of native education. In various ways, the controversies that embroiled Harvard and Trinity in the 1650s and the attempts by puritans of various stripes to found new colleges were part of a longer trajectory that saw higher educational institutions wielded to correct wider societal ills. They were also indicative of the ways puritans tried to realise rival visions of orderly, idealised societies. These events underline the colleges' strategic place as contested institutions, where during the 1650s rival groups clashed both within and beyond the universities to exercise effective control over higher learning.

This chapter is organised into three parts. The first part examines how both Harvard and Trinity confronted the tensions surrounding Protestant sects and heterodoxy in New England and Ireland. It focuses on the controversy surrounding Henry Dunster's ouster from Harvard due to his adoption of Baptist beliefs. It also examines Trinity's Independent turn under Provost Samuel Winter, which marked a crucial transformation at a critical time, for it occurred as Henry Cromwell began to court the favour the 'Old Protestant' New English, not the Independents.[3] These controversies raised existential questions about the health of the extramural communities that the colleges served. They also provide vital grounding to understanding the plans to found new colleges in the 1650s. The second part thus examines the schemes to found new institutions in New England – at Harvard, with the Indian College, and in the New Haven colony – Dublin, and Durham, England, in light of broader religious controversies at established educational institutions. These plans not only highlight how rivals attempted to realise their competing visions of healthy commonwealths, but they also indicate the ways in which the contests and disputes within the universities fuelled much of the energy behind new foundations. This chapter then concludes with an examination

---

Empire, chap. 3; Timothy L. Wood, *Agents of Wrath, Sowers of Discord: Authority and Dissent in Puritan Massachusetts, 1630–1655* (New York, 2006).

[2] For foundational studies on these developments, see e.g., Barnard, *Cromwellian Ireland*, pp. 206–18, chap. 8; Webster, *Great Instauration*, pp. 222–45.

[3] On the 'Old Protestant' New English and 'New Protestants' represented by followers of the new sects, see Gribben, *God's Irishmen*, p. 40; S.J. Connolly, *Religion, Law, and Power: The Making of Protestant Ireland 1660–1760* (Oxford, 1992), pp. 114–15; Aidan Clarke, *Prelude to Restoration in Ireland: The End of the Commonwealth, 1659–1660* (Cambridge, 1999), p. ix; Toby Barnard, 'Planters and Policies in Cromwellian Ireland', in *Irish Protestant Ascents and Descents, 1641–1770* (Dublin, 2004), pp. 1–34, at 2–3.

of the charged confessional politics in the period immediately preceding the Restoration. It examines the ways, and the extent to which, Harvard and Trinity were embroiled in the upheaval that saw the manifestation of a new political order rooted in the restored monarchy.

Controversy at Harvard and Trinity

In October 1652, the Massachusetts General Court issued a declaration for 'the advauncment of learninge in New England'. The main thrust of the declaration was that both the teaching of the liberal arts and increased provisions for the college were crucial 'for the better discharge of our trust for the next generation, & so to posterity'. It cut to the core of higher education's central utility to provide personnel essential to the long-term endurance of the wider state. In order to continue this process of social engineering, funding for teachers, students, and graduates was crucial. This was especially pressing because as the New England plantation expanded, and as student numbers increased, Harvard's graduates, once they were 'ready for publicke use', tended to leave New England for 'imployment elsewhere'. The General Court ordered voluntary collections be taken to maintain 'timely provision' for the president, fellows, and poor scholars in order avoid 'the ruine of this common wealth'.[4] It subsequently made a series of grants to Harvard out of the contested Pequot lands in Connecticut before creating a committee in September 1653 to examine Harvard's estate and collect contributions from settlements within Massachusetts.[5] A month later the committee issued a circular to the towns of Massachusetts requesting contributions to the college for the 'enlargement of learning'.[6] Over the next several months, settlements in Massachusetts – and York, Maine – donated funds, while the General Court would continue to urge towns to contribute to the upkeep of the college.[7]

As highlighted in Chapter 4, Harvard graduates had from early on left New England to staff the secular and religious structures of the Parliamentarian and later Cromwellian state. While a potential boon for the republican imperial state, the departure of would-be ministers and magistrates from the plantation clashed with the General Court's intention to perpetuate a learned, godly society for future generations in New England. The North American commonwealth required these men, socialised to the authorised norms of New England society, to sustain its existence. In addition to increased funding to provide more opportunities to keep Harvard graduates in New England, the General

---

[4] MA, MS 58, fols 21–2; *Massachusetts Records*, III, pp. 279–80, IV.1, pp. 100–1.
[5] Morison, *HCSC*, I, p. 31; *HCR*, IV, p. 10–11; *Massachusetts Records*, III, pp. 296, 299, 331–2, IV.1, pp. 136, 178–80.
[6] MA, MS 58, fol. 23r.
[7] Ibid., fol. 24r; HUA, UAI 5.120, Box 1, Folder 3; *Massachusetts Records*, III, p. 348, IV.1, pp. 182–3, 186–7.

Court was also bent on maintaining religious orthodoxy.[8] In May 1654, the Court issued an order against heterodoxy that targeted educators specifically. Because the welfare of the commonwealth was rooted in educating youths in 'good literature' and 'sound doctrine', the General Court commanded the Overseers and town selectmen not to 'admit or suffer any such to be contynued in the office or place of teaching, educating, or instructing of youth or child, in the colledge or schooles, that have manifested themselves unsound in fayth, or scandelous in theire lives'.[9] This order echoed those issued in England, Scotland, and Ireland in the previous three decades – those deemed heterodox were unfit to train New England's future churchmen and statesmen. Additionally, the context of the General Court's actions was key and came with added urgency, for by May 1654, the General Court and the Overseers had become aware of Henry Dunster's rejection of infant baptism.

President Dunster had guided Harvard's fiscal, administrative, and intellectual development in the aftermath of the Eaton controversy. At or around the time he came under suspicion of heterodoxy, he was at work on bringing Harvard's course of study for a bachelor's degree in line with the four-year residency requirement practiced in the English universities.[10] Indeed, months before his heterodoxy came to light, the committee appointed to examine Harvard's finances had lauded Dunster's 'rare strength & labour' in educating students and administering the college's affairs.[11] But his abilities as an educator and administrator – as the chief moulder of New England youths – were called into question when he failed to produce his fourth child for baptism in October 1653. Dunster had previously espoused orthodox defences of the practice of infant baptism, and in New England, it was an important part of membership into the church of the elect.[12] But by 1653 his views had changed. Scholars have debated as to whether Dunster's repudiation of infant baptism represented a logical development of his understanding of contemporary theological debates or a more direct indictment of the entire New England system.[13] Regardless of Dunster's motives, his rejection of infant baptism violated the Cambridge Platform and the laws of Massachusetts.[14] This sparked an existential crisis for colonial authorities. Harvard's president,

---

[8] See e.g., *Massachusetts Records*, III, p. 317.
[9] *Ibid.*, III, pp. 343–4.
[10] See Dunster's '*Quadriennium* Memoir' in *HCR*, III, pp. 279–300.
[11] HUA, UAI 5.120, Box 1, Folder 4.
[12] MHS, MS N-1143, pp. 145–53. See also Kirsten MacFarlane, 'Why Did Henry Dunster Reject Infant Baptism? Circumcision and the Covenant of Grace in the Seventeenth-Century Transatlantic Reformed Community', *Journal of Ecclesiastical History*, 72:2 (2021), 323–51, at 337–8.
[13] MacFarlane, 'Why Did Henry Dunster Reject Infant Baptism', pp. 343–5. On Dunster's ideological development and the broader scholarly debates, see also Jonathan Den Hartog, '"National and Provinciall Churches Are Nullityes": Henry Dunster's Puritan Argument against the Puritan Established Church', *Journal of Church and State*, 56:4 (2014), 691–710.
[14] *Massachusetts Records*, II, p. 85.

the most influential educator at the top of the colonial educational apparatus, espoused heterodox ideas, thus threatening to debase the entire New England social order.

In January 1654 the General Court wrote to the Overseers that Dunster's 'practice and opinion against infant baptisme rendred himself offensive to this government'. The Court thus pressed the Harvard Overseers to act 'for the preventing or removing of that which may tend to the prejudice of the colledge and scandall of the Country'.[15] In May, it issued its order against unorthodox schoolmasters. Dunster understood its implications, and in June he submitted a letter of resignation to the General Court, in which he took the time to also signal his misgivings with the process surrounding his ouster. He cited the illegality of the recent committee to examine Harvard's finances – which he believed superseded the Harvard Corporation's authority – as prompting his decision. He did, however, note that he would maintain his duties 'for some few weeks or months… if the Society in the interim fall not to pieces in our hands'.[16] Dunster clearly felt that his removal did more harm than good for the college, but he would gain no supporters by lambasting the General Courts' decisions. Unsurprisingly, authorities disagreed, and again commanded the Overseers 'to make provision, in case [Dunster] persist in his resolution more then moneth… for some meete person to carry an end that worke for the present'.[17] The Overseers made one last effort to reason with Dunster, but his public disavowal of infant baptism in late June sealed his fate.[18] While it is unclear if he presided over the 1654 commencement, Dunster does seem to have remained active in the college until his formal removal. For instance, in a 3 October 1654 letter to John Winthrop Jr, the Harvard tutor Thomas Dudley noted that he had been consulting with Dunster about his cousin Fitz-John Winthrop's fitness to be admitted a student.[19] But on 24 October, at a meeting of the Overseers, he formally resigned.[20]

Dunster's dissent was scandalous in orthodox New England, but it was not unique in a wider transatlantic context that the saw the increase of and practice of heterodox ideas.[21] When understood as part of a process of state formation within a settler society, Dunster's ultimate removal, despite his service to the college, is analogous with other, similar removals throughout the British Atlantic in the mid-seventeenth century, in which capable educators deviated from the authorised norms that buttressed church and state power and thus had to be marginalised.[22] Most immediately, the Covenanters in the

---

[15] MA, MS 58, fol. 27r; Morison, *HCSC*, I, pp. 307–8.
[16] Morison, *HCSC*, I, pp. 309–10; Chaplin, *Dunster*, pp. 125–6.
[17] *Massachusetts Records*, III, p. 352.
[18] Morison, *HCSC*, I, p. 311; Chaplin, *Dunster*, pp. 129–30.
[19] *Winthrop Papers*, VI, pp. 442–3.
[20] Morison, *HCSC*, I, p. 311.
[21] *Dunster Papers*, p. 195.
[22] On this point, see Cipriano, 'Ejected Academics'.

preceding decade had shown how university masters who deviated too far from accepted orthodoxies faced expulsion, regardless of their abilities as educators and administrators. Indeed, the issue for Dunster and for New England's authorities was that he occupied a post of considerable influence at a college that was singularly tasked with producing orthodox ministers to sustain an ordered society. The Massachusetts resident Edward Holyoke noted in a letter to Dunster that 'Much may be sayd concerning your calling, place estieme in N. England: and the great offense to Christ his spouse that you will lay in his peoples wayes a stumbling blocke'.[23] Despite the proliferation of religious radicalism during the Interregnum, New England was not a society interested in experimenting with novel ideas, especially those regarding baptism. Thus a week before Dunster's ouster, the General Court prohibited anyone 'unsound in judgment concerninge the mayne poynts of Christian religion as they have bin held forth & acknowledged by the generallitie of the Protestant orthodox writers' from serving in the civil administration.[24] The Court then appointed four new Overseers – John Allen, John Norton, Samuel Whiting, and Thomas Cobbet – four days prior to Dunster's resignation.[25] Dunster, an esteemed academic and cleric who reared the college into maturity, was removed and became a pariah.[26]

For New England's authorities – who again had to appoint a new college head in the wake of a scandal – it was essential that Dunster's successor adhere to the colony's rigid orthodoxy. In October 1654, the Overseers ordered Richard Mather and John Norton to appeal to Charles Chauncy, then minister at Plymouth, to accept the presidency.[27] Chauncy held a bachelor of divinity from Trinity College, Cambridge, where he had also lectured in Hebrew and Greek before eventually falling out with Laudian authorities.[28] He accepted Harvard's post, though not before the Overseers and General Court increased their offered salary in a bid to keep Chauncy from returning to England.[29] On 27 November, a month after Dunster resigned, Chauncy 'was solemnly inaugurated into the place of President' at a meeting of the Overseers.[30]

Tellingly, Dunster was offered an opportunity to abscond to Ireland, where Baptist sympathies had found a more welcome, if still contentious, environment and where the Cromwellian tenet of liberty of conscience had

---

[23] The letter is reproduced in MacFarlane, 'Why Did Henry Dunster Reject Infant Baptism', pp. 346–51, quotation at 350.
[24] *Massachusetts Records*, III, p. 357.
[25] MA, MS 58, fol. 28r; *Massachusetts Records*, III, p. 368.
[26] On the difficulties Dunster faced following his resignation, see Morison, HCSC, I, pp. 311–19; Chaplin, *Dunster*, chaps 11–12.
[27] HCR, I, p. 206.
[28] Francis J. Bremer, 'Chauncy, Charles (bap. 1592, d. 1672)', ODNB; Morison, *Founding*, pp. 89–91; idem, HCSC, I, pp. 320–3.
[29] MA, MS 58, fol. 29r. On Chauncy's compensation, see also MA, MS 58, fol. 31r; *Massachusetts Records*, IV.1, p. 216.
[30] HCR, I, p. 207.

manifested more fully. In May 1655, Dunster received a letter from Edward Roberts, an official in the Cromwellian administration in Dublin. Roberts wrote that, because Dunster had suffered in New England for his beliefs, Lord Deputy Charles Fleetwood, who favoured the Baptists and whom he depended upon to maintain power, was ready to 'provide for you in this Land'. Dunster 'may through mercy have free Liberty of your Conscience; and opportunity of Associateing with Saints and free publishing the Ghospell of Truth which [is] greatly wanted amongst us there being but few able and painefull men who make the service of god theire worke'.[31] Dunster remained in Massachusetts, but the letter underscores the extent to which sects had multiplied in Cromwellian Ireland and as a result tensions and controversies were endemic to the realm. In William Petty's estimation, Protestants, outnumbered by Catholics by more than two to one, were divided between 'Episcopalls', 'presbiterians', and a small minority of 'ffanatiques'.[32] That the administration of Fleetwood, an Independent and a champion of liberty of conscience for Protestants, emboldened these 'ffanatiques' – and especially the Baptists who were concentrated in the army – exacerbated conflicts between Protestants.[33] If New England's social order can be characterised as one built on a rigid and homogenised orthodoxy where deviancy and heterodoxy was quickly stamped out, the Ireland of the 1650s was at the opposite end of the spectrum.

Dunster's doctrinal transgression was not anomalous. It was part of a wider tide of intra-Protestant controversy that was endemic to the Interregnum, into which the universities were embroiled. In Ireland, Trinity stood at the apex of a society riven by religious discord. Provost Samuel Winter remained mindful of government religious policy, and in his notebook he included articles 35 to 38 of the Instrument of Government, which dealt specifically with the propagation of the gospel.[34] He likely interpreted the Instrument's articles as a remit to promote Independency.[35] However, in February 1655 Fleetwood pressed the fellows and scholars of Trinity 'to give their Master the reverence and honour due unto his office agreeable to the statutes of the Colledge and strict discipline of like places, whereby his just authority may not be enervated'.[36] This indicated that the fellows and students did not hold Winter in high regard, and given the fact that he was installed unilaterally by the regime, this is unsurprising. A month later, Fleetwood urged the fellows and scholars to lead godly lives and attend diligently to their responsibilities

---

[31] HUA, UAI 15.850, Box 1, Folder 26. On Fleetwood's Baptist sympathies and his tenure in Ireland, see, generally, Terry Clavin, 'Fleetwood, Charles', *DIB*.

[32] 'Commonwealth Records (Continued)', *Archivium Hibernicum*, 7 (1918–21), 20–66, at 61.

[33] *Thurloe State Papers*, III, pp. 70, 145, 183, 245–6; Barnard, *Cromwellian Ireland*, pp. 100–7.

[34] TCD, MS 805, fols 32v–33r.

[35] Gardiner, *Constitutional Documents*, p. 416; Gribben, *God's Irishmen*, pp. 144–5.

[36] Urwick, *Trinity College Dublin*, p. 63.

while 'instructing and admonishing one another to edifye each other that they may increase in the saving knowledge of Christ'.[37] Any member who disobeyed – by blaspheming, breaking the Sabbath, or frequenting taverns – was subject to expulsion by the provost.[38] Fleetwood thus empowered Winter to expel 'corrupt persons' after their first offense, giving Winter greater authority to deal with refractory fellows.[39]

As the concurrent situation in Scotland indicated – with the formation of committees to visit the universities, the formation of a governing Council of Scotland, and consistent petitioning to and from London – structures of power during the Interregnum regularly changed. In Ireland, Fleetwood's actions highlight how Cromwellian power dynamics in Ireland, and particularly the power of the lord deputy, directly impacted the university. Anticipating changes to this position of authority would be in Trinity's favour. Thus in March 1654, Provost Winter hosted Henry Cromwell at Trinity, where he was 'entertained with copyes of verses, speeches, and disputations'.[40] He was thereafter elected to Trinity's chancellorship over the exiled marquis of Ormond.[41] This was strategic on the part of Winter, who courted Henry in an attempt to build favour for Independents.[42] Henry was installed as the commander of the army in Ireland in December 1654, and he became effective chief governor in September 1655, after Fleetwood returned to England. Henry was later elevated to the lord deputyship in 1657.[43] Winter's machinations seem to have worked, for after his visit to Ireland in March 1654 Henry wrote disparagingly of the Baptists, while noting that others, including Winter's Independents, were 'abundantly satisfied and well pleased with the present government in Englande'.[44] This did not necessarily mean that Henry would favour the Independents when he assumed power in September 1655. On the one hand, he had proven to be something of a religious moderate.[45] On the other, when Henry assumed control of the Irish government, his chaplain Thomas Harrison, a London Independent who had ministered in New England, accompanied him.[46] But Henry's tendency for moderation

---

[37] TCD, MUN/V/5/1, p. 81; Corcoran, *State Policy in Irish Education*, p. 75.
[38] TCD, MUN/V/5/1, p. 81.
[39] *Ibid.*
[40] *Thurloe State Papers*, II, p. 163; Peter Gaunt, 'Cromwell, Henry (1628–1674)', *ODNB*.
[41] TCD, MUN/P/1/378a; TCD, MUN/V/5/1, p. 83.
[42] Barnard, *Cromwellian Ireland*, pp. 112–14.
[43] *Ireland under the Commonwealth*, II, pp. 468–9; *Thurloe State Papers*, II, pp. 697, 728–9, IV, pp. 327–8, VI, pp. 446–7.
[44] *Thurloe State Papers*, II, pp. 149–50.
[45] *Ibid.*, III, pp. 132–3.
[46] Edmund Calamy, *The Nonconformist's Memorial: Being an Account of the Ministers, Who Were Ejected or Silenced after the Restoration*, ed. Samuel Palmer, 3rd edn (3 vols, London, 1802–03), I, p. 330.

would prove central to his policies, and upon his arrival in Ireland, he attempted to steer a middle course.⁴⁷

Provost Winter's manoeuvrings with the soon-to-be lord deputy paralleled his efforts to build Trinity into an Independent seminary. Though Winter had increased authority and the support of Fleetwood's government, he did not have like-minded fellows with whom to collaborate in propagating an Independent order for Ireland and a college to support it. This began to change in March 1655, several months before Henry Cromwell returned to Ireland. In a petition to Fleetwood, 'The delegates of the Congregational Churches of Ireland' pressed the Dublin government as to the 'the want of godly Fellows in the college at Dublin for the pious, as well as learned, education of youth'. The 'delegates' proposed a group of men for fellowships, with Provost Winter and two Cromwellian-appointed ministers, Claudius Gilbert and Henry Wootton, tasked with considering candidates.⁴⁸ This letter was crucial, and it marked the beginning of Trinity's fleeting, Independent transformation.⁴⁹

The petition requested that Independent fellows be installed at Trinity was submitted by a group of ministers to be considered by the provost and two imported ministers with no association to the college.⁵⁰ This request underlined the existence of a practice that saw extramural authorities take quick action to calibrate institutions of higher education towards a particular doctrinal vision, an action most recently taken in New England with Dunster's Baptist turn. It also situates comfortably within a longer tradition, dating back to the Laudian intrusion of the 1630s, that saw English officials ignore Trinity's established laws and privileges in order to plant amenable fellows. The importance of the individuals who staffed these fellowships was again brought to the fore. According to Trinity's statutes, the election of fellows was an internal procedure, the authority of the provost in collaboration with a quorum of senior fellows.⁵¹ Winter's committee with Gilbert and Wootton violated this stricture, which recalled similar measures from previous decades, such as Laud's importation of English fellows and the Irish Parliament's reestablishment of the 'native' interest. More immediately, the March 1655 petition was a significant effort to consolidate Independency's position in Ireland and reconfigure Trinity's ethos to sustain the burgeoning congregational communities in Ireland.⁵²

---

⁴⁷ Hall, *Puritans*, p. 298; Barnard, *Cromwellian Ireland*, pp. 105–6; idem, 'Planters and Policies', p. 14.
⁴⁸ BL, Egerton MS 1762, fol. 150v.
⁴⁹ Gribben, *God's Irishmen*, pp. 146–7.
⁵⁰ In May, Trinity granted Gilbert the bachelor of divinity, but this was certainly after deliberations on the election of Independent fellows had taken place. See TCD, MUN/V/5/1, p. 82.
⁵¹ MacDonnell, *Chartæ et Statuta*, pp. 35–6, 97–8; Bolton, *Statutes*, pp. 32, 108–9.
⁵² See especially Barnard, *Cromwellian Ireland*, pp. 114–15; Gribben, *God's Irishmen*, pp. 44–5, 75, 81.

The petition and Winter, Gilbert, and Wootton's subsequent actions also underscore the reality of Trinity's strategic existence as a contested space. If the actions of Trinity's trustees in staffing the college mainly with Trinity alumni represented a pragmatic approach from the state to maintain order and control over the seminary, Winter's plans challenged this status quo and represented a rival exertion of growing Independent power in Ireland and, more immediately, in the college. Indeed, the list of names in the petition included recent Trinity graduates educated under Winter as well as associates and congregants of Winter's Dublin church.[53] Among the list were Winter's two sons, Samuel Jr and Josiah, the latter of whom received his BA from Trinity in May 1655, and Francis Saunders, a member of Winter's congregation.[54] Other recent graduates included William Burton, Gamaliel Marsden, William Oliver, John Price, and Joseph Scott.[55] The list also included William Leckey, Robert Norbury, and Edward Veele, who, with their fellow Englishman Marsden, were later ejected for nonconformity following the Restoration.[56] Many of these men would go on to serve as fellows between 1655 and 1660.[57] As Winter's plans were realised, New England's influence was also felt. Harvard alumnus Samuel Mather received an MA from Trinity in 1655, after he had travelled to Ireland with Henry Cromwell, Thomas Harrison, and Nathaniel Brewster, a graduate of Harvard's inaugural class.[58] Mather's name does not appear in the register, but according to James Ware he was made a senior fellow in 1656.[59] Mather's younger brother Increase, a Harvard alumnus and Harvard's future president, also received his MA from Trinity in 1658.[60] The influx of Harvard educated ministers and academics into Trinity, even following the controversy surrounding Dunster's resignation, was among the clearer signals of Trinity's broader Independent transformation.

This transformed Trinity's old order, as the influx of Independents also spelled the end of the tenures of fellows who were already at the college.[61]

---

[53] Barnard, *Cromwellian Ireland*, p. 203, n. 90–5.
[54] TCD, MUN/V/5/1, p. 82; Seymour, *Puritans in Ireland*, p. 105; Barnard, *Cromwellian Ireland*, p. 203; *Alumni Dublinenses*, p. 890.
[55] TCD, MUN/V/5/1 p. 75; Seymour, *Puritans in Ireland*, p. 105; *Alumni Dublinenses*, pp. 120, 555, 637, 682, 739.
[56] Calamy, *Nonconformist's Memorial*, I, pp. 210–11, 341, II, p. 599, III, pp. 436–7; *Alumni Dublinenses*, pp. 489, 621, 837; Urwick, *Trinity College Dublin*, pp. 75–6; Alexander Gordon, 'Veal, Edward (1632/3–1708)', rev. Caroline L. Leachman, *ODNB*.
[57] See TCD, MUN/V/5/1, pp. 85, 86, 88, 89, 90, 91, 93, 94, 96, 97, 99. See also *Alumni Dublinenses*, p. 621; Urwick, *Trinity College Dublin*, p. 75; Fry, *Dublin University Calendar*, p. 576.
[58] *Thurloe State Papers*, III, pp. 559, 660; Sibley, *Biographical Sketches*, I, pp. 68–71.
[59] *Alumni Dublinenses*, p. 561; Fry, *Dublin University Calendar*, p. 576; Harris, *Ware Works*, II, p. 345; Murray, *Dublin University*, pp. 19–20; Morison, *HCSC*, I, pp. 15–16.
[60] *Alumni Dublinenses*, p. 561; Sibley, *Biographical Sketches*, I, pp. 412–13; Murray, *Dublin University*, pp. 26–7; Morison, *HCSC*, I, p. 300, n. 1.
[61] TCD, MUN/V/5/1, pp. 75–80.

These fellows' systematic exclusion from the college is another indicator of the exertion of Independent authority at Trinity. Adam Cusack was forced to leave Trinity in 1655, and thereafter entered Lincoln's Inn.[62] Miles Symner was then appointed to a commission to settle soldiers following the completion of the Down Survey, which drew him away from the college for long stretches.[63] Joseph Travers' name, meanwhile, does not appear in the Trinity register as one of the fellows after May 1655.[64] Winter likely removed Travers for his persistent opposition.[65] Similar to the situation in the Scottish universities, Trinity was operating, but the continued presence of Winter's opponents, and Travers' antagonisms most of all, spread disaffection in the college.[66] The army officer Humphrey Barrow urged Henry Cromwell, to 'be moved to a speedy Rectification, and rescue of [Trinity] from Disorder'.[67] It is likely that because of this upheaval Henry contacted John Owen about revising Trinity's constitution, though nothing came of this effort.[68] Despite Winter's energies, however, Trinity was not completely transformed.[69] Two fellows, Caesar Williamson, a former episcopal minister, and John Stearne, who dedicated his medical writings to deposed bishops remained throughout the latter half of the 1650s.[70] There is also evidence that episcopal sympathies remained. Cotton Mather wrote that upon his father Increase's examination for the MA, he was assessed by 'some of the Fellows, who were Prelatically Disposed, [who] gave him all the Discouragement they could'.[71] Nevertheless, 1655 did represent something of a watershed for the college. Whereas opposition in the Scottish universities had materialised among professors and students whose tenures predated the Cromwellian conquest, the pre-1655 fellows, including Travers, owed their places to the regime. This is another indicator that Winter's actions represented a new effort to systematically alter Trinity's ethos and to transform the college, to whatever extent possible, more acutely into an institution that supported Ireland's Independent churches.

---

[62] His name makes a final appearance in the College register in January 1656. TCD, MUN/V/5/1, p. 85. See also Ball, *History of the County Dublin*, pp. 145–6.
[63] BL, Add MS 19845, fols 1v–2v; HP, 33/1/1B; *Ireland under the Commonwealth*, II, p. 609.
[64] TCD, MUN/V/5/1, p. 84.
[65] Barnard, *Cromwellian Ireland*, p. 202.
[66] TCD, MUN/V/5/1, p. 81; Urwick, *Trinity College Dublin*, p. 63.
[67] Humphrey Barrow, *The Relief of the Poore and Advancement of Learning Proposed* (London, 1656), p. 7.
[68] Peter Gaunt (ed.), *The Correspondence of Henry Cromwell, 1655–1659: From the British Library Lansdowne Manuscripts* (Cambridge, 2007), pp. 316–17.
[69] Barnard, *Cromwellian Ireland*, pp. 204–5.
[70] TCD, MUN/V/5/1, pp. 84–91. See also Barnard, *Cromwellian Ireland*, p. 202; Harris, *Ware Works*, II, p. 343; Belcher, *Memoir of John Stearne*, p. 34.
[71] Increase Mather and Cotton Mather, *Two Mather Biographies: Life and Death and Parentator*, ed. William J. Scheick (London, 1989), p. 93.

Table 6.1. Trinity College, Dublin Staff, c. 1655–60.

Provosts
Samuel Winter, c. 1651–60
Thomas Seele, 1660–75

Fellows and Associated Offices Where Known
Nathaniel Hoyle (1631), Vice Provost (1658–59)
Miles Symner (1652), Mathematics (1652)
John Stearne (c. 1651–52), Registrar (1652–58)
Caesar Williamson (c. 1654), Divinity Lecturer (1660)
Edward Veele (c. 1654)
William Leckey (c. 1655)
John Price (c. 1655)
Joshua Cowley (c. 1655)
Gamaliel Marsden (c. 1655)
Joseph Scott (c. 1655)
Samuel Mather (c. 1655)
Josiah Winter (c. 1655)
Francis Saunders (1656)
Joseph Wilkins (1656)
Patrick Sheridan (1659)

Sources: Fry, *Dublin University Calendar*; TCD, MUN/V/5/1, MUN/V/5/2; Mahaffy, *Epoch in Irish History*; *Alumni Dublinenses*.

Trinity's pivot towards Independency was not, nor would it ever be, complete, and its transformation highlighted the extent to which competing doctrinal visions and their corresponding power structures entangled and clashed in Irish higher education. It also, more immediately, underlined Winter and the Independents' consolidation of power in Dublin. Winter had done much to ingratiate Ireland's Independent party, and by extension the college, to the new governor, and Henry Cromwell was a close friend of other leading Independents in Ireland, including Harrison and Mather. But close personal ties did not make for sound policy. Following Henry Cromwell's arrival in late 1655, official religious policy began to be reformulated along non-sectarian lines. Though initially conciliatory towards the Independents, Henry's chief goal was to consolidate conquest, especially by sewing discord among Protestants. This first meant breaking the power of the Baptists.[72] In December 1656, Henry reported to Secretary Thurloe that 'the Anabaptists

[72] Barnard, 'Planters and Policies', p. 14.

and others, whose way and principles were inconsistent with settlement and our interest, do find themselves disabled from doing much harm'.[73] In his campaign against the sects, Henry also removed Quakers from positions of civil authority in Ireland.[74]

On the back of Winter's intrigues, the stage was set for the Independents to assume greater influence with Henry Cromwell's administration, but this was not to be.[75] In early 1658 Henry Cromwell noted that his time in Ireland had exposed him 'more and more' to the 'vanitys' of the sects.[76] He and the Irish council would thereafter commune largely with the 'Old Protestant' New English, the community the regime believed to be most able to secure Cromwellian rule in Ireland.[77] He placated New English fears of territorial and political dislocation and ensured they received a privileged place in Cromwellian government. The New English's 'Old Protestantism' was also central to Henry's religious policy. Historians have highlighted that this resulted in a 'conservative shift' in religious policy.[78]

The irony is that the Cromwellian regime in Ireland would begin to favour the New English at the moment Trinity shifted towards Independency. In New England, the Massachusetts General Court had rooted out the threat of religious division by ejecting Dunster. In Ireland, division was virtually entrenched through Trinity's Independent transformation, which raised questions about the order of the wider commonwealth. As Trinity consolidated around an Independent ethos the central government pursued a contrasting religious policy, which amplified a tension between important institutions, and representations, of state power. The controversies and machinations on both sides of the Atlantic were emblematic of the broader, existential questions about the nature of society and what constituted an ordered state. During this era, rival authorities also channelled these competing visions into pursuing the foundation of new colleges.

College Schemes in New England, Ireland, and Northern England

Following the 1655 Harvard commencement, Charles Chauncy preached a sermon that spelled out his conception of the university. The university was, at its core, an institution to produce a pious ministry. In New England,

---

[73] *Thurloe State Papers*, V, p. 710.
[74] ibid., IV, pp. 508–9; *Ireland under the Commonwealth*, II, pp. 563, 637–8; Gribben, *God's Irishmen*, pp. 140, 142–3.
[75] Barnard, *Cromwellian Ireland*, pp. 114–15; idem, 'Planters and Policies', pp. 14–15; Gribben, *God's Irishmen*, pp. 45–6.
[76] *Thurloe State Papers*, VI, pp. 774, VII, pp. 198–9.
[77] Barnard, 'Planters and Policies', pp. 6–13, 16; John Cunningham, *Conquest and Land in Ireland: The Transplantation to Connacht, 1649–1680* (Woodbridge, 2011), pp. 124–7.
[78] Hall, *Puritans*, p. 298; Gillespie, 'The Crisis of Reform', pp. 212–13.

Chauncy emphasised that 'schools of learning, and meanes of education for our children' were meant to perpetuate 'some comfortable supply & succession in the Ministry'.[79] Schools and universities were 'approved and appointed of God, and of great importance for the benefit of Gods people'. And, within the context of the religious and intellectual disputes ensnaring Britain, Ireland, and New England, Chauncy emphasised that 'there is much more need of schools now'.[80] Chauncy addressed one radical critic of university learning, the New Model Army chaplain William Dell, specifically. Dell proposed a 'reformation of learning' that would dislodge the study of the liberal arts from the university. Dell had also sought to remove Oxford and Cambridge's seminary function.[81] Chauncy picked apart Dell's ideas and defended 'humane learning'. He emphasised university learning's scriptural antecedents and argued for the necessity of divinity, logic, rhetoric, and linguistic study to 'furnish' a sufficient ministry.[82]

Chauncy's sermon underlined the function of the university as a vital organ of the state and its role in fuelling the pipeline of clerics that provided legitimacy to the structures of political power through the distillation of 'true' learning and religion.[83] Conceptions of what constituted 'true' religion differed greatly in this era, but ideologues as far apart as Chauncy and William Laud would agree on the university's essential power in socialising students to a standardised corpus of authorised knowledge to breed societal homogeneity and guard against deviancy that would degrade society.[84] Additionally, in addressing William Dell outright, Chauncy's sermon also struck at the wider intellectual movement that had gained momentum in the 1640s and 1650s. The universities of Scotland, Ireland, and New England had already, to varying degrees, integrated into their curricula the philosophies and pedagogies of Ramus, Comenius, and other Reformed intellectuals. But the adoption of new pedagogical and philosophical ideas did not signal an alteration to the course of university learning; rather, it adapted the Aristotelian course to meet the needs of Reformed communities.[85] Directly related to these developments was the expansion of scientific and educational initiatives rooted in inductive experimentation to gain, and indeed produce, knowledge. Critics of the traditional university, such as the polymath Samuel Hartlib, wished to transform how knowledge was acquired – by shifting from reliance on the ancients to experiential learning – to understand the world around them. At a rudimentary level, they advocated for practical pedagogical and scientific

---

[79] Charles Chauncy, *Gods Mercy, Shewed to His People in Giving Them a Faithful Ministry and Schooles of Learning for the Continual Supplyes Therof* (Cambridge, MA, 1655), pp. 5, 14.
[80] Ibid., p. 33.
[81] Hill, 'Radical Critics', pp. 119–26.
[82] Chauncy, *Gods Mercy*, pp. 34–43.
[83] Braddick, *State Formation*, p. 287; Hammerstein, 'Relations with Authority', pp. 114–15.
[84] Foucault, *Discipline and Punish*, p. 184.
[85] See especially Hotson, 'A Generall Reformation', pp. 195–206.

improvements at the universities.[86] Ireland witnessed such endeavours, much of which stemmed from the energies of Hartlib and his associates.[87] At Trinity, this saw the creation in 1652 of a professorship of mathematics.[88] The senior fellow John Stearne, who served as professor of physic, also sought to establish a separate faculty of medicine in 1654.[89] And, across the Atlantic, scholars have highlighted the compatibility between puritanism and empiricism, with intellectuals such as John Cotton, John Norton – both Harvard Overseers – and John Winthrop Jr having integrated Baconian methods of induction into their spiritual work.[90] Beyond these influences, in the 1650s neither Trinity nor Harvard – nor the Scottish universities, for that matter – adopted these innovative initiatives for the 'advancement of learning' in any comprehensive fashion.[91] Chauncy's conception of the university as an institution that preserved and perpetuated a known body of inherited knowledge to sustain the wider social order endured.[92]

The foundation of new colleges represented another path by which to pursue innovations in new learning within the confines of a university setting. And, in the 1650s, several colleges were proposed in New England, Ireland, and northern England. These schemes, save for one – the Durham College project – were born from the exigencies of providing 'true' religion and learning to sustain godly communities. In other words, they were firmly rooted in the traditional conception of a university as the model, and moulder, of the extramural social order. The examples from the 1650s represent how the forces behind the disputes, controversies, and power struggles that were seemingly a hallmark of the early modern university were catalysed to the pursuit of new higher educational projects. These schemes that dotted the British Atlantic world were often sparked by the contests for authority and control of religion and learning – microcosms of the existential disputes over the wider social order – that had disrupted established institutions. The new colleges provided an opportunity to correct the failings – real or imagined – of the existing universities, and thus afforded another channel through which to pursue the realisation of a godly social order.

---

[86] Rivka Feldhay, 'Religion', in Katharine Park and Lorraine Daston (eds), *The Cambridge History of Science: Volume 3, Early Modern Science* (Cambridge, 2006), pp. 725–55.
[87] Barnard, *Cromwellian Ireland*, pp. 216–43; idem, 'The Hartlib Circle and the Origins of the Dublin Philosophical Society', *Irish Historical Studies*, 19:73 (1974), 56–71.
[88] Barnard, 'Miles Symner', pp. 129–30.
[89] TCD, MUN/V/5/1 pp. 84, 87; TCD, MUN/P/1/403e; Belcher, *Memoir of John Stearne*, pp. 15–16; Davis Coakley, 'Stearne, John (1624–1669)', *ODNB*.
[90] Hutchins, 'Building Bensalem', pp. 581–9; Woodward, *Prospero's America*, chap. 2; Rivett, *Science of the Soul*, pp. 5–16.
[91] Chauncy's successor as president, Leonard Hoar (1672–5), would attempt to 'rededicate' the college to the advancement of learning, but Hoar's visions, and his presidency, were abortive. See Morison, *HCSC*, II, pp. 400–1.
[92] See e.g., Robinson-Hammerstein, 'Common Good', pp. 74–5.

In New England, the scandal over Dunster's Baptist turn and the wider questions it raised about both Harvard and the health of New England society reignited calls for founding a college in New Haven. Chief among the project's architects was John Davenport, one of Harvard's first Overseers and a correspondent with Hartlib who was steeped in Comenian educational ideas.[93] Davenport long harboured a desire to found a college in New Haven, but the New Haven General Court's lack of action forced him to focus on sending New Haven youth, including Nathaniel Brewster, among Harvard's first graduates, to study at the Cambridge college.[94] In the wake of Dunster's ouster, however, planning for a college resumed. While the project had been proposed in the 1640s, in May 1654, as the Massachusetts General Court issued orders against scandalous schoolmasters in the wake of the Dunster controversy, John Winthrop Jr, governor of New Haven, was notified 'that there is some motion againe on foote concerning the setting up of a Colledg, here at Newhaven'.[95] Coupled with this renewed push was President Chauncy's adoption of Dunster's four-year residency requirement, which created difficulties when graduates refused to pay commencement fees.[96] These issues did not go unnoticed in New Haven, where the college project was again revived among the colony's magistrates. The town records for May 1655 stating that 'some disturbanc being at present at the Colledg in the bay [Harvard], and it is now intended to be propounded to the Gen. Court; therefore this Town may declare that they will doe by the way of Incouragement for the same'. Leading this charge before New Haven's magistrates were Davenport and his associate, minister William Hooke.[97] At subsequent meetings, the General Court highlighted the importance of higher education for the endurance of the godly New Haven settlement and agreed to a £60 annual contribution for 'furtheranc of the Colledg worke, a busines of much concernment for the good of posteritie'.[98]

To lead the college, Davenport and his associates appealed to William Leverich, an Emmanuel-educated minister who had recently settled at Oyster Bay on Long Island. Leverich had previously ministered throughout Massachusetts and had conducted missionary work among Native Americans in Plymouth and Cape Cod.[99] In October 1655 Harvard student John

---

[93] See e.g., HP, 6/5/1A–2B. In general, see Francis J. Bremer, 'Davenport, John (bap. 1597, d. 1670)', *ODNB*.
[94] Francis J. Bremer, *Building a New Jerusalem: John Davenport, a Puritan in Three Worlds* (New Haven, CT, 2012), pp. 203–4.
[95] Franklin Bowditch Dexter (ed.), *New Haven Town Records, 1649–1662* (New Haven, CT, 1917), pp. 213–14.
[96] Morison, *HCSC*, I, p. 328.
[97] Dexter, *New Haven Town Records*, pp. 241–2.
[98] *Ibid.*, 248–49; Charles J. Hoadly (ed.), *Records of the Colony or Jurisdiction of New Haven, from May, 1653 to the Union* (Hartford, CT, 1858), pp. 141–2.
[99] Kellaway, *New England Company*, p. 105; Morison, *Founding*, pp. 387–8.

Haynes wrote to his classmate Fitz-John Winthrop that 'I hear you are to be at New-Haven & I think so shall I, because there is a Colledg to be sttled there, Mr Leveredg is chosen President.'[100] Leverich seems to have been engaged with planning the college, but his wife was evidently opposed to his involvement. Davenport wrote to Winthrop Jr in November that her 'violent averseness from his settling in the Colledg, he saith, causeth him to desist from that buisnes. So, that worke must waite for a better season.'[101]

About the same time that Harvard's difficulties precipitated the planning of a college at New Haven, planning for a second college in Dublin commenced. The March 1650 ordinance for the advancement of the gospel in Ireland had called for the founding of another college to complement Trinity. The trustees were tasked with 'erecting, setling and maintenance of one other Colledge in the said City of Dublin, and of a Master, Fellows, Scholars and Officers therein, and of publique Profesors in the University there'.[102] The second college was envisioned as a constituent of the University of Dublin, of which Trinity was the 'Mother' institution.[103] It would not be until 1656, however, under the rule of Henry Cromwell, that planning of the second college commenced.

Given the Irish ordinance's evangelising thrust, the second college was likely envisioned as another seminary – but one that would provide a foil to the direction being pursued by Provost Winter at Trinity. According to Toby Barnard, the college was meant to 'balance Winter's Independent seminary at Trinity'.[104] Henry Cromwell, a driving force behind the planned college, was alive to the political machinations of Winter and the Independents.[105] But the planned college also stoked the aspirations of Ireland's intelligentsia. In a letter to Samuel Hartlib in November 1656, Robert Wood, a mathematician who served in Henry Cromwell's household, wrote that 'My Lord Henry Cromwell, the Chancellor of this University, is about a very noble Designe of making another Colledge in this City, & putting things into a better way for the Advancement of ingenuous Learning.'[106] The English minister and Hartlib Circle member John Beale also emphasised that students in the new college be 'of Naturall philosophy, & allowd freedome to engage in the way of Aristotle, or of the Academies or Sceptiques, as far as to notion of Ultimityes & Principles or elements, or in the way of Democritus & any

---

[100] Robert C. Winthrop, Jr, 'John Haynes to Fitz-John Winthrop', *Proceedings of the Massachusetts Historical Society*, 2nd series, 1 (1884–5), 118–31, at 120.
[101] Isabel M. Calder (ed.), *Letters of John Davenport, Puritan Divine* (New Haven, CT, 1937), p. 108.
[102] *Acts and Ordinances*, II, p. 356.
[103] Mahaffy, *Epoch in Irish History*, p. 63; *Chartae et Statuta Collegii Sacrosanctae et Individue Trinitatis Reginae Elizabethae Juxta Dublin* (Dublin, 1839), pp. 1–2.
[104] Barnard, *Cromwellian Ireland*, pp. 206–7, 210.
[105] *Thurloe State Papers*, VII, pp. 198–9.
[106] HP, 33/1/7A–8B. On Robert Wood, see Barnard, *Cromwellian Ireland*, pp. 48–9, 223–4.

moderne proposalls of Lord Bacon, Gassendus, Synertus &c'. Dublin's students should be steeped in anatomy, astronomy, chemistry, geography, mathematics, mechanics, medicine, and physics.[107] But in the end, ambitions for a college on the vanguard of science amounted to wishful thinking.

Like the New Haven project vis-à-vis Harvard, plans for a second college in Dublin can be viewed as a reaction to developments at Trinity. In Robert Wood's estimation, Henry Cromwell, a 'passionat & great lover of Learning', was a diligent steward of the college project.[108] As Dublin University's chancellor – Trinity being the only constituent college – he had a hand in forming a second college. He was also instrumental in purchasing James Ussher's library at a cost of £2,500, the 'great Magazeen of learning', which was to be housed in Cork House in Dublin, Henry's residence. Ussher's books were to serve as the basis for the library of the second college.[109] But beyond obtaining Ussher's library, the work on the second college also signalled a concerted effort to exercise control over the socialisation of future civil servants of the Cromwellian regime as Henry Cromwell envisioned it, and thereby contest the influence of Winter's Trinity.

In November 1657, Oliver Cromwell issued orders to the lord deputy and council in which he repeated instructions to ensure the propagation of the gospel and the education of youths in 'piety and literature'.[110] In December 1658, Wood reported to Hartlib that the 'businesse of the New Colledge here seems to be seriously minded, a Committee was this weeke appointed by my Lord Lieutenant & Council to consider of several particulars'.[111] The committee 'mett often' between December and February 1659, at which time it produced a proposal for both Trinity and the second college.[112] The committee was concerned mainly with deriving adequate funding for both colleges, as Trinity received few recorded benefactions during the Interregnum.[113] To this effect the committee proposed sequestering lands belonging to St Patrick's for use at the two institutions. It also proposed setting aside grounds near St Stephen's Green for the new college.[114] The report was a comprehensive account of the practicalities of both founding a new college and maintaining Trinity. What

---

[107] HP, 31/1/77A–80B. The names mentioned include the ancient Greek atomist Democritus and the early modern scientists Francis Bacon and Pierre Gassendi. See Mark Greengrass, Michael Leslie, and Timothy Raylor, 'Introduction', in Mark Greengrass, Michael Leslie, and Timothy Raylor (eds), *Samuel Hartlib and Universal Reformation: Studies in Intellectual Communication* (Cambridge, 1994), pp. 1–26, at 16–17.

[108] HP, 33/1/11A–B.

[109] CSPD 1655–56, p. 370; CSPD 1655–57, p. 199; TCD, MS 2160/7/1; HP, 33/1/9A–10B, 39A. See also Fox, *Trinity College Library*, pp. 25–9; Toby Barnard, 'The Purchase of Archbishop Ussher's Library in 1657', *Long Room*, 4 (1971), 9–14.

[110] CSPI 1647–60, pp. 849–50; *Cromwell Writings*, III, pp. 406–12.

[111] HP, 33/1/36A.

[112] HP, 33/1/39A, 33/1/39/44A–B.

[113] TCD, MS 571, fol. 3r.

[114] Urwick, *Trinity College Dublin*, pp. 64–8.

is more, the proposed college would mirror Trinity's composition completely. It would have a provost, vice-provost, and sixteen fellows. The senior fellows' posts included a divinity lecturer, English lecturer, catechist, bursar, senior dean, junior dean, and senior lecturer. The new college would also have seventy scholars, thirty of whom were to be 'natives'. The committee also earmarked allowances for several public professors to be shared by the two colleges, including professors of divinity, civil law, rhetoric, mathematics, and a 'Physick Professor who is to reade Natural Philosophy'.[115] While the latter two suggest potential turn towards new learning, both professorships predated the committee's proposals: Miles Symner had held the mathematics professorship since 1652 and John Stearne had been professor of 'physicke' since at least 1655.[116] In the draft bill establishing the second college, there were no suggestions as to the college's character beyond its role in 'the Advancement of the Protestant Religion in Ireland and more particularly the Completing of those pious intencons' set out in March 1650. In a final note that spoke to the political order that the college was to serve, the college was to be named 'the Colledge of his late most Serene Highnes Oliver Lord Protector of the Comonwealth of England Scotland and Ireland'.[117]

As historians have previously highlighted, the new college was to be a Protestant seminary, rooted in a 'traditional', Aristotelian course, with a mission similar to Trinity's.[118] Yet the individuals involved in the planning of the college provide important clues as to the new college's tenor. Based on the composition of the planning committee, the college, had it progressed beyond the design phase, would have challenged the Independents' grip on Irish higher learning. The group that planned the second Dublin college was more 'moderate' in makeup and marked the growing cooperation between Henry Cromwell and the New English in Ireland. Chief among the committee was Edward Worth, erstwhile dean of Cork, who had been a Trinity scholar in 1638, and who had been drawn into public life because of his opposition to the sects.[119] In 1657, but possibly earlier, Worth and other ministers formed the Cork Association to examine expectants, a regional commission for Munster that they envisioned as the basis of a national church rooted in uniformity and adherence to gospel ordinances.[120] Worth and his allies opposed the

---

[115] Urwick, *Trinity College Dublin*, pp. 67–8.
[116] TCD, MUN/V/5/1 pp. 84, 95; Belcher, *Memoir of John Stearne*, pp. 14–16; Barnard, *Cromwellian Ireland*, p. 208; Webster, *Great Instauration*, pp. 228–9.
[117] TCD, MUN/P/1/376.
[118] Barnard, *Cromwellian Ireland*, p. 208; Mahaffy, *Epoch in Irish History*, p. 314; Murphy, *History of Trinity College Dublin*, p. 119; Webster, *Great Instauration*, p. 231.
[119] TCD, MUN/V/5/1 p. 63; *Thurloe State Papers*, V, pp. 353–4; *Ireland under the Commonwealth*, II, p. 648. On Worth, see also *Alumni Dublinenses*, p. 895; Toby Barnard, 'Worth, Edward (c. 1620–1669)', *ODNB*.
[120] *The Agreement and Resolution of Severall Associated Ministers in the County of Corke for the Ordaining of Ministers* (Cork, 1657). See also Gribben, *God's Irishmen*, pp. 115–22.

Independents, and as the leader of a committee to plan Dublin's anti-Trinity, he was joined by other 'Old' Protestants like Dudley Loftus, James Ware, and Henry Jones, all Trinity alumni.[121]

The planning committee did not signal their intent to offer a new model of higher learning. Rather, they drew on the familiar model of the existing college, Trinity, but used it to plan an institution of higher learning that would serve a competing Protestant interest in Ireland. New England witnessed a similar situation, though, unlike the situation in Ireland, the calls for a new college in New Haven did not appear to engender any great animosity towards Harvard.[122] Both the Massachusetts and New Haven plantations also operated largely within the same puritan framework. There is also little to suggest the New Haven project would differ substantially from Harvard, beyond the fact that Harvard had been tainted with heterodoxy.[123] The fact that William Leverich was proposed as 'president', thus adopting a Harvard-style office, suggests New Haven would resemble Harvard's organisation. Davenport's exhortations to the New Haven General Court also reiterated the broader goal of training students for 'publick serviceableness' through a college and attached grammar school to sustain the order of the extramural community.[124] Lack of funding, however, frustrated his plans.[125] Ultimately, the conditions surrounding the proposed colleges in New Haven and Dublin demonstrate the ways in which contests over the direction of higher education expanded beyond the walls of the institutions and manifested in proposals for the new colleges. There was nothing radical about these proposals, which underlines that competing power structures – in these cases, clerical factions backed by local governing bodies – viewed universities, in their traditional guise, as tools to re-orient students towards their understandings of 'true' religion to the benefit of society.

If the New Haven and Dublin projects were marked by their conventionality, other contemporary schemes for the founding of new colleges highlighted the innovatory impulses that also existed in higher learning. These projects were pursued in New England, at Harvard itself, and at Durham in the north of England. At Harvard, the broader missionary compulsion drove the founding of a new college. Harvard's 1650 charter highlighted its existence 'for the education of English and Indian youth'.[126] President Dunster, a supporter of Native American education, routinely pressed the United Colonies and the New England Company for additional funding for Harvard in this regard. Meanwhile, in September 1651, the United Colonies wrote to Edward

---

[121] Urwick, *Trinity College Dublin*, p. 68; *Alumni Dublinenses*, pp. 446–7, 509, 854, 895.
[122] Calder, *Davenport Letters*, p. 163.
[123] See e.g. HP, 32/1/1A–5B; Calder, *Davenport Letters*, pp. 141–2, 172–4, 175–6.
[124] Calder, *Davenport Letters*, pp. 161–6; Hoadly, *New Haven Records*, pp. 370–4; Dexter, *New Haven Town Records*, pp. 457–8.
[125] HP, 6/5/1A–2B.
[126] *Massachusetts Records*, III, pp. 195–6, IV.1, pp. 12–14.

Winslow about the importance of enlarging Harvard to educate natives.[127] It was not until September 1653 that New England Company commissioners assented to having 'six hopfull Indians youthes' take up residence at Harvard, and in September 1655 the Company purchased a sizable library to be used 'in preaching unto or teaching the Indians'.[128] The 'Indian College' project, which resulted in the construction of a new building in Harvard Yard, would work in concert with the missionary effort then being led by the likes of John Eliot and Thomas Mayhew, who were tasked with identifying indigenous youths fit to be trained in the college.[129] Alongside New England Company-sponsored proselytisation efforts, which included Eliot's translation efforts and the formation of 'Praying Towns' of Native American catechumens, the Indian College represented another way to spread the gospel, and thus civilise, New England's indigenous peoples.[130]

The Indian College was based on the premise that Native Americans educated among students at Harvard – where they would intermix culturally and linguistically – would later serve as teachers and ministers to their indigenous brethren.[131] Creating teachers and preachers from within the native community represented another flank on which to exercise authority over New England's native peoples, and thus to bring them into the bounds of state power. Practically for the natives, beyond possessing the Algonquian tuition to preach to other natives, education at Harvard would provide the foundational knowledge of Biblical languages to comprehend and distil God's word.[132] Dunster had harboured such aspirations in the 1640s, but it was only at the end of his presidency that such schemes began to take shape. Scholars have shown that proselytising efforts in 1640s and 1650s New England, in which the Indian College was an important part, was a key arena that conditioned civil servants who would pursue similar policies in Ireland and Scotland under the Cromwellian regime.[133] However, when viewed in the context of wider trajectory of higher education transformations in the mid-seventeenth century, the main parallel to the Indian College effort was the Covenanters' schemes in the 1640s to funnel Gaelophone students from the Gaidhealtachd to the Scottish universities. This did not see the founding of a new college

---

[127] *Plymouth Records*, IX, p. 198.

[128] *HCR*, I, p. lxxxii; *Plymouth Records*, X, p. 107. Quotation at Wells, 'Prelude to Empire', p. 47. See also Morison, *HCSC*, I, pp. 342–3.

[129] *Plymouth Records*, X, pp. 128–9, 164–5; *Massachusetts Records*, III, p. 275.

[130] MA, MS 30, fols 21, 81; *Plymouth Records*, X, p. 106; *Massachusetts Records*, III, p. 246. See also Morison, *HCSC*, I, pp. 345–6; Szasz, *Indian Education*, pp. 106–28; Christina J. Hodge, '"A Small Brick Pile for the Indians": The 1655 Harvard Indian College as Setting', in Mary Carolyn Beaudry and Travis G. Parno (eds), *Archaeologies of Mobility and Movement* (New York, 2013), pp. 217–36. On the proselytisation efforts overseen by the New England Company, see also Wells, 'Prelude to Empire', pp. 45–51.

[131] Kellaway, *New England Company*, p. 110.

[132] Gray, *New World Babel*, pp. 44, 65–6, 70–3.

[133] An argument most revealingly put in Wells, 'Prelude to Empire', pp. 49–51.

specifically for Scottish Gaels; rather, the Covenanting regime drew on an established tradition that saw Glasgow and Aberdeen universities, specifically, serve as conduits for the sons of powerful Gaelic nobles. A logic similar to the Indian College scheme informed the Covenanting program: train select indigenous peoples in the universities to be the chief purveyors of conversion, after which they would inculcate the civilising impulse of God's word – according to the state's authorised norms – thereby extending the authority, and legitimacy, of the state over diverse peoples.[134] And, like the Indian College, the Covenanting program was also one largely dependent on the munificence of Anglophone donors.[135] By contrast, in Ireland, neither a higher educational institution specifically for Ireland's Gaelic population, nor a concerted effort to integrate Catholic native Irish into existing structures, seems to have been considered. Henry Cromwell did seek £500 per year for the education of Irish-speaking boys 'in order to the propagating civilitie as well as Religion among the Irish hereafter, who tis hoped will harken to their owne country men with lesse prejudice then the English, against whom they have something of a national antipathy'.[136] But nothing came of this scheme; indeed, whether monarchy or republic, the education of the native Irish was an afterthought.

The schemes for Harvard's Indian College were pursued as Dunster faced expulsion for heterodoxy, yet this controversy appeared to have factored little into the plans for a native seminary. Tellingly, New England's wider ambivalence to conversion, despite funding from the New England Company and the efforts of a crop of ministers, also translated to apathy to teaching natives in the college. The commissioners of the United Colonies identified two brothers, John and Thomas Stanton, sons of Thomas Stanton Sr, who had previously served as an interpreter for the Pequots in Connecticut, to serve as translators. But neither had completed their university studies and there is little suggestion of specialised instruction for native students. As Dunster's earlier struggles with indigenous languages indicate, Harvard did not possess multilingual faculty to teach native learners.[137] Chauncy was able to testify to the progress of several Native American youths in Elijah Corlet's grammar school, but none entered Harvard before 1660.[138] Chauncy, the Overseers, and Massachusetts' magistrates were instead more concerned with improving the college's finances, and appealed directly to Cromwell in early 1656 for

[134] See Cipriano, 'Students Who Have the Irish Tongue', pp. 72–9.
[135] *Ibid.*, pp. 80–6.
[136] HP, 33/1/13B.
[137] *Plymouth Records*, X, pp. 128–9; Morison, HCSC, I, p. 342; Vaughan, *New England Frontier*, pp. 281–2; James Axtell, 'Babel of Tongues: Communicating with the Indians in Eastern North America', in Edward G. Gray and Norman Fiering (eds), *The Language Encounter in the Americas, 1492–1800: A Collection of Essays* (New York, 2000), pp. 15–60, at 49.
[138] *Plymouth Records*, X, pp. 217–18; Kellaway, *New England Company*, p. 111; Morison, HCSC, I, pp. 352–5.

increased maintenance.[139] Chauncy would soon after propose that the new Indian College house 'English' students.[140] In the end, Harvard gained a new building, and for a fleeting moment emerged as a site of a potentially unique and innovatory college project focused specifically on native education within the wider British Atlantic. But ultimately the scheme failed to materialise.[141]

While the Indian College project was rooted in a civilising impulse, the new, scientific impulse drove the Durham College project. Alongside its ordinances for Ireland, Wales, and New England, Parliament passed an act for advancing the gospel in northern England in 1650 in order to propagate the gospel in England's 'darker' regions.[142] Furthermore, in 1650, and again in January 1656, the inhabitants of Durham submitted a petition for the establishment of a college for 'religious education'.[143] Colonel Robert Lilburne was optimistic that a college in the north would 'turne to the greate renowne of his highnes [Cromwell], and very much affect the inhabitants of that poore county and city to him and the government'.[144] Early suggestions for a Durham college bore the marks of a traditional early modern university, an institution to advance true religion and learning and promote obedience and conformity to the authorised norms of state power. But soon after these initial calls, the Durham scheme was co-opted for another purpose: the advancement of learning.[145] At about the time petitions for a college at Durham were submitted to the Cromwellian administration in London, Samuel Hartlib wrote in his diary about the 'founding of a Mechanical schoole' and the 'designe of founding a College of Sciences with several schooles and a library and a worke-house in Durham'.[146] A committee, which included Francis Rous and Thomas Goodwin, was named in February 1656 to draw up statutes for Durham, and throughout the spring and summer of 1656, it met continuously to establish laws for the college.[147] In August, Hartlib and minister Israel Tonge were elected to the committee, and progress on the statutes continued into the autumn and winter.[148] In March 1657, Robert Wood thanked Hartlib for inviting him to accept Durham's proposed professorship of mathematics.[149]

---

[139] Morison, HCSC, II, p. 366.
[140] Plymouth Records, X, pp. 168, 190.
[141] Morison, HCSC, I, pp. 359–60.
[142] CJ, VI, pp. 366, 370, 374, 396.
[143] CSPD 1655–56, pp. 140, 156.
[144] Thurloe State Papers, IV, p. 442.
[145] Feldhay, 'Religion', pp. 746–9; R.W. Serjeantson, 'Proof and Persuasion', Cambridge History of Science, pp. 132–76, at 134–5. On Durham College, see J.T. Fowler, Durham University: Earlier Foundations and Present Colleges (London, 1904), pp. 15–21; G.H. Turnbull, 'Oliver Cromwell's College at Durham', Durham Research Review, 3 (1952), 1–7.
[146] HP, 29/5/2B.
[147] CSPD 1655–56, pp. 218, 262, 288, 297, 325.
[148] CSPD 1656–57, pp. 66, 100, 191; Turnbull, 'Oliver Cromwell's College at Durham', pp. 1–2.
[149] HP, 33/1/11A–12B.

In the same month, Cromwell issued letters patent for the founding of a college that bore his name at Durham. The college's stated purpose and provisions were familiar: it would benefit the 'northern parts' of England through the 'promoting of the Gospel, as the religious and prudent education of young men there', and it would be funded by the rents formerly belonging to Durham Cathedral. It would consist of a provost, two preachers, and twelve fellows: four to serve as professors, four as tutors, and four as schoolmasters for the attached free school.[150]

But a closer look at the personnel who were proposed for these positions exposes Durham's scientific focus. Of the twelve fellows, half were Hartlib associates, including three professors: Thomas Vaughan, an alchemist; Johannes Sibertus Kuffeler, a German chemist; and the aforementioned Robert Wood.[151] The Bohemian Georg Ritschel, an associate of Comenius, was among the tutors,[152] while Richard Russell, another tutor, worked with chemical medicines and translated alchemical texts.[153] Moreover, according to Tonge, the master Philip Hunton, a political polemicist, was an 'indisputable scholar', while William Sprigg, one of the proposed schoolmasters, was described as 'excellent for drawing and painting and very optical also'.[154] The staff's character was captured in the commentaries of the minister John Beale, who referred to Durham in September 1657 as a 'newe Colledge of Advancement of Learning'.[155] Despite the conventionality its laws constitution, Durham College seems to have been an institution focused on science and empiricism.[156]

Durham, however, was eventually founded as an independent college that did not have power to grant degrees. In England, that authority was still confined to Oxford and Cambridge, whose masters lobbied against proposals to confer university status on Durham in April 1659; amidst the Restoration, the college ultimately closed.[157] That Oxford and Cambridge's governors would oppose Durham highlighted the potential threat that the college posed to conventional conceptions of higher education – not as an institution to provide the statesmen and churchmen to sustain a well-ordered society, but as a rogue space in which to produce new ideas to upset the social order that the universities were supposed to play a vital role in affirming. Granting

---

[150] *Cromwell Writings*, IV, pp. 522–8; John Towill Rutt (ed.), *Diary of Thomas Burton Esq., 1653–1659* (4 vols, London, 1828), II, pp. 531–43.
[151] Webster, *Samuel Hartlib*, p. 62; Turnbull, 'Oliver Cromwell's College at Durham', pp. 2–5. On Vaughan, see HP, 29/6/17A; Jennifer Speake, 'Vaughan, Thomas (1621–1666)', ODNB. On Kuffeler, see HP, 29/7/8B.
[152] HP, 1/33/87A; John T. Young, 'Ritschel, Georg (1616–1683)', ODNB.
[153] Stanton J. Linden, 'Russell, Richard (b. before 1640, d. 1686x97)', ODNB.
[154] HP, 29/6/17A; Turnbull, 'Oliver Cromwell's College at Durham', p. 2.
[155] HP, 31/1/59A.
[156] Webster, *Great Instauration*, pp. 232–42, 528–32.
[157] Fowler, *Durham University*, p. 21; Turnbull, 'Oliver Cromwell's College at Durham', pp. 5–6.

Durham the power to issue degrees would provide an extra layer of legitimacy to potentially disruptive graduates.[158]

Save for the Durham experiment, given the flurry of new college foundations in the 1650s, the conventional university – or rather, a Reformed academy the likes of which had already been established in Scotland, Ireland, and New England – reigned supreme. This section has highlighted how religious controversy and heterodoxy in the academy, which constituted existential threats to the wider social order, drove foundations, especially in New Haven and Dublin, and where controversy did not precipitate foundation, the impulse to spread learning and religion to marginal populations, for various reasons – as in northern England and New England – emerged as a primary driver for founding colleges. In the Interregnum, contested political, religious, and intellectual spaces on either side of the Atlantic provided the conditions for opponents with different visions of orthodoxy and learning to pursue their educational projects. These schemes were still tied to the contests for authority between rival factions, as they had been in the previous three decades.

Harvard, Trinity, and Late Interregnum Politics

In the final years of the Interregnum, authorities in Ireland and New England continued to wrestle with sects, which provided persistent threats to self-fashioned godly societies. In Massachusetts, the growth of the Quaker population in the second half of the 1650s both revealed Harvard's shortcomings in providing capable ministers for New England and reinforced the fact that it had to be a bulwark of orthodoxy.[159] In October 1656 and 1657, the General Court issued draconian penalties against Quakers and their writings, including whipping, forced labour, and ear and tongue lacerations.[160] In Ireland, meanwhile, Henry Cromwell's aversion to the fissiparous state of Irish Protestantism further reinforced the second college's purpose in serving the 'moderate' New English interest and, likewise, Trinity's emergence as an Independent hub. In January 1658 he issued two proclamations that sought to curb unauthorised preaching and prohibit ejected ministers from

---

[158] Durham was, in its brief history, ultimately more akin to Eton, as an independent collegiate foundation, and to London's Gresham College. See Webster, *Samuel Hartlib*, p. 62; Francis R. Johnson, 'Gresham College: Precursor of the Royal Society', *Journal of the History of Ideas*, 1:4 (1940), 413–38.

[159] Carla Gardina Pestana, 'The City upon a Hill under Siege: The Puritan Perception of the Quaker Threat to Massachusetts Bay, 1656–1661', *New England Quarterly*, 56:3 (1983), 323–53.

[160] *Massachusetts Records*, III, pp. 415–16, IV.1, pp. 314–15.

preaching or teaching in schools.[161] These efforts aimed to prevent further division among Ireland's Protestants.[162]

In both New England and Ireland wider religious settlements were proposed in order to neutralise radical sects and strengthen central authority. In New England, the Massachusetts General Court facilitated an assembly of ministers from the Bay colony and Connecticut in June 1657 to again deliberate on manners of church membership.[163] New England's strict parameters for church membership had been fortified earlier in the Cambridge Platform. One of the main issues at hand in the later 1650s was that non-church members – the baptised children of the New England's first generation, who had not yet demonstrated the signs of conversion necessary for church membership – were susceptible to the corrupting influences of radicals.[164] The 1657 assembly, consisting of just thirteen divines, decided that baptised children of church members were permitted to maintain their membership among the congregation without having to undertake the requirements for full membership.[165] This first step towards a 'halfway covenant', which would be ensconced in 1662, represented an innovative solution to the problem of church membership that sought to maintain the authority of New England's clerical elite.[166]

Yet the decision was met with opposition from many of New England's ministers, including John Davenport and Charles Chauncy.[167] This is unsurprising. Harvard, as a pillar of orthodoxy, had served as the institutional bedrock of a godly state built on strict membership. While expanding membership did not have immediate ramifications for the college, the wider issue of 'unchurched' colonists and the corresponding shortage of godly clerics to lead congregations underlined the issues that had plagued Harvard since Dunster's tenure began: the lack of monies to support scholars and graduates.[168] While Massachusetts' authorities continued to empower Chauncy to exercise strict discipline over students, this did not effectuate the production of graduates who received ordination or remained in New England society to minister to its growing population.[169] Students did not remain in the college

---

[161] Robert Steele (ed.), *Tudor and Stuart Proclamations 1485–1714, Volume II: Scotland and Ireland* (Oxford, 1910), pp. 72–3.

[162] Kilroy, 'Radical Religion in Ireland', p. 215.

[163] *Massachusetts Records*, III, p. 419. See also Robert G. Pope, *The Half-Way Covenant: Church Membership in Puritan New England* (Princeton, NJ, 1969), pp. 25–7.

[164] Staloff, *American Thinking Class*, p. 135; Katharine Gerbner, 'Beyond the "Halfway Covenant": Church Membership, Extended Baptism, and Outreach in Cambridge, Massachusetts, 1656-1667', *New England Quarterly*, 85:2 (2012), 281–301, at 285–6.

[165] Walker, *Creeds and Platforms*, pp. 288–300.

[166] Gerbner, 'Beyond the Halfway Covenant', p. 287; Staloff, *American Thinking Class*, pp. 134–6.

[167] Pope, *Half-Way Covenant*, pp. 30–1.

[168] Morison, HCSC, I, pp. 329–30.

[169] *Massachusetts Records*, III, p. 417, IV.1, pp. 278–9, 315; HCR, I, p. xxxvi, III, p. 340;

to train for their master's degrees, and thus did not receive additional divinity training from Chauncy and the fellows, the latter of whom regularly left the college after short tenures. The shortage of fellows, whether for lack of maintenance or non-residence, was detrimental to the college.[170] The state of affairs was reinforced in 1662, when the commencement orator remarked that 'Mother Academy has had a miscarriage in the birth of Masters.'[171] Harvard was faulty machinery, failing in its production of churchmen to sustain the wider commonwealth.

Table 6.2. Harvard College Staff, c. 1654–60.

President
Charles Chauncy, 1654–72

Treasurer
Thomas Danforth, 1650–68

Fellows and Tutors*
Thomas Dudley, 1654–5
Samuel Hooker, 1654–6(?)
Nehemiah Ambrose, 1654–7
Thomas Shepard, 1654–73
Samuel Nowell, 1656(?)
Joshua Moody, 1656–8
Samuel Bradstreet, 1656–7
Zachariah Symmes, 1657–63(?)
Zachariah Brigden, 1657–60(?)
Gershom Bulkeley, 1658–61(?)

Sources: HCR; Sibley, *Biographical Sketches*.

In Ireland, clerical maintenance was central in the drive towards a religious settlement in the latter 1650s. As has been stated, Henry Cromwell preferred Ireland's pre-conquest Protestant communities – Worth's Cork Association and Ulster's Presbyterians – but in early 1658 he intended to accommodate as wide a swath of Ireland's Protestants as possible. This was prudent, for despite the Independents' polarising drive for power in Ireland, Winter remained

---

Morison, HCSC, I, p. 330.
[170] See e.g., Morison, HCSC, I, p. 330; Sibley, *Biographical Sketches*, I, pp. 360–1, 367; HCR, I, p. cliv.
[171] George Lyman Kittredge, 'A Harvard Salutatory Oration of 1662', PCSM, 28 (1930–3), 1–24, at 14.

strong in Dublin and well-connected in England, while Independency in general showed few signs of waning.[172] Henry Cromwell thus summoned about twenty ministers from across Ireland to Dublin in late April 1658 in order to settle 'several things relating the worke of the Gospel'.[173] The most contentious issue, clerical maintenance, dominated this Dublin Convention. Worth argued for a return to tithing, while Winter defended the Civil List, the Cromwellian directory of state-funded preachers.[174] By late May only two of the nineteen delegates – Winter and the Waterford minister Edward Wale – dissented from reinstating tithing.[175] Ultimately, the most significant outcome of the Dublin Convention was the solidification of Worth's party as the preeminent Protestant interest in Ireland.[176] The Convention also made clear that it had sought to reconcile a number of pressing issues, including ordering discipline, ordination, and education. The result, exemplified by the return of tithing, was anti-sectarian.[177] The exact contents of the Dublin Convention's resolutions are unclear, but given the sectaries' enmity and the decision to restore tithing, it is likely it echoed the Cork Association.[178] This association was established to evaluate ministers in Munster and stem the rise of 'intruders', which led to the spread of heterodoxy.[179] Henry Cromwell thus endorsed a religious settlement built upon the scaffolding of the Cork Association, a settlement that would require Ireland's higher educational apparatus to follow suit.[180]

This burgeoning contest between Worth's moderates and Winter's Independents was exported to England. Henry Cromwell sent Worth to England in summer 1658 to promote the settlement, where he ingratiated himself to the lord protector and found favour with the masters of Oxford and Cambridge universities.[181] Not to be eclipsed, Winter also travelled to England to drum up Independent support and undermine Worth's efforts, much to the irritation of Henry Cromwell.[182] Winter was also privy to the English Independents' Savoy Declaration of September 1658, a new Independent confession of faith influenced by Thomas Goodwin and John Owen that drew on the Westminster Confession and New England's Cambridge Platform. It

---

[172] Barnard, 'Winter, Samuel'.
[173] HP, 15/4/5A.
[174] TNA, SP 63/287, fol. 176r; HP, 15/4/3A, 5B. See also Barnard, *Cromwellian Ireland*, pp. 126–7; Kilroy, 'Radical Religion in Ireland', pp. 215–16.
[175] *Thurloe State Papers*, VII, p. 145; James Seaton Reid, *The History of the Presbyterian Church in Ireland, Volume II* (London, 1837), p. 502.
[176] *Thurloe State Papers*, VII, p. 162.
[177] Reid, *Presbyterian Church in Ireland*, p. 501; *Thurloe State Papers*, VII, pp. 153, 161–2.
[178] Richard L. Greaves, *God's Other Children: Protestant Nonconformists and the Emergence of Denominational Churches in Ireland, 1660–1700* (Stanford, CA, 1997), p. 13.
[179] *Agreement and Resolution, Cork*, pp. 11–21.
[180] Gribben, *God's Irishmen*, pp. 99–128.
[181] HP, 15/4/8A–9B, 15/4/10A–B; Gaunt, *Correspondence of Henry Cromwell*, pp. 397–8.
[182] *Thurloe State Papers*, VII, p. 243; Barnard, *Cromwellian Ireland*, p. 128.

added Independent revisions, including asserting the autonomy of congregations and the supremacy of Scripture.[183] Upon returning to Ireland, Winter integrated this confession into his founding in February 1659 of a rival association of Dublin and Leinster ministers. The Dublin Association, particularly with its adoption of the Savoy Declaration, had an Independent bent, especially in its emphasis that congregations comprise 'visible saints' – thus adopting the New England model of church membership, laid out in the Cambridge Platform, at a time when the New England model was being reassessed.[184] Winter's goal was to build his own coalition against the lord deputy and Worth.[185] Henry had sought to remedy the religious situation in Ireland in calling the Dublin Convention in April 1658; yet, less than a year later, Irish Protestantism was still divided by two clerical factions, one of which received the regime's support, the other of which was founded in direct opposition.

Religious settlements like these directly impacted higher education. As the evidence of the previous three decades demonstrate – Laud's initiatives; the Covenanters' reforms; Irish Parliament' actions at Trinity – large-scale religious policies issued from central authorities were nearly always complemented by concurrent university reforms. In New England, the 1657 assembly that recommended the 'halfway' covenant of church membership, which underscored the lack of clerical and scholarly maintenance in the plantation, spurred additional action. In May 1659, the president and fellows convinced the General Court to again appeal to England in order to support the 'Inlargement of University Learning'.[186] A broadside printed in support of the scheme extolled the foundation of a 'Seminary of Learning' in New England's imagined wilderness and the 'endeavours of those, who have been trained up in their Cambridg, of whom some are eminently useful among themselves at this present'. Because of the funding strictures established by the New England Company, support for university learning had of late become subordinate to 'furtherance of Preaching to the Indians'. The broadside thus stated rather plainly that the 'increase of Children' of the colonists demanded further support for education.[187] The General Court appointed a group of trustees in England, which included many repatriated New Englanders and associates of Harvard, including Richard Saltonstall, Herbert Pelham, and William Hooke,

---

[183] Gribben, *John Owen*, pp. 196–9.
[184] *The Agreement and Resolution of the Ministers of Christ Associated within the City of Dublin, and Province of Leinster* (Dublin, 1659), pp. 5, 9–14; Bremer, *Puritan Experiment*, p. 127; Gribben, *God's Irishmen*, pp. 122–6.
[185] Barnard, *Cromwellian Ireland*, p. 129.
[186] Morison, HCSC, II, p. 367.
[187] MA, MS 58, fol. 38r; Albert Matthews, 'A Proposal for the Enlargement of University Learning in New England, 1658–1660', *Proceedings of the Massachusetts Historical Society*, 41 (1908), 301–8, at 302–5.

to raise funds.[188] The proposal saw early success through the supposed £1,000 donation of Roger Hill, baron of the exchequer, 'towards the education of youths in University learning'.[189] But this was too good to be true. While Saltonstall did secure additional funds for the university in March 1660 – a more modest £220 – Harvard's appeal to England came as the Protectorate was unravelling.[190] The days in which Harvard could potentially depend on sympathetic allies in positions of power in England were numbered.

In respect to the universities, the political and religious spasms that marked the fall of the Protectorate and the beginnings of the Restoration were most clearly felt in Dublin. In the months leading up to the death of Cromwell and the ineffectual rule of his son Richard, in Ireland, Henry Cromwell possessed the authority as chancellor to intervene in Trinity's affairs – such as removing Provost Winter – in order make the college conform to his visions. According to the Laudian statutes, which still governed Trinity, Henry alone could undertake this given his role as primary visitor.[191] There may have been an opportunity to intervene sometime in 1658, when he received a petition from the college against Winter. It is unclear who wrote the petition, but its authors seem to have taken exception to Winter's narrow Independent focus. They wrote, 'Our faith is not so tied to think all entered into the Fellowship of the Church should be of the College too.' The petitioners also argued that Winter had committed numerous 'crimes' and objected to the provost's animosity towards the lord deputy.[192] This petition shows that despite Winter's increased power, opposition still existed in the college. But nothing came of this petition, and it is likely that Henry opted for moderation by intervening only superficially in Trinity's affairs.[193]

Yet at precisely at the point the schisms between Worth and Winter's parties widened with the formation of the Dublin Association, Henry revived the proposal for a second college in Dublin. As discussed above, the planning committee consisted of Trinity alumni, including Worth, who was also a member of the Dublin Convention.[194] Worth, the architect of the Dublin Convention, thus had a hand in planning a second college to support his religious settlement. If Winter's Trinity was at least momentarily antithetical to promoting the wider aims of the Dublin Convention, the second college would support, and thus legitimise, the government-endorsed religious policy. By contrast, with the Dublin Association, Winter and his allies formulated

---

[188] *Massachusetts Records*, IV.1, p. 362
[189] Matthews, 'Proposal for the Enlargement of University Learning', p. 306; Morison, HCSC, II, p. 368.
[190] HCR, I, p. 198; Morison, HCSC, II, pp. 369–70.
[191] MacDonnell, *Chartæ et Statuta*, pp. 26–7; Bolton, *Statutes*, pp. 21–2.
[192] Seymour, *Puritans in Ireland*, pp. 30–1.
[193] This included allowing Winter and the fellows to increase their incomes. See TCD, MUN/P/1/388.
[194] Reid, *Presbyterian Church in Ireland*, p. 502; Urwick, *Trinity College Dublin*, p. 68.

a coherent Independent vision of the Irish social order for Trinity to serve. Their focus on the abilities of the ministry evinces the importance of a college to serve the Independent churches.[195] By early 1659, therefore, the University of Dublin had, on paper, two colleges that served two divergent social orders.

The plans for the second college, and the potential for two colleges promoting two different agendas, were short-lived, as the Protectorate fell in spring 1659.[196] Following the restoration of the Rump in May, Parliament recalled Henry to England.[197] On 7 June, the army appointed commissioners to govern Ireland, punish scandalous ministers, and prevent episcopacy's revival and the use of the Book of Common Prayer.[198] Army officers reasserted control under the new commander-in-chief, Edmund Ludlow, who oversaw a purge of officials.[199] These measures rejuvenated Ireland's religious radicals, who had been increasingly stifled under Henry Cromwell. Independents and Baptists were appointed as chaplains, and Winter seems to have been favoured by Ludlow.[200] The fluid religious climate led Samuel Mather to urge his younger brother Increase, the Harvard and Trinity alumnus who had recently departed Ireland for England, to return to Dublin.[201] Samuel wrote to Increase that 'I should bee glad to see you here & to have you settled in Dublin, if it were in my power to effect it… to the publike good also of this poore city & nation.'[202]

Despite these events, Trinity's operations continued apace. In June 1659, Provost Winter and the fellows approved a measure requiring entrants to have a 'competent proficiency in the Greeke tongue'.[203] Shortly thereafter, Henry Cromwell, in his final act as chancellor, increased John Stearne's salary for the Hebrew professorship, though Winter and his cadre refused the increase. Stearne, who had been among the college's remaining non-Independent fellows, subsequently left in November.[204] Earlier, in October, at about the time the army dissolved the Rump, commissioners for Ireland instructed Ludlow to review Trinity's operations in relation to the 1649 act for the advancement of the gospel in Ireland, as its current government was not 'suitable or sufficient for carrying on the intent of the Parliament therein'.[205] To this effect, on 9 December the English commissioners examined the proposals for Trinity and

---

[195] *Agreement and Resolution*, Dublin, pp. 10–11.
[196] Clarke, *Prelude to Restoration*, pp. 21–55; idem, '1659 and the Road to Restoration', *Ireland from Independence to Occupation*, pp. 241–64.
[197] Dunlop, *Ireland under the Commonwealth*, II, p. 696; *Thurloe State Papers*, VII, pp. 683–4.
[198] *Acts and Ordinances*, II, pp. 298–9.
[199] Clarke, *Prelude to Restoration*, pp. 76–8.
[200] *CJ*, VII, p. 757; *Ireland under the Commonwealth*, II, p. 704; Clarke, *Prelude to Restoration*, pp. 84–6; Seymour, *Puritans in Ireland*, pp. 175–6.
[201] Sibley, *Biographical Sketches*, I, pp. 412–13.
[202] 'The Mather Papers', *Collections of the Massachusetts Historical Society*, 4th series, 8 (Boston, MA, 1868), p. 550.
[203] TCD, MUN/V/5/1, p. 89.
[204] *Ibid.*, pp. 88–91; Belcher, *Memoir of John Stearne*, pp. 13–14.
[205] BL, Stowe MS 142, fol. 137r.

the second college and ordered Winter and five senior fellows 'as are now resident there' to appear before the council five days later 'to consider all due ways and means for the advancement of learning and training of youth up in piety'.[206] This is a clear indication that Ludlow and the commissioners sought to seize control of Trinity to promote their vision and agenda. Even in this fevered period, Trinity's place was contested as power factions aimed to assert their power in the universities.

But the review of Trinity would never take place. Ludlow's rule in Ireland and the expulsion of the Rump in England had proved disillusioning to New English army officers and powerful elites, including Lord Broghill and Charles Coote.[207] On 13 December, these parties seized Dublin Castle, established lines of communication with General Monck in Scotland, and called for the restoration of the Rump.[208] Immediately following this seizure of power, the coup's officers drafted seventeen articles for settling the Irish church and state. The proposed religious settlement, discussed in article four, did not reveal a new, detailed program, but it did emphasise that Ireland's ministers be 'orthodox' and 'learned'. And, like the litany of instructions for promoting the gospel that preceded them, the instructions also sought to encourage the maintenance of both Trinity and schools to educate youths in piety and literature; there was no reference to the second college.[209] These efforts sought to bring a measure of stability to a tumultuous situation and to provide guidance to Irish higher education. According to Worth, it was also meant to silence the 'prophane Rabble' of the sectaries.[210] Broghill, Coote, and other leaders of the December coup called for a convention to meet in Dublin beginning in March 1660 to create a settlement for Ireland. In February, Broghill and Coote declared their antipathy for the sects and what they held to be arbitrary military rule.[211] Coote attacked the heresies of the sectaries and the dislocation of 'Godly Minsters of the Gospel'.[212] Broghill's declaration is especially telling for its commentary on religion:

> And whilst we seemingly aspired to perfectness, we actually lost that charity, which is the bond of it, becoming thereby a reproach to ourselves,

---

[206] Urwick, *Trinity College Dublin*, pp. 68–9. The fellows were likely Caesar Williamson, Edward Veele, John Price, Gamaliel Marsden, and Josiah Winter, all recently elected to new offices in late November. See TCD, MUN/V/5/1, p. 91.
[207] Little, *Lord Broghill*, pp. 170–5.
[208] Connolly, *Religion, Law and Power*, pp. 5–10; James McGuire, 'The Dublin Convention, the Protestant Community and the Emergence of an Ecclesiastical Settlement in 1660', in Art Cosgrove and James McGuire (eds), *Parliament and Community* (Belfast, 1983), pp. 121–46, at 122–9.
[209] TCD, MS 808, fols 160–2.
[210] Harvard University, Houghton Library, Orrery Papers, MS Eng 218/22F/15.
[211] McGuire, 'Dublin Convention', pp. 124–9.
[212] *The Declaration of Sir Charles Coot…and the Rest of the Council of Officers of the Army in Ireland, Present at Dublin* (London, 1660).

and a derision to that Protestant part of the world, unto which, whilst our supreme authority was inviolated, we were a bulwark; the universities and schools of learning in our nations having been looked more after to poison them than to keep them sound, that not only our streams might be impure, but even our fountains. Many have been imployed to teach, who stood in need to be taught; and the legal maintenance of the ministry of the gospel conferred on men unable, unwilling, or unfit to dispense it, who had less ill deserved a maintenance for their silence, than their speaking.[213]

It further hoped for a quick and 'happy settlement' built on 'godly, learned and orthodox ministers of the gospel maintained by their tythes' who were supported by the 'universities and all other seminaries of learning'.[214] These sentiments prefigured the direction of the ensuing General Convention: anti-sectarian and 'moderate'. At the same time, it linked the ills of the ministry in part to the university: by drawing on the familiar trope of university-as-fountain, Broghill's declaration opined that the 'stream' of the Irish ministry had sprung from a 'poisoned' and 'impure' fountain. The declaration also laid bare the university's role as an organ of state power that sustained extramural community. Certainly, Broghill's assertions overstated the Independents' ultimate influence, but they did draw attention to the fact that if a lasting religious settlement was to be entrenched in Ireland, Trinity required reform.

The General Convention at Dublin began in early March 1660, a few weeks before the restoration of the Long Parliament, and included 137 members; Broghill served as Trinity's representative.[215] It was focused primarily on producing a religious and political settlement agreeable to the interests of 'Old Protestant' New English elites, thus laying the foundations of Ireland's Restoration settlement.[216] In securing the New English interest in Ireland, the Convention need not have veered too far from Henry Cromwell's favourable policies. Tellingly, the Convention appointed Henry Jones, Dudley Loftus, and Robert Gorges to 'enquire where the obstruction lyeth that hinders the said College [the second college] from being erected', as well as to decide on a 'fit place' for Archbishop Ussher's library.[217] That the Convention would consider the schemes for the second college is further evidence of its role as an anti-Independent seminary. Yet the Convention also, ultimately, failed to bring the college into existence.[218] More pressing was the need to reconcile matters at Trinity if a lasting religious settlement was to be entrenched.

---

[213] *Thurloe State Papers*, VII, p. 817.
[214] *Ibid.*, VII, p. 819.
[215] Clarke, *Prelude to Restoration*, pp. 169–230, 321–5.
[216] Barnard, *Cromwellian Ireland*, p. 71; Little, *Lord Broghill*, pp. 175–7; McGuire, 'Dublin Convention', p. 130.
[217] *An Account of the Chief Occurrences of Ireland. Together with Some Particulars from England. From Monday 12 of March, to Monday the 19 of March* (Dublin, 1660), p. 35.
[218] Barnard, *Cromwellian Ireland*, p. 211.

Provost Winter and most of the fellows were antithetical to the Convention's aims. On 13 March, Trinity's scholars submitted a petition to the Convention against Winter.[219] The Convention subsequently commanded Winter to deliver Trinity's charter to the senior fellows Caesar Williamson and Francis Saunders and ordered Saunders to deliver to Winter the provost's oath of demission.[220] The Convention thus removed Winter as it pursued a broader reconstruction of the Irish religious order.[221]

While both Trinity and Harvard experienced controversies, heresies, and political machinations throughout the 1650s, the political revolution portended the divergent trajectories the institutions would take in the post-Restoration environment. Though there was no widespread migration of radicals and regicides to New England, three regicides – Edward Whalley, William Goffe, and John Dixwell – did abscond across the Atlantic, with Whalley and Goffe residing with the Harvard Overseer Daniel Gookin in Cambridge before departing for New Haven.[222] At Trinity, by contrast, it was prudent among remaining fellows and students to exhibit immediate fidelity to the restored monarchy should they wish to maintain their places. According to a June 1660 petition that Trinity's students sent to the duke of Ormond – whom they greeted as chancellor – the petitioners emphasised the 'sad and perishing Condicon' of Trinity under the 'ravenous Usurpers', and entreated Ormond to remedy the situation.[223] The petition is short on details, but it is probable that the college faced financial insecurity.[224] The petition clearly meant to establish the loyalty of its signees, especially as the two leading signatories – Joseph Travers and John Stearne – had served under the Cromwellian regime.[225] The following month, Ormond, as chancellor, ordered that letters be prepared for appointing Thomas Seele, the Trinity alumnus who had previously served as a senior fellow in the 1630s and 1640s, as provost.[226] Whereas Harvard continued as a puritan seminary, at the Restoration, Trinity's fleeting courtship with Independency came to an end.

---

[219] TCD, MUN/V/5/1, p. 92; *Chief Occurrences*, p. 36; Mahaffy, *Epoch in Irish History*, p. 306.
[220] TCD, MUN/V/5/1, p. 92; MacDonnell, *Chartæ et Statuta*, p. 34; Bolton, *Statutes*, pp. 30–1.
[221] Toby Barnard, 'Trinity at Charles II's Restoration in 1660: A Loyal Address', *Hermathena*, 109 (1969), 44–50, at 48.
[222] Morison, *HCSC*, I, pp. 334–5.
[223] Barnard, 'Trinity at Charles II's Restoration', pp. 46–8.
[224] TCD, MUN/P/1/391.
[225] Barnard, 'Trinity at Charles II's Restoration', p. 47.
[226] *CSPI 1660–62*, p. 11.

Conclusion

This chapter has sought to highlight the ways in which higher education experienced the upheavals of the 1650s, and particularly the ways in which controversy, heterodoxy, and political intrigues reverberated in the universities of Ireland and New England. The religious and intellectual climate of the British Atlantic during this era presented numerous challenges to established orders, and as institutions whose role it was to produce the men who governed and sustained ordered societies, the universities were integrated into the tumult in revealing ways. As authorities wrestled with controversies at Harvard and Trinity, new college projects were pursued to correct the failings these institutions. These projects, which ultimately never materialised, revealed how governing elites, both secular and religious, envisioned new colleges as an antidote for the poisoned, pre-existing institutions. After all, disorder in the academy had the potential knock-on effect of debasing the wider society. Thus Henry Cromwell's push to found a second college can be viewed as an attempt to counter Winter's consolidation of power at Trinity, while the New Haven project was proposed on the heels of Dunster's heterodox turn at Harvard. Both represented potential threats to the ways in which ruling authorities conceptualised a godly, ordered society.

In Ireland, specifically, the central paradox of Cromwellian policy after 1655 is that the regime came to support the New English interest. Henry Cromwell's courting of this community – sanctioning its land claims, its political influence, and, in the end, its religious character – was considered the best way to solidify Cromwellian rule in Ireland. Here lies one of the major differences between Ireland and Scotland, and certainly New England. In Scotland, the Restoration would undo the Covenanting and Cromwellian revolutions, and the universities would be recast as seminaries to promote the newly ascendant monarchical state and episcopal Church of Scotland. In Ireland, the opposite was true: the General Convention's efforts, coupled with the Cromwellian land revolution, fostered the conditions that rekindled New English authority in Ireland and precipitated the rise of the Restoration Protestant interest.[227] Unlike the Scottish universities, neither Trinity nor Harvard, which was an ocean away, would be the site of royalist retribution, despite the monarchy's insistence that New England incorporate the parameters of the Church of England.[228] Instead, as Harvard, and New England, grappled with both the demands of the monarchy growing religious pluralism after 1660, in Ireland, Trinity would reassume its role as a bulwark of the Protestant, formerly New English interest and the established church.[229]

---

[227] Barnard, 'Planters and Policies', pp. 33–4; Cunningham, *Conquest and Land*, pp. 148–9.
[228] Bremer, *Puritan Experiment*, chap. 10.
[229] Toby Barnard, *A New Anatomy of Ireland: The Irish Protestants, 1649–1770* (New Haven, CT, 2004), pp. 104–14.

Conclusion

This book has endeavoured to highlight the role of higher education in the construction of early modern states and in the maintenance of healthy, ordered societies across the British Atlantic. As part of the wider matrix of state governance that exercised political, religious, and social power, universities acted as the models of order and conformity to authorised norms for the wider extramural community in a way that aimed to legitimise and buttress state power. Crucially, the university was also tasked with educating and training the students who would go on to constitute and control the levers of governing power, thereby perpetuating the wider social order for future generations. This was often a messy and contingent process, marked by pronounced conflict and resistance. Rival structures of power – the monarchy, clerical factions, settler communities, and others – attempted to exert their power and authority in the universities. They clashed in these contested spaces, as competing conceptions of what defined an ideal type of societal homogeneity – such as 'true' religion, sober learning, and political conformity – were imposed, resisted, debated, and coerced. Such actions show how the universities figured into the conflicts endemic to early modern state formation, but also how higher education reckoned in the minds of the authorities bent on holding and promoting power.

This study has also suggested that the mid-seventeenth-century Civil Wars amplified the universities' function in the construction of emerging states and societies on either side of the Atlantic, and thus their utility to realising competing visions of healthy commonwealths in an era of particular upheaval. It has pursued an interpretive framework rooted in examining the understudied higher educational institutions of Scotland, Ireland, and New England, institutions that shared structural commonalities as Reformed academies, and served Reformed communities regularly opposed to central power. But while the upheavals of the period between 1625 and 1660 magnified the universities' strategic significance, this is not necessarily a story that has an arbitrary cut-off at the Restoration. The Restoration saw the universities pressed into the service of the new monarchical state. A brief overview of events at the outset of the Restoration reveals how many of the same ideas and actions that were implemented, and in some areas refined, during the Civil Wars and Interregnum – the focus on staffing academic posts with amenable individuals, the understanding of the university as both model and machinery – were deployed immediately on Charles II's accession to power.

At Trinity, Charles II ordered the new provost, Thomas Seele, to govern according to the Laudian statutes and installed new senior fellows, including several signatories of the petition sent to the duke of Ormond expressing loyalty to the crown.[1] In August 1661, Ormond, who viewed Trinity as a 'seminary for loyalists in state and church', urged Protestants to send their sons there but barred anyone not conformable 'to the Doctrine & Discipline of the Church, as it is now established by law'.[2] Among the scholars at Trinity in April 1661, nearly every student betrayed the 'Old' Protestant, New English origins that had constituted the college's 'native' interest.[3] Purged of nonconformists, Trinity re-emerged as an institution that undergirded Irish Protestants' religious and political power in the kingdom.

In Scotland, a Parliamentary visitation of King's College, Aberdeen in February 1661 reveals how resurgent royal authorities sought to suppress 'schism and heresy' and ensure 'due obedience and allegiance to his majesty' by placing 'sober, learned, well-qualified and loyal persons' in professorships.[4] Officials purged Cromwellian collaborators – Protesters, mainly – from their posts, including Patrick Gillespie, Samuel Rutherford, John Row, and William Muir.[5] Resolutioner principals were maintained, while Robert Baillie replaced Gillespie as principal of Glasgow.[6] Alexander Colville was made principal of St Mary's, while at Edinburgh, William Colville, initially nominated in 1652, replaced Robert Leighton, who was translated to the bishopric of Dunblane.[7] The restored mechanisms of royal power co-opted the General Assembly's previously held authority in university affairs, and in June 1662 Parliament re-established metropolitan oversight of the universities, mandated that all members submit to 'the government of the church by archbishops and bishops', and ordered all entrants to take oaths of allegiance to the crown.[8] The Covenant had been eclipsed in the state's seminaries – the universities were transformed to uphold the new Restoration social order.

In New England, magistrates formally recognised the monarchy in August 1661, though Charles II attempted to usher in a wholesale revolution that

---

[1] *CSPI 1660–62*, p. 11; TCD, MUN/V/5/2, pp. 47, 49; Carte, *Ormond*, IV, pp. 17–18. These included Joshua Cowley, Richard Lingard, William Vincent, and Patrick Sheridan. See Barnard, 'Trinity at Charles II's Restoration', pp. 48–9.
[2] TCD, MUN/V/5/2, p. 63.
[3] TCD, MUN/P/1/407.
[4] AUL, MSK 266; *Fasti Aberdonenses*, pp. 313–15; *RPS*, 1661/1/79.
[5] Scott, *Fasti*, VII, pp. 357–8, 366, 395, 418–19.
[6] Gillespie attempted to plead his case, but the Privy Council sequestered his salary, declared that the post had been vacant since John Strang's death in 1654, and installed Robert Baillie as replacement. See e.g., Baillie, *L&J*, III, pp. 417–18, 422–3, 454, 455; MAUG, II, pp. 329–30, 331–2; GUL, MS Gen 1769/1/13, 17, 39.
[7] Scott, *Fasti*, VII, pp. 381, 411, 420.
[8] MAUG, II, pp. 332–3; *RPS*, 1662/5/21. On Restoration oaths of allegiance in Scotland, see Alasdair Raffe, *The Culture of Controversy: Religious Arguments in Scotland, 1660–1714* (Woodbridge, 2012), 68–9.

would subvert the New England social order. In a June 1662 letter, the king signalled his desire to abolish all laws inconsistent with the monarchy, institute freedom of worship for adherents to the Church of England, and administer oaths of allegiance to the monarchy.[9] In addition to this uneasy relationship with the restored monarchy, New England authorities continued to wrestle with growing religious diversity, highlighted by the growth of Quaker and Baptist communities, and with internal divisions among the puritan elite, especially after a contentious synod formalised the 'halfway covenant' in 1662.[10] At Harvard, the Restoration era saw the failure of the Indian College project, with just two students attending – Joel Iacoomis and Caleb Cheeschmaumuk, the latter of whom graduated in 1665 – which prompted President Chauncy to petition the New England Company for compensation for 'Tutors in the Colledge for every Indian', an ultimately futile endeavour.[11] Authorities were mainly focused on ensuring Harvard's survival as a puritan seminary to serve the burgeoning colony. That is not to say that Harvard remained withdrawn from the broader social and political transformations that were unfolding. In 1664, Chauncy headlined a petition to the king outlining Cambridge's resistance to 'arbitrary' government.[12] And, a year earlier, the fellow John Mitchell called for the creation of a committee of trustees consisting of the Overseers and ministers and magistrates to administer scholarships and identify, select, and support fellows to teach Harvard's scholars.[13] It is telling that Mitchell would draw on a strategy employed by Cromwellian authorities in the previous decade, for similar committees had been proposed for Trinity and the planned colleges in Dublin and Durham.

One can continue this narrative through the reigns of Charles II, James VII/II, and William and Mary. These examples demonstrate the ways in which universities continued to be contested spaces where socialisation could be controlled and political and religious allegiances crafted, refined, and employed to promote state power. As such, the universities' status as purveyors of ideological and political power that legitimised governing structures did not necessarily transform – partisans of all religious and political stripes regularly exploited their utility to mould religious and political

---

[9] *Massachusetts Records*, IV.2, pp. 31–2, 164–6. See also Bremer, *Puritan Experiment*, pp. 143–5.
[10] Bremer, *Puritan Experiment*, chap. 11; Pestana, *Protestant Empire*, pp. 108–20.
[11] Morison, HCSC, I, pp. 354–9; HCR, I, p. 85. For Chauncy's letters to the New England Company, see John W. Ford (ed.), *Some Correspondence between the Governors and Treasurers of the New England Company in London and the Commissioners of the United Colonies in America* (London, 1896), pp. 5–10.
[12] Adrian Chastain Weimer, 'The Resistance Petitions of 1664–1665: Confronting the Restoration in Massachusetts Bay', *New England Quarterly*, 92:2 (2019), 221–62, at 243–4.
[13] MA, 240, fols 142–51; HCR, III, pp. 303–22; Morison, HCSC, II, pp. 370–3. Mitchell's tract recalled an earlier, English text by the minister Matthew Poole. See Matthew Poole, *A Model for the Maintaining of Students of Choice Abilities at the University, and Principally in Order to the Ministry* (London, 1658).

loyalties. The nature of these loyalties – and of the wider societies that the universities were to help create and sustain – could take varying forms, while ascendant powers could take different approaches to wielding higher education to their ends.

In underlining the universities' utility within the broader, almost existential power struggle that upended life across the British Atlantic, this study has also sought to integrate the study of the established universities, beyond just those of England, into our understanding of the Civil War era. From Aberdeen to Massachusetts, each of the universities examined in this study resembled the smaller, Protestant academies that had proliferated in early modern Europe. Howard Hotson has argued that these types of institutions of higher learning, and the distinctive Reformed pedagogies that they employed, were tailor-made for communities on frontiers and in smaller states, but they were also more susceptible to external control and intervention because of their size.[14] In many ways, their malleability was on full display in the mid-seventeenth century. By probing the ways in which competing authorities wielded and contested for control of these seminaries, this study has emphasised that universities were not cloistered backwaters divorced from events unfolding beyond their walls that earlier historiography, and arguably the preponderance of institutional histories, would suggest. If anything, this book has suggested that we stand to learn much about how early modern churchmen and statesmen conceptualised wider society and imagined their ideal versions of a healthy commonwealth by examining how they approached higher education. By employing an episodic, comparative framework in the examination of three specific locales, this study has also highlighted the ways in which common ideas surrounding higher education developed in the quite different contexts of the mid-seventeenth-century British Atlantic world.

Charles I and William Laud's university policies aimed to create the conditions within Scotland and Ireland that would mould conformity, and eventual uniformity, to the sacramental Church of England that the monarchy endorsed. Such efforts were part of ecclesiastical policies in both realms. This was a crucial feature of university policy throughout the mid-seventeenth century: university reform was either pursued alongside or directly following religious reform. But it also spurred opponents not only to fortify their own universities with agreeable academics, but to impel the founding of colleges abroad – in the Netherlands and New England – to sustain expatriate communities who opposed the established churches. A pattern is discernible: Laud orchestrated the reform of Trinity following the Irish Convocation of 1634; Charles pursued Scottish university reform as work pressed ahead on the new Canons and Prayer Book; the Covenanters inaugurated a robust reform of the universities in support of the newly renovated Church of Scotland; the New English in Ireland aimed to return Trinity to its pre-Laudian ethos as

---

[14] Hotson, 'Generall Reformation', pp. 203–5.

it dismantled the Laudian reforms through the Irish Parliament; and settlers in New England founded a college to support and perpetuate a social order built on specific conditions for church membership – initially formalised via the Cambridge Platform – that diametrically opposed Laudian policy. Even the Cromwellian regime, whose state and imperial formation in its conquered realms betrayed an approach that was conditioned by localised realities, followed a similar pattern, especially at the outset of the 1650s, when agreeable principals and provosts were installed in order to build conformity to the republican Commonwealth.

This book has thus aimed to provide one such comparative investigation of early modern higher education. In conceiving of the universities as instruments of state power, in several ways this book has also shown the coercive power of universities as technologies of repression and forced acculturation. Universities necessarily assisted in creating socially constructed boundaries between those who adhered to normative knowledge and customs that bred purity, conformity, and order, on the one hand, and those whose deviant behaviours risked poisoning and thereby debasing society, on the other.[15] The proposed college at Henrico, the Indian College at Harvard, the founding impetus of Trinity, and the Covenanters' removal of Gaelophone students to the universities represented types of cultural and linguistic violence exacted upon marginalised and subjugated populations. This was in addition to the African and indigenous peoples that were coerced and enslaved into the service of these institutions.[16] There already exists a scholarly literature that has examined the imperial nature of education and its use in engineering cultural conformity, particularly in American spaces.[17] But, as this study has shown, ascendant powers did not just wield the university as tools of oppression in colonial spaces – they were equally as coercive in the metropole. The appeals of ministers and magistrates to the university's ability to provide for the 'common good' had grave implications depending on the specific political, religious, and social conditions of the environment in which universities were founded, yet they nevertheless arrived at some idiosyncratic interpretation of true religion and learning, much to the detriment of localised cultures, Christian or otherwise. As our understanding of higher education continues to evolve, we need to further rethink the university's

---

[15] Foucault, *Discipline and Punish*, pp. 170–93. On ideas around purity and deviancy, see also Mary Douglas, *Purity and Danger: An Analysis of Concepts of Pollution and Taboo* (London, 2002), pp. 1–7.

[16] See Wilder, *Ebony and Ivy*, chap. 1.

[17] See e.g., Szasz, *Indian Education*; Bobby Wright, '"For the Children of Infidels?": American Indian Education in the Colonial Colleges', in Lester F. Goodchild and Harold S. Wechsler (eds), *The History of Higher Education*, 2nd edn (Needham Heights, MA, 1997), 72–9; Margaret Connell Szasz, *Scottish Highlanders and Native Americans: Indigenous Education in the Eighteenth-Century Atlantic World* (Norman, OK, 2007).

purpose and probe more deeply higher education's potentially destructive power, in addition to its utilities.

This study has also re-contextualised the founding of Harvard through the lens of imperial Laudianism in the 1630s. While scholars have examined the nature of *translatio studii*, whereby imperial states founded European-style institutions, like the university, in colonial spaces, an institution like Harvard was not endorsed by the monarchy – it was the precise type of institution Charles and Laud wished to suppress. Harvard is an example not just of how religious tensions in European states filtered out into the Atlantic World, but also how distinctive ideas about the nature and purpose of higher learning were repurposed and employed to meet the needs of migrants. There is, therefore, opportunity to evaluate the geographies and the ideas surrounding higher learning, and how they developed, evolved, and travelled with refugees and migrants – intellectuals, clerics, teachers, and students – at a time of widespread migration and displacement within Europe and beyond.[18]

The common theme running through this book is the centrality of early modern universities to the building of ordered societies. The universities of Scotland, Ireland, and New England were very much alive to the vicissitudes of the mid-seventeenth century – indeed, Harvard is the offspring of such upheaval. The Civil War era was a particularly critical moment that evinced the universities' essential utility in Britain, Ireland, and New England. In examining the universities in the context of archipelagic and wider Atlantic revolution of the mid-seventeenth century, this study has revealed that Trinity College, Dublin, the Scottish universities, and Harvard College served practical political and religious functions and responded to specific societal needs at a formative moment in the making of the early modern British state and empire.

---

[18] Work has begun in this regard, with a particular emphasis on exiled religious communities, particularly in the Catholic world. See e.g., Chambers and O'Connor, *College Communities Abroad*; Nicholas Terpstra, *Religious Refugees in the Early Modern World: An Alternative History of the Reformation* (Cambridge, 2015); Peter Burke, *Exiles and Expatriates in the History of Knowledge, 1500–2000* (Waltham, MA, 2017), chap. 3.

Bibliography

Primary Sources

Manuscripts

Aberdeen University Library, Special Collections
MS 635, Diary, or 'Spiritual Exercises', of John Forbes of Corse
MSK 36, King's College Minutes
MSK 231, Documents Concerning the Dispute between King's and Marischal, 1659
MSK 266, Commission for Visiting the Colleges of Aberdeen, February 1661
MSM 91, Marischal College Visitation Papers, 1636–1717

British Library, London
Add MS 4274, Thomas Birch Manuscripts, Letters
Add MS 4276, Thomas Birch Manuscripts, Letters and Papers
Add MS 4460, Thomas Birch Manuscripts, Ralph Thoresby Transcripts
Add MS 4771, Milles Collection, Minutes of English Parliamentary Committees for Irish Affairs
Add MS 19845, Registers of Orders in Council in Ireland, 1655–9
Add MS 23111, Papers and Correspondence of John Maitland, Second Earl of Lauderdale
Add MS 46927, Correspondence and Papers, Ireland, 1628–47
Egerton MS 1761, Orders, English Parliamentary Commissioners for Irish Affairs, 1650–4
Egerton MS 1762, Orders, English Parliamentary Commissioners for Irish Affairs, 1651–5
Egerton MS 2553, Miscellaneous Warrants Relating to Ireland, 1628–41
Sloane MS 427, Manuscripts Relating to Natural Philosophy
Stowe MS 142, Miscellaneous Historical Letters, 1375–1810

Edinburgh University Archives
IN1/ADS/STA/2/1, Edinburgh University Matriculation Album, 1627–1703

Edinburgh University Library, Special Collections
Dc.1.4/1, Papers Illustrating the History and Constitution of Edinburgh University

Dc.5.5, Extracts from the City Records regarding Edinburgh University, 1636–58

Dc.5.122, Dictates of Thomas Craufurd, Mathematics Professor, 1652–4

Gen.1965, Dictates by Robert Ranken taken down by Zurishaddai Lang, 1636–7

La.I.296/2, General Demands Concerning the Late Covenant, 38

La.I.305/2, Notes from Acts of the General Assembly, 1586–1641

La.I.306, Paper Containing Observations on the Large Declaration, c. 1642

La.I.314, Letter, John Row, 'About Independency', 27 May 1652

La.I.321, Papers of the Relations between the Commonwealth and Kirk, 1652–8

La.II.89, Collection of Papers on the Presbyterians and Covenanters, 1634–1700

La.III.179, John Row, Praxis on Hebrew Grammar, c. 1651

La.III.207, James Ferguson's Minutes of the Glasgow Assembly, 1638

La.IV.25/34, Extracts of the Records of Glasgow University

Glasgow University Archives
26621, Faculty Meeting Minutes, 1642–8, and Visitation Reports, 1638–43

26627, Accounts relative to the New Buildings, 1655–8

26754, Report by the Commissioners of Visitation on Glasgow University, 1641–95

26790, Register of the Commissioners of the Four Scottish Universities, 1647–9

Glasgow University Library, Special Collections
MS Gen 210, Correspondence of James Sharp, 1660
MS Gen 1769/1, Papers Relating to Patrick Gillespie

Harvard University Archives
UAI 5.120, Harvard Corporation Papers, First Series
UAI 15.850, Papers of Henry Dunster

Henry E. Huntington Library, San Marino, CA
EL 7055, Ellesmere Manuscripts, Table for the Settlement of Ulster, c. 1610
HA 14039-15973, Hastings Irish Papers, Correspondence

Houghton Library, Harvard University
MS Eng 218/22F/15, Orrery Papers, Edward Worth to Lord Broghill, January 1660

Massachusetts Archives, Boston, MA
MS 30, Indian Papers
MS 58, Literary Papers
MS 240, Hutchinson Papers

BIBLIOGRAPHY

Massachusetts Historical Society, Boston, MA
MS N-1143, Henry Dunster Notebook

National Archives, Kew, London
CO 1, State Papers Colonial
PC 2, Privy Council Registers
SP 16, State Papers Domestic, Charles I
SP 18, Council of State, Navy Commission, and Related Bodies Orders and Papers
SP 25, Council of State, Books and Accounts
SP 63, State Papers Ireland
SP 84, State Papers Foreign, Holland

National Library of Ireland, Dublin
MS 9607, Journal of the Irish House of Lords

National Library of Scotland, Edinburgh
Adv. MS 19.3.4, Latin Epigram, Samuel Colville to Col. Robert Lilburne, 7 May 1653
Adv. MS 31.1.1 vol. 12, Letter, Professors of Leiden to the Covenanters, 1638
MS 1908, Robert Baillie Papers and Letters, 1637–43
MS 3430, Papers and Correspondence of the General Assembly, 1637–1725
Wod.Fol.XXVI, Church and State Papers, 1654–1709
Wod.Fol.XXX, Papers Relating to the Protester-Resolutioner Controversy, 1650–60
Wod.Fol.XXXI, Church and State Papers, 1618–85
Wod.Fol.XLIII, Church and State Papers, 1560–8
Wod.Fol.L, Church and State Papers, 1216–1687
Wod.Fol.LIX, Letters of Robert McWard, Minister of Rotterdam, 1648–81
Wod.Fol.LXII, Church Papers, Mainly Concerning the Glasgow Assembly, c. 1638
Wod.Fol.LXIII, Church and State Papers, 1638–9
Wod.Fol.LXIV, Church and State papers, 1638–41
Wod.Qu.XXV, Covenanter Papers, 1636–41
Wod.Qu.XXVI, Papers Relating to Presbyterian Dissent, 1622–85
Wod.Qu.XXIX, Church and State Papers and Letters, 1636–71
Wod.Qu.XXXIII, Papers Relating to the Protester-Resolutioner Controversy, 1652–5
Wod.Qu.LXXVI, Papers of David Calderwood, c. 1614–38
Wod.Qu.CVI, Eighteenth-Century Transcripts of Church and State Papers, 1636–40

National Records of Scotland, Edinburgh
GD45/1/65, Address to King by the Masters of St Andrews, 12 November 1641

GD112/39/73/19, Letter, Robert Campbell of Glenfalloch to his brother, 27 August 1639
GD214/214, Petition to the Commissioners for the Universities of Scotland, 21 April 1656
GD305/1/167/13, Reasons for the Illegality of the Visitation of Aberdeen University, June 1650
GD406/1, Hamilton Correspondence
RH9/12/4, Grant of Oliver Cromwell to the University of Edinburgh, 22 July 1658

New College Library, Edinburgh
Baill 2, Robert Baillie's Letters and Journals Transcripts, 1701
Baill 4, Robert Baillie's Letters and Journals Contemporary Transcripts

Riksarkivet, Stockholm
E748, Oxenstiernska Samlingen (Axel Oxenstierna Collection)

St Andrews University Library, Special Collections
UYSL 156, 'Pringle's Book', Records of the University and St Leonard's College
UYSM/B18/P2, Acts of the Visitation of the University of St Andrews
UYSS 110/AG, Visitation Papers
UYSS 110/AI, Laws, Statutes, and Acts Relating to St Salvator's College
UYSS 110/C, Royal Grants and Confirmations, 1578–1633
UYUY 152/3, Copies of Bulls, Charters, Etc.
UYUY 412, Faculty of Arts Bursars' Book
UYUY 459/2, Oliver Cromwell's Grant to St Andrews University, 24 March 1657
UYUY 812, Register of Visitations of the University of St Andrews, 1642–9

Trinity College, Dublin, Manuscripts and Archives Library
MS 543, Irish Historical Manuscripts
MS 571, Account of the Founders and Benefactors of Trinity College, 1591–1661
MS 805, Provost Samuel Winter's Notebook, c. 1652–60
MS 808, Irish Historical Manuscripts
MS 833, 1641 Depositions
MS 840, 1641 Depositions
MS 1038, Records of Convocation, c. 1634
MS 2160, Documents Concerning Trinity College Library
MS 3571/1-2, Letters, James Ussher to John Bramhall, 1641
MS 3812, Letter, James Ussher to William Bedell, 9 June 1628
MUN/P/1, Chronological Muniments Relating to the Administration of Trinity College
MUN/P/22, Papers Relating to Trinity College Estates
MUN/V/5/1, Registers of the Board of Trinity College, 1627–60

MUN/V/5/2, Registers of the Board of Trinity College, 1660–1740
MUN/V/23/1, Admissions Records, 1637–1725

Yale University Library, Manuscripts and Archives, New Haven, CT
OSB MS 16794, Osborn Collection, Newsletter sent to Samuel Hartlib, 24 December 1645
OSB MS 16799, Osborn Collection, William Petty to Samuel Hartlib, 13 October 1652
OSB MS 16807, Osborn Collection, William Petty to Samuel Hartlib, 1 March 1653

Printed Primary Sources

Contemporary Books, Declarations, and Pamphlets

An Account of the Chief Occurrences of Ireland. Together with Some Particulars from England. From Monday 12 of March, to Monday the 19 of March (Dublin, 1660).
The Agreement and Resolution of Severall Associated Ministers in the County of Corke for the Ordaining of Ministers (Cork, 1657).
The Agreement and Resolution of the Ministers of Christ Associated within the City of Dublin, and Province of Leinster (Dublin, 1659).
Barrow, Humphrey, *The Relief of the Poore and Advancement of Learning Proposed* (London, 1656).
By the Commissioners for Visiting and Regulating the Universities, and Other Affairs, Relating to the Ministry of Scotland (Leith, 1652).
Canons and Constitutions Ecclesiasticall Gathered and Put in Forme, for the Government of the Church of Scotland (Aberdeen, 1636).
[Charles I], *A Large Declaration Concerning the Late Tumults in Scotland* (London, 1639).
Chauncy, Charles, *Gods Mercy, Shewed to His People in Giving Them a Faithful Ministry and Schooles of Learning for the Continual Supplyes Therof* (Cambridge, MA, 1655).
Constitutions and Canons Ecclesiasticall, Treated upon by the Archbishops, and Bishops, and the Rest of the Cleargie of Ireland…Anno Dom. 1634 (Dublin, 1635).
A Declaration of the Commissioners for the Visitation of Universities, and for Placing and Displacing Ministers in Scotland (Leith, 1653).
The Declaration of Sir Charles Coot…and the Rest of the Council of Officers of the Army in Ireland, Present at Dublin (London, 1660).
Generall Demands, Concerning the Late Covenant, Together with the Answeres of Those Reverend Brethren to the Sayd Demands: As Also the Replyes of the Foresayd Ministers and Professors to Their Answeres (Aberdeen, 1638).
Heylyn, Peter, *Cyprianus Anglicus* (London, 1671).

Lechford, Thomas, *Plaine Dealing: Or, Newes from New-England* (London, 1642).
New Englands First Fruits (London, 1643).
Poole, Matthew, *A Model for the Maintaining of Students of Choice Abilities at the University, and Principally in Order to the Ministry* (London, 1658).
Roch, Patrick, *A True Copie of a Letter Sent from Patrick Roch, a Romish Priest in Ireland, to Doctor Washington, Provost of the College of Dublin, and to the Whole Society* (London, 1641).
Shepard, Thomas, *The Clear Sunshine of the Gospel Breaking Forth Upon the Indians in New-England* (London, 1648).
Strang, John, *De Interpretatione & Perfectione Scripturæ* (Rotterdam, 1663).
W[eaver], J[ohn], *The Life and Death, of the Eminently Learned, Pious, and Painful Minister of the Gospel, Dr. Samuel Winter, Sometime Provost of Trinity Colledge near Dublin in Ireland* (London, 1671).
Winslow, Edward, *The Glorious Progress of the Gospel Amongst the Indians in New England* (London, 1649).

Edited Primary Sources

Abbott, W.C. (ed.), *The Writings and Speeches of Oliver Cromwell* (4 vols, Cambridge, MA, 1937–47).
Airy, Osmund (ed.), *Lauderdale Papers Vol. 1: 1639–1667* (London, 1884).
Aymon, Jean, (ed.), *Tous Les Synodes Nationaux Des Églises Réformées de France* (2 vols, The Hague, 1710).
Birch, Thomas (ed.), *A Collection of the State Papers of John Thurloe* (7 vols, London, 1742).
Bonar, Andrew A. (ed.), *Letters of Samuel Rutherford* (Edinburgh, 1891).
Boran, Elizabethanne (ed.), *The Correspondence of James Ussher, 1600–1656* (3 vols, Dublin, 2015).
Botfield, Beriah (ed.), *Original Letters Relating to the Ecclesiastical Affairs of Scotland, 1603–1625* (2 vols, Edinburgh, 1851).
Brown, P. Hume (ed.), *The Register of the Privy Council of Scotland, 1635–1637*, 2nd series, 6 (Edinburgh, 1905).
Cadbury, Henry J., 'John Harvard's Library', *Publications of the Colonial Society of Massachusetts*, 34 (1940), 353–77.
Calamy, Edmund, *The Nonconformist's Memorial: Being an Account of the Ministers, Who Were Ejected or Silenced after the Restoration*, ed. Samuel Palmer, 3rd edn (3 vols, London, 1802–03).
Calder, Isabel M. (ed.), *Letters of John Davenport, Puritan Divine* (New Haven, CT, 1937).
Calderwood, David, *The History of the Kirk of Scotland*, ed. David Laing and Thomas Thomson (8 vols, Edinburgh, 1842–9).
Calendar of State Papers, Domestic Series, of the Reign of Charles I and the Interregnum (36 vols, London, 1858–97).

Cameron, James K. (ed.), *The First Book of Discipline: With Introduction and Commentary* (Edinburgh, 1972).

Carte, Thomas, *The Life of James Duke of Ormond*, new edn (6 vols, Oxford, 1851).

Cipriano, Salvatore (ed.) 'The Principal of Glasgow Against the Covenant (1638)', in *Miscellany of the Scottish History Society, Volume XVI*, 6th series (Woodbridge, 2020), pp. 95–142.

'Commonwealth Records (Continued)', *Archivium Hibernicum*, 7 (1918–21), 20–66.

Cooper, Charles Henry (ed.), *Annals of Cambridge* (5 vols, Cambridge, 1842–1908).

Corcoran, Timothy (ed.), *State Policy in Irish Education A.D. 1536 to 1816* (Dublin, 1916).

Cramond, William (ed.), *Extracts from the Records of the Synod of Moray* (Elgin, 1906.)

Craufurd, Thomas, *History of the University of Edinburgh, from 1580 to 1646* (Edinburgh, 1808).

Dexter, Franklin Bowditch (ed.), *New Haven Town Records, 1649–1662* (New Haven, CT, 1917).

Donaldson, Gordon (ed.), *Scottish Historical Documents* (Glasgow, 1999).

Dunlop, Robert (ed.), *Ireland under the Commonwealth: Being a Selection of Documents Relating to the Government of Ireland from 1651 to 1659* (2 vols, Manchester, 1913).

Dunn, Richard S., James Savage, and Laetitia Yeandle (eds), *The Journal of John Winthrop, 1630–1649* (Cambridge, MA, 1996).

'The Dunster Papers', *Collections of the Massachusetts Historical Society*, 4th series, 2 (Boston, MA, 1864), pp. 191–9.

Elrington, Charles R. (ed.), *The Whole Works of the Most Rev. James Ussher, D.D.* (17 vols, Dublin, 1847–64).

Empey, Mark (ed.), 'The Diary of Sir James Ware, 1623–66', *Analecta Hibernica*, 45 (2014), 53–146.

'February Meeting. William Pynchon, Founder of Springfield; Hugh Peter in the Netherlands', *Proceedings of the Massachusetts Historical Society*, 3rd series, 64 (1931), 66–111.

Felt, Joseph B, 'Memoir of Hugh Peters', *New England Historical and Genealogical Register* 5:3 (1851), 275–94.

Fincham, Kenneth (ed.), *The Further Correspondence of William Laud* (Woodbridge, 2018).

Firth, C.H. (ed.), *Scotland and the Commonwealth: Letters and Papers Relating to the Military Government of Scotland, from August 1651 to December 1653* (Edinburgh, 1895).

——— (ed.) *Scotland and the Protectorate: Letters and Papers Relating to the Military Government of Scotland from January 1654 to June 1659* (Edinburgh, 1899).

——— (ed.) 'Thomas Shepard to Hugh Peter, 1645', *American Historical Review* 4:1 (1898), 105–7.

Firth, C.H., and R.S. Rait (eds), *Acts and Ordinances of the Interregnum* (3 vols, London, 1911).

Ford, Alan, 'Correspondence between Archbishops Ussher and Laud', *Archivium Hibernicum*, 46 (1992), 5–21.

Ford, John W. (ed.), *Some Correspondence between the Governors and Treasurers of the New England Company in London and the Commissioners of the United Colonies in America*, (London, 1896).

Gardiner, S.R. (ed.), *The Constitutional Documents of the Puritan Revolution, 1625–1660* (Oxford, 1906).

Gaunt, Peter (ed.), *The Correspondence of Henry Cromwell, 1655–1659: From the British Library Lansdowne Manuscripts* (Cambridge, 2007).

Goold, William H (ed.), *The Works of John Owen* (24 vols, Edinburgh, 1850–5).

Gordon, James, *History of Scots Affairs, from 1637 to 1641*, ed. Joseph Robertson and George Grub (3 vols, Aberdeen, 1841).

Griffiths, John (ed.), *Statutes of the University of Oxford Codified in the Year 1636 Under the Authority of Archbishop Laud* (Oxford, 1888).

Haddan, A.W. (ed.), *The Works of the Most Reverend Father in God, John Bramhall, D.D.* (5 vols, Oxford, 1842–5).

Harris, Walter (ed.), *The Whole Works of Sir James Ware Concerning Ireland* (2 vols, Dublin, 1739–45).

Hetherington, W.M. (ed.), *The Works of Mr. George Gillespie, Minister of Edinburgh* (2 vols, Edinburgh, 1846).

HMC, *Calendar of the Manuscripts of the Marquess of Ormonde*, new series (8 vols, London, 1902–20).

———, *The Manuscripts of the House of Lords Vol. XI: 1514-1714*, ed. Maurice F. Bond, new series (London, 1962).

———, *Report on the Manuscripts of the Earl of Egmont Volume I: 1573–1661* (London, 1905).

Hoadly, Charles J. (ed.), *Records of the Colony or Jurisdiction of New Haven, from May, 1653 to the Union* (Hartford, CT, 1858).

Jaffray, Alexander, *Diary of Alexander Jaffray*, ed. John Barclay, 3rd edn (Aberdeen, 1856).

Jansson, Maija (ed.), *Proceedings in the Opening Session of the Long Parliament, House of Commons Volume 1: 3 November–19 December 1640* (Rochester, NY, 2000).

Johnston, Archibald, *Diary of Sir Archibald Johnston of Wariston, Volume I 1632–1639*, ed. George Morison Paul (Edinburgh, 1911).

——— *Diary of Sir Archibald Johnston of Wariston, Volume II 1650–1654*, ed. David Hay Fleming (Edinburgh, 1919).

The Journals of the House of Commons, 1547–1660 (7 vols, London, 1802).

The Journals of the House of Commons of the Kingdom of Ireland, Vol. I, 1613–1666 (Dublin, 1796).

Journals of the House of Lords of the Kingdom of Ireland, Vol. I, 1634–1698 (Dublin, 1779).

Kingsbury, Susan M. (ed.), *The Records of the Virginia Company of London* (4 vols, Washington, DC, 1906–35).

Kinloch, George R. (ed.), *Selections from the Minutes of the Presbyteries of St. Andrews and Cupar, 1641–1698* (Edinburgh, 1837).

Kirk, James (ed.), *The Second Book of Discipline: With Introduction and Commentary* (Edinburgh, 1980).

Kittredge, George Lyman, 'A Harvard Salutatory Oration of 1662', *Publications of the Colonial Society of Massachusetts*, 28 (1930–3), 1–24.

Knowler, William (ed.), *The Earl of Strafforde's Letters and Despatches* (2 vols, London, 1739).

Laing, David (ed.), 'Extracts from the Presbytery Records of Dalkeith, Relating to the Parish of Newbattle, During the Incumbency of Mr Robert Leighton, 1641–1653', in *Proceedings of the Society of Antiquaries of Scotland, Vol. IV Part II* (Edinburgh, 1863), pp. 459–92.

—— (ed.), *The Letters and Journals of Robert Baillie* (3 vols, Edinburgh, 1841).

Lamont, John, *The Diary of Mr. John Lamont of Newton 1649–1671*, ed. George R. Kinloch (Edinburgh, 1830).

Landrum, Robert H. (ed.), 'Records of the Anglo-Scottish Union Negotiations, 1652–1653', in *Miscellany of the Scottish History Society, Volume XV*, 6th series (Woodbridge, 2014), pp. 153–293.

Langley, Chris R. (ed.), *The Minutes of the Synod of Lothian and Tweeddale, 1648–1659* (Edinburgh, 2016).

Lawlor, Hugh J. (ed.), *The Registers of Provost Winter (Trinity College, Dublin), 1650 to 1660* (Exeter, 1907).

Lyon, C.J., *History of St. Andrews, Episcopal, Monastic, Academic, and Civil* (2 vols, Edinburgh, 1843).

MacTavish, Duncan C. (ed.), *Minutes of the Synod of Argyll, 1639–1661* (2 vols, Edinburgh, 1943–4).

Mahaffy, Robert Pentland (ed.), *Calendar of State Papers Relating to Ireland, 1625–1660* (3 vols, London, 1900–08).

Martin, R. Thomson (ed.), *Sermons, Prayers, and Pulpit Addresses by Alexander Henderson, 1638* (Edinburgh, 1867).

Marwick, J.D. (ed.), *Extracts from the Records of the Burgh of Glasgow, A.D. 1573–1642* (Glasgow, 1876).

—— (ed.), *Extracts from the Records of the Burgh of Glasgow, A.D. 1630–1662* (Glasgow, 1881).

Mather, Cotton, *Magnalia Christi Americana*, ed. Thomas Robbins and Lucius F. Robinson (2 vols, Hartford, CT, 1853).

Mather, Cotton, and Increase Mather, *Two Mather Biographies: Life and Death and Parentator*, ed. William J. Scheick (London, 1989).
'The Mather Papers', *Collections of the Massachusetts Historical Society*, 4th series, 8 (Boston, MA, 1868).
Matthews, Albert, 'A Proposal for the Enlargement of University Learning in New England, 1658–1660', *Proceedings of the Massachusetts Historical Society*, 41 (1908), 301–8.
McCrie, Thomas, *The Life of Mr Robert Blair, Minister of St Andrews* (Edinburgh, 1848).
Mitchell, Alexander F., and James Christie (eds), *The Records of the Commissions of the General Assemblies of the Church of Scotland* (3 vols, Edinburgh, 1892–1909).
Mitchell, Stewart, Allyn B. Forbes, and Malcolm Freiberg (eds), *The Winthrop Papers* (6 vols, Boston, MA, 1929–92).
Nicoll, John, *A Diary of Public Transactions and Other Occurrences, Chiefly in Scotland from January 1650 to January 1667* (Edinburgh, 1836).
Peterkin, Alexander (ed.), *Records of the Kirk of Scotland, Containing the Acts and Proceedings of the General Assemblies from the Year 1638 Downwards* (Edinburgh, 1843).
Potter, Alfred C., 'Catalogue of John Harvard's Library', *Publications of the Colonial Society of Massachusetts*, 21 (1919), 190–230.
Rogers, Charles (ed.), *The Earl of Stirling's Register of Royal Letters Relative to the Affairs of Scotland and Nova Scotia from 1615 to 1635* (2 vols, Edinburgh, 1885).
Rothes, John Leslie, earl of, *A Relation of Proceedings Concerning the Affairs of the Kirk of Scotland, from August 1637 to July 1638* (Edinburgh, 1830).
Row, John, *The History of the Kirk of Scotland, from the Year 1558 to August 1637*, ed. David Laing (Edinburgh, 1842).
Rutt, John Towill (ed.), *Diary of Thomas Burton Esq., 1653–1659* (4 vols, London, 1828).
Sainsbury, Noel (ed.), *Calendar of State Papers, Colonial Series Volume 1: 1574–1660* (London, 1860).
Scot, W., and J. Bliss, (eds), *The Works of the Most Reverend Father in God, William Laud* (7 vols, Oxford, 1847–60).
Selement, George, and Bruce C. Woolley (eds), 'Thomas Shepard's Confessions', *Publications of the Colonial Society of Massachusetts*, 58 (1981).
Shuckburgh, E.S. (ed.), *Two Biographies of William Bedell, Bishop of Kilmore* (Cambridge, 1902).
Shurtleff, Nathaniel B. (ed.), *Records of the Governor and Company of the Massachusetts Bay in New England* (5 vols, Boston, MA, 1853–4).
Shurtleff, Nathaniel B., and David B. Pulsifer (eds), *Records of the Colony of New Plymouth in New England* (12 vols, Boston, MA, 1855–61).
Spalding, John, *Memorialls of the Trubles in Scotland and in England, A.D. 1624–A.D. 1645*, ed. John Stuart (2 vols, Aberdeen, 1850–1).

Stearns, Raymond P. (ed.), 'Letters and Documents by or Relating to Hugh Peter', *Essex Institute Historical Collections*, 72:1 (1936), 43–72.

Steele, Robert (ed.), *Tudor and Stuart Proclamations 1485–1714, Volume II: Scotland and Ireland* (Oxford, 1910).

Stephen, William (ed.), *Register of the Consultations of the Ministers of Edinburgh and Some Other Brethren of the Ministry, 1652–1660* (2 vols, Edinburgh, 1921–30).

Stevenson, David (ed.), *The Government of Scotland under the Covenanters, 1637–1651* (Edinburgh, 1982).

Stock, Leo Francis (ed.), *Proceedings and Debates of the British Parliaments Respecting North America, Vol. 1: 1542–1688* (Washington, DC, 1924).

Stuart, John (ed.), *Extracts from the Council Register of the Burgh of Aberdeen. 1643–1747* (Edinburgh, 1872).

—— (ed.), *Selections from the Records of the Kirk Session, Presbytery, and Synod of Aberdeen* (Aberdeen, 1846).

Stubbings, Frank H. (ed.), *The Statutes of Sir Walter Mildmay for Emmanuel College* (Cambridge, 1983).

Terry, C.S. (ed.), *The Cromwellian Union: Papers Relating to the Negotiations for an Incorporating Union between England and Scotland 1651–1652* (Edinburgh, 1902).

Toon, Peter (ed.), *The Correspondence of John Owen (1616–1683), With an Account of His Life and Work* (Cambridge, 1970).

—— (ed.), *The Oxford Orations of Dr. John Owen* (Callington, 1971).

Treadwell, Victor (ed.), *The Irish Commission of 1622: An Investigation of the Irish Administration, 1615–1622, and Its Consequences, 1623–1624* (Dublin, 2006).

Tuttle, Julius H, 'Thomas Weld's Receipts and Disbursements', *Publications of the Colonial Society of Massachusetts*, 14 (1911), 121–6.

Walker, Williston (ed.), *The Creeds and Platforms of Congregationalism* (New York, 1893).

Walne, Peter, 'The Collections for Henrico College, 1616–1618', *Virginia Magazine of History and Biography*, 80:3 (1972), 259–66.

Winthrop, Jr., Robert C., 'John Haynes to Fitz-John Winthrop', *Proceedings of the Massachusetts Historical Society*, 2nd Series, 1 (1884–5), 118–31.

Wodrow, Robert, *Analecta: Or, Materials for a History of Remarkable Providences* (4 vols, Glasgow, 1842–3).

Wood, Marguerite (ed.), *Extracts from the Records of the Burgh of Edinburgh, 1626 to 1641* (Edinburgh, 1936).

—— (ed.), *Extracts from the Records of the Burgh of Edinburgh, 1642 to 1655* (Edinburgh, 1938).

—— (ed.), *Extracts from the Records of the Burgh of Edinburgh, 1655 to 1665* (Edinburgh, 1940).

Young, Alexander (ed.), *Chronicles of the First Planters of the Colony of Massachusetts Bay, from 1623–1636* (Boston, MA, 1846).

University Collections

Anderson, P.J. (ed.), *Officers and Graduates of University and King's College Aberdeen, MVD–MDCCCLX* (Aberdeen, 1893).

Anderson, P.J., and J.F.K. Johnstone (eds), *Fasti Academiae Mariscallanae Aberdonensis: Selections from the Records of Marischal College and University, MDXCIII–MDCCCLX* (3 vols, Aberdeen, 1889).

Bolton, Robert (ed.), *A Translation of the Charter and Statutes of Trinity College, Dublin* (Dublin, 1749).

Burtchaell, George D., and Thomas U. Sadleir (eds), *Alumni Dublinenses: A Register of the Students, Graduates, Professors and Provosts of Trinity College in the University of Dublin (1593–1860)* (Dublin, 1935).

Chartae et Statuta Collegii Sacrosanctae et Individue Trinitatis Reginae Elizabethae Juxta Dublin (Dublin, 1839).

A Collection of All the Papers Relating to the Proposal for Uniting the King's and Marischal Colleges of Aberdeen (London, 1787).

Evidence, Oral and Documentary, Taken and Received by the Commissioners Appointed by His Majesty George IV., July 23d 1826; and Re-Appointed by His Majesty William IV., October 12th, 1830; for Visiting the Universities of Scotland (4 vols, London, 1837).

Fry, M.W.J. (ed.), *The Dublin University Calendar, Vol. III. Being a Special Supplemental Volume for the Year 1912–1913* (Dublin, 1913).

Harvard College Records 1: Publications of the Colonial Society of Massachusetts, 15 (1925).

Harvard College Records 2: Publications of the Colonial Society of Massachusetts, 16 (1925).

Harvard College Records 3: Publications of the Colonial Society of Massachusetts, 31 (1935).

Harvard College Records 4: Publications of the Colonial Society of Massachusetts, 49 (1975).

Innes, Cosmo (ed.), *Fasti Aberdonenses: Selections from the Records of the University and King's College of Aberdeen* (Aberdeen, 1854).

——— (ed.), *Munimenta Alme Universitatis Glasguensis: Records of the University of Glasgow, from Its Foundation till 1727* (4 vols, Glasgow, 1854).

Laing, David (ed.), *A Catalogue of the Graduates of the Faculties of Arts, Divinity, and Law of the University of Edinburgh, Since Its Foundation* (Edinburgh, 1858).

MacDonnell, Hercules H.G. (ed.), *Chartæ et Statuta Collegii Sacrosanctæ et Individuæ Trinitatis Reginæ Elizabethæ, Juxta Dublin* (Dublin, 1844).

Mahaffy, John Pentland (ed.), *The Particular Book of Trinity College, Dublin: A Facsimile from the Original* (London, 1904).

——— (ed.), *The Plate in Trinity College, Dublin: A History and a Catalogue*. London, 1918.

Smart, Robert N. (ed.), *Alphabetical Register of the Students, Graduates, and Officials of the University of St Andrews, 1579–1747* (St Andrews, 2012).

Wood, Anthony à, *The History and Antiquities of the University of Oxford* (2 vols, Oxford, 1796).

Secondary Sources

Adams, Sharon, 'The Making of the Radical South-West: Charles I and His Scottish Kingdom, 1625–1649', *Celtic Dimensions of the British Civil Wars*, 53–74.

Adams, Sharon, and Julian Goodare (eds), *Scotland in the Age of Two Revolutions* (Woodbridge, 2014).

Adamson, John (ed.), *The English Civil War: Conflict and Contexts, 1640–49* (Basingstoke, 2009).

Aiton, John, *The Life and Times of Alexander Henderson* (Edinburgh, 1836).

Allan, David, '"For the Advancement of Religion and Learning": University and Society in Seventeenth-Century Scotland', *Scottish Philosophy in the Seventeenth Century*, pp. 11–32.

——, 'The Universities and the Scottish Enlightenment', *Edinburgh History of Education in Scotland*, pp. 97–113.

Andersen, Per, Pia Letto-Vanamo, Kjell Äke Modeer, and Helle Vogt (eds), *Liber Amicorum Ditlev Tamm. Law, History and Culture* (Copenhagen, 2011).

Anderson, Robert, Mark Freeman, and Lindsay Paterson (eds), *The Edinburgh History of Education in Scotland* (Edinburgh, 2015).

Anderson, Virginia DeJohn, 'Migrants and Motives: Religion and the Settlement of New England, 1630–1640', *New England Quarterly*, 58:3 (1985), 339–83.

——, 'New England in the Seventeenth Century', *Oxford History of the British Empire*, pp. 193–217.

David Armitage, *The Ideological Origins of the British Empire* (Cambridge, 2000).

——, 'Three Concepts of Atlantic History', *British Atlantic World*, pp. 11–27.

Armitage, David and Michael J. Braddick (eds) *The British Atlantic World, 1500-1800*, 1st edn (New York, 2002).

Armstrong, Robert, and Tadhg Ó hAnnracháin (eds), *Insular Christianity: Alternative Models of the Church in Britain and Ireland, c. 1570–c. 1700* (Manchester, 2012).

Ash, Eric H., 'Introduction: Expertise and the Early Modern State', *Osiris*, 25:1 (2010), 1–24.

Axtell, James, 'Babel of Tongues: Communicating with the Indians in Eastern North America', *Language Encounter in the Americas*, pp. 15–60.

——, *The School Upon a Hill: Education and Society in Colonial New England* (New Haven, CT, 1974).

——, *Wisdom's Workshop: The Rise of the Modern University* (Princeton, NJ, 2016).

Bailyn, Bernard, *The Barbarous Years: The Peopling of British North America: The Conflict of Civilizations, 1600–1675* (New York, 2012).
——, *Education in the Forming of American Society: Needs and Opportunities for Study* (New York, 1960).
——, 'The Idea of Atlantic History', *Itinerario*, 20:1 (1996), 19–44.
Baker, Derek (ed.), *Church, Society and Politics* (Oxford, 1975).
Baldwin, John W., and Richard A. Goldthwaite (eds), *Universities in Politics: Case Studies from the Late Middle Ages and Early Modern Period* (Baltimore, MD, 1972).
Ball, Francis Elrington, *A History of the County Dublin: The People, Parishes and Antiquities from the Earliest Times to the Close of the Eighteenth Century. Part Second* (Dublin, 1903).
Barnard, Toby, *Cromwellian Ireland: English Government and Reform in Ireland, 1649–1660* (Oxford, 1975).
——, 'The Hartlib Circle and the Origins of the Dublin Philosophical Society', *Irish Historical Studies*, 19:73 (1974), 56–71.
——, *Improving Ireland? Projectors, Prophets and Profiteers, 1641–1786* (Dublin, 2008).
——, *Irish Protestant Ascents and Descents, 1641–1770* (Dublin, 2004).
——, 'Miles Symner and the New Learning in Seventeenth-Century Ireland', *Journal of the Royal Society of Antiquaries of Ireland*, 102:2 (1972), 129–42.
——, *A New Anatomy of Ireland: The Irish Protestants, 1649–1770* (New Haven, CT, 2004).
——, 'Planters and Policies in Cromwellian Ireland', *Irish Protestant Ascents and Descents*, pp. 1–34.
——, 'The Purchase of Archbishop Ussher's Library in 1657', *Long Room*, 4 (1971), 9–14.
——, 'Trinity at Charles II's Restoration in 1660: A Loyal Address', *Hermathena*, 109 (1969), 44–50.
Beaudry, Mary Carolyn, and Travis G. Parno (eds), *Archaeologies of Mobility and Movement* (New York, 2013).
Belcher, T.W., *Memoir of John Stearne, M. & J.U.D., S.F.T.C.D., Founder and First President of the College of Physicians* (Dublin, 1865).
Bendall, Sarah, Christopher Brooke, and Patrick Collinson, *A History of Emmanuel College, Cambridge* (Woodbridge, 1999).
Bennett, Martyn, 'God's Wall of Brass: Cromwell's Generals in Ireland, 1649–1650', *Cromwell and Ireland*, pp. 135–56.
Bennett, Martyn, Raymond Gillespie, and R. Scott Spurlock (eds), *Cromwell and Ireland: New Perspectives* (Liverpool, 2021).
Black, George F., 'The Beginnings of the Study of Hebrew in Scotland', *Studies in Jewish Bibliography*, pp. 463–78.
Bondos-Greene, Stephen A., 'The End of an Era: Cambridge Puritanism

and the Christ's College Election of 1609', *Historical Journal*, 25:1 (1982), 197–208.

Boran, Elizabethanne, 'Malignancy and the Reform of the University of Oxford in the Mid-Seventeenth Century', *History of Universities*, 17 (2002), 19–46.

———, 'Perceptions of the Role of Trinity College, Dublin, from 1592 to 1641', *Università in Europa*, pp. 257–66.

———, 'Ramism in Trinity College, Dublin, in the Early Seventeenth Century', *Influence of Petrus Ramus*, pp. 177–99.

Boran, Elizabethanne, and Crawford Gribben (eds), *Enforcing Reformation in Ireland and Scotland, 1550–1700* (Aldershot, 2006).

Boran, Elizabethanne, and Helga Robinson-Hammerstein, 'The Promotion of "Civility" and the Quest for the Creation of a "City of Peace": The Beginnings of Trinity College, Dublin and of Harvard College, Cambridge, Mass', *Paedagogica Historica*, 34:2 (1998), 479–505.

Boulliot, L'Abbé, *Biographie Ardennaise, Ou Histoire Des Ardennais, Tome Premier* (Paris, 1830).

Bower, Alexander, *The History of the University of Edinburgh; Chiefly Compiled from Original Papers and Records, Never before Published* (2 vols, Edinburgh, 1817).

Bowie, Karin, *Public Opinion in Early Modern Scotland, c. 1560–1707* (Cambridge, 2020).

Braddick, Michael J., 'Administrative Performance: The Representation of Authority in Early Modern England', *Negotiating Power in Early Modern Society*, pp. 166–87.

——— (ed.), *The Oxford Handbook of the English Revolution* (Oxford, 2015).

———, *State Formation in Early Modern England, c. 1550–1700* (Cambridge, 2000).

Braddick, Michael J., and David L. Smith (eds), *The Experience of Revolution in Stuart Britain and Ireland: Essays for John Morrill* (Cambridge, 2011).

Braddick, Michael J. and John Walter (eds), *Negotiating Power in Early Modern Society: Order, Hierarchy and Subordination in Britain and Ireland* (Cambridge, 2001).

Bradshaw, Brendan, and John Morrill (eds), *The British Problem, c. 1534–1707: State Formation in the Atlantic Archipelago* (New York, 1996).

Bradshaw, Brendan, and Peter Roberts (eds), *British Consciousness and Identity: The Making of Britain, 1533–1707* (Cambridge, 1998).

Bradstock, Andrew, *Radical Religion in Cromwell's England: A Concise History from the English Civil War to the End of the Commonwealth* (London, 2011).

Brady, Ciaran (ed.), *Worsted in the Game: Losers in Irish History* (Dublin, 1989).

Brady, Ciaran, and Jane H. Ohlmeyer (eds), *British Interventions in Early Modern Ireland* (Cambridge, 2005).

Brandmüller, Walter, Herbert Immenkötter, and Erwin Iserloh (eds.), *Ecclesia*

Militans: Studia Zur Konzilien Und Refomartionsgeschichte Remigius Bäumer Zum 70. Geburtstag Gewidmet (Paderborn, 1988).

Bremer, Francis J., *Building a New Jerusalem: John Davenport, a Puritan in Three Worlds* (New Haven, CT, 2012).

———, *John Winthrop: America's Forgotten Founding Father* (New York, 2003).

———, 'The New England Way Reconsidered: An Exploration of Church Polity and the Governance of the Region's Churches', *Church Polity and Politics in the British Atlantic World*, pp. 155–73.

——— (ed.), *Puritanism: Transatlantic Perspectives on a Seventeenth-Century Anglo-American Faith* (Boston, MA, 1993).

———, 'The Puritan Experiment in New England, 1630–1660', *Cambridge Companion to Puritanism*, pp. 127–42.

———, *The Puritan Experiment: New England Society from Bradford to Edwards*, rev. edn (Hanover, NH, 1995).

Bremer, Francis J., and Lynn A. Botelho (eds), *The World of John Winthrop: Essays on England and New England, 1588–1649* (Boston, MA, 2005).

Broadie, Alexander (ed.), *Scottish Philosophy in the Seventeenth Century* (Oxford, 2020).

Brock, Michelle, 'Keeping the Covenant in Cromwellian Scotland', *Scottish Historical Review*, 99 (2020), 392–411.

———, '"The Man Will Shame Me": Women, Sex and Kirk Discipline during the Cromwellian Occupation', *Scottish Historical Review*, 51:2 (2022), 133–56.

Brockliss, Laurence, 'Curricula', *History of the University in Europe*, pp. 565–620.

Brooke, Christopher, and Victor Morgan, *A History of the University of Cambridge, Vol. II 1546–1750* (Cambridge, 2004).

Brown, Keith M, 'Scottish Identity in the Seventeenth Century', *British Consciousness and Identity*, pp. 236–58.

Brown, Keith M., and Alan R. MacDonald (eds), *Parliament in Context, 1235–1707* (Edinburgh, 2010).

Brown, Keith M., and Alaistar J. Mann (eds), *Parliament and Politics in Scotland, 1567–1707* (Edinburgh, 2005).

Buchanan, Kate, Lucinda H.S. Dean, and Michael Penman (eds), *Medieval and Early Modern Representations of Authority in Scotland and the British Isles* (New York, 2016).

Buckroyd, Julia M., *The Life of James Sharp, Archbishop of St Andrews, 1618–1679: A Political Biography* (Edinburgh, 1987).

———, 'Lord Broghill and the Scottish Church, 1655–1656', *Journal of Ecclesiastical History*, 27:4 (1976), 359–68.

———, 'The Resolutioners and the Scottish Nobility in the Early Months of 1660', *Church, Society and Politics*, pp. 245–52.

Bulloch, John M., *A History of the University of Aberdeen 1495–1895* (London, 1895).

Burg, B.R., 'The Cambridge Platform: A Reassertion of Ecclesiastical Authority', *Church History*, 43:4 (1974), 470–87.
Burgess, Glenn (ed.), *The New British History: Founding a Modern State 1603–1715* (London, 1999).
Burke, Peter, *Exiles and Expatriates in the History of Knowledge, 1500–2000* (Waltham, MA, 2017).
Burns, Ryan, 'Unrepentant Papists: Catholic Responses to Cromwellian Toleration in Interregnum Scotland', *History*, 103:355 (2018), 243–61.
Butler, Dugald, *The Life and Letters of Robert Leighton: Restoration Bishop of Dunblane and Archbishop of Glasgow* (London, 1903).
Campbell, Alexander D., *The Life and Works of Robert Baillie (1602–1662): Politics, Religion and Record-Keeping in the British Civil Wars* (Woodbridge, 2017).
Campbell, Ian W.S., 'Calvinist Absolutism: Archbishop James Ussher and Royal Power', *Journal of British Studies*, 53:3 (2014), 588–610.
Campbell, R.H., and Andrew S. Skinner (eds), *The Origins and Nature of the Scottish Enlightenment* (Edinburgh, 1982).
Campi, Emidio, Simone De Angelis, Anja-Silvia Goeing, and Anthony Grafton (eds), *Scholarly Knowledge: Textbooks in Early Modern Europe* (Geneva, 2008).
Cañizares-Esguerra, Jorge, *Puritan Conquistadors: Iberianizing the Atlantic, 1550–1700* (Stanford, CA, 2006).
Canny, Nicholas, 'Identity Formation in Ireland: The Emergence of the Anglo-Irish', *Colonial Identity in the Atlantic World*, pp. 159–212.
———, 'The Ideology of English Colonization: From Ireland to America', *William and Mary Quarterly*, 30:4 (1973), 575–98.
———, 'Irish, Scottish and Welsh Responses to Centralisation, c. 1530–c. 1640: A Comparative Perspective', *Uniting the Kingdom*, pp. 147–69.
———, *Kingdom and Colony: Ireland in the Atlantic World, 1560–1800* (Baltimore, MD, 1988).
———, *Making Ireland British, 1580–1650* (Oxford, 2001).
——— (ed.), *The Oxford History of the British Empire, Vol. I: The Origins of Empire* (Oxford, 1998).
Canny, Nicholas, and Anthony Pagden (eds), *Colonial Identity in the Atlantic World, 1500–1800* (Princeton, NJ, 1987).
Cant, Ronald G., *The College of St Salvator: Its Foundation and Development Including a Selection of Documents* (Edinburgh, 1950).
———, 'Origins of the Enlightenment in Scotland: The Universities', *Origins and Nature of the Scottish Enlightenment*, pp. 42–64.
———, 'The Scottish Universities in the Seventeenth Century', *Aberdeen University Review*, 43:143 (1970), 223–33.
———, *The University of St Andrews: A Short History*, 2nd edn (Edinburgh, 1970).

Capern, Amanda L., 'The Caroline Church: James Ussher and the Irish Dimension', *Historical Journal*, 39:1 (1996), 57–85.
Carlton, Charles, *Archbishop William Laud* (London, 1987).
Carlton, Eric, *Ideology and Social Order* (London, 1977).
Carter, Jennifer J., and Donald J. Withrington (eds), *Scottish Universities: Distinctiveness and Diversity* (Edinburgh, 1992).
Chambers, Liam, and Thomas O'Connor (eds), *College Communities Abroad: Education, Migration and Catholicism in Early Modern Europe* (Manchester, 2017).
Chaplin, Jeremiah, *Life of Henry Dunster: First President of Harvard College* (Boston, MA, 1872).
Christie, George, 'James Durham as Courtier and Preacher', *Records of the Scottish Church History Society*, 4 (1930), 66–80.
Cipriano, Salvatore, 'Ejected Academics: Marginalised Scottish University Professors between the Reformation and Revolution', in *Deviance and Marginality in Early Modern Scotland*, ed. Allan Kennedy (Woodbridge, forthcoming).
———, 'The Engagement, the Universities and the Fracturing of the Covenanter Movement, 1647–51', *National Covenant in Scotland*, pp. 145–60.
———, 'The Scottish Universities and Opposition to the National Covenant, 1638', *Scottish Historical Review*, 97:1 (2018), 12–37.
———, '"Students Who Have the Irish Tongue": The Gaidhealtachd, Education, and State Formation in Covenanted Scotland, 1638–1651', *Journal of British Studies*, 60:1 (2021), 66–87.
Clapp, Clifford B., 'Christo et Ecclesiae', *Publications of the Colonial Society of Massachusetts*, 25 (1922), 59–83.
Clarke, Aidan, '1659 and the Road to Restoration', *Ireland from Independence to Occupation*, pp. 241–64.
———, 'Bishop William Bedell (1571–1642) and the Irish Reformation', *Worsted in the Game*, pp. 61–72.
———, 'The Breakdown of Authority, 1640–41', *New History of Ireland*, pp. 270–88.
———, 'Colonial Identity in Early Seventeenth-Century Ireland', *Nationality and the Pursuit of National Independence*, pp. 57–71.
———, *The Old English in Ireland, 1625–42* (Ithaca, NY, 1966).
———, *Prelude to Restoration in Ireland: The End of the Commonwealth, 1659–1660* (Cambridge, 1999).
Cobban, A.B., *The Medieval Universities: Their Development and Organization* (London, 1975).
Coffey, John, *Politics, Religion and the British Revolutions: The Mind of Samuel Rutherford* (Cambridge, 1997).
Coffey, John, and Paul C.H. Lim., 'Introduction', *Cambridge Companion to Puritanism*, pp. 1–15.

―――― (eds), *The Cambridge Companion to Puritanism* (Cambridge, 2008).

Cohen, Charles L., 'Conversion Among Puritans and Amerindians: A Theological and Cultural Perspective', *Puritanism: Transatlantic Perspectives*, pp. 233–56.

Collins, Jeffrey R., 'The Church Settlement of Oliver Cromwell', *History*, 87:285 (2002), pp. 18–40.

Collinson, Patrick, *The Elizabethan Puritan Movement* (Oxford, 1967).

――――, 'Sects and the Evolution of Puritanism', *Puritanism: Transatlantic Perspectives on a Seventeenth-Century Anglo-American Faith*, pp. 147–66.

Como, David R., 'Predestination and Political Conflict in Laud's London', *Historical Journal*, 46:2 (2003), 263–94.

Connolly, S.J., *Religion, Law, and Power: The Making of Protestant Ireland 1660–1760* (Oxford, 1992).

Cosgrove, Art, and James McGuire (eds), *Parliament and Community* (Belfast, 1983).

Cotton, Henry, *Fasti Ecclesiæ Hibernicæ: The Succession of the Prelates and Members of the Cathedral Bodies of Ireland* (6 vols, Dublin, 1851–78).

Coutts, James, *A History of the University of Glasgow From Its Foundation in 1451 to 1908* (Glasgow, 1909).

Coward, Barry, *The Cromwellian Protectorate* (Manchester, 2002).

Cremin, Lawrence A., *American Education: The Colonial Experience, 1607–1783* (New York, 1970).

Crome, Andrew, 'The Jewish Indian Theory and Protestant Use of Catholic Thought in the Early Modern Atlantic', *Puritans and Catholics*, pp. 112–30.

Crook, J. Mordaunt, *Brasenose: The Biography of an Oxford College* (Oxford, 2008).

Cross, Arthur Lyon, *The Anglican Episcopate and the American Colonies* (New York, 1902).

Cunningham, John, *Conquest and Land in Ireland: The Transplantation to Connacht, 1649–1680* (Woodbridge, 2011).

Curtis, Mark H., *Oxford and Cambridge in Transition, 1558–1642: An Essay on Changing Relations between the English Universities and English Society* (Oxford, 1959).

Dalzel, Andrew, *History of the University of Edinburgh from Its Foundation* (2 vols, Edinburgh, 1862).

Darwall-Smith, Robin, *A History of University College, Oxford* (Oxford, 2008).

Davies, Julian, *The Caroline Captivity of the Church: Charles I and the Remoulding of Anglicanism, 1625–1641* (Oxford, 1992).

Davis, Jonathan. 'The Ideal Student: Manuals of Student Behaviours in Early Modern Italy', *Scholarly Self-Fashioning*, pp. 21–37.

Delahaye, Agnès, *Settling the Good Land: Governance and Promotion in John Winthrop's New England (1620–1650)* (Leiden, 2020).

Den Hartog, Jonathan, '"National and Provinciall Churches Are Nullityes":

Henry Dunster's Puritan Argument against the Puritan Established Church', *Journal of Church and State*, 56:4 (2014), 691–710.

Denlinger, Aaron Clay, '"Men of Gallio's Naughty Faith?": The Aberdeen Doctors on Reformed and Lutheran Concord', *Church History and Religious Culture*, 92:1 (2012), 57–83.

———, 'Swimming with the Reformed Tide: John Forbes of Corse (1593–1648) on Double Predestination and Particular Redemption', *Journal of Ecclesiastical History*, 66:1 (2015), 67–89.

Dennehy, Coleman, *The Irish Parliament, 1613–89: The Evolution of a Colonial Institution* (Manchester, 2019).

———, 'The Irish Parliament after the Rebellion, 1642–48', *Ireland in Crisis*, pp. 100–18.

———, 'Some Manuscript Alternatives to the Printed Irish Parliamentary Journals', *Parliaments, Estates and Representation*, 30:2 (2010), 129–43.

Dennison, E. Patricia, David Ditchburn, and Michael Lynch (eds), *Aberdeen Before 1800: A New History* (East Linton, 2002).

DesBrisay, Gordon, '"The Civill Warrs Did Overrun All": Aberdeen, 1630–1690', *Aberdeen Before 1800*, pp. 238–66.

Devine, T.M. and Jenny Wormald (eds), *The Oxford Handbook of Modern Scottish History* (Oxford, 2012).

Dhondt, Pieter, and Elizabethanne Boran (eds), *Student Revolt, City, and Society in Europe: From the Middle Ages to the Present* (London, 2018).

Dhondt, Pieter, and Laura Kolbe, 'Students as Agents of Change?', *Student Revolt, City, and Society*, pp. 1–8.

Ditchburn, David, 'Educating the Elite: Aberdeen and Its Universities', *Aberdeen Before 1800*, pp. 327–46.

Doan, James E., '"An Island in the Virginian Sea": Native Americans and the Irish in English Discourse, 1585–1640', *New Hibernia Review*, 1:1 (1997), 79–99.

Donald, Peter, *An Uncounselled King: Charles I and the Scottish Troubles, 1637–1641* (Cambridge, 1990).

Donaldson, Gordon, 'Aberdeen University and the Reformation', *Northern Scotland*, 1:2 (1973), 129–42.

——— (ed.), *Four Centuries Edinburgh University Life: 1583–1983* (Edinburgh, 1983).

———, *The Making of the Scottish Prayer Book of 1637* (Edinburgh, 1954).

———, *Scottish Church History* (Edinburgh, 1985).

Dow, Frances D., *Cromwellian Scotland 1651–1660* (Edinburgh, 1979).

Dugre, Neal T., 'Repairing the Breach: Puritan Expansion, Commonwealth Formation, and the Origins of the United Colonies of New England, 1630–1643', *New England Quarterly*, 91:3 (2018), 382–417.

Durkan, John, *Scottish Schools and Schoolmasters 1560–1633*, ed. Jamie Reid-Baxter (Woodbridge, 2013).

Durkheim, Émile, *Education and Sociology*, trans. Sherwood D. Fox (New York, 1956).
Durnin, Richard G., 'The Role of Presidents in the American Colleges of the Colonial Period', *History of Education Quarterly*, 1:2 (1961), 23–31.
Durston, Christopher, and Judith Maltby (eds), *Religion in Revolutionary England* (Manchester, 2006).
Elliott, J.H., *Empires of the Atlantic World: Britain and Spain in America 1492–1830* (New Haven, CT, 2006).
——, 'A Europe of Composite Monarchies', *Past & Present*, 137 (1992), 48–71.
——, 'Religions on the Move', *Religious Transformations in the Early Modern Americas*, pp. 25–45.
Ellis, Steven G., and Sarah Barber (eds), *Conquest and Union: Fashioning a British State, 1485–1725* (London, 1995).
Emerson, Roger L., *Academic Patronage in the Scottish Enlightenment: Glasgow, Edinburgh, and St Andrews Universities* (Edinburgh, 2008).
——, 'Scottish Cultural Change 1660–1710 and the Union of 1707', *Union for Empire*, pp. 121–44.
——, 'Scottish Universities in the Eighteenth Century, 1690–1800', *Studies on Voltaire and the Eighteenth Century*, 167 (1977), 453–74.
Empey, Mark, Alan Ford, and Miriam Moffitt (eds), *The Church of Ireland and Its Past: History, Interpretation and Identity* (Dublin, 2017).
Feingold, Mordechai, Joseph S. Freedman, and Wolfgang Rother (eds), *The Influence of Petrus Ramus* (Basel, 2001).
Feldhay, Rivka, 'Authority, Political Theology, and the Politics of Knowledge in the Transition from Medieval to Early Modern Catholicism', *Social Research*, 73:4 (2006), 1065–92.
——, 'Religion', *Cambridge History of Science*, pp. 725–55.
Fincham, Kenneth, 'Avant-Garde Conformity and the English Church, c. 1590–1625', *Altars Restored*, pp. 74–125.
—— (ed.), *The Early Stuart Church, 1603–1642* (Stanford, CA, 1993).
——, 'Oxford and the Early Stuart Polity', *History of the University of Oxford*, pp. 179–210.
Fincham, Kenneth, and Nicholas Tyacke (eds), *Altars Restored: The Changing Face of English Religious Worship, c. 1547–1700* (Oxford, 2007).
Fletcher, Anthony, and Peter Roberts (eds), *Religion, Culture and Society in Early Modern Britain: Essays in Honour of Patrick Collinson* (Cambridge, 1994).
Fletcher, John M., and Hilde de Ridder-Symoens (eds), *Lines of Contact* (Gent, 1994).
Ford, Alan, 'Apocalyptic Ireland: 1580–1641', *Irish Theological Quarterly*, 78:2 (2013), 123–48.
——, 'The Church of Ireland, 1558–1634: A Puritan Church?', *As By Law Established*, pp. 52–68.

———, 'The Church of Ireland: Power and Distance in the Early-Seventeenth-Century Atlantic', *The Seventeenth Century* (2023), 1–22.

———, 'Dependent or Independent? The Church of Ireland and Its Colonial Context, 1536–1649', *The Seventeenth Century*, 10 (1995), 163–87.

———, 'James Ussher and the Creation of an Irish Protestant Identity', *British Consciousness and Identity*, pp. 185–212.

———, *James Ussher: Theology, History, and Politics in Early-Modern Ireland and England* (Oxford, 2007).

———, *The Protestant Reformation in Ireland, 1590–1641*, 2nd edn (Dublin, 1997).

———, 'Shaping History: James Ussher and the Church of Ireland', *Church of Ireland and Its Past*, pp. 19–35.

———, '"That Bugbear Arminianism": Archbishop Laud and Trinity College, Dublin', *British Interventions in Early Modern Ireland*, pp. 135–60.

———, 'Who Went to Trinity? The Early Students of Dublin University', in *European Universities in the Age of Reformation and Counter Reformation*, pp. 53–74.

Ford, Alan, and John McCafferty (eds), *The Origins of Sectarianism in Early Modern Ireland* (Cambridge, 2005).

Ford, Alan, James McGuire, and Kenneth Milne (eds), *As By Law Established: The Church of Ireland Since the Reformation* (Dublin, 1995).

Ford, J.D., *Law and Opinion in Scotland during the Seventeenth Century* (Oxford, 20070.

Ford, Worthington C., 'New Englands First Fruits', *Proceedings of the Massachusetts Historical Society*, 43 (1909), 259–66.

Foster, Stephen, *The Long Argument: English Puritanism and the Shaping of New England Culture, 1570–1700* (Chapel Hill, NC, 1991).

Foucault, Michel, *Discipline and Punish: The Birth of the Prison*, trans. Alan Sheridan, 2nd edn (New York, 1995).

———, *Security, Territory, Population: Lectures at the Collége de France, 1977–1978*, ed. Michel Senellart, trans. Graham Burchell (New York, 2007).

Fowler, J.T., *Durham University: Earlier Foundations and Present Colleges* (London, 1904).

Fox, Peter, *Trinity College Library Dublin: A History* (Cambridge, 2014).

Frijhoff, Willem, 'Graduation and Careers', *History of the University in Europe*, pp. 355–415.

———, 'Patterns', *History of the University in Europe*, pp. 43–110.

———, 'Was the Dutch Republic a Calvinist Community? The State, the Confessions, and Culture in the Early Modern Netherlands', *Republican Alternative*, pp. 99–122.

Games, Alison, 'Atlantic History: Definitions, Challenges, and Opportunities', *American Historical Review*, 111:3 (2006), 741–57.

———, 'Beyond the Atlantic: English Globetrotters and Transoceanic Connections', *William and Mary Quarterly*, 63:4 (2006), 675–92.

———, *Migration and the Origins of the English Atlantic World* (Cambridge, MA, 1999).

———, *The Web of Empire: English Cosmopolitans in an Age of Expansion, 1560–1660* (Oxford, 2008).

Geiger, Roger L., *The History of American Higher Education: Learning and Culture from the Founding to World War II* (Princeton, NJ, 2014).

Gellera, Giovanni, 'The Reception of Descartes in the Seventeenth-Century Scottish Universities: Metaphysics and Natural Philosophy (1650–1680)', *Journal of Scottish Philosophy*, 13:3 (2015), 179–201.

———, 'The Scottish Faculties of Arts and Cartesianism (1650–1700)', *History of Universities*, 29:2 (2016), 166–87.

Gerbner, Katharine, 'Beyond the "Halfway Covenant": Church Membership, Extended Baptism, and Outreach in Cambridge, Massachusetts, 1656–1667', *New England Quarterly*, 85:2 (2012), 281–301.

Gillespie, Raymond, 'The Crisis of Reform, 1625–60', *Christ Church Cathedral*, pp. 195–217.

Ginzburg, Louis (ed.), *Studies in Jewish Bibliography and Related Subjects* (New York, 1929).

Goatman, Paul, and Andrew Lind, 'Glasgow and the National Covenant in 1638: Revolution, Royalism and Civic Reform', *National Covenant in Scotland*, pp. 39–52.

Goeing, Anja-Silvia, 'Sixteenth Century Higher Education in Zurich and Its Ties to the City-State Government', *Early Modern Universities*, pp. 63–82.

Goeing, Anja-Silvia, Glyn Parry, and Mordechai Feingold (eds), *Early Modern Universities: Networks of Higher Learning* (Leiden, 2021).

Goodare, Julian, 'The Rise of the Covenanters, 1637–1644', *Oxford Handbook of the English Revolution*, pp. 43–59.

———, 'The Scottish Revolution', *Scotland in the Age of Two Revolutions*, pp. 79–96.

Goodchild, Lester F., and Harold S. Wechsler (eds), *The History of Higher Education*, 2nd edn (Needham Heights, MA, 1997).

Gorski, Philip S., 'Calvinism and State-Formation in Early Modern Europe', *State/Culture*, pp. 147–81.

Grant, Alexander, *The Story of the University of Edinburgh during Its First Three Hundred Years* (2 vols, London, 1884).

Grant, Alexander, and Keith J. Stringer (eds), *Uniting the Kingdom? The Making of British History* (New York, 1995).

Gray, Edward G., *New World Babel: Languages and Nations in Early America* (Princeton, NJ, 1999).

Gray, Edward G., and Norman Fiering (eds), *The Language Encounter in the Americas, 1492–1800: A Collection of Essays* (New York, 2000).

Greaves, Richard L., *God's Other Children: Protestant Nonconformists and the*

Emergence of Denominational Churches in Ireland, 1660–1700 (Stanford, CA, 1997).

Greengrass, Mark, Michael Leslie, and Timothy Raylor, 'Introduction', *Samuel Hartlib and Universal Reformation*, pp. 1–26.

——— (eds), *Samuel Hartlib and Universal Reformation: Studies in Intellectual Communication* (Cambridge, 1994).

Gregerson, Linda, 'The Commonwealth of the Word: New England, Old England, and the Praying Indians', *Empires of God*, pp. 70–83.

Gregerson, Linda and Susan Juster (eds), *Empires of God: Religious Encounters in the Early Modern Atlantic* (Philadelphia, PA, 2011).

Gregory, Brad S., *The Unintended Reformation: How a Religious Revolution Secularized Society* (Cambridge, MA, 2012).

Grendler, Paul, 'The Universities of the Renaissance and Reformation', *Renaissance Quarterly*, 57:1 (2004), 1–42.

Gribben, Crawford, *God's Irishmen: Theological Debates in Cromwellian Ireland* (Oxford, 2007).

———, *John Owen and English Puritanism: Experiences of Defeat* (New York, 2016).

———, 'Preaching the Scottish Reformation, 1560–1707', *Oxford Handbook of the Early Modern Sermon*, pp. 271–86.

———, 'Robert Leighton, Edinburgh Theology and the Collapse of the Presbyterian Consensus', *Enforcing Reformation*, pp. 159–83.

Gribben, Crawford, and R. Scott Spurlock (eds), *Puritans and Catholics in the Trans-Atlantic World 1600–1800* (New York, 2016).

Gura, Philip F., *A Glimpse of Sion's Glory: Puritan Radicalism in New England, 1620–1660* (Middletown, CT, 1984).

Ha, Polly, and Patrick Collinson (eds), *The Reception of Continental Reformation in Britain* (Oxford, 2010).

Haefeli, Evan, *Accidental Pluralism: America and the Religious Politics of English Expansion, 1497–1662* (Chicago, IL, 2021).

Hall, David D., *The Puritans: A Transatlantic History* (Princeton, NJ, 2019).

———, *A Reforming People: Puritanism and the Transformation of Public Life in New England* (Chapel Hill, NC, 2011).

Halsey, A.H., Jean Floud, and C. Arnold Anderson (eds), *Education, Economy, and Society: A Reader in the Sociology of Education* (New York, 1961).

Hammerstein, Notker, 'Relations with Authority', *History of the University in Europe*, pp. 114–53.

———, 'Universitäten - Territorialstaaten - Gelehrte Rätem', *Die Rolle Der Juristen Bei Der Entstehung de Mondernen Staates*, pp. 687–737.

———, 'The University of Heidelberg in the Early Modern Period: Aspects of Its History as a Contribution to Its Sexcentennary', *History of Universities*, 6 (1986), 105–33.

Harris, Tim, *Rebellion: Britain's First Stuart Kings, 1567–1642* (Oxford, 2014).

Henderson, G.D., 'The Aberdeen Doctors', *The Burning Bush*, pp. 75–93.

———, *The Burning Bush: Studies in Scottish Church History* (Edinburgh, 1957).

Herbst, Jurgen, *From Crisis to Crisis: American College Government, 1636–1819* (Cambridge, MA, 1982).

———, 'Translatio Studii: The Transfer of Learning from the Old World to the New', *History of Higher Education Annual*, 12 (1992), 85–99.

Hessayon, Ariel, and David Finnegan (eds), *Varieties of Seventeenth- and Early Eighteenth Century English Radicalism in Context* (Farnham, 2011).

Hill, Christopher, 'The Radical Critics of Oxford and Cambridge in the 1650s', in *Universities in Politics*, pp. 107–32.

Hindle, Steve, *The State and Social Change in Early Modern England, 1550–1640* (Basingstoke, 2000).

Hodge, Christina J., '"A Small Brick Pile for the Indians": The 1655 Harvard Indian College as Setting', *Archaeologies of Mobility and Movement*, pp. 217–36.

Holenstein, André, Thomas Maissen, and Maarten Prak (eds), *The Republican Alternative: The Netherlands and Switzerland Compared* (Amsterdam, 2008).

Hölscher, Steffen, 'Moving Out! Student Identity and Symbolic Protest at Eighteenth-Century German Universities', *Student Revolt, City, and Society*, pp. 120–35.

Hood, Nathan C.J., 'Corporate Conversion Ceremonies: The Presentation and Reception of the National Covenant', *National Covenant in Scotland*, pp. 21–38.

Horn, D.B., *A Short History of the University of Edinburgh 1556–1889* (Edinburgh, 1967).

Horning, Audrey, *Ireland in the Virginian Sea: Colonialism in the British Atlantic* (Chapel Hill, NC, 2013).

Hotson, Howard, *Commonplace Learning: Ramism and Its German Ramifications, 1543–1630* (Oxford, 2007).

———, '"A Generall Reformation of Common Learning" and Its Reception in the English-Speaking World, 1560–1642', *Reception of Continental Reformation*, pp. 193–228.

———, 'The Ramist Roots of Comenian Pansophia', *Ramus, Pedagogy and the Liberal Arts*, pp. 227–52.

———, *The Reformation of Common Learning: Post-Ramist Method and the Reception of the New Philosophy, 1618–1670* (Oxford, 2020).

Houston, R.A., *Literacy in Early Modern Europe: Culture and Education 1500–1800* (London, 2002).

Howard, Thomas A., and Mark A. Noll (eds), *Protestantism after 500 Years* (Oxford, 2016).

Hoyle, David, *Reformation and Religious Identity in Cambridge, 1590–1644* (Woodbridge, 2007).

Hughes, Ann, '"The Public Profession of These Nations": The National

Church in Interregnum England', *Religion in Revolutionary England*, pp. 93–114.

Hunter, Ian, *The Secularisation of the Confessional State: The Political Thought of Christian Thomasius* (Cambridge, 2007).

Hutchins, Zachary McLeod, 'Building Bensalem at Massachusetts Bay: Francis Bacon and the Wisdom of Eden in Early Modern New England', *New England Quarterly*, 83:4 (2010), 577–606.

———, *Inventing Eden: Primitivism, Millennialism, and the Making of New England* (Oxford, 2014).

Hutton, Ronald, *The British Republic, 1649–1660*, 2nd edn (New York, 2000).

Irving, David, *The History of Scottish Poetry*, ed. John Aitken Carlyle (Edinburgh, 1861).

Jackson, Clare, *Restoration Scotland, 1660–1690: Royalist Politics, Religion and Ideas* (Woodbridge, 2003).

Jackson Williams, Kelsey, *The First Scottish Enlightenment: Rebels, Priests, and History* (Oxford, 2020).

James, Leonie, *'This Great Firebrand': William Laud and Scotland, 1617–1645* (Woodbridge, 2017).

Jansson, Maija (ed.), *Realities of Representation: State Building in Early Modern Europe and European America* (New York, 2007).

Jensma, G.T., F. Smit, and F. Westra (eds), *Universiteit Te Franeker, 1585–1811: Bijdragen Tot de Geschiedenis van de Friese Hogeschool* (Leeuwarden, 1985).

Johnson, Francis R., 'Gresham College: Precursor of the Royal Society', *Journal of the History of Ideas*, 1:4 (1940), 413–38.

Jones, Martin et al., *An Introduction to Political Geography: Space, Place and Politics* (London, 2015).

Kearney, Hugh, *Scholars and Gentlemen: Universities in Pre-Industrial Britain, 1500–1700* (Ithaca, NY, 1970).

———, *Strafford in Ireland, 1633–41: A Study in Absolutism* (Manchester, 1959).

Kellaway, William, *The New England Company, 1649–1776: Missionary Society to the American Indians* (London, 1961).

Kenny, Kevin (ed.), *Ireland and the British Empire* (Oxford, 2004).

Kerr-Peterson, Miles, *A Protestant Lord in James VI's Scotland: George Keith, Firth Early Marischal (1554–1623)* (Woodbridge, 2019).

Kidd, Colin, *British Identities before Nationalism: Ethnicity and Nationhood in the Atlantic World, 1600–1800* (Cambridge, 1999).

Kilroy, Phil, 'Radical Religion in Ireland, 1641–1660', *Ireland from Independence*, 201–17.

Kim, Joong-Lak, 'Firing in Unison? The Scottish Canons of 1636 and the English Canons of 1640', *Records of the Scottish Church History Society*, 28 (1998), 55–76.

———, 'The Scottish-English-Romish Book: The Character of the Scottish Prayer Book of 1637', *Experience of Revolution*, pp. 14–32.

Kirk, James, '"Melvillian" Reform in the Scottish Universities', *Renaissance in Scotland*, pp. 276–300.
Kirk, Stephanie, and Sarah Rivett (eds), *Religious Transformations in the Early Modern Americas* (Philadelphia, PA, 2014).
Kirwan, Richard, 'Introduction: Scholarly Self-Fashioning and the Cultural History of Universities', *Scholarly Self-Fashioning*, pp. 1–20.
——— (ed.), *Scholarly Self-Fashioning and Community in the Early Modern University* (Burlington, VT, 2013).
Kirwan, Richard, and Helga Robinson-Hammerstein, 'University Ritual and the Construction of the Scholar', *Liber Amicorum Ditlev Tamm*, pp. 107–20.
Klingenstein, Grete, Heinrich Lutz, and Gerard Stourzh (eds), *Bildung, Politik Und Gesellschaft* (Vienna, 1978).
Knight, Sarah, and Emma Annette Wilson (eds), *The European Contexts of Ramism* (Turnhout, 2019).
Kupperman, Karen O., 'How to Make a Successful Plantation: Colonial Experiment in America', *Ireland, 1641*, pp. 219–35.
———, *Indians and English: Facing Off in Early America* (Ithaca, NY, 2000).
Lake, Peter, 'The Laudian Style: Order, Uniformity and the Pursuit of the Beauty of Holiness in the 1630s', *Early Stuart Church, 1603–1642*, pp. 161–86.
Land, Robert Hunt, 'Henrico and Its College', *William and Mary Quarterly*, 18:4 (1938), 453–98.
Landrum, Robert H., 'Convincing Aberdeen, 1638: The Nation's Reluctant Converts', *Aberdeen University Review*, 60:210 (2003), 80–95.
Langley, Chris R., *Cultures of Care: Domestic Welfare, Discipline and the Church of Scotland, c. 1600–1689* (Leiden, 2020).
———, '"Diligence in His Ministrie": Languages of Clerical Sufficiency in Mid-Seventeenth-Century Scotland', *Archiv Für Reformationsgeschichte*, 104:1 (2013), 272–96.
——— (ed.), *The National Covenant in Scotland, 1638–1689* (Woodbridge, 2020).
———, 'Reading John Knox in the Scottish Revolution, 1638–50', *National Covenant in Scotland*, pp. 89–104.
———, *Worship, Civil War and Community, 1638–1660* (London, 2016).
Lenihan, Pádraig, *Consolidating Conquest: Ireland 1603–1727* (London, 2008).
Lennon, Colm, 'Education and Religious Identity in Early Modern Ireland', *Paedagogica Historica*, 35, supplement (1999), 57–75.
———, *Sixteenth-Century Ireland: The Incomplete Conquest* (New York, 1995).
Lind, Andrew, 'Battle in the Burgh: Glasgow during the British Civil Wars, c. 1638–1651', *Journal of the Northern Renaissance*, 12 (2021).
Lindberg, Bo (ed.), *Early Modern Academic Culture* (Stockholm, 2019).
Little, Patrick (ed.), *Ireland in Crisis: War, Politics and Religion, 1641–50* (Manchester, 2020).

———, 'The Irish "Independents" and Viscount Lisle's Lieutenancy of Ireland', *Historical Journal*, 44:4 (2001), 941–61.
———, *Lord Broghill and the Cromwellian Union with Ireland and Scotland* (Woodbridge, 2004).
———, 'Michael Jones and the Survival of the Church of Ireland, 1647–9', *Irish Historical Studies*, 43:163 (2019), 12–26.
Lloyd-Jones, Hugh, Valerie Pearl, and Blair Worden (eds.), *History and Imagination: Essays in Honour of H.R. Trevor-Roper* (London, 1981).
Lotz-Heumann, Ute, 'Confessionalisation in Ireland: Periodisation and Character, 1534–1649', *Origins of Sectarianism in Early Modern Ireland*, pp. 24–53.
Lynch, Michael, 'The Origins of Edinburgh's "Toun College": A Revision Article', *Innes Review*, 33 (1982), 3–14.
Maag, Karin, 'The Huguenot Academies: Preparing for an Uncertain Future', *Society and Culture in the Huguenot World*, pp. 139–56.
———, 'The Reformation and Higher Education', *Protestantism after 500 Years*, pp. 121–37.
———, *Seminary or University? The Genevan Academy and Reformed Higher Education, 1560–1620* (Aldershot, 1995).
MacDonald, Alan R., *The Jacobean Kirk, 1567–1625: Sovereignty, Polity, and Liturgy* (Aldershot, 1998).
———, 'James VI and I, the Church of Scotland, and British Ecclesiastical Convergence', *Historical Journal*, 48:4 (2005), 885–903.
MacDonald, Alasdair A., Michael Lynch, and Iain B. Cowan (eds), *The Renaissance in Scotland: Studies in Literature, Religion, History and Culture* (Leiden, 1994).
MacFarlane, Kirsten, 'Why Did Henry Dunster Reject Infant Baptism? Circumcision and the Covenant of Grace in the Seventeenth-Century Transatlantic Reformed Community', *Journal of Ecclesiastical History*, 72:2 (2021), 323–51.
Macinnes, Allan I., *The British Revolution, 1629–1660* (Basingstoke, 2005).
———, *Charles I and the Making of the Covenanting Movement 1625–1641* (Edinburgh, 1991).
———, *Clanship, Commerce and the House of Stuart, 1603–1788* (East Linton, 1996).
———, 'The Scottish Constitution, 1638–51: The Rise and Fall of Oligarchic Centralism', *Scottish National Covenant in Its British Context*, pp. 106–33.
———, 'The "Scottish Moment", 1638–45', *English Civil War: Conflict and Contexts*, pp. 125–52.
Macinnes, Allan I., and Jane H. Ohlmeyer (eds), *The Stuart Kingdoms in the Seventeenth Century: Awkward Neighbours* (Dublin, 2002).
MacKenzie, Kirsteen M., 'A Contested Space: Demonstrative Action and the Politics of Transitional Authority in Glasgow 1650–1653', *Medieval and Early Modern Representations of Authority*, pp. 68–82.

———, *The Solemn League and Covenant of the Three Kingdoms and the Cromwellian Union, 1643–1663* (London, 2017).

Mackie, J.D., *The University of Glasgow 1541–1951: A Short History* (Glasgow, 1954).

MacMillan, Donald, *The Aberdeen Doctors* (London, 1909).

MacMillan, Ken, *The Atlantic Imperial Constitution: Center and Periphery in the English Atlantic World* (New York, 2011).

Mahaffy, John Pentland, *An Epoch in Irish History: Trinity College, Dublin, Its Foundation and Early Fortunes, 1591–1660* (London, 1903).

———, 'The Library of Trinity College, Dublin: The Growth of a Legend', *Hermathena*, 12:28 (1902), 68–78.

Mann, Michael, *The Sources of Social Power, Volume I: A History of Power from the Beginning to A.D. 1760* (Cambridge, 1986).

Marshall, Peter, *Reformation England 1480–1642*, 2nd edn (New York, 2012).

Mason, Roger A. (ed.), *Scotland and England, 1286–1815* (Edinburgh, 1987).

Matthews, Albert, 'Comenius and Harvard College', *Publications of the Colonial Society of Massachusetts*, 21 (1919), 146–90.

McAlister, Kirsty F., and Roland J. Tanner, 'The First Estate: Parliament and the Church', *Parliament in Context*, pp. 31–66.

McCabe, W. Gordon, 'The First University in America, 1619–1622', *Virginia Magazine of History and Biography*, 30:2 (1922), 133–56.

McCafferty, John, *The Reconstruction of the Church of Ireland: Bishop Bramhall and the Laudian Reforms* (Cambridge, 2007).

McCallum, John (ed.), *Scotland's Long Reformation: New Perspectives on Scottish Religion, c. 1500–c. 1660* (Leiden, 2016).

McCormack, Danielle, 'Highland Lawlessness and the Cromwellian Regime', *Scotland in the Age of Two Revolutions*, pp. 115–33.

McCoy, Florence N., *Robert Baillie and the Second Scots Reformation* (Berkeley, CA, 1974).

McCullough, Peter, and Hugh Adlington (eds), *The Oxford Handbook of the Early Modern Sermon* (Oxford, 2011).

McDougall, Jamie, 'Allegiance, Confession and Covenanting Identities, 1638–51', *National Covenant in Scotland*, pp. 71–87.

McDowell, R.B., and D.A. Webb, *Trinity College Dublin 1592–1952: An Academic History* (Dublin, 2004).

McGrath, Bríd, 'The Irish Elections of 1640–1641', *British Interventions in Early Modern Ireland*, pp. 186–206.

———, 'Parliament Men and the Confederate Association', *Kingdoms in Crisis*, pp. 90–105.

McGuire, James, 'The Dublin Convention, the Protestant Community and the Emergence of an Ecclesiastical Settlement in 1660', *Parliament and Community*, pp. 121–46.

McInally, Tom, *The Sixth Scottish University: The Scots Colleges Abroad: 1575 to 1799* (Leiden, 2012).

McLaren, Colin A., *Aberdeen Students 1600–1860* (Aberdeen, 2005).

———, 'Affrichment and Riot: Student Violence in Aberdeen, 1659–1669', *Northern Scotland*, 10:1 (1990), 1–17.

———, 'Discipline and Decorum: The Law-Codes of the Universities of Aberdeen, 1605–86', *Scottish Universities: Distinctiveness and Diversity*, pp. 128–37.

———, 'New Work and Old: Building at the Colleges in the Seventeenth Century', *Aberdeen University Review*, 53:183 (1990), 208–17.

McOmish, David, 'The Scientific Revolution in Scotland Revisited: New Sciences in Edinburgh', *History of Universities*, 31:2 (2018), 153–72.

Mentzer, Raymond A., and Andrew Spicer (eds), *Society and Culture in the Huguenot World 1559–1685* (Cambridge, 2002).

Mijers, Esther, '"Addicted to Puritanism": Philosophical and Theological Relations between Scotland and the United Provinces in the First Half of the Seventeenth Century', *History of Universities*, 29:2 (2016), 69–95.

Miller, Perry, *The New England Mind: The Seventeenth Century* (Cambridge, MA, 1983).

Milne, Kenneth (ed.), *Christ Church Cathedral, Dublin: A History* (Dublin, 2000).

Moody, T.W. (ed.), *Nationality and the Pursuit of National Independence* (Belfast, 1978).

Moody, T.W., F.X. Martin, and F.J. Byrne (eds), *A New History of Ireland, Vol. III: Early Modern Ireland 1534–1691* (Oxford, 1976).

Morgan, Edmund S., *Visible Saints: The History of a Puritan Idea* (Ithaca, NY, 1963).

Morgan, John, *Godly Learning: Puritan Attitudes towards Reason, Learning and Education, 1560–1640* (Cambridge, 1986).

Morgan, Victor, 'Approaches to the History of the English Universities in the Sixteenth and Seventeenth Centuries', *Bildung, Politik Und Gesellschaft*, pp. 138–64.

———, 'The Electoral Scene and the Court: Royal Mandates 1558–1640', *History of the University of Cambridge*, pp. 388–436.

Morison, Samuel Eliot, *The Founding of Harvard College* (Cambridge, MA, 1935).

———, *Harvard College in the Seventeenth Century* (2 vols, Cambridge, MA, 1936).

———, *Three Centuries of Harvard, 1636–1936* (Cambridge, MA, 1936).

Morrill, John, 'A British Patriarchy? Ecclesiastical Imperialism Under the Early Stuarts', *Religion, Culture and Society in Early Modern Britain*, pp. 209–38.

——— (ed.), *Oliver Cromwell and the English Revolution* (London, 1990).

———, 'The Puritan Revolution', *Cambridge Companion to Puritanism*, pp. 67–88.

——— (ed.), *The Scottish National Covenant in Its British Context* (Edinburgh, 1990).

———, 'Seventeenth-Century Scotland', *Journal of Ecclesiastical History*, 33:2 (1982), 266–71.
Mullan, David G., *Scottish Puritanism 1590–1638* (Oxford, 2000).
Murdoch, Steve, and Alexia Grosjean, *Alexander Leslie and the Scottish Generals of the Thirty Years' War, 1618–1648* (London, 2016).
Murphy, Harold L., *A History of Trinity College Dublin from Its Foundation to 1702* (Dublin, 1951).
Murray, James, 'St Patrick's Cathedral and the University Question in Ireland c. 1547–1585', *European Universities in the Age of Reformation and Counter Reformation*, pp. 1–33.
Murray, Robert H., *Dublin University and the New World* (London, 1921).
Nash, Roderick Frazier, *Wilderness and the American Mind*, 5th edn (New Haven, CT, 2014).
Newton, Russell, 'United Opposition? The Aberdeen Doctors and the National Covenant', *National Covenant in Scotland*, pp. 53–70.
Norton, Arthur O., 'Harvard Text-Books and Reference Books in the Seventeenth Century', *Publications of the Colonial Society of Massachusetts*, 28 (1933), 361–438.
Nugent, Janay, and Elizabeth Ewan (eds), *Children and Youth in Premodern Scotland* (Woodbridge, 2015).
Ó Siochrú, Micheál, *Confederate Ireland: A Constitutional and Political Analysis* (Dublin, 1999).
———, *God's Executioner: Oliver Cromwell and the Conquest of Ireland* (London, 2009).
——— (ed.), *Kingdoms in Crisis: Ireland in the 1640s: Essays in Honour of Dónal Cregan* (Dublin, 2001).
Ó Siochrú, Micheál, and Jane H. Ohlmeyer (eds), *Ireland, 1641: Contexts and Reactions* (Manchester, 2013).
O'Brien, J.J., 'Commonwealth Schemes for the Advancement of Learning', *British Journal of Educational Studies*, 16:1 (1968), 30–42.
O'Connor, Thomas, 'The Domestic and International Roles of Irish Overseas College, 1590–1800', *College Communities Abroad*, pp. 90–114.
Ogilvie, J.D., 'The Aberdeen Doctors and the National Covenant', *Papers of the Edinburgh Bibliographical Society*, 11 (1912), 73–86.
Ohlmeyer, Jane H. (ed.), *Ireland from Independence to Occupation, 1641–1660* (Cambridge, 1995).
———, 'The Irish Peers, Political Power and Parliament, 1640–1641', *British Interventions in Early Modern Ireland*, pp. 161–85.
———, 'A Laboratory for Empire? Early Modern Ireland and English Imperialism', *Ireland and the British Empire*, pp. 26–60.
———, *Making Ireland English: The Irish Aristocracy in the Seventeenth Century* (New Haven, CT, 2012).
———, 'Power, Politics and Parliament in Seventeenth-Century Ireland', in *Realities of Representation*, pp. 113–32.

———, 'Seventeenth-Century Ireland and the New British and Atlantic Histories', *American Historical Review*, 104:2 (1999), 446–62.

Orme, William, *Memoirs of the Life, Writings, and Religious Connexions, of John Owen, D.D* (London, 1820).

Orr, Robert L., *Alexander Henderson: Churchman and Statesman* (London, 1919).

Padgett, John F., and Walter W. Powell (eds), *The Emergence of Organizations and Markets* (Princeton, NJ, 2012).

———, 'The Problem of Emergence', *Emergence of Organizations and Markets*, pp. 1–29.

Park, Katharine, and Lorraine Daston (eds), *The Cambridge History of Science: Volume 3, Early Modern Science* (Cambridge, 2006).

Parsons, Talcott, 'The School Class as a Social System: Some of Its Functions in American Society', *Education, Economy, and Society*, pp. 434–55.

Pedersen, Olaf, *The First Universities: Studium Generale and the Origins of University Education in Europe*, trans. Richard North (Cambridge, 1997).

———, 'Tradition and Innovation', *History of the University in Europe*, pp. 452–88.

Peile, John, *Biographical Register of Christ's College, 1505–1905, and of the Earlier Foundation, God's House, 1448–1505* (Cambridge, 1910).

Perceval-Maxwell, Michael, *The Outbreak of the Irish Rebellion of 1641* (Montréal, 1994).

Pestana, Carla Gardina, 'The City upon a Hill under Siege: The Puritan Perception of the Quaker Threat to Massachusetts Bay, 1656–1661', *New England Quarterly*, 56:3 (1983), 323–53.

———, *The English Atlantic in the Age of Revolution, 1640–1661* (Cambridge, MA, 2004).

———, *Protestant Empire: Religion and the Making of the British Atlantic World* (Philadelphia, PA, 2009).

Peterson, Mark A., 'The Practice of Piety in Puritan New England: Contexts and Consequences', *World of John Winthrop*, pp. 75–110.

Peyran, Charles, *Histoire de l'Ancienne Académie Réformée de Sedan* (Strasbourg, 1846).

Phillipson, Nicholas (ed.), *Universities, Society and the Future* (Edinburgh, 1983).

Pocock, J.G.A., 'The Atlantic Archipelago and the War of the Three Kingdoms', *British Problem*, pp. 172–91.

———, 'British History: A Plea for a New Subject', *Journal of Modern History*, 47:4 (1975), 601–21.

———, 'The Limits and Divisions of British History', *American Historical Review*, 87:2 (1982), 311–36.

Pope, Robert G., *The Half-Way Covenant: Church Membership in Puritan New England* (Princeton, NJ, 1969).

Prögler, Daniela, *English Students at Leiden University, 1575–1650: 'Advancing*

Your Abilities in Learning and Bettering Your Understanding of the World and State Affairs' (Burlington, VT, 2013).

Quane, Michael, 'City of Dublin Free School', *Journal of the Royal Society of Antiquaries of Ireland*, 90:2 (1960), 163–89.

Quincy, Josiah, *The History of Harvard University* (Cambridge, MA, 1840).

Quinn, David Beers 'Ireland and Sixteenth-Century European Expansion', in *Historical Studies I*, ed. T.D. Williams (London, 1958), pp. 20–32.

Raffe, Alasdair, 'Academic Specialisation in the Early Modern Scottish Universities', *Early Modern Academic Culture*, pp. 177–88.

———, *The Culture of Controversy: Religious Arguments in Scotland, 1660–1714* (Woodbridge, 2012).

———, 'Intellectual Change before the Enlightenment: Scotland, the Netherlands and the Reception of Cartesian Thought, 1650–1700', *Scottish Historical Review*, 94:238 (2015), 24–47.

Rait, Robert S., *The Universities of Aberdeen: A History* (Aberdeen, 1895).

Rashdall, Hastings, *The Universities of Europe in the Middle Ages* (2 vols, Oxford, 1895).

Reid, Henry M.B., *The Divinity Principals in the University of Glasgow 1545–1654* (Glasgow, 1917).

Reid, James Seaton, *The History of the Presbyterian Church in Ireland, Volume II* (London, 1837).

Reid, Steven J., 'Aberdeen's "Toun College": Marischal College, 1593–1623', *Innes Review*, 58:2 (2007), 173–95.

———, '"Ane Uniformitie in Doctrine and Good Order": The Scottish Universities in the Age of the Covenant, 1638–1649', *History of Universities*, 29:2 (2016), 13–41.

———, *Humanism and Calvinism: Andrew Melville and the Universities of Scotland, 1560–1625* (Aldershot, 2011).

———, 'On the Edge of Reason: The Scottish University between Reformation and Enlightenment, 1560–1660', *Scottish Philosophy in the Seventeenth Century*, pp. 33–49.

———, 'The Parish of Govan and the Principals of the University of Glasgow, 1577–1621', *The Society of Friends of Govan Old* (2012), 1–23.

———, 'Reformed Scholasticism, Proto-Empiricism and the Intellectual "Long Reformation" in Scotland: The Philosophy of the "Aberdeen Doctors", c. 1619–c. 1641', *Scotland's Long Reformation*, pp. 149–78.

Reid, Steven J., and Emma Annette Wilson (eds), *Ramus, Pedagogy and the Liberal Arts: Ramism in Britain and the Wider World* (Aldershot, 2011).

Reid-Baxter, Jamie, 'Elizabeth Melville, Lady Culross: Two Letters to Her Son James', *Children and Youth in Premodern Scotland*, pp. 205–20.

Reynolds, Matthew, *Godly Reformers and Their Opponents in Early Modern England: Religion in Norwich c. 1560–1643* (Woodbridge, 2005).

Ridder-Symoens, Hilde de (ed.), *A History of the University in Europe, Volume II: Universities in Early Modern Europe (1500–1800)* (Cambridge, 1996).

Rivett, Sarah, *The Science of the Soul in Colonial New England* (Chapel Hill, NC, 2011).
Roberts, John, Águeda M. Rodríguez Cruz, and Jurgen Herbst, 'Exporting Models', *History of the University in Europe*, pp. 256–82.
Robertson, Barry, 'The Covenanting North of Scotland, 1638–1647', *Innes Review*, 61:1 (2010), 24–51.
———, *Royalists at War in Scotland and Ireland, 1638–1650* (Burlington, VT, 2014).
Robertson, John (ed.), *A Union for Empire: Political Thought and the British Union of 1707* (Cambridge, 1995).
Robinson-Hammerstein, Helga, 'Archbishop Adam Loftus: The First Provost of Trinity College, Dublin', *European Universities in the Age of Reformation and Counter Reformation*, pp. 34–52.
———, 'Aspects of the Continental Education of Irish Students in the Reign of Elizabeth I', *Historical Studies*, 8 (1971), 137–54.
———, 'Commencement Ceremonies and the Public Profile of a University: Trinity College, Dublin, the First One Hundred Years', *Università in Europa*, pp. 239–55.
———, 'The "Common Good" and the University in the Age of Confessional Conflict', *British Interventions in Early Modern Ireland*, pp. 73–96.
——— (ed.), *European Universities in the Age of Reformation and Counter Reformation* (Dublin, 1998).
———, 'Royal Policy and Civic Pride: Founding a University in Dublin', *Treasures of the Mind*, pp. 1–16.
———, 'Trinity College, Dublin, in the Early Seventeenth Century: Institutional Isolation and Foreign Contacts', *Lines of Contact*, pp. 43–56.
Romano, Andrea (ed.), *Università in Europa: Le Istituzioni Universitarie Del Medio Evo Ai Nostri Giorni Strutture, Organizzazione, Funzionamento* (Messina, 1995).
Roper, L.H., *Advancing Empire: English Interests and Overseas Expansion, 1613–1688* (Cambridge, 2017).
Roy, Ian, and Dietrich Reinhart, 'Oxford and the Civil Wars', *History of the University of Oxford*, pp. 687–731.
Rüegg, Walter, 'Foreword', *History of the University in Europe*, pp. xix–xxiii.
———, 'Themes', *History of the University in Europe*, pp. 3–42.
Russell, Conrad, *The Causes of the English Civil War* (Oxford, 1990).
———, *The Fall of the British Monarchies, 1637–1642* (Oxford, 1991).
Ryrie, Alec, *The Origins of the Scottish Reformation* (Manchester, 2006).
Sachse, William L., 'The Migration of New Englanders to England, 1640–1660', *American Historical Review*, 53:2 (1948), 251–78.
Schindling, Anton, 'Schulen Und Universitäten Um 16. Und 17. Jahrhundert. Zehn Thesen Zu Bildungsexpansion, Laienbildung Und Konfessionalisierung Nach Reformation', *Ecclesia Militans*, pp. 561–70.

Schnur, Roman (ed.), *Die Rolle Der Juristen Bei Der Entstehung de Mondernen Staates* (Berlin, 1986).

Schultz, Karie, 'Protestant Intellectual Culture and Political Ideas in the Scottish Universities, ca. 1600–50', *Journal of the History of Ideas*, 83:1 (2022), 41–62.

Scott, David (ed.), *Treasures of the Mind: Trinity College, Dublin Quatercentenary Exhibition Catalogue* (London, 1992).

Scott, Hew, *Fasti Ecclesiæ Scoticanæ: The Succession of Ministers in the Church of Scotland from the Reformation* (7 vols, Edinburgh, 1915–28).

Serjeantson, Richard, 'Preaching Regicide in Jacobean England: John Knight and David Pareus', *English Historical Review*, 134:568 (2019), 553–88.

———, 'Proof and Persuasion', *Cambridge History of Science*, pp. 132–76.

Seymour, St John D., *The Puritans in Ireland, 1647–1661*, 2nd edn (Oxford, 1969).

Sharp, Joanne P. et al. (eds), *Entanglements of Power: Geographies of Domination/Resistance* (New York, 2000).

———, 'Entanglements of Power: Geographies of Domination/Resistance', *Entanglements of Power*, pp. 1–42.

Sharpe, Kevin, 'Archbishop Laud and the University of Oxford', *History and Imagination*, pp. 146–64.

———, *The Personal Rule of Charles I* (New Haven, CT, 1992).

Shaw, Duncan, *The General Assemblies of the Church of Scotland, 1560–1600: Their Origins and Development* (Edinburgh, 1964).

Shepherd, Christine M., 'A National System of University Education in Seventeenth-Century Scotland?', *Scottish Universities: Distinctiveness and Diversity*, pp. 26–33.

———, 'Newtonianism in Scottish Universities in the Seventeenth Century', *Origins and Nature of the Scottish Enlightenment*, pp. 65–85.

———, 'University Life in the Seventeenth Century', *Four Centuries Edinburgh University Life*, pp. 1–15.

Sher, Richard B., *Church and University in the Scottish Enlightenment: The Moderate Literati of Edinburgh* (Edinburgh, 1985).

Sibley, John L., *Biographical Sketches of Graduates of Harvard University, in Cambridge, Massachusetts* (3 vols, Cambridge, MA, 1873–85).

Simone, Maria Rosa di, 'Admission', *History of the University in Europe*, pp. 285–325.

Sletcher, Michael, 'Historians and Anachronisms: Samuel E. Morison and Seventeenth-Century Harvard College', *History of Universities*, 19:2 (2004), 188–220.

Smyth, Jim, 'Empire-Building: The English Republic, Scotland and Ireland', *Varieties of Seventeenth- and Early Eighteenth-Century English*, pp. 129–44.

Sommerville, J.P., *Politics and Ideology in England, 1603–1640* (London, 1986).

Sprunger, Keith L., 'Archbishop Laud's Campaign Against Puritanism at the Hague', *Church History*, 44:3 (1975), 308–20.

——, *Dutch Puritanism: A History of English and Scottish Churches of the Netherlands in the Sixteenth and Seventeenth Centuries* (Leiden, 1982).

——, *The Learned Doctor William Ames: Dutch Backgrounds of English and American Puritanism* (Urbana, IL, 1972).

——, 'William Ames and the Franeker Link to English and American Puritanism', *Universiteit Te Franeker*, pp. 264–74.

——, 'William Ames and the Settlement of Massachusetts Bay', *New England Quarterly*, 39:1 (1966), 66–79.

Spurlock, R. Scott, '"Anie Gospell Way": Religious Diversity in Interregnum Scotland', *Records of the Scottish Church History Society*, 37 (2007), 89–119.

——, *Cromwell and Scotland: Conquest and Religion, 1650–1660* (Edinburgh, 2007).

——, 'Polity, Discipline and Theology: the Importance of the Covenant in Scottish Presbyterianism, 1560–c. 1700', *Church Polity and Politics in the British Atlantic World*, pp. 80–103.

Spurr, John, *The Post-Reformation: Religion, Politics and Society in Britain 1603–1714* (London, 2006).

Staloff, Darren, *The Making of an American Thinking Class: Intellectuals and Intelligentsia in Puritan Massachusetts* (New York, 1998).

Stearns, Raymond P., *The Strenuous Puritan: Hugh Peters, 1598–1660* (Urbana, IL, 1954).

——, 'The Weld-Peter Mission to England', *Publications of the Colonial Society of Massachusetts*, 32 (1934), 188–246.

Steinmetz, George (ed.), *State/Culture: State-Formation after the Cultural Turn* (Ithaca, NY, 1999).

Stevenson, Andrew, *The History of the Church and State of Scotland, from the Accession of King Charles I to the Year 1649* (3 vols, Edinburgh, 1840).

Stevenson, David, 'Cromwell, Scotland and Ireland', *Oliver Cromwell and the English Revolution*, pp. 149–80.

——, 'Deposition of Ministers in the Church of Scotland under the Covenanters, 1638–1651', *Church History*, 44:3 (1975), 321–35.

——, 'The Early Covenanters and the Federal Union of Britain', *Scotland and England, 1286–1815*, pp. 163–81.

——, *King's College, Aberdeen, 1560–1641: From Protestant Reformation to Covenanting Revolution* (Aberdeen, 1990).

——, *Revolution and Counter-Revolution in Scotland, 1644–1651* (London, 1977).

——, *The Scottish Revolution 1637–1644: The Triumph of the Covenanters* (Newton Abbot, 1973).

Stewart, David, 'The "Aberdeen Doctors" and the Covenanters', *Records of the Scottish Church History Society*, 22 (1986), 35–44.

Stewart, Laura A.M., 'Authority, Agency and the Reception of the Scottish National Covenant of 1638', *Insular Christianity*, pp. 88–106.

———, *Rethinking the Scottish Revolution: Covenanted Scotland, 1637–1651* (Oxford, 2016).

———, 'The "Rise" of the State?', *Oxford Handbook of Modern Scottish History*, pp. 220–35.

Stone, Lawrence, 'Social Control and Intellectual Excellence: Oxbridge and Edinburgh, 1560–1983', *Universities, Society and the Future*, pp. 3–30.

Storey, David, *Territories: The Claiming of Space*, 2nd edn (London, 2012).

Stout, Harry S, 'The Morphology of Remigration: New England University Men and Their Return to England, 1640–1660', *Journal of American Studies*, 10:2 (1976), 151–72.

———, 'University Men in New England 1620–1660: A Demographic Analysis', *Journal of Interdisciplinary History*, 4:3 (1974), 375–400.

Strauss, Gerald, *Luther's House of Learning: Indoctrination of the Young in the German Reformation* (Baltimore, MD, 1978).

Stubbs, John William, *The History of the University of Dublin, from Its Foundation to the End of the Eighteenth Century* (Dublin, 1889).

Szasz, Margaret Connell, *Indian Education in the American Colonies, 1607–1783*, 2nd edn (Lincoln, NE, 2007).

———, *Scottish Highlanders and Native Americans: Indigenous Education in the Eighteenth-Century Atlantic World* (Norman, OK, 2007).

Terpstra, Nicholas, *Religious Refugees in the Early Modern World: An Alternative History of the Reformation* (Cambridge, 2015).

Tilly, Charles, *Coercion, Capital and European States: AD 990–1990* (Oxford, 1990).

———, *The Formation of National States in Western Europe* (Princeton, NJ, 1975).

———, 'Reflections on the History of European State-Making', *Formation of National States*, pp. 3–83.

Todd, Margo, *The Culture of Protestantism in Early Modern Scotland* (New Haven, CT, 2002).

———, 'The Problem of Scotland's Puritans', *Cambridge Companion to Puritanism*, pp. 174–88.

Toomer, G.J., *Eastern Wisedome and Learning: The Study of Arabic in Seventeenth-Century England* (Oxford, 1996).

Tremml-Werner, Birgit and Dorothée Goetze, 'A Multitude of Actors in Early Modern Diplomacy', *Journal of Early Modern History*, 23 (2019), 407–22.

Trevor-Roper, Hugh, *Archbishop Laud, 1573–1645*, 3rd edn (London, 1988).

———, *History and the Enlightenment*, ed. John Robertson (New Haven, CT, 2010).

———, *Religion, the Reformation and Social Change* (London, 1967).

———, 'Scotland and the Puritan Revolution', *Religion, the Reformation and Social Change*, pp. 392–444.

———, 'The Scottish Enlightenment', *History and the Enlightenment*, pp. 17–33.

Tröhler, Daniel, 'The Knowledge of Science and the Knowledge of the Classroom: Using the Heidelberg Catechism (1563) to Examined Overlooked Connections', *Scholarly Knowledge*, pp. 75–85.

Tucker, Marie-Claude, 'Scottish Masters in Huguenot Academies', *History of Universities*, 29:2 (2016), 42–68.

———, 'Scottish Philosophy Teachers at the French Protestant Academies in the Seventeenth Century', *Scottish Philosophy in the Seventeenth Century*, pp. 50–72.

Turnbull, G.H., 'Oliver Cromwell's College at Durham', *Durham Research Review*, 3 (1952), 1–7.

Tuttle, Julius H., 'The Library of Dr. William Ames', *Publications of the Colonial Society of Massachusetts*, 14 (1911), 63–6.

Twigg, John, 'The Limits of 'Reform': Some Aspects of the Debate on University Education during the English Revolution', *History of Universities*, 4 (1984), 99–114.

———, *The University of Cambridge and the English Revolution, 1625–1688* (Woodbridge, 1990).

Tyacke, Nicholas, *Anti-Calvinists: The Rise of English Arminianism c. 1590–1640* (Oxford, 1987).

———, 'Archbishop Laud', *Early Stuart Church, 1603–1642*, pp. 51–70.

——— (ed.), *The History of the University of Oxford, Vol. IV Seventeenth-Century Oxford* (Oxford, 1997).

———, 'Religious Controversy', *History of the University of Oxford*, pp. 569–619.

Urwick, William, *The Early History of Trinity College Dublin 1591–1660, As Told in Contemporary Records on Occasion of Its Tercentenary* (Dublin, 1892).

Vandermeersch, Peter A., 'Teachers', *History of the University in Europe*, pp. 210–55.

Vaughan, Alden T., *New England Frontier: Puritans and Indians, 1620–1675*, 3rd edn (Norman, OK, 1995).

Vernon, Elliot, and Hunter Powell (eds), *Church Polity and Politics in the British Atlantic World, c. 1635–66* (Manchester, 2020).

Visscher, Hugo, *Guilielmus Amesius: Zihn Leven En Werken* (Haarlem, 1894).

Webster, Charles, *The Great Instauration: Science, Medicine, and Reform, 1626–1660*, 2nd edn (New York, 2002).

——— (ed.), *Samuel Hartlib and the Advancement of Learning* (Cambridge, 1970).

Weimer, Adrian Chastain, 'The Resistance Petitions of 1664–1665: Confronting the Restoration in Massachusetts Bay', *New England Quarterly*, 92:2 (2019), 221–62.

Wellmon, Chad, *Organizing Enlightenment: Information Overload and the Invention of the Modern Research University* (Baltimore, MD, 2015).

Wells, Jennifer, 'English Law, Irish Trials and Cromwellian State Building in the 1650s', *Past & Present*, 227 (2015), 77–119.

Wilder, Craig Steven, *Ebony and Ivy: Race, Slavery, and the Troubled History of America's Universities* (New York, 2013).

Williams, George H., *First Light: The Formation of Harvard College in 1636 and Evolution of a Republic of Letters in Cambridge* (Göttingen, 2014).

Wilson, Emma Annette, 'The International Nature of Britannic Ramism', in *The European Contexts of Ramism*, pp. 109–31.

Wood, Paul, 'Defining the Scottish Enlightenment', *Journal of Scottish Philosophy*, 15:3 (2017), 299–311.

Wood, Timothy L., *Agents of Wrath, Sowers of Discord: Authority and Dissent in Puritan Massachusetts, 1630–1655* (New York, 2006).

Woodward, Walter W., *Prospero's America: John Winthrop, Jr., Alchemy, and the Creation of New England Culture, 1606–1676* (Chapel Hill, NC, 2010).

Woolrych, Austin, *Britain in Revolution 1625–1660* (Oxford, 2002).

Worden, Blair, 'Cromwellian Oxford', *History of the University of Oxford*, pp. 733–72.

———, *God's Instruments: Political Conduct in the England of Oliver Cromwell* (Oxford, 2013).

———, 'Toleration and the Cromwellian Protectorate', in *Persecution and Toleration*, ed. W.J. Sheils, Studies in Church History, vol. 21 (Oxford, 1984), pp. 199–233.

Wormald, Jenny, 'Introduction', *Seventeenth Century*, pp. 1–12.

——— (ed.), *The Seventeenth Century: The Short Oxford History of the British Isles* (Oxford, 2008).

Wright, Bobby, '"For the Children of Infidels?": American Indian Education in the Colonial Colleges', *History of Higher Education*, pp. 72–9.

Young, John R. (ed.), *Celtic Dimensions of the British Civil Wars* (Edinburgh, 1997).

———, 'Charles I and the 1633 Parliament', *Parliament and Politics in Scotland*, pp. 101–37.

Zamick, Morris, 'Julius Conradus Otto: Manuscripts Remains in the University Library', *University of Edinburgh Journal*, 4 (1931), 229–35.

Unpublished Theses

Holfelder, K.D., 'Factionalism in the Kirk during the Cromwellian Invasion and Occupation of Scotland, 1650 to 1660: The Protester-Resolutioner Controversy' (unpublished PhD thesis, University of Edinburgh, 1998).

Landrum, Robert H., 'Vast Visions and Intransigent Realities: The Anglo-Scottish Union of 1651–60' (unpublished PhD thesis, University of Wisconsin, Madison, 1999).

Lind, Andrew, '"Bad and Evill Patriotts?" Royalism in Scotland during the British Civil Wars, c. 1638–1651' (unpublished PhD thesis, University of Glasgow, 2020).

McDougall, Jamie, 'Covenants and Covenanters in Scotland 1638–1679' (unpublished PhD thesis, University of Glasgow, 2018).

McGrath, Bríd, 'A Biographical Dictionary of the Membership of the Irish House of Commons 1640–1641' (2 vols, unpublished PhD thesis, Trinity College, Dublin, 1998).

Shepherd, Christine M., 'Philosophy and Science in the Arts Curriculum of the Scottish Universities in the 17th Century' (unpublished PhD thesis, University of Edinburgh, 1974).

Wells, Jennifer, 'Prelude to Empire: State Building in the British Archipelago and Its Global Repercussions, 1620–1688' (unpublished PhD thesis, Brown University, 2016).

Web-Based Sources

Brown, Keith M., *et al.* (eds), *The Records of the Parliaments of Scotland to 1707* (St Andrews, 2007–17) [www.rps.ac.uk/].

Dictionary of Irish Biography (Cambridge, 2009) [http://dib.cambridge.org/].

Greengrass, Mark, *et al.* (eds), *The Hartlib Papers* (Sheffield, 2013) [www.hrionline.ac.uk/hartlib/].

Oxford Dictionary of National Biography (Oxford, 2004) [www.oxforddnb.com/].

Virginia Company Archives [http://virginiacompanyarchives.amdigital.co.uk/].

Index

Page numbers in italics refer to tables

Abbott, George, archbishop of
  Canterbury   24–5, 49, 53
Aberdeen
  bishopric   74
    see also Forbes, Patrick, bishop of
      Aberdeen
  and Independency   161–3, 179
  synod   89, 162
  University of *see* King's College,
    Aberdeen; Marischal College,
    Aberdeen
Aberdeen Doctors
  opposition to National
    Covenant   64–6
  purged from universities   86–9
  see also General Assembly
Adamson, John   66, 69, 70, 71, 93, 94,
  159, 169
Addis, William   109 n.90
Aidie, William   63
Allen, James   *186*
Allen, John   204
Alsted, Johan Heinrich   122
Alumni Dublinenses   109
Ambrose, Nehemiah   225
Ames, William   48–51, 56, 118, 122,
  129
Anabaptists/Anabaptism   130, 210
  see also Baptists
Anderson, Hugh   187
Antinomian Controversy   56, 117, 118
Argyll, marquis of *see* Campbell,
  Archibald, first marquis of Argyll
Argyll synod   92–3, 95
  see also Gaidhealtachd (Scotland)
Aristotle/Aristotelianism   3, 10, 16, 78,
  193, 212, 215, 217
  Organon   9, 122
  and the Scottish universities   17, 78

and Trinity   38, 107
see also Ramism
Armagh, archbishop of *see* Ussher,
  James, archbishop of Armagh
Armine, Mary   123
Arminianism   22, 40, 49, 95, 160
  and the Scottish universities   68, 76,
    77, 88
  and Trinity   27, 30, 33–5, 99–100,
    103, 107
  see also Chappell, William
Arminius, Jacobus   49, 100
Armour, John   63
Ayr synod   82

Bacon, Francis   122, 213, 216, 216
  n.107
Baillie, Henry   173, 190
Baillie, Robert   65 n.26, 66, 69, 70, 70
  n.59, 72, 74 n.90, 79, 80–1, 85,
  90, 122, 163, 164, 166, 168, 169,
  179, 182, 185, *186*, 187–9, 192
  appointed Glasgow principal   235
  and creation of a unified
    curriculum for the Scottish
    universities   92–5
  opposition to Cromwellian
    regime   157–9, 187–9
  opposition to Protesters   153–5
  proposals for the reform of
    Glasgow   76–8
  protest of Patrick Gillespie's
    principalship   173–4, 173 n.28,
    177–8, 181, 189–91
  translation to Glasgow divinity
    professorship   82–3
Baker, George   37
Balcanquhall, Walter, dean of
  Rochester   65, 73, 89

281

INDEX

Baptists 175, 200, 207, 214, 236
   in Ireland 204–6, 210–11, 229
   see also Dunster, Henry
Barebones Parliament 155
Barlow, Randolph, archbishop of
     Tuam 100
Barnard, Tobias 123
Barnard, Toby 215
Baron, John 62, 64, 66, 69–70, 70
     n.59, 85, 151, 163, 187
Baron, Robert 63, 64, 67, 78, *91*
   see also Aberdeen Doctors
Barrow, Humphrey 209
Battle of Dunbar 153, 162
Battle of Naseby 89
Battle of Preston 150
Battle of Worcester 153, 155, 160, 163
Beale, John 215, *222*
Beckwith, Christopher 37, 106, *115*
Bedell, William 33, 34, 35, 38, 99,
     106, 149
   translation to bishopric of Kilmore
     and Ardagh 30–1
   Trinity provostship 28–30, 29 n.40
Belgic Confession 49
Bellingham, Richard *125*
Bellingham, Samuel 123
Binning, Hugh 85
Birnie, Andrew 162, *187*
Bishop, James 37, 115, *115*
Bishops' Wars 73, 86, 104, 119
Blackhall, William 63, *91*
Blair, James *186*
Blair, Robert 72, 82, 82 n.146, 83, 90,
     93, 155, 157, 163, 176, 179, 197
Book of Common Prayer 26, 48, 51,
     141, 229
   use at Scottish universities 40, 42–4
   use at Trinity 39, 116
   see also Charles I; Laud, William/
     Laudianism
Booth, Gilbert 109 n.91
Boran, Elizabethanne 19, 28 n.38, 98
Borlase, John 111–14
Boswell, Dudley 37
Boyd, Zachary 93, 158
Boyle, Roger, Lord Broghill 180, 189

and appointment of Scottish
     university staff 185, 188
conciliates with Protesters and
     Resolutioners 183–4
and General Convention
     (Dublin) 230–1
   see also Council of Scotland
Boyle, Roger, Trinity lecturer 115, *116*
Braddick, Michael 4–5
Bradstreet, Samuel 225
Bramhall, John, bishop of Derry 26,
     32, 36, 102–3, 104
Brewster, Nathaniel 123, 208, 214
Brigden, Zachariah 225
Briscoe, John 109, 109 n.88
Briscoe, Nathaniel 118, *126*
Brodie, John *187*
Broun, John 62, 63, 71, 86, *91*
Bruce, Andrew 62, 64, 66, 85
Bruce Jr, Andrew *186*
Bruce, David *186*
Buckeridge, John 22 n.2
Buckworth, Theophilus, bishop of
     Dromore 35
Bulkeley, Gershom 225
Bulkeley, John 123, 124, *126*, 127
Burnet, Andrew 177 n.55, 179, *187*
Burnet, Robert, professor of medicine, St
     Salvator's College *186*
Burnet, Robert, regent, Marischal
     College *187*
bursar/bursaries (Scottish universities)
   see under General Assembly
Burton, William 208
Butler, James, first duke of
     Ormond 113, 115, 206
   Trinity chancellorship 114–15, 206,
     232, 235
Bysse, John 107
Bysse, Robert 108

Calderwood, David 65
Calvinism/Calvinists 5, 16, 42, 44,
     49, 77
   and perceptions of Scottish
     Covenanters 60–1
   see also Arminianism; Puritans/

282

INDEX

Puritanism; Reformed
    Protestantism
Cambridge, Massachusetts   55, 117,
    118, 236
Cambridge Platform   130–1, 202, 224,
    226, 227, 238
Campbell, Archibald, first marquis of
    Argyll   151
Campbell, William   85, 186, 187–8
Cant, Andrew   65–6, 88, 175–6, 187
Cant, Ronald   71 n.71, 167
Canterbury, archbishop of see
    Abbott, George, archbishop
    of Canterbury; Laud, William/
    Laudianism
Carey, Valentine   33
Carleton, Dudley   31, 49
Carlton, Eric   2, 4
Cartesianism   193
Cary, Henry, viscount Falkland   29–31
Catholicism/Catholics   239 n.18
    in Ireland   13–14, 19, 54, 98, 144,
        147, 205, 220
        grievances of Irish
            Catholics following Irish
            Rebellion   110–11
        and Trinity's statutes   39
    universities   10, 16, 51
Chalmers, James   187
Chappell, John   101–3
Chappell, William   31, 31 n.55, 32, 36,
    110, 111, 112, 115, 147
    and Arminianism   33–4, 99–100,
        103
    installed as Trinity provost   32–3
    prosecuted by Irish
        Parliament   105–8, 108 n.83,
        113, 116
    role in fellowship dispute at
        Trinity   34–6, 113
    translation to bishopric of Cork and
        Ross   98, 100–2, 103
Charles I   1, 13, 20, 30, 47, 53, 59, 73,
    100, 103–4, 113–14, 136, 143,
    150, 165, 169, 177, 237, 239
    execution   139, 152, 172
    imposes Prayer Book on Scotland   61

and nature of religious policy for
    British Isles   22–3
    see also Laud, William/Laudianism
Scottish coronation   39–40
and the Scottish universities   13,
    39–47, 73–5, 237
and Trinity   27–8, 31, 33, 103
    see also Laud, William/Laudianism
Charles II   153, 157, 236
    Restoration   195–6, 234–5
Charteris, Laurence   186
Chauncy, Charles   214, 220–1, 224–5,
    225, 236
    appointed Harvard president   204
    defence of universities   211–13
Cheeschmaumuk, Caleb   236
Child, Robert   130–1
Christopher, David   37
Church of England   13, 14, 22–3, 25–6,
    32, 39, 41, 57, 99, 233, 236
    and communities overseas   47–8, 51
    and Oxford   54, 103
    see also Book of Common Prayer;
        Laud, William/Laudianism
Church of Ireland   14, 24, 31, 104, 107
    and Cromwellian conquest   141–3,
        144
    reform and alignment with Church
        of England   23, 24–7, 32, 39,
        52, 99
        see also Bramhall, John, bishop
            of Derry; Irish Canons (1634);
            Laud, William/Laudianism;
            Wentworth, Thomas, first earl of
            Strafford
    and Trinity   38, 116, 131, 233
    see also Irish Articles (1615);
        New English; Ussher, James,
        archbishop of Armagh
Church of Scotland   13, 17, 21, 40, 84,
    90, 150–1, 157, 172, 237
    under the Covenanters   59, 68–72,
        95
    see also General Assembly; National
        Covenant
    and Cromwellian conquest   163–4,
        178, 180, 183–4

283

INDEX

Church of Scotland and Cromwellian conquest (*continued*)
  see also Council of Scotland; Gillespie's Charter
  episcopacy and   13, 39–40, 84
    Covenanting opposition to   59, 65–8
    and Restoration   196–7, 233
  Presbyterianism and   13, 17, 20, 40, 96, 156, 196
    renovated under Covenanters   72
  reform and alignment with Church of England   23, 40–1, 43, 46–7
    see also Charles I; Scottish Canons (1636); Scottish Prayer Book; Laud, William/Laudianism
  and the Scottish universities   74, 83, 166
  see also Commission of the General Assembly of the Church of Scotland; Covenanters/Covenanting movement; General Assembly
Civil List (Ireland)   226
Clopton, William   34 n.87, *37*, 106
Cobbet, Thomas   204
Cocke, Robert   106, 115
Collins, John   140
Colville, Alexander   85, 90, 93, 94, 159, 163, *186*
  appointed principal of St Mary's   235
  clashes with Samuel Rutherford over vacant St Mary's divinity professorship   194–5
  nominated for Edinburgh principalship   159
  translated to St Mary's divinity professorship   80, 80 n.132
Colville, John   186
Colville, Samuel   163
Colville, William
  appointed Edinburgh principal   235
  initial nomination for Edinburgh principalship   159–61
Comenius, John Amos   122, 212, 222
  and recruitment to Harvard   119, 120

commencements   123
  see under Harvard College; Trinity College, Dublin; University of Edinburgh; University of Glasgow; University of St Andrews
Commission for Visiting and Regulating the Universities (Cromwellian)   166–7, 173, 176, 182, 184, 185, 191, 193, 194
  duties and membership   156–7
  intervention at Glasgow, Aberdeen, Edinburgh, and St Andrews   157–63
  opponents call for abolition   178, 189
Commission of the General Assembly of the Church of Scotland   154–5
  issues Public Resolutions (1650)   153
Committee for Foreign Plantations (Charles I)   53
Committee for Foreign Plantations (Parliament)   127
Committee of Estates (Scotland)   75
Confederation of Kilkenny   110
Convention Parliament (England)   195
Conway, Robert   34, *37*
Cooper, Thomas   183
Coote, Charles   230
Corbett, Miles   144
Cork Association   217, 225–6
  see also Worth, Edward
Cork House   216
Corlet, Elijah   122, 220
Cottingham, George   29 n.39, *37*
Cotton, John   52, 56, 120, *125*, 145, 213
Coughlan, Richard   115, *116*
Council of Scotland   180, 193, 194, 195, 206
  intervention in Scottish university affairs   183–5, 188–9, 191
  see also Boyle, Roger, Lord Broghill
Council of State (Cromwellian)   177, 184

INDEX

Council of State (Netherlands) 50
Covenanters/Covenanting
    movement 20, 59–61, 96, 101,
    103–4, 118, 119, 135, 152, 157,
    161, 163, 190, 191–2, 203–4,
    219, 227, 237, 238
  curriculum for Scottish
    universities 17, 76–9, 193
  unified curriculum for Scottish
    universities 92–5, 189
  see also Baillie, Robert; General
    Assembly
  initial reform of universities 67–72,
    75
  see also General Assembly
  schism following the
    Engagement 150–1
  see also Engagement, the (1647);
    Protester-Resolutioner
    Controversy
  subscription campaign in Scottish
    universities 61–6
  see also National Covenant (1638);
    Tables, the
  visitations; planting and purging of
    professors *see* General Assembly
Coward, Barry 166
Cowley, Joshua 210, 235 n.1
Craufurd, Thomas 86, 94, *187*
  dictates with student notes supporting
    Charles I 169–70
  nominated for Edinburgh
    principalship 159
Cromwell, Henry 143, 207, 208, 209,
    220, 223, 228–9, 231, 233
  elected Trinity chancellor 206
  favours religious moderates in
    Ireland 210–11, 225
  and the proposed second college in
    Dublin 215–218, 228
  summons Dublin Convention
    (1658) 226–7
  see also Dublin Convention (1658)
Cromwell, Oliver 142, 145, 150, 153,
    162, 172, 192, 220, 226, 228
  conquest and incorporation of
    Scotland 133, 150, 153, 155
  Scottish religious
    settlement 175–6, 180
  see also Gillespie's Charter
  see also Tender of Union
  conquest of Ireland 133
  and Durham College 221–2
  see also Durham College
  and the English universities 134–6
  and the proposed second college in
    Dublin 216–17
  religious policy in Ireland 141–2
  and the Scottish universities 158,
    177–8, 181–2, 184, 189, 191,
    193–4
  see also Commission for Visiting
    and Regulating the Universities
    (Cromwellian); Council of
    Scotland
Cromwell, Richard 192, 228
Cullen, Charles 34–6, 36 n.104, 37,
    107
Cunningham, William, ninth earl of
    Glencairn 196
  rising 172
curriculum 3, 107, 212
  see also Aristotle/Aristotelianism;
    Ramism; Scholastics/
    Scholasticism
  see under Covenanters/Covenanting
    movement; Harvard College;
    Trinity College, Dublin
Cusack, Adam 146, 147, *148*, 209

Dalkeith
  Cromwellian union negotiations
    at 155
  presbytery 161
Dalrymple, James 85
Danforth, Samuel 126, 140, *140*, 141
    n.41
Danforth, Thomas 140, *140*, 225
Davenport, John 47, 56, *125*, 224
  and proposed college at New
    Haven 214–15, 218
  see also New Haven
Deane, Richard 156
Dell, William 134, 212

285

INDEX

Derry, bishop of *see* Bramhall, John, bishop of Derry
Desborough, Samuel   156, 162, 183
  see also Commission for Visiting and Regulating the Universities (Cromwellian)
Dickson, Alexander   185, *187*, 188
Dickson, David   65, 72, 85, 90, 94, 157, 159, 160, 164, 168, 172, 179, 185, *187*, 188, 189
  translation to Edinburgh divinity professorship   154
  translation to Glasgow divinity professorship   79, 80–2, 83
Directory of Worship *see under* Westminster Assembly
Dixwell, John   232
Douglas, Robert   95, 151, 176, 179, 185, 188, 189, 195
Douglas, William   86, 93, *187*
Dow, Frances   156
Downing, Emmanuel   52, 55, 56
Downing, George   123, 124, *126*, 127
Dublin   52, 88, 111, 123, 142, 144, 145, 146, 205, 228, 229
  archbishop of   38, 143
  Castle   230
  county   108 n.76
  fall to Parliamentary forces   112–14, 116
  grammar schools in   109
  Independents in   207–8, 210, 225–6
    see also Winter, Samuel
  mayor of   38
  proposed second college   143, 199–200, 215–18, 223, 228–9, 236
  University of *see* Trinity College, Dublin
Dublin Association (1659)   227, 228
Dublin Convention (1658)   226–7, 228
Dudley, Thomas   *125*, 203, *225*
Dun, Patrick   63, 78, 85
Dunster, Henry   53, 120, 122, *125*, 128, 138–9, *140*, 141, 146, 156 n.136, 164, 220, 224, 233
  and education of Native Americans   122, 220
    see also Native Americans; *New Englands First Fruits* (1643)
  elected Harvard president   119
  and Harvard charter   139–40, 149
    see also Harvard College
  and the Indian College   218, 219
    see also Harvard College
  rejection of infant baptism and resignation from Harvard   200, 202–5, 207, 208, 211, 214
  requests funding for Harvard   124, 129
Durham, bishop of *see* Neile, Richard, bishop of Durham
Durham College   200, 213, 218, 221–3, 223 n.158, 236
Durham, James   154–5
Durkheim, Émile   2, 3

Eaton, Nathaniel   122, *125*, 128, 202
  Harvard mastership   56, 118–19
Eaton, Samuel   140, *140*, 141 n.41
Edinburgh   59, 61, 62, 80, 82, 89, 93–4, 180, 195
  bishop of *see* Forbes, William, bishop of Edinburgh
  town council   41, 80 n.132, 81, 169, 171
    as authority in Edinburgh University's affairs   11, 71, 86, 182, 185, 193
    and Edinburgh principalship   159–60
    withholds Edinburgh college mace   171
    see also University of Edinburgh
  University of *see* University of Edinburgh
Edward, Alexander   85, 151, *152*, 186
Eliot, John   120, 121, 137, 139, 219
Endecott, John   55, 120
Engagement, the (1647)   89–90, 150
  anti-Engager visitations and purges of Scottish universities   150–3
    see also General Assembly
English Parliament *see* Barebones

INDEX

Parliament; Convention
  Parliament; Long Parliament;
  Rump Parliament
English Privy Council   51
Episcopacy/Episcopalians
  in Ireland   205, 209, 229
  in Scotland *see under* Church of
    Scotland
Erskine, Robert   187
Eton College   181, 223 n.158

Feasant, Thomas   34–6, *37*, 107
Fenwick, George   156, 162, 163
Fife synod   195–6
First Book of Discipline (1560)   73, 80,
  92
Fitzgerald, William   29
Fleetwood, Charles   205–7
Floyd, John   28–9, 28 n.38
Floyd, William   28–9, 28 n.37, *37*
Forbes, John, of Corse   45, 63, 91, 93
  deposed by Covenanters   88–9
  initial opposition to National
    Covenant   64
  see also Aberdeen Doctors
Forbes, Patrick, bishop of Aberdeen   41
  reforms of King's College   44–5
Forbes, Robert   85, *186*
Forbes, William, bishop of
    Edinburgh   40, 41, 88
Forbes, William, King's College
    student   88
Forbes, William, regent, University of
    Edinburgh   187
Ford, Alan   27, 28
Forrester, Duncan   86, 94, *187*
Forret, David   62
Forsyth, David   85
Fubbings, John   37
Fyeagh, James   109

Gaidhealtachd (Scotland)   95, 219
Games, Alison   7
Gardyne, Alexander   63, 86, 87
Garthwaite, John   34 n.87, *37*
Gassendi, Pierre   216 n.107
General Assembly   13, 46, 60, 61, 96,
  125, 160, 184, 189, 191, 196, 235

and bursars/bursaries   92–3, 95
censures and expels Protesters   153,
  158
disbandment by Robert
  Lilburne   163–4, 172, 178
Glasgow Assembly (1638)   67–72,
  75
  Glasgow Declaration   68, 76
  and Glasgow University's contested
    commission   69–70
  see also Hamilton, James, third
    marquis of Hamilton; Strang,
    John
  issues visitation commissions for
    Aberdeen and Glasgow   70–2,
    71 n.71
  prosecutes Patrick Panter   68–9
    see also Panter, Patrick
  repudiates episcopacy, High
    Commission, Prayer Book   67–8
  revives acts for visitations of
    universities   67–8
nature of early Covenanting
  visitations   70–2, 75–80, 78
  n.117
orders and oversees creation of unified
    curriculum   92–5
  see also Covenanters/Covenanting
    movement
and overtures to Scottish
    Parliament   73–4
planting of professors in Scottish
    universities   80–4
  see also Baillie, Robert; Dickson,
    David; Rutherford, Samuel
purging of professors opposed to
    National Covenant   84–91
  purges Aberdeen Doctors   86–9
visitations of Scottish universities
  anti-Engager visitations and
    purges   151–2
  see also Commission of the General
    Assembly of the Church of
    Scotland
General Convention, Dublin
  (1660)   230–2
Geneva Academy   77
Gilbert, Claudius   207–8, 207 n.50

287

INDEX

Gilbert, William 105
Gillespie, George 62
Gillespie, Patrick 153, 172, 183, *186*, 194–5
  collusion with Cromwellian commissioners 161, 162
    see also Commission for Visiting and Regulating the Universities (Cromwellian)
  and the Glasgow principalship 154–5, 179, 189, 190–1
  clashes with Robert Baillie 173–4
  installed as principal by Cromwellians 158–9
  removed at Restoration 235, 235 n.6
  secures funding for Glasgow 181
  and proposed religious settlement of Scotland 175–6, 178
  see also Gillespie's Charter
Gillespie's Charter 168, 175–81, 183, 184, 195, 197
Ginnings, Thomas 37
Glasgow
  archbishop *see* Lindsay, Patrick, archbishop of Glasgow
  Blackfriars Church 82, 154
  burgh 6, 67, 80–1, 168 n.6, 171, 190–1
  Cathedral/High Church 64, 81, 82, 154
  presbytery 158
  University of *see* University of Glasgow
Glasgow Assembly *see under* General Assembly
Glasgow Declaration *see under* General Assembly
Gleg, Thomas 85, 151, *151*
Glen, John 179
Glencairn, earl of *see* Cunningham, William, ninth earl of Glencairn
Goffe, William 232
Goodwin, Thomas 141, 144, 175 n.39, 221, 226
Gookin, Daniel 232
Gordon, George 187

Gordon, Patrick 86, 94, *152*
Gordon, William 45, 63, 87
Gorges, Robert 231
Gorski, Philip 5
Gorton, Samuel 137
'Great Migration' (New England) 47, 52
Greek
  instruction at Harvard 122, 123
  instruction at the Scottish universities 77, 78
  requirement for entry to Trinity 229
Gresham College 223 n.158
Guild, William 64, 66, 67, 86, *151*
  installed as King's principal by Covenanters 87
  removed as King's principal by anti-Engagers 151
  replaced as King's principal by Cromwellians 162
Gurdon, John (or Brampton) 138
Guthrie, James 63, 151, 173, 175, 176, 180
Guthrie, John, bishop of Moray 45

Hachting, Johannes 49
Haggis, George 109 n.90
'halfway' covenant 224, 227, 236
Hamilton, Archibald 30–1, 107, 108
Hamilton, James, third marquis of Hamilton 65, 67, 70
Hamilton, William 63, 85
Harding, John 34, 36, 37, 102, 108, 108 n.76, 112
Harlakenden, Roger *125*
Harrison, Thomas 206, 208, 210
Hartlib Circle 134, 199–200, 213
  and Durham College 221–2
  and the proposed second college in Dublin 215–16
  see also Hartlib, Samuel
Hartlib, Samuel 50, 102, 130, 138, 147, 212, 214, 215, 221
Harvard College 9, 13, 15, 18–19, 20–1, 53, 58, 59, 93, 97–9, 107, *125*–6, 136, 138, *140*, 146, 157, 198, 199–201, 208, 211, 213, *225*, 232

288

INDEX

Board of Overseers 11–12, 56, 118, 124–5, 126, 127, 128, 140, 141, 149, 202–4, 220–1, 236
  Charles Chauncy appointed president 204
    see also Chauncy, Charles
  Charter of 1650 139–41, 149, 218
  controversy over Dunster's rejection of infant baptism 202–4
    see also Dunster, Henry
  donations to college 123–4, 227–8
  early curriculum and library 122–3, 129
    see also New Englands First Fruits (1643)
  and education and conversion of Native Americans 57, 120, 121, 139
  Indian College 57 n.235, 218–21, 236, 238
  first commencement 123, 171
    see also New Englands First Fruits (1643)
  'Formula of Admission' 128
  founding and early years 11, 24, 48, 55–7, 117–18, 239
    Dunster appointed first president 119
  graduates leave New England to staff republican government 139–40, 164, 201–2
  and New England society 129–32, 135, 223–5
    relations with Massachusetts General Court 56, 125–6, 202–4
    relations with United Colonies 125–7, 128–30
  and New Haven college project 214–15, 216, 218
  and Ramism 10
  and the Restoration 236
Harvard, John 55
Hatfield, Alexander 34, 37, 106, 108, 108 n.76
Hay, James 63, 85

Haynes, John 214–15
Hebrew
  instruction at Harvard 122, 139
  instruction at the Scottish universities 77, 78, 79, 177 n.162, 189
  professorship at Edinburgh 80, 83, 185
    see also Dickson, Alexander; Otto, Julius Conradus
  instruction at Trinity 107
  professorship at Trinity 102, 229
    see also Ravius, Christian; Stearne, John
Heidelberg Catechism 49, 76
Heidelberg University 77
Henderson, Alexander 61, 65–6, 68–9, 71 n.71, 72, 78, 83, 83 n.156, 90, 194
  rectorship at Edinburgh 83–4, 93
Henrico College 53–5, 57, 238
Henrietta Maria 49
Hepburn, Andrew 63
Herbert, William, third earl of Pembroke 1
Herbertsone, John 159
Hibbins, William 120
Higginson, Francis 52
High Commission (Ireland) 104,
High Commission (Scotland) 40, 67, 72, 180
Hill, Roger 228
Hindle, Steve 10
Hoar, Leonard 213 n.91
Holyoke, Edward 204
Honeyman, Robert 85
Hooke, William 214, 227
Hooker, Samuel *225*
Hooker, Thomas 52
Horgan, Malachy 109
Hotson, Howard 5, 9, 123, 237
Howard, Charles 183
Howie, Robert 62, 66, 82, *91*
  demits St Mary's principalship 89
  initial opposition to National Covenant 64
Howlett, Richard 102–3
Hoyle, Joshua 52

289

INDEX

Hoyle, Nathaniel 34–6, *37*, 106, 111, 114–15, *115*, 115 n.29, 121, 146, 147, *148*, *210*
Hubbard, William 123
Huguenots 59, 92
  academies 77, 79, 92
  see also Sedan, Academy of
Humphrey, John *125*
Hunton, Philip 222
Hutchinson, Daniel 145

Iacoomis, Joel 236
Ince, Randal 36
Ince, William 34, *37*
Independents/Independency 125, 128, 135, 136, 156
  in Ireland 141, 146, 148, 149, 200, 205, 211, 218, 225–7, 229, 231
  and Trinity 206–10, 207 n.50, 211, 212, 217, 223, 228, 232
  see also Dublin Association (1659); Winter, Samuel
  in Scotland 151, 161–3, 166, 175, 176, 179, 189
  see also Aberdeen
Innes, Patrick 63, 67, 86, 87
Instrument of Government (1653) 155, 175, 205
Ireton, Henry 144
Irish Articles (1615) 14, 26, 27, 31
Irish Canons (1634) 26, 35, 38, 46
  educational codes 26–7
  see also Irish Convocation (1634); Laud, William/Laudianism
Irish Convocation (1634) 26, 32, 39, 113, 237
Irish Parliament 98, 103, 111, 113–14, 116, 130, 227
  prosecution of Laud's Trinity reforms 58, 104–10, 108 n.83, 112, 238
  see also Chappell, William
Irish Privy Council 112, 113
Irish Rebellion (1641) 98–9, 103, 108, 110, 120, 131, 147
  impact on Trinity 111–12, 114, 117
Irvine presbytery 81

Jaffray, Alexander 162
James VI/I 23, 46, 60, 61, 76
  and Henrico College 53–4
  and the Scottish universities 40–1, 43, 44, 66
  and Trinity 24–5, 28, 145
James VII/II 236
Jameson, Alexander *186*, 194
Johnston, Archibald, of Wariston 61, 66, 83 n.156, 161, 173, 175, 180
Johnston, William 63, *187*
Jones, Henry 143, 218, 231
Jones, John 144
Jones, Michael 114, 116
Jordan, Richard 29, 36

Keckermann, Bartholomäus 10, 122
Keith, George, fifth earl Marischal 45
Keith, Robert 85
Kerdiff, Christopher 108,
Kerdiff, John *37*, 113, 115, *115*
Kerr, Gilbert 194
Kilmore and Ardagh, bishop of *see* Bedell, William
King's College, Aberdeen 15, 41, 63, 71, 74, 86, 168, 181, 182, *187*, 220
  anti-Engager visitation and purges 151, *151*–2
  commissioners to Glasgow Assembly 67, 69
  Cromwellian visitation and planting of principalship 157, 162
  see also Commission for Visiting and Regulating the Universities (Cromwellian); Row, John
  founding 11
  General Assembly visitation and purge of Aberdeen Doctors 86–9, *91*
  see also Aberdeen Doctors; General Assembly
  granted rents of bishopric of Aberdeen 74, 74 n.93
  and 'King Charles University' 74
  New Foundation and Bishop Forbes' reforms 44–5, 44 n.150, 71

290

relationship with Marischal College   45
opposition to National Covenant   64, 73
see also Aberdeen Doctors
and the Restoration   235
staff contributes to Covenanter unified curriculum   93
see also Covenanters/Covenanting movement
student violence with Marischal   191–2
see also Marischal College, Aberdeen
King's Covenant (1638)   65, 89
see also National Covenant (1638); Strang, John
Kirk *see* Church of Scotland
Kuffeler, Johannes Sibertus   222

Lamont, John   169
Lang, Zurishaddai   169 n.8
Large Declaration (1639)   73
see also Charles I
Laud, William/Laudianism   1–2, 22–3, 47, 57, 65, 117, 136, 141, 165, 212, 237, 239
accedes to archbishopric of Canterbury   48
and Church of England   13, 23, 32, 41
and English universities   22, 55, 56, 133, 142, 204
Oxford chancellorship   22, 32, 69
and Irish Canons   26–7, 35
see also Bramhall, John, bishop of Derry; Irish Canons (1634); Irish Convocation (1634); Wentworth, Thomas, first earl of Strafford
library of   129
and puritans in Netherlands and New England   24, 47–8, 51, 54, 56, 139
appointed to lead Committee for Foreign Plantations   53
reforms prosecuted by Irish Parliament   104–7, 110

see also Chappell, William; Irish Parliament
and Scottish Canons   46–7
see also Scottish Canons (1636)
and Scottish Prayer Book   43, 58, 59, 62
see also Scottish prayer Book
and the Scottish universities   39–42, 45
visit to St Andrews with Charles I   43
visit to St Andrews with James VI/I   40–1
trial   47
and Trinity   20, 27, 30–9, 44, 49, 51, 99–103, 116, 131, 237
appointed chancellor   24, 25, 32
succeeded by Ormond   114
plants Chappell and sympathetic fellows   32–5
statutes   36–9, 111, 114, 115, 228, 235
see also Trinity College, Dublin
laureations *see* commencements
Learmonth, Robert   186
Leckey, William   208, *210*
Leiden University   48, 49, 50
Leighton, Alexander   160
Leighton, Robert   182, 185, *187*, 190
installed as Edinburgh principal by Cromwellians   160–1
see also Colville, William; Commission for Visiting and Regulating the Universities (Cromwellian)
translated to bishopric of Dunblane   235
Leslie, Alexander   86
Leslie, John, earl of Rothes   196
Leslie, William   63, 64, 67, *91*
deposed by Covenanters   87
see also Aberdeen Doctors
Leverich, William   214–15, 218
Lilburne, Robert   163, 172–3, 221
Lincoln's Inn   147, 209
Lindsay, David   82, 94
Lindsay, Patrick, archbishop of Glasgow   41, 45

INDEX

Lingard, Richard   235 n.1
Livingston, John   176, 178
Locke, Thomas   113, *116*
Lockhart, George   158
Lockhart, William   183
Loftus, Dudley   112, *115*, 218, 231
Long Parliament   103
  Irish Committee   105, 114
  reform of Oxford and Cambridge   133–6
  relations with New England   118, 120, 128, 129, 130
  restoration   195, 231
Lothian and Tweeddale synod   160
Lovelock, George   37
Ludlow, Edmund   144, 229–30
Lundie, John   63, 67, 69, 71, 86, 87
Lutheranism   76
  universities   10
Lyon, Patrick   *186*
Lysaght, John   109
Lysaght, Thaddeus   29

Maag, Karin   9
Maccovius, Johannes   143
MacKenzie, John   63
MacKenzie, Kirsteen   6
Mahaffy, J.P.   148
Maine, Robert   63, 78 n.117, 85, *91*
March, John   156
  see also Commission for Visiting and Regulating the Universities (Cromwellian)
Marischal College, Aberdeen   15, 41, 63, 72, 81, 85, *91*, 94, 151, 175, 181, 182, *186–7*
  and Aberdeen Doctors   64
  constitutional relationship with King's College   45
  founding   11
  General Assembly visitation   78
    see also General Assembly
  granted provisions in Gillespie's Charter   177
  granted rents of bishopric of Aberdeen   74, 74 n.93
  and Independency   162, 178, 179, 189

  and 'King Charles University'   74
  student violence with King's College   191–2
    see also King's College, Aberdeen
Marsden, Gamaliel   208, *210*, 230 n.206
Marshall, Thomas   34, 36, 47
Martin, Anthony, bishop of Meath   35, 145
  assumes Trinity's provostship   113–16
  testifies against Chappell in Irish Parliament   108
Martine, George   62, 64, 66
Martine Jr, George   63, 85, 151, *152*, 188
Massachusetts Bay Company   49, 55, 57
  and Massachusetts charter   52–3, 54, 118, 120
Massachusetts General Court   11, 93, 117, 118, 120, 124–5, 128, 214, 223, 224, 227
  and the Board of Overseers   56, 126
  and the Cambridge Platform   130–1
  and Dunster's rejection of infant baptism   201–4, 211
  grants Harvard Charter   140–1, 149
  and Harvard's founding   55
  and United Colonies   126, 130, 137
Mather, Cotton   117, 209
Mather, Increase   208, 229
Mather, Richard   204
Mather, Samuel   126, 127, 140, *140*, 141, 141 n.41, 208, *210*, 210, 229
Mathew, Tobias, archbishop of York   53
Maxwell, George, of Pollock   177 n.55
Maxwell, John, bishop of Ross   45
Maxwell, Patrick   63
Mayhew, Thomas   139, 219
McCafferty, John   26
McGowen, James   *187*
McWard, Robert   179, *187*
Meade, Garrett   37
Meath, bishop of   38
  see also Martin, Anthony
Mede, Joseph   27, 30, 31, 102–3

INDEX

Meldrum, George *187*
Melville, Andrew 17, 43, 44, 44 n.150, 45, 78, 78 n.117
Melville, Elizabeth, lady Culross 163
Menzies, John 63, 85, 151, *186*
 and Aberdeen Independents 162
 and Gillespie's Charter 175–8
Mercer, James 63
Mercer, Robert 88
Middleton, Alexander 63, 86, 87, 151, *152*
Middleton, George 86
Miller, Perry 18, 123
Mitchell, Jonathan *126*, 140, *140*, 141 n.41, 236
Mocket, Richard 46
Monck, George 172, 180, 181, 183, 192, 195, 230
Moody, Joshua *225*
Moore, Andrew *187*
Moray, bishop of *see* Guthrie, John, bishop of Moray
Morison, Samuel Eliot 15, 18, 98, 119, 138
Morrill, John 23, 26, 176 n.49
Moseley, Edward 156, 158, 159, 161, 162
 see also Commission for Visiting and Regulating the Universities (Cromwellian)
Moulson, Ann 123
Muir, William 85, 94, 181, *186*
 and Aberdeen Independents 162
 purged from Marischal principalship at Restoration 235
Munro, David 63, 85
Munster 217, 226
 Trinity College, Dublin's land in 145–6, 148 n.91
Murray, Patrick 151, *152*

National Covenant (1638) 13, 20, 59, 60–2, 128, 161
 Cromwellians outlaw subscription in universities 176
 outlawed at the Restoration 196
 Scottish universities' opposition to 64–7, 73
 subscription mandated in Scottish universities 72, 76, 77
 see also Covenanters/Covenanting movement; General Assembly; King's Covenant (1638); Solemn League and Covenant (1643)
Native Americans
 conversion and education of 120–2, 123, 137–9, 142, 200, 214, 218, 219
 and Harvard 57
  Indian College 219–21
 and Henrico College 53–4
 see also New England Company; *New Englands First Fruits* (1643)
 see also Pequot War; Powhatan Uprising
Native Irish 13–14, 110, 121, 149
 and Trinity 15, 24, 25, 111, 144, 220
 students 106, 109, 109 n.87
Negative Confession (1581) 65–6, 68
Neile, Richard, bishop of Durham 30
Nevay, David 85, 94, 151, *151*
New College, St Andrews *see* St Mary's College, St Andrews
New England Company 121, 137–8, 141, 149, 218, 236
New Englands First Fruits (1643) 117, 123–5, 131, 138, 171
 account of Harvard's early curriculum and library 122–3
 account of Harvard's first commencement 123
 and the conversion of Native Americans 120–1
New English 7, 14, 103, 104, 118, 121, 148, 230
 favoured by Henry Cromwell 200, 211, 217, 223, 244
 'Old Protestants' 142, 200, 211, 218, 231, 235
 and Trinity 20, 28, 33, 34, 99, 101, 106–7, 131, 141, 149, 237–8
 students 25, 29, 109–10, 130
New Haven 126

293

New Haven (*continued*)
  proposed college   200, 214–16, 218, 223, 233
  see also Davenport, John
Newman, William   32, 34, 37
Neyland, Daniel   115, *116*
Nichols, Richard   37
Norbury, Robert   208
Norie, Robert   85
Norton, John   204, 213
Nowell, Samuel   *225*
Nye, Philip   175 n.39

Oakes, Urian   *140*, 141 n.41
Ogilvie, Robert   63, 87
Old English   13–14, 110
  and Trinity   29, 106
  students   109, 109 n.88
Oliver, William   208
Ormond, duke of *see* Butler, James, first duke of Ormond
Otto, Julius Conradus   80, 80 n.132, 86, 185, *187*
Owen, Andrew   156, 162
  see also Commission for Visiting and Regulating the Universities (Cromwellian)
Owen, John   134, 149, 162, 175 n.39, 189, 226
  and Trinity   142–5, 209

Panter, Patrick   62, 64, 66, 89
  deposed from St Mary's divinity professorship   68–9, 71, 77, 82, 91
Pareus, David   76
Parsons, Talcott   2
Parsons, William   111–14
Patterson, John   186
Pelham, Herbert   124, *125*, 227
Pemberton, John   84
Pemberton, Samuel   84
Pembroke, earl of *see* Herbert, William, third earl of Pembroke
Pepper, Christopher   106, *116*
Pepper, Gilbert   37, *115*
Pequot War   117, 118

Perceval, Thomas   37, *115*
Perth Articles (1618)   39, 42, 64, 65, 67, 68, 87
Pestana, Carla   8, 137
Peter, Hugh   56, 120, 123, 125, *125*, 129
  and Rotterdam college project   49–51
Petty, William   147, 205
Peyran, Charles   194 n.155
Pillans, James   86, *187*
Pitcairn, Alexander   186
Plymouth colony   126
Pocock, J.G.A.   7–8
Poole, Matthew   236 n.13
Powhatan Uprising   54
Prendergast, Paul   109, 109 n.88
Presbyterians/Presbyterianism   175, 189
  in Ireland   142, 205, 225
  repudiated in New England   126, 130
  see also Cambridge Platform
  in Scotland *see under* Church of Scotland
  see also Engagement, the (1647); Solemn League and Covenant (1643); Westminster Assembly
Preston, John   145,
Preston, William   186
Price, John   208, *210*, 230 n.206
Price, Thomas   36
Protester-Resolutioner Controversy   153, 161, 167, 173–4, 175–6, 178, 181, 183, 197
Protesters (Remonstrants)   153, 160, 161–2, 166, 172, 184, 193, 195, 196, 235
  and the Scottish universities   153–5, 158–9, 167, 168, 173, 179–80, 187–9, 194–5
  see also Gillespie, Patrick
Public Resolutions (1650)   153, 154
  see also Resolutioners
Puritans/Puritanism   12–13, 14, 19, 23, 30, 33, 57, 58, 121, 160, 200
  and advancement of learning   134–5, 213

and Harvard 55, 98, 232, 236
in the Netherlands 48, 50–1
and New England 47–8, 49, 52,
    55–6, 117–18, 126–8, 131, 218
and Trinity 112–13, 148

Quakers 142, 211, 223, 236

Rae, John 63
Rait, Robert 88
Rait, William 86, 194–6
Ramism 10, 18, 44, 57, 58
    and Harvard 56, 122
    and the Scottish universities 17, 122
    and Trinity 14, 38, 52, 107
    and the University of Franeker 49, 51
    see also Ramus, Petrus
Ramsay, Andrew 93
Ramsay, Robert 82–3, 154–5
Ramus, Petrus 10, 17, 58, 212
Ranken, Robert 62, 63, 71, 86, *91*
Ravius, Christian 102, 138, 139
Ray, John 63, 85
Raymond, William 37, 115, *116*
Reformed Protestantism 21, 61, 92, 96, 121, 165,
    and Church of Ireland 14, 107
    and Church of Scotland 13
    and Harvard 56, 118, 125, 129, 141
    and higher education 5, 7, 9–10, 12, 24, 49, 51, 58, 59, 212, 223, 234, 237
    and the Scottish universities 44, 60, 66, 69, 71, 76–7, 79
    and sects 199, 205
    and Trinity 25, 28, 30, 33, 39, 52, 55, 103, 148
    see also Calvinism/Calvinists; Puritans/Puritanism
regents/regenting (Scottish universities) 11, 17, 78, 152
Reid, James, of Pitlethie 94
Reid, Steven 17
Resolutioners 153, 155, 160, 172, 176, 184, 185, 188, 196

and the Scottish universities 153–4, 167, 168, 172, 174, 179–80, 187, 189, 194–5, 235
see also Public Resolutions (1650)
Rhodes, Edward 183
Rich, Robert, second earl of Warwick 127
Ritschel, Georg 222
Roberts, Edward 205
Robertson, Richard 158, 173, *186*
Robinson-Hammerstein, Helga 15, 19, 98
Roch, Patrick 111
Rogers, Ezekiel 145
Ross, Alexander 64
    see also Aberdeen Doctors
Ross, bishop of see Maxwell, John, bishop of Ross
Ross, Gilbert 63, 87, *91*
Rothes, earl of see Leslie, John, earl of Rothes
Rotterdam
    proposed college 50–1, 55, 56, 57
    see also Peter, Hugh
Rous, Francis 157, 221
Row, John 162 n.178, 181, *187*
    and Aberdeen Independents 162
    installed as King's principal by Cromwellians 162
    see also Commission for Visiting and Regulating the Universities (Cromwellian); Guild, William
    and legal code for King's 191–2
    purged from King's principalship at Restoration 235
Rule, Gilbert 162, *187*
Rump Parliament 136, 150, 175 n.39, 195, 229, 230
    Act for Promoting and Propagating the Gospel of Jesus Christ in New England (1649) 137–9
    see also New England Company
    Act for the Advancement of the Gospel and Learning in Ireland (1650) 142–4
    establishes trustees to oversee Trinity 143

INDEX

Rump Parliament (*continued*)
  commissioners in Ireland intervene in Trinity's affairs   144, 146–7
  and the Scottish universities *see* Commission for Visiting and Regulating the Universities (Cromwellian)
Russell, Conrad   23 n.4
Russell, Richard   222
Rutherford, Samuel   72, 85, 89, 90, 94, 153, 161, 175, 179, 180, *186*, 187
  and dispute over vacant St Mary's divinity professorship   194–6
  purged from St Mary's principalship at Restoration   235
  translation to St Mary's divinity professorship   69, 81–2, 83

St Andrews   82, 171
  archbishop *see* Spottiswoode, John, archbishop of St Andrews; Sharp, James
  presbytery   68, 69, 72, 163, 195–6
  University of *see* University of St Andrews
St Giles Cathedral (Edinburgh)   41
St Leonard's College, St Andrews   62–3, 64, 78, 85, 94, 163, *186*, 194
  anti-Engager visitation and purges   151, *151–2*
  founding   11
  initial opposition to National Covenant   64
  see also University of St Andrews
St Mary's College, St Andrews   43, 44, 62, 68, 79, 81, 85, 89, 90, 91, 153, 163, *186*, 194 n.155, 235
  as Scotland's principal seminary   80, 80 n.133
  dispute over vacant divinity professorship   193–7
  see also Rutherford, Samuel; Sharp, James
  founding   11
  initial opposition to National Covenant   64

  see also University of St Andrews
St Salvator's College, St Andrews   41, 62–3, 78, 85, 163, 179, *186*
  anti-Engager visitation and purges   151, *151–2*
  founding   11
  initial opposition to National Covenant   64
  James Wood's translation to vacant principalship   187–8, 194, 195
  see also University of St Andrews
Saltonstall, Henry   123, 138, 156 n.136
Saltonstall, Richard   52, 138, 227–8
Saltonstall Jr, Richard   156, 156 n.136, 157, 159
  see also Commission for Visiting and Regulating the Universities (Cromwellian)
Sandilands, James   63, 87, *91*
Sandilands, Patrick   85, 86, *187*, 192
Saunders, Francis   208, *210*, 232
Savoy Declaration   226–7
Schmitt, Charles   7
Scholastics/Scholasticism   3, 69, 77, 129
Scott, Alexander   62, 85
Scott, Joseph   208, *210*
Scottish Canons (1636)   24, 44, 67, 237
  educational codes   46
  see also Laud, William
Scottish Parliament   60, 61, 104
  Act of Classes (1649)   150–1
  Coronation Parliament   39, 44
  and the Covenanting settlement   73–5
  see also General Assembly
  'Education Act' (1646)   93
  and the Restoration   235
  Act of Rescissory (1661)   196
Scottish Prayer Book   40, 43, 44, 47, 58, 59, 61–2, 67, 237
  see also Charles I; Laud, William/ Laudianism
Scottish Privy Council   61, 235 n.6
Scougal, Patrick   194
Scroggie, Alexander   63, 64, 87, *91*
  see also Aberdeen Doctors

INDEX

Scroope, Adrian 183
Second Book of Discipline (1578) 66
Sedan, Academy of 80, 194, 194 n.155
Seele, Thomas 37, 106, 115, *115*, *210*, 235
   appointed Trinity provost 232
Semple, William 85
Sharp, James 85, 188–9, 192
   appointed archbishop of St Andrews 197
   and the St Mary's divinity professorship 194–7
Sharp, John 63, 86
Sharpe, Kevin 1
Shepard, Thomas 56, 117, *125*, 129–30, 225
   Clear Sunshine of the Gospel (1648) 138
Sheridan, Patrick *210*, 235 n.1
Shortall, Leonard 109 n.91
Sibbald, James 63, 64, 67, 88, *91*
   see also Aberdeen Doctors
Sibbes, Richard 27
Sinclair, George 179, *187*
Sinclair, John 85
Smith, Hugh *187*
Smyth, George 156, 159, 162
   see also Commission for Visiting and Regulating the Universities (Cromwellian)
Society for the Propagation of the Gospel in New England *see* New England Company
Solemn League and Covenant (1643) 75, 126, 128, 150, 155, 176, 196
Spang, William 66, 80, 94, 166, 188
Spottiswoode, John, archbishop of St Andrews 41, 42
Spreule, John 159
Sprigg, William 222
Stanton, John 220
Stanton, Thomas 220
Stanton Sr, Thomas 220
Starr, Comfort *126*, 140, *140*, 141 n.41
States General (Netherlands) 48
Stearne, John 146, 147, *148*, 209, *210*, 213, 217, 229, 232

Steele, William 137
Stevenson, Andrew 63
Stevenson, David 43, 84
Stoughton, Israel *125*
Stoughton, John 57
Stout, Harry 52
Strachan, John *187*
Strachan, William 63
Strafford, earl of *see* Wentworth, Thomas, first earl of Strafford
Strang, John 63, 79, 81, 82, 85, *91*, 94, *151*, 154, 174, 235 n.6
   contested Glasgow Assembly commission 70
   examination of dictates and forced retirement 89–90, 93
   opposition to National Covenant and treatise on King's Covenant 64–5, 66
Suttie, Andrew 94, *187*
Swinton, John 183
Syler, Edmund 156
   see also Commission for Visiting and Regulating the Universities (Cromwellian)
Symmes, Zachariah 225
Symner, Miles 146–7, *148*, 209, *210*, 217
Synod of Dort 49, 51, 76, 100

Tables, the 58, 64, 73
   bans use of prayer book in Scottish universities 62
Teate, Faithful 112–13, 112 n.109, 114, *115*
   appointed Trinity provost 112
Temple, William 25, 27, 28, 29, 106 n.61, 113
Tender of Union 155, 157, 171 n.17
   Scots refuse to subscribe in the universities 169, 171–2
Thomas, David 29
Thomson, John *186*
Thurloe, John 189, 210
Tilly, Charles 5
Tonge, Israel 221, 222
Travers, Joseph 146, 147, *148*, 209, 232

INDEX

Treaty of Breda 153
Treaty of London 73
Trinity College, Dublin 9, 11, 15–16, 19, 20–1, 27–30, 36–7, 44, 47, 55, 59, 97, 98–9, *115–16*, 116–17, 118, 119, 121, 124, 131–2, 139, 141, *148*, 157, 164, 198, 199–201, *210*, 213, 227, 229, 236, 237, 238, 239
  and Catholics/Catholicism 16, 39, 110–11
  and colonial colleges 54–5
  and Cromwellian trustees 142–9, 156, 183, 208, 215
    see also Rump Parliament
  curriculum 38–9, 52, 107, 217
    Irish language instruction 28, 106–110, 148
  founding 11
  and General Convention (Dublin) 230–2
  Henry Cromwell elected chancellor 206
  and Independency 200, 205–6, 207–11, 223
    see also Winter, Samuel
  and Irish Parliament 58, 136
    prosecutes Laudian reforms 104–10
  and Irish Rebellion 111–12, 114, 117
    lack of commencements post-Rebellion 123
  and James VI/I 24–5
  John Owen proposes reforms of 141–2, 144
  and Laud 24, 25–6, 27, 30–9, 40–1, 45, 48, 49, 51, 99–103
    appointed chancellor 24, 25–6, 32
    plants Chappell and sympathetic fellows 32–5
    statutes 36–9, 42, 105, 111, 114, 115, 128, 228, 235
    see also Chappell, William; Laud, William/Laudianism; Ussher, James, archbishop of Armagh; Wentworth, Thomas, first earl of Strafford
  and Native Irish 15–16, 24–5
  and New English 14, 106, 110, 130, 135, 148
    disputes over fellowships 28–9
  Ormond appointed chancellor 114
  and proposed second college in Dublin 215–18, 227–8
  provost 11, 24–5, 27–33, 34–6, 38, 99–101, 103, 105, 108–10, 112–14, 116, 145–6, 206, 207, 228, 232, 235
    see also Bedell, William; Chappell, William; Martin, Anthony; Seele, Thomas; Teate, Faithful; Temple, William; Ussher, Robert; Washington, Richard; Winter, Samuel
  and Ramism 10, 38, 52, 56, 107
  and the Restoration 232, 235
  students 109–10, 109 n.88–91, 112–13, 232
  visitors 29, 34–6, 38, 105
Tucker, Marie-Claude 194 n.155
Tullideph, William 186
Tweedie, William 85, 86, *187*

Ulster
  plantation 24, 24 n.10, 54
    Scottish settlers in 13
  Trinity's lands in 145–6, 148 n.91
United Colonies 126–7, 129, 130, 131, 137, 138, 139, 218, 220
University of Cambridge 2, 9, 11, 22, 22 n.3, 40, 41, 43, 52, 66, 98, 105, 119, 123, 133–4, 164, 181, 212, 222, 226
  Christ's College 31, 48
    provides amenable fellows to Laudian Trinity 33–4, 36, 106
  Emmanuel College 16, 28, 29, 113, 145, 214
    Harvard's connection to 55, 56, 57
  Magdalene College 199
  St Catharine's College 84

INDEX

Sidney Sussex College   102, 147
Trinity College   16, 148, 204
University of Dublin *see* Trinity College, Dublin
University of Edinburgh   15, 41–2, 44, 63, 78, 80 n.133, 86, 154, 157, 177, 178, 184, *187*, 188
   Cromwellian visitation and planting of principalship   157, 159–61
   English students request to attend   83
   see also Colville, William; Commission for Visiting and Regulating the Universities (Cromwellian); Leighton, Robert
   founding   11
   granted rents of bishoprics of Edinburgh and Orkney   74, 83
   Hebrew professorship   80, 83, 185
   see also Council of Scotland; Dickson, Alexander; Otto, Julius Conradus
   initial reception of National Covenant   62
   expulsion of regents opposed to National Covenant   71, 73, 86, *91*
   see also Broun, John; Ranken, Robert
   library   82–3
   see also Henderson, Alexander
   opposition to Cromwellian regime   168, 169, 174
   commencements held in private under Cromwellian regime   169–71
   see also Craufurd, Thomas
   petitions Cromwellian regime for aid   182
   and the Restoration   235
   staff contributes to Covenanter unified curriculum   93–4
   see also Covenanters/Covenanting movement
University of Franeker   48–50, 56, 118
University of Glasgow   15, 41–2, 44, 63, 73, 85, 89, *91*, *151*, 152 n.105, 157, 162, 175, 179, 184, 186–7, 188, 220
   contested commission at Glasgow Assembly   69–70, 72
   see also General Assembly; Strang, John
   Cromwellian visitation and planting of principalship   157–9
   see also Commission for Visiting and Regulating the Universities (Cromwellian); Gillespie, Patrick
   deterioration of learning under Gillespie   189–91
   divinity professorships   80–3, 153–5, 158
   see also Baillie, Robert; Dickson, David; Durham, James; Young, John
   founding   11
   General Assembly visitations   71, 78
   orders divinity teaching   79
   revives regenting   78
   and Gillespie's Charter   177–8, 180–1, 182
   granted rents of bishopric of Galloway   74
   initial opposition to National Covenant   64–5, 66
   see also Strang, John; Wilkie, William
   Melvillian *Nova Erectio*   44 n.150
   opposition to Cromwellian regime   168, 173–4
   commencements not held under Cromwellian regime   169, 171
   student disobedience   174
   see also Baillie, Robert
   and the Restoration   235
   Robert Baillie's proposals for the reform of   76–8
   see also Baillie, Robert
   staff contributes to Covenanter unified curriculum   93–4
   see also Covenanters/Covenanting movement

INDEX

University of Oxford   1, 9, 22, 27, 38, 41, 43, 47, 54, 56, 66, 69, 76, 110, 123, 133–4, 164, 181, 212, 222, 226
  Brasenose College   54, 115, 147
  Corpus Christi College   54
  Laud's chancellorship   1, 2, 22, 25, 32, 39, 40–1
  Magdalen College   141, 144
  Queen's College   142
  St John's College   22, 22 n.2
  University College   54, 103
University of Paris   17
University of St Andrews   15, 41–4, 44 n.150, 62–3, 71, 71 n.71, 72, 81–2, 84, 85, 91, 152, 153, 155, 177, 178, 179, 184, 186, 187, 193, 194
  anti-Engager visitation and purges   151–2, 151–2
  Cromwellian visitation   162–3
  founding   11
  General Assembly visitations   77–9
    see also General Assembly
  granted rents of archbishopric of St Andrews   74, 74 n.92
  initial opposition to National Covenant   64–6, 73
  and James VI/I   40, 43, 44
  opposition to Cromwellian regime   174
    commencements held in private under Cromwellian regime   169, 171
    students support Glencairn's rising   172–3
    petitions Cromwellian regime for aid   182
    staff contributes to Covenanter unified curriculum   93–4
    see also Covenanters/Covenanting movement
  see also St Leonard's College; St Mary's College; St Salvator's College
University of Utrecht   48
Urquhart, Walter   88

Ussher, James, archbishop of Armagh   105, 107, 113, 147
  and Irish Protestant identity   14
  library of   216, 231
  and Trinity   25, 27–9, 29 n.40, 30–1, 38, 100–2, 109, 139
    clashes with Provost Chappell   35–6, 103
    recommends Laud assume Trinity's chancellorship   32
    testifies against Chappell in Irish Parliament   108
Ussher, Robert   27–8, 28 n.38, 32, 36, 118
  elected Trinity provost   31
  translated to archdeaconry of Meath   33

Vale, Thomas   115, 116
Vaughan, Thomas   222
Veele, Edward   148, 208, 210, 230 n.206
Veitch, James   158, 177 n.55, 187
Vincent, William   235 n.1
Virginia Company   53–4
  see also Henrico College
Vorstius, Conrad   49
Vossius, Gerardus   51

Wale, Edward   226
Walker, Ithiel   37
Walker, Thomas   103
Ward, Samuel   50, 100, 147
Ware, Arthur   34–5, 36, 37
Ware, James   105, 108, 112, 208, 218
Warwick, earl of see Rich, Robert, second earl of Warwick
Washington, Richard   36, 108, 110, 111, 115
  appointed Trinity provost   103
Watson, John   37
Weaver, John   144, 146
Weld, Thomas   120, 123, 125, 125
Welsh, Nicholas   116
Wemyss, George   62, 85, 94, 186
Wemyss, James, regent, St Leonard's College   186

Wemyss, James, regent, St Salvator's College   186
Wentworth, Thomas, first earl of Strafford   26, 31, 103, 104, 111
  prosecuted by Irish Parliament   103, 104, 110, 131
  and Trinity   32–3, 34, 36, 100–2
Western Remonstrance   153
  see also Gillespie, Patrick; Protesters
Westminster Assembly   89–90, 128
  Confession   130, 226
  Directory of Worship   94, 130, 133
Whalley, Edward   232
Whetham, Nathaniel   183
Whiggamore Raid   150
White, Alexander   88, *187*
Whiting, Samuel   204
Wigglesworth, Michael   140
Wilkie, William   63, 65, 89–90
Wilkins, Joseph   210
William and Mary   236
Williams, Roger   137
Williamson, Caesar   146, 147, *148*, 209, *210*, 230 n.206, 232
Wilson, John, Harvard graduate   123, *125*
Wilson, John, Trinity student   109 n.90
Winslow, Edward   121, 137, 218–19
  Glorious Progress of the Gospel Amongst the Indians in New England (1649)   138
Winter, Josiah   208, *210*, 230 n.206
Winter, Samuel   *148*, 148 n.91, 164, 206, *210*, 215, 225–6, 228 n.193, 229–30, 233
  appointed Trinity provost   145–6
  and the Dublin Association (1659)   227–8
  expelled from provostship by General Convention (Dublin)   232
  and Independency at Trinity   148, 149, 200, 207–10, 211, 216
  petitions against Winter's Independent focus   228
Winter Jr, Samuel   208
Winthrop, Fitz-John   203, 215
Winthrop, John   49, 52, 55, 56, 123, *125*
Winthrop Jr, John   52, 120, 203, 213, 214, 215
Wiseman, James   71, 86, 94, *187*
Wishart, John   *187*
Wood, James   63, 85, 90, 153, 157, 159, 164, 168, 179, *186*, 188, 194
  translation to St Salvator's provostship   187–8, 194, 195
Wood, Robert   215, 216, 221, 222
Woodbridge, Benjamin   123
Wootton, Henry   207–8
Wootton, Matthew   147, 147 n.82, *148*
Worden, Blair   135
Worsley, Benjamin   138
Worth, Edward   217, 225–7, 228, 230
  see also Cork Association
Wright, James   63, 71, 86
Wylie, Thomas   158

York, archbishop of *see* Matthew, Tobias, archbishop of York
Young, George   158, 117 n.55
Young, John   85, 158, 173, 174, 117 n.55, 179, *186*
Young, Patrick   158, *187*, 190–1
Youngson, Andrew   85, 86
Yule, Robert   151, *152*

STUDIES IN EARLY MODERN CULTURAL, POLITICAL AND SOCIAL HISTORY

Details of volumes I–XXX can be found on the Boydell & Brewer website.

XXXI
Stuart Marriage Diplomacy
Dynastic Politics in their European Context, 1604–1630
Edited by Valentina Caldari and Sara J. Wolfson

XXXII
National Identity and the Anglo-Scottish Borderlands, 1552–1652
Jenna M. Schultz

XXXIII
Roguery in Print: Crime and Culture in Early Modern London
Lena Liapi

XXXIV
Politics, Religion and Ideas in Seventeenth- and Eighteenth-Century Britain
Essays in Honour of Mark Goldie
Edited by Justin Champion, John Coffey, Tim Harris and John Marshall

XXXV
The Hanoverian Succession in Great Britain and its Empire
Edited by Brent S. Sirota and Allan I. Macinnes

XXXVI
Age Relations and Cultural Change in Eighteenth-Century England
Barbara Crosbie

XXXVII
The National Covenant in Scotland, 1638–1689
Chris R. Langley

XXXVIII
Visualising Protestant Monarchy
Ceremony, Art and Politics after the Glorious Revolution (1689–1714)
Julie Farguson

XXXIX
Blood Waters
War, Disease and Race in the Eighteenth-Century British Caribbean
Nicholas Rogers

XL
The State Trials and the Politics of Justice in Later Stuart England
Edited by Brian Cowan and Scott Sowerby

XLI
Africans in East Anglia, 1467–1833
Richard C. Maguire

XLII
Royalism, Religion and Revolution: Wales, 1640–1688
Sarah Ward Clavier

XLIII
Painting for a Living in Tudor and Early Stuart England
Robert Tittler

XLIV
Scotland and the Wider World: Essays in Honour of Allan I. Macinnes
Edited by Alison Cathcart and Neil McIntyre

XLV
Urban Government and the Early Stuart State
Provincial Towns, Corporate Liberties, and Royal Authority in England, 1603–1640
Catherine F. Patterson

XLVI
The National Covenant and the Solemn League and Covenant, 1660–1696
James Walters

XLVII
The Restraint of the Press in England, 1660–1715: The Communication of Sin
Alex W. Barber

XLVIII
Conspiracy Culture in Stuart England
The Mysterious and Strange Death of Sir Edmund Berry Godfrey
Andrea McKenzie

XLIX
Contesting the English Polity, 1660–1688
Religion, Politics, and Ideas
Mark Goldie

L
Civil Religion in the Early Modern Anglophone World, 1550–1700
Edited by Adam Morton and Rachel Hammersley

LI
Radical Ideas and the Crisis of Christianity in England, 1640–1740:
The Politics of Religion
Edited by Alex W. Barber, Katherine A. East

Printed in the United States
by Baker & Taylor Publisher Services